Mar
Law
she
She
held
and
Mar
the
auth
Hus
(she
the
and
She

The Penguin Book of Hindu Names for Girls

MANEKA GANDHI

PENGUIN BOOKS

PENGUIN BOOKS
Published by the Penguin Group
Penguin Books India Pvt. Ltd, 11 Community Centre, Panchsheel Park, New Delhi 110 017, India
Penguin Group (USA) Inc., 375 Hudson Street, New York, New York 10014, USA
Penguin Group (Canada), 10 Alcorn Avenue, Toronto, Ontario, Canada M4V 3B2 (a division of Pearson Penguin Canada Inc.)
Penguin Books Ltd, 80 Strand, London WC2R 0RL, England
Penguin Ireland, 25 St Stephen's Green, Dublin 2, Ireland (a division of Penguin Books Ltd)
Penguin Group (Australia), 250 Camberwell Road, Camberwell, Victoria 3124, Australia (a division of Pearson Australia Group Pty Ltd)
Penguin Group (NZ), cnr Airborne and Rosedale Roads, Albany, Auckland 1310, New Zealand (a division of Pearson New Zealand Ltd)
Penguin Group (South Africa) (Pty) Ltd, 24 Sturdee Avenue, Rosebank, Johannesburg 2196, South Africa

Penguin Books Ltd, Registered Offices: 80 Strand, London WC2R 0RL, England

First published by Penguin Books India 2004

10 9 8 7 6 5 4 3 2

Typeset by Vans Information Limited, Mumbai

Printed at Pauls Press, New Delhi

To Aaryaman, the reason for this book

Introduction

This book started with the realization that I did not know the meaning of my name. All I knew was that Menaka (I spell it Maneka) was the name of an apsara in the court of Indra. No one I had encountered knew the meaning of their names either. Like me, they had been named after historical or mythological people. I hunted for a book, but while the libraries are full of information about the gods, I did not come across one book in India which gave the meaning of the name. What does Sarasvati mean? No, not 'learning' even though she is the goddess of that, but 'full of water'. Chandrashekhar does not mean Shiva but one who bears the moon on his forehead. I waited for someone to write a book but the two that emerged listed 'Menaka' as 'apsara'. When my sister announced that a baby was on the way, I decided to compile the dictionary myself.

The Vedic rishis believed that the name defined the child's character—its face, figure, temper, morals, tastes and profession. The name Anamika or 'without a name' for instance, would ensure that the child's future was what she wanted to make it—since she was not hedged in by any preordained limitations. Most of us look for phonetically pleasing names without realizing their significance. But Minna means 'fat' and Ambika means 'little mother', Sita means 'furrow', Mina means 'fish' and Draupadi has no meaning other than 'daughter of Drupada'. A number of names which are very common do not have any meaning at all. Anita, Lina, Rina and Tina for instance, come from languages other than Indian. If Roma is of Indian origin it means 'hairy'! The Phul, Sona and Pyar family (Phulvati, Phulrani, Sonalika, Soriam, Pyari) have no roots in Sanskrit, Pali or any of the classical Indian languages. Rishma and Rashmini simply do not exist. Malvika is a combination name that has no meaning. (There is however a plant of the Ipomoea family called Malvika.) My mother's name Amteshwar is a corruption of, I think, Amritesvara or lord of the amrita. Alternatively it has no meaning at all Names like Bina are distortions of Vina (the musical instrument), Bihari is not from Bihar, for instance, but from Vihari or roamer. I have left out the local versions of the classical name (Poonam comes from Purnima, Rakhi from Rakshaka, for instance) or the local diminutives or corruptions (e.g. Lacchman or Lakha for Lakshman, Upinder for Upendra, Vanti for Vati). The only exception I have made is for Rima which is a corruption of Hrim—since this happened to be my copy editor's name!

A lot of the names in India are combination names. Two primary names (usually of two gods or of a god and goddess) taken and made into one. For instance Ramakrishna or Radheshyam and in some cases, the conjoining of two gods produces an entirely new deity. I have tried to give as many combinations as possible, especially where there is a historical or mythological person with that compound. However the compounds can be infinite—and a lot of distortion of the primary names takes place in the mixture. Punjab is full of Gurveens, Tarveens, Harleens, Hargurbirinders and Harkirats. Some combinations are unique to certain regions in the country. The suffixes of Jit, Mita and Inder/Indra to the main name are usually from Punjab, Haryana and Rajasthan. Swamy, Appa, Amma show Tamil Nadu and Karnataka. The nagas or serpents who formed such an integral part of pre-Vedic and Vedic mythology are now confined to south and east India—e.g. Seshan, Nagabhushan, Phenamani. Even Manasa, the goddess of serpents, is a name far more common in Bengal than anywhere else in India.

The entries in this dictionary have been designed so that each entry is divided into three categories:

1. The exact or literal meaning. For instance Menaka means 'daughter of Mena'.

2. The intended meaning or rather, the meaning of the meaning. Menaka's intended meaning is 'of the mountains' because, in Indian mythology, Mena is the consort of Himavan who is the lord of the Himalayas.

3. This is divided into two sub-categories. The first is the locating of the name in mythology, history, literature, botany or ornithology. If the name denotes a person out of mythology, history or literature I have tried to give the name of the mythological consort, the children and the name of the dynasty, as well as the names of Sanskrit Vedic commentators, grammarians and playwrights. I have included the names that come from plants, trees, birds and animals along with their Latin and English names.

The last sub-category is 'another name for—'. In Menaka's case, it is 'another name for Parvati' as Parvati was born a daughter of Himavan in her incarnation as Uma. (The name Parvati also means of the mountains.)

I have read the *Mahabharata*, the *Ramayana*, the *Kathasaritsagara*, the *Panchatantra*, the listings of all the Vedas and Upanishads, books on Sanskrit plants and birds, the catalogues that list the thousand names of each major god, Vedic and Puranic encyclopaedias and the Buddhist and Jaina mythologies and histories and, of course, Sanskrit dictionaries to unearth the meanings of the names in this book. Very often the meaning of the name sounds bizarre unless one knows the context. Aparna which is another name for Parvati in her incarnation as Himavan's daughter means 'leafless'. This is explained by the legend of Parvati fasting to marry Shiva.

One result of this search has been new and unexpected perceptions into the traditional Indian way of life. For instance, what is truth? Or again, what is right and what is wrong? Jaya and Vijaya were the two door-keepers of Vishnu's palace in Vaikuntha. One day they were cursed by Lakshmi to be reborn on the earth as mortals. Vishnu modified the curse on his two devoted servants by saying that if they were killed thrice by him, they could come back to Vaikuntha. Jaya and Vijaya chose to be reborn as the most evil (or what we define as evil within the parameters of morality set by our religion) asuras or anti-gods Hiranyaksha and Hiranyakashipu, Ravana and Kumbhakarna, Shisupala and Dantavaktra so that their deaths at the hands of Vishnu—in his incarnation of Narasimha, Rama and Krishna—became quick and inevitable. So were these asuras good or bad? It was inevitable that Sita be separated from Rama for she had imprisoned a pregnant female parrot and had been cursed by the consort of the parrot to suffer the same fate. So, is Rama to be blamed for listening to the jibes of a washerman or was his action inevitable? Krishna means dark or black and Arjuna fair or white. They are reborn from Nara and Narayana or man and superman/god. Do they represent people or the Eastern philosophy of yin and yang, two opposites that fuse to complete? I find my attitude towards people and current affairs, goals and achievements, and even the pursuit of happiness or rather the diminishing of pain has changed with the unfolding of the history of each mythological character.

I would like to thank all the people who helped me in the preparation of this book. The friends who brought in the odd name in the beginning, those who pitched in to type the manuscript over and over again, the pandits and Sanskrit teachers who corrected my mistakes, the editors at Penguin who put the work into order and spent hours proof-reading and inserting new words till the last minute. I have used the Sanskrit classical style of spelling with diacritical marks, to help in the correct pronunciation of the names.

New Delhi *Maneka Gandhi*

Guide to the Use of the Book

How to Read an Entry

1. All Sanskrit words are marked (S).
2. Genders are differentiated as follows—(F) denotes Female.
3. The definition of each name is listed in a numbered sequence in the following order: the subdivision marked '1' gives the literal meaning; '2' is the implied or intended meaning and '3' places the name in its specific mythological/literary/botanical context. Some entries do not feature all the subdivisions as these are not required.
4. All books and scriptures referred to in abbreviated form in the entries are expanded in full at the end of the book.

Pronunciation

ā	—	f*a*ther
ī	—	eagle/pol*i*ce
ū	—	r*u*de
ṛ	—	mer*r*ily
ṅ	—	ki*ng*
ć	—	*ch*ick
ćh	—	*ch*hota
ñ	—	si*n*ge
ṭ	—	*t*omato
ṭh	—	an*th*ill
ḍ	—	*d*rum
ḍh	—	red*h*aied
ṇ	—	no*n*e
ś	—	*s*ure
ṣ	—	*sh*un
ṇ or ṁ	—	nasal sound

A

Ābhā (S) (F) splendour; light; colour; appearance; beauty; reflected image; resemblance; likeness.

Ābhāti (S) (F) splendour; light.

Abherī (S) (F) **1.** fearless. **3.** a rāgiṇī.

Abhibhā (S) (F) glittering.

Ābhidhā (S) (F) **1.** literal meaning. **2.** name; word; sound.

Abhidhyā (S) (F) of thought; wish; longing; desire.

Abhigūrtī (S) (F) chants of praise.

Abhijitī (S) (F) victory.

Abhijñā (S) (F) **1.** knowing; recollection; skilful; clever. **2.** remembrance.

Abhikhyā (S) (F) beauty; splendour; fame; glory.

Abhilāṣā (S) (F) desire; wish; affection.

Abhilāṣin (S) (F) one who desires.

Abhimukhī (S) (F) turned towards; facing.

Abhinīti (S) (F) **1.** that which has already been performed. **2.** one who has achieved perfection; gesture; friendship; civility.

Abhiprī (S) (F) gladdening; refreshing.

Abhiprīti (S) (F) **1.** full of love. **2.** that which is pleasing; that which causes pleasure.

Abhipuṣpam (S) (F) an excellent flower.

Abhirakṣā (S) (F) one who protects.

Abhirati (S) (F) pleasure.

Abhīrkā (S) (F) wife of a cowherd.

Abhiruċi (S) (F) **1.** delighting in pleasures. **2.** deep interest.

Abhiśri (S) (F) **1.** surrounded by glory. **2.** one who is glorious; worthy; shining; powerful.

Abhiśvarā (S) (F) **1.** invocation. **2.** a song or hymn of praise.

Abhīti (S) (F) fearlessness.

Abhivādakā (S) (F) **1.** one who pays homage. **2.** a devotee.

Abhivibhā (S) (F) illuminating.

Abhragaṅgā (S) (F) **1.** Gaṅgā of the sky. **2.** the Ākāśagaṅgā (the celestial Gaṅgā).

Abhramū (S) (F) **1.** steady; clear. **3.** the female elephant of the east who is also the mate of Airāvata (*V. D. Ćaritam*).

Abhrāntī (S) (F) without perplexity; without error.

Abhrayantī (S) (F) **1.** forming clouds. **2.** bringing rain. **3.** one of the 7 kṛttikās (*T. Samhitā*).

Abjā (S) (F) **1.** born in water. **2.** water lily (*Nymphaea alba*).

Abjinī (S) (F) a multitude of lotuses.

Abolī (S) (F) a flower.

Aċalā (S) (F) **1.** immovable. **2.** the earth. **3.** a mother in Skanda's retinue (*Sk. Purāṇa*).

Aċċhodā (S) (F) **1.** with clear water. **3.** a river; a daughter of the Pitṛs reborn as Satyavatī the mother of Vyāsa, Ćitrāṅgada and Viċitravīrya (*M. Bh.*).

Aċċhuptā (S) (F) **1.** inactive. **3.** one of the 16 Jaina vidyādevīs (*J. Koṣa*).

Aċirā (S) (F) **1.** brief; instantaneous. **2.** swift; fast; active; prompt. **3.** a queen of Hastināpura and mother of Śāntinātha Jaina Tīrthaṅkara (*J. S. Koṣa*).

Ādevī (S) (F) devoted to the gods; one who performs meritorious rites.

Adhṛṣyā (S) (F) **1.** invincible. **3.** a river (*M. Bh.*).

Adhyā (S) (F) **1.** beyond perception. **2.** the 1st creator. **3.** one of the 10 Durgās (*D. Purāṇa*).

Ādilakṣmī (S) (F) **1.** the primal Lakṣmī. **3.** Lakṣmī as the wife of Ādinārāyaṇa.

Ādimātā (S) (F) **1.** the primal mother. **3.** another name for Manasā.

Ādiśakti (S) (F) **1.** the primal energy. **3.** another name for Pārvatī and Māyā.

Āditā (S) (F) the first root.

Aditī (S) (F) **1.** freedom. **2.** security; safety; immensity; abundance; perfection; creative power; cow; milk; speech. **3.** a primal Indian goddess; the daughter of Dakṣa; wife of Kaśyapa, mother of the ādityas, rudras and vasus (*M. Bh.*); the incarnation of Pṛṣnī later reborn as Devakī and the mother of lord Viṣṇu in his incarnation as the dwarf Vāmana (*V. Purāṇa*); another name for the earth.

Adrijā (S) (F) **1.** of the mountain. **3.** another name for Pārvatī.

Adrikā (S) (F) **1.** small mountain. **3.** an apsarā who was the mother of Matsya and Satyavatī (*M. Bh.*).

Adṛśyantī (S) (F) **1.** invisible. **3.** the wife of sage Śakti daughter-in-law of Vasiṣṭha and mother of sage Parāśara (*M. Bh.*).

Advaitavādinī (S) (F) propounder of the uniqueness of the absolute.

Ādyā (S) (F) **1.** first. **2.** unparalleled; excellent. **3.** goddess Durgā; the earth.

Agajā (S) (F) **1.** produced on a mountain. **3.** another name for Pārvatī.

Agnajitā (S) (F) **1.** one who has conquered fire. **3.** wife of Kṛṣṇa (*Bhāgavata*).

Agnāyī (S) (F) **1.** fiery. **3.** the wife of Agni (*A. Parāṇa*).

Āgneyī (S) (F) **1.** daughter of fire. **3.** a daughter of Agni and the wife of Ūru (*Ś. Brāhmaṇa*); the wife of Kuru, the son of Manu and the mother of Aṅga, Sumanas, Khyāti, Kratu, Aṅgiras and Śibi (*V. Parāṇa*).

Agnidurgā (S) (F) **1.** Durgā in her fiery form.

Agnimukhī (S) (F) **1.** fire faced. **3.** the Common Marking Nut tree (*Semecarpus anacardium*); the *Gloriosa superba* creeper.

Agnivardhinī (S) (F) **1.** increasing fire. **3.** the Lovage plant (*Carum copticum*).

Agrajā (S) (F) **1.** born first. **2.** elder daughter.

Agrayī (S) (F) **1.** primal. **3.** a wife of Agni, who is also the goddess of fire and the daughter of Dakṣa (*A. Purāṇa*).

Ahalyā (S) (F) **1.** agreeable. **3.** the daughter of Mudgala, wife of sage Gautama, mother of sage Śatānanda, who according to the Rāmāyaṇa, supposed to have been the first woman created by Brahmā and is one of the 5 women renowned for their chastity and purity (*V. Rāmāyaṇa*).

Ahanā (S) (F) **1.** one who cannot be killed; one who is immortal. **2.** one who is born in the day.

Ahī (S) (F) heaven and earth conjoined.

Ahilyā (S) (F) **1.** unploughed. **2.** maiden; pious; sacred.

Ahiṁsā (S) (F) **1.** not injuring. **3.** a wife of Dharma (*V. Purāṇa*).

Ahitā (S) (F) **1.** hostile; evil. **3.** a river (*M. Bh.*).

Āhlāditā (S) (F) delighted.

Āhū (S) (F) calling; invoking.

Ahukā (S) (F) **1.** offerer; sacrificer. **3.** another name for Damayantī.

Āhūti (S) (F) **1.** calling; summoning; offering. **2.** a solemn rite.

Aikṣvākī (S) (F) **1.** produced from sugarcane. **2.** very sweet. **3.** the wife of Suhotra and the mother of Ajamīdha, Sumīdha and Purumīdha (*M. Bh.*).

Aindrī (S) (F) **1.** belonging to the senses. **3.** another name for Indrāṇi, consort of Indra; the *Amomum subulatum* herb; *Cucumis prophetarum*.

Aingīnī (S) (F) **1.** agitated. **2.** inviting; welcoming. **3.** consort of Gaṇeśa.

Aiśvaryā (S) (F) wealth; fame; riches; glory.

Ajā (S) (F) **1.** not born. **2.** one who is self existent. **3.** another name for Prākṛtī and Māyā.

Ajālā (S) (F) **1.** eternal; birthless and deathless. **3.** the daughter of Prākṛtī (*V. Purāṇa*); another name for the earth.

Ajamukhī (S) (F) **1.** goatfaced. **3.** an asura daughter of Kaśyapa and Surasā and the wife of Durvāsas (*Sk. Purāṇa*).

Ājānī (S) (F) of noble birth.

Ajarā (S) (F) **1.** ever young. **3.** another name for the river Sarasvatī.

Ajathyā (S) (F) the yellow jasmine (*Jasminum humile*).

Ajayā (S) (F) **1.** one who cannot be conquered; Indian Hemp (*Cannabis *sativa*). 3. a friend of Durgā also known as Māyā (*D. Bhāgavata*).

Ajirā (S) (F) **1.** not slow. **2.** agile; quick; rapid. **3.** a river (*D. Bhāgavata*); another name for Durgā.

Ākālikī (S) (F) lightning.

Akalkā (S) (F) **1.** free from impurity. **2.** moonlight.

Ākāṅkṣā (S) (F) desire; wish.

Ākāśadīpa (S) (F) **1.** a lamp in the sky. **2.** a lamp lit in honour of Lakṣmī at the Divāli festival.

Ākāśagaṅgā (S) (F) the celestial Gaṅgā; the Milky Way.

Ākāśī (S) (F) **1.** all pervading. **2.** the atmosphere.

Ākrānti (S) (F) might; valour; force.

Ākṛtī (S) (F) form; figure; shape; appearance; a constituent part; a Vedic metre consisting of 4 lines with 22 syllables each; ancient mathematicians substituted Ākṛtī for the number 22 which remains one of its meanings.

Akṣamālā (S) (F) **1.** a rosary of Rudrākṣa seeds (*Eleocarpus ganitrus*). **3.** the mother of Vatsa (*Ś. Purāṇa*); another name for Arundhatī.

Akṣasutrā (S) (F) **1.** bearer of knowledge. **3.** wife of sage Āpastamba (*Ā. Samhitā*).

Akṣāvalī (S) (F) a string of Akṣa (*Eleocarpus ganitrus*) seeds.

Akṣayā (S) (F) **1.** undecaying. **3.** another name for Pṛthvī, the goddess of earth.

Akṣayiṇī (S) (F) **1.** undecaying. **3.** another name for Pārvatī.

Akṣī (S) (F) abode; existence; a possession; the eye.

Akṣitī (S) (F) imperishability.

Akūpārā (S) (F) **1.** unbounded. **2.** free; independent. **3.** a daughter of sage Aṅgiras (*P. Brāhmaṇa*).

Ākūtā (S) (F) **1.** not of the earth. **3.** another name for Parvati.

Ākūtī (S) (F) **1.** intention. **3.** wish personified as the daughter of Manu Svāyambhuva and Śatarūpā (*V. Samhitā*), the wife of Prajāpati Ruċi and the mother of Yajña and Dakṣiṇā (*V. Purāṇa*); the wife of Pṛthuśena (*Bhā. Purāṇa*).

Alakā (S) (F) **1.** girl; curl; lock of hair. **3.** city of Kubera (*M. Bh.*).

Alakanandā (S) (F) **1.** young girl. **3.** the celestial Gaṅgā (*A. Koṣa*); a river (*M. Bh.*).

Alakarāvatī (S) (F) **1.** loving. **2.** with adorable hands. **3.** wife of King Naravāhanadatta who was emperor of the vidyādharas (*K. Sāgara*).

Alambuśā (S) (F) **1.** a line not to be crossed. **2.** a barrier; the *Sphaeranthus indicus* herb. **3.** an apsarā daughter of Kaśyapa and Prādhā who married King Tṛṇabindu and was the mother of Ilabilā, Viśālā, Śunyabandhu and Dhūmraketu (*Bhā. Purāṇa*).

Alamelā (S) (F) **1.** extremely intelligent. **3.** another name for Rukminī the consort of Kṛṣṇa.

Alamelū (S) (F) **1.** very sportive. **2.** extremely merry.

Ālāpinī (S) (F) a lute.

Alātākṣī (S) (F) **1.** fire eyed. **3.** a mother in Skanda's retinue (*M. Bh.*).

Alin (S) (F) **1.** that which possesses a sting. **3.** the zodiac sign of Scorpio.

Alīśā (S) (F) grand; stately.

Allā (S) (F) **1.** mother. **2.** the Supreme Spirit.

Alpanā (S) (F) delighted; glad.

Amalā (S) (F) **1.** spotless. **2.** pure; shining. **3.** another name for Lakṣmī; Bombay Hemp plant (*Hibiscus cannabinus*).

Amanī (S) (F) **1.** road; way. **2.** one who shows the path; a leader; a preceptor.

Amarajā (S) (F) daughter of the gods.

Amarāṅganā (S) (F) celestial damsel.

Amarataṭinī (S) (F) **1.** river of deathless beings. **3.** the Gaṅgā which is considered the river of immortals.

Amarāvatī (S) (F) **1.** abode of the eternal. **3.** city of Indra (*D. Bhāgavata*).

Amari (S) (F) **1.** eternal **3.** couch grass (*Cynodon dactylon*).

Amartā (S) (F) immortality.

Amati (S) (F) **1.** beyond intellect. **2.** that which cannot be perceived; form; shape; splendour; lustre; time.

Amāvasya (S) (F) **1.** dwelling together. **2.** a moonless night in which neither the sun nor the moon can be spotted as they are considered to be dwelling together.

Ambā (S) (F) **1.** mother. **2.** a good woman. **3.** daughter of the king of Kāśī, the sister of Ambikā and Ambālikā, later reborn as Śikhaṅḍi to seek revenge on Bhīṣma (*M. Bh.*); one of the 7 kṛttikās (*T. Samhitā*); an apsarā (*A. Koṣa*); a river which is part incarnation of princess Ambā of Kāśī (*M. Bh.*); another name for Durgā.

Ambālā (S) (F) **1.** mother. **2.** sensitive; compassionate; loving.

Ambālī (S) (F) **1.** mother. **2.** sensitive; compassionate; loving.

Ambālikā (S) (F) **1.** mother. **2.** one who is sensitive. **3.** a daughter of the king of Kāśī, the sister of Ambā and Ambikā, the wife of Vićitravīrya and the mother of Pāṇḍu through sage Vyāsa (*M. Bh.*); Bombay Hemp plant (*Hibiscus cannabinus*).

Ambaraprabhā (S) (F) light of the sky.

Ambayā (S) (F) mother.

Ambhīnī (S) (F) **1.** born of water. **3.** the preceptress who transmitted the *Yajur Veda* to Vāćā (*Y. Veda*).

Ambhojinī (S) (F) **1.** an assemblage of lotuses. **2.** fragrant; auspicious; venerated; dear to the gods.

Ambī (S) (F) **1.** mother. **2.** sensitive; compassionate; loving.

Ambikā (S) (F) **1.** mother. **2.** sensitive; compassionate; loving; a good woman; the harvest in the most productive season; Bombay Hemp (*Hibiscus cannabinus*) **3.** a daughter of the king of Kāśī, the sister of Ambā and Ambālikā, the wife of Vićitravīrya and the mother of Dhṛtarāṣṭra through sage Vyāsa (*M. Bh.*); a Matṛ or village goddess who represents a fierce class of yoginīs (*Y. Veda*); a goddess formed from the energies of all the gods to defeat the asuras (*D. Bhāgavata*); a sister of Rudra (*V. Samhitā*); a mother in Skanda's retinue (*M. Bh.*); the wife of Rudra Ugraretas (*Bhā Purāṇa*); Jaina deity (*A. Koṣa*); another name for Pārvatī.

Ambujākṣī (S) (F) **1.** lotus eyed. **2.** with beautiful eyes.

Ambujānanā (S) (F) **1.** lotus faced. **3.** a tutelary deity (*Brah. Purāṇa*).

Ambumatī (S) (F) **1.** containing water. **3.** a river (*M. Bh.*).

Ambupadma (S) (F) **1.** lotus of the water. **2.** Indian Lotus (*Nelumbo nucifcra*).

Ambuvāhinī (S) (F) **1.** carrying water. **3.** a holy river (*M. Bh.*).

Amiṣā (S) (F) free from guile or deceit.

Amiteśvarī (S) (F) with unlimited wealth; goddess of the infinite.

Amiti (S) (F) **1.** immeasurable. **2.** boundless; divine.

Amiya (S) (F) **1.** full of tenderness. **2.** nectar.

Ammavaru (Tamil) (F) **1.** the primal mother. **3.** tutelary goddess of Madras once regarded the primary Śakti.

Āmodinī (S) (F) fragrant; famous.

Āmohanikā (S) (F) fragrance.

Amoghā (S) (F) **1.** unerring; unfailing; productive; fruitful; the Trumpet flower (*Bignonia suaveolens*). **3.** a wife of Śantanu (*M. Bh.*); a mother in Skanda's retinue (*Sk. Purāṇa*); another name for Durgā and the night; the Black Myrobalan tree (*Terminata chebula*).

Amoghākṣī (S) (F) **1.** of unerring eye. **3.** Dākṣāyaṇī (*M. Purāṇa*).

Āmramañjarī (S) (F) the mango blossom.

Amṛtā (S) (F) **1.** beyond death; immortal; nectar like. **2.** a goddess. **3.** daughter of a king of Magadha who was the wife of Anaśya and the mother of Parīkṣit (*M. Bh.*); a sister of Amṛtodana (*B. Literature*); a digit of the moon (*Brah. Purāṇa*); a Dākṣāyaṇī (*M. Purāṇa*).

Amṛtamā (S) (F) food obtained from the Ocean of Milk.

Amṛtamālinī (S) (F) **1.** with an everfresh garland. **3.** another name for Durgā.

Anabhrā (S) (F) **1.** cloudless. **2.** clear in visage and mind.

Anādyā (S) (F) **1.** without a beginning. **2.** one who has always been there; immortal; divine. **3.** an apsarā (*M. Bh.*).

Anāgā (S) (F) **1.** sinless. **3.** a river.

Anāgaiammā (S) (F) **1.** formless mother; angry mother. **3.** a Coimbatore deity known for her anger.

Analā (S) (F) **1.** composed of fire. **2.** without a blemish. **3.** a daughter of Dakṣa, wife of Kaśyapa and mother of trees and creepers (*V. Rāmāyaṇa*); a daughter of Rohiṇī and granddaughter of Surabhī (*M. Bh.*); a daughter of Mālyavān and Sundarī, the wife of Viśvavasu and the mother of Kumbhināśi (*V. Rāmāyaṇa*).

Analapriyā (S) (F) beloved of fire; wife of Agni.

Anāmikā (S) (F) without a name (since the name of a person reflects the virtues desired, one without a name is considered without limitations of virtues associated with a particular name, therefore one who has all the virtues); ring finger.

Ānamrā (S) (F) bent; humble; modest; propitious.

Ānandabhairavī (S) (F) **1.** consort of Śiva. **3.** another name for Gaurī.

Ānandalakṣmī (S) (F) **1.** goddess of happiness. **2.** always happy.

Ānandamayī (S) (F) full of bliss.

Ānandaparṇa (S) (F) **1.** with wings of joy. **2.** one who spreads happiness and joy.

Ānandaprabhā (S) (F) **1.** spreading pleasure. **3.** an apsarā (*M. Bh.*).

Ānandī (S) (F) **1.** bestower of pleasure. **3.** another name for Gaurī.

Anaṅgadevī (S) (F) **1.** formless goddess. **2.** divine; immortal. **3.** a queen of Kāśmira (*R. Taraṅgiṇī*).

Anaṅgalekhā (S) (F) **1.** a love-letter. **2.** a personification of love. **3.** a queen of Kāśmira (*R. Taraṅgiṇī*).

Anantā (S) (F) **1.** endless. **2.** eternal; divine. **3.** a wife of King Janamejaya; another name for Pārvatī, the earth.

Anantalakṣmī (S) (F) **1.** eternal Lakṣmī. **2.** eternally fortunate.

Anantaśīrṣā (S) (F) **1.** with an immortal mind. **2.** eternal; divine. **3.** Vāsuki's wife.

Anantyā (S) (F) **1.** endless. **2.** eternal; divine; a god.

Ananyā (S) (F) **1.** without a second. **2.** sole; unique; peerless.

Anasūyā (S) (F) **1.** without spite or envy. **3.** a daughter of Kardama and Devahutī, the wife of ṛṣi Atri, the mother of Dattātreya, Durvāsas and Ćandra (*V. Purāṇa*), who after practising great austerities found miraculous powers and irrigated the earth with the water of the Gaṅgā after a drought (*M. Bh.*); a friend of Śakuntalā (*K. Granthāvali*); a daughter of Dakṣa (*M. Bh.*).

Anatā (S) (F) **1.** not bent. **3.** a daughter of Atri and Anasūyā and the mother of fruit (*M. Bh.*).

Ānati (S) (F) **1.** bent. **2.** modest; respectful; humble.

Anaupamyā (S) (F) **1.** without comparison. **2.** unique; peerless. **3.** wife of Bāṇāsura (*P. Purāṇa*).

Anavadyā (S) (F) **1.** faultless. **3.** an apsarā.

Ānavī (S) (F) **1.** humane. **2.** kind to people.

Anāyuṣā (S) (F) **1.** with a short life. **3.** mother of Bala and Vṛtta (*Bhā. Purāṇa*).

Aṇḍalā (T) (F) **1.** eggless; partless; petalless. **2.** whole; perfect. **3.** a Tamil poetess of the Bhakti cult and adopted daughter of Periyalvar.

Aṇḍikā (S) (F) elder sister.

Aṅgajā (S) (F) **1.** born of the body. **2.** a daughter.

Aṅgālamma (S) (F) **1.** mother with a form. **3.** wife of Vīrabhadra who hauls up the spirits of the dead; an idol of goddess Ambā.

Aṅganā (S) (F) **1.** with a beautiful form; a beautiful woman. **2.** the zodiac sign of Virgo.

Aṅgāravatī (S) (F) **1.** having fire. **2.** that which is hot, destructive and unperishable. **3.** a daughter of the asura Aṅgāraka, and mother of Gopālaka, Pālaka and Vāsavadattā who married King Udayana (*K. Sāgara*).

Aṅgāritā (S) (F) **1.** a luminous plant; blossom of the Kiṇśuka tree (*Butefrondosa*). **3.** a river (*A. Koṣa*).

Aṅgirā (S) (F) **1.** of indescribable form. **2.** celestial; divine. **3.** mother of Bṛhaspati (*Mu. Upaniṣad*).

Aṅgurī (S) (F) finger; finger ring.

Aṅhatī (S) (F) gift.

Aṅhitī (S) (F) gift; donation.

Anindā (S) (F) irreproachable.

Anindinī (S) (F) who does not speak ill of others; who is not spoken ill of.

Aninditā (S) (F) **1.** who is never spoken ill of. **2.** virtuous; irreproachable; venerated.

Anindyā (S) (F) beyond reproach.

Anīśā (S) (F) without night; nightless.

Anita (S) (F) **1.** without guile; not driven. **2.** a leader.

Anitābhā (S) (P) **1.** with guileless charm. **3.** a *Ṛg Veda* river.

Añjanā (S) (F) **1.** collyrium coloured. **2.** grey; swarthy; dusky. **3.** daughter of the monkey King Kuñjara and wife of Kesarī (*Br. Purāṇa*); mother of Hanumān through Vāyu, and incarnation of apsara Puñjikāsthalā (*Rāmāyaṇa*).

Añjanam (S) (F) collyrium; paint used as a cosmetic; lampblack; antimony; night; fire.

Añjasī (S) (F) **1.** not dark; not crooked. **2.** honest; upright; deceitless. **3.** a celestial river (*Ṛg Veda*).

Añjī (S) (F) a blessing; who blesses.

Añjinī (S) (F) blessed.

Añkalammā (S) (F) **1.** goddess with an auspiciously marked body. **3.** another name for the goddess Śītaladevī.

Aṅkitā (S) (F) with auspicious marks.

Aṅkolikā (S) (F) **1.** an embrace. **2.** who personifies love; affection; respect.

Aṅkuśī (S) (F) **1.** one who exercises restraint. **3.** one of the 24 Jaina goddesses.

Annadā (S) (F) **1.** one who gives food. **3.** another name for Durgā.

Annalakṣmī (S) (F) **1.** who bestows grain; giver of grain. **3.** another name for Lakṣmī.

Annammā (Kannada) (F) goddess of food.

Annapatni (S) (F) goddess of food.

Annapūrṇā (S) (F) **1.** one who bestows food to the fullest. **3.** a goddess who is a form of Durgā (*D. Bhāgavata*).

Annī (S) (F) shortened name for Annapūrṇā.

Annīśvarī (S) (F) **1.** goddess of food. **3.** Bhairavī, a fearsome form of Durgā.

Anokhī (S) (F) unique; unparalleled.

Anomā (S) (F) **1.** illustrious. **3.** a river (*H. Koṣa*).

Anṛtām (S) (F) **1.** lie. **3.** a daughter of Adharma and Hiṁsā and mother of Bhaya and Naraka (*A. Purāṇa*).

Aṅśrutā (S) (F) **1.** unheard of; unique; whose fame is pearless. **3.** wife of Aṅgiras (*M. Bh.*).

Aṅśumālā (S) (F) **1.** a garland of rays; a halo. **2.** as glorious as the sun.

Aṅśumatī (S) (F) **1.** bearer of rays. **2.** resplendent; glorious; wise. **3.** daughter of the gandharva King Dramila (*A. Koṣa*); another name for the Yamunā river (*Bhāgavata*); a shrub (*Desmodium gangeticum*).

Āntikā (S) (F) elder sister.

Antinī (S) (F) living in a hermitage.

Anubhā (S) (F) one who follows glory.

Aṇubhā (S) (F) lightning.

Anūcānā (S) (F) **1.** devoted to learning; well behaved. **3.** an apsarā (*M. Bh.*).

Anugā (S) (F) **1.** one who follows behind. **2.** a companion. **3.** an apsarā (*Bhāgavata*).

Anugītā (S) (F) after song; overtly praised.

Anukā (S) (F) **1.** one who follows the earth; backbone; spine; follows the principles of nature; who supports. 3. an apsarā (*Ś. Brāhmaṇa*).

Anukānkṣā (S) (F) desire; wish.

Anulā (S) (F) 1. not wild. 2. gentle; agreeable. 3. a female Arhat or Buddhist saint (*B. Literature*); a river in Kāśmira (*R. Taraṅgiṇī*).

Anulekhā (S) (F) one who follows destiny.

Anulī (S) (F) 1. homage. 2. respected; respectful.

Anumatī (S) (F) 1. assent; sanction. 3. approval personified as a goddess (*Ṛg Veda, A. Veda*); the 15th day of the moon personified as a daughter of Aṅgiras and Smṛtī (*V. Purāṇa*); a goddess who is invoked to bestow wealth, inspiration, offspring and longevity (*Bhāgavata*); a goddess present at the time of Skanda's crown-ceremony (*M. Bh.*).

Anumloćā (S) (F) 1. very flexible. 2. agreeable. 3. an apsarā (*Purāṇas*).

Anumoditā (S) (F) 1. pleased. 2. delighted; applauded.

Anūnā (S) (F) 1. not inferior. 2. superior; entire; whole. 3. an apsarā (*H. Purāṇa*).

Anunāyikā (S) (F) 1. submissive. 2. humble; modest.

Anunīta (S) (F) 1. disciplined; obtained. 2. respected; learned; wise.

Anunītī (S) (F) 1. supplication. 2. courtesy.

Anupallavī (S) (F) 1. like a petal. 2. that which is young; tender; soft; fragrant.

Anupamā (S) (F) 1. matchless. 2. peerless; unique; rare. 3. the elephant of the southwest quarter (*Br. Purāṇa*).

Anuprabhā (S) (F) followed by glory.

Anupriyā (S) (F) beloved; very dear.

Anurādhā (S) (F) 1. who bestows welfare. 3. the 17th lunar asterism.

Anurakti (S) (F) devotion; affection; love.

Anurati (S) (F) love; affection; attachment.

Anurimā (S) (F) attached; fond of.

Anusara (S) (F) 1. full of desires. 3. a rākṣasa (*M. Bh.*).

Anuṣṇā (S) (F) 1. not hot. 2. cool; soothing; pacifying. 3. a river (*M. Bh.*); the Blue Lotus (*Nymphaea stellata*).

Anuśobhinī (S) (F) 1. shining; follows grace. 2. bright; dignified; lluminating.

Anuśrī (S) (F) glorious; famous.

Anutaptā (S) (F) 1. heated; filled with regret. 3. a river (*V. Purāṇa*).

Anuvindā (S) (F) 1. one who finds or discovers. 3. a wife of Kṛṣṇa (*P. purāṇa*).

Anuvṛndā (S) (F) 1. surrounded by a crowd. 2. with many friends; moving in a group. 3. a queen of Kṛṣṇa (*Bhāgavata*).

Anvākṛti (S) (F) 1. shaping after. 2. one who imitates.

Anvitā (S) (F) reached by the mind; connected with; linked to; understood.

Anviti (S) (F) following after.

Anyā (S) (F) inexhaustible.

Apaćitī (S) (F) 1. honouring; reverence; loss. 2. incurs expenditure. 3. a daughter of Marīći (*Vā. Purāṇa*).

Apagā (S) (F) 1. flowing water. 3. a holy river (*M. Bh.*).

Apālā (S) (F) 1. unguarded. 2. undefended. 3. a daughter of Atri (*Ṛg Veda*).

Apārā (S) (F) 1. boundless; with no rival or second. 2. inexhaustible; unequalled; divine. 3. a wife of Vasudeva (*Vā. Purāṇa*).

Aparājitā (S) (F) 1. never been conquered. 3. a form of Durgā worshipped on Vijayādaśamī or Dussera; the Blue Pea plant which serves as an amulet (*Clitoria ternatea*); a yoginī (*M. Bh.*); a river of Śāka Dvīpa (*Bhāgavata*); the northeast quarter.

Aparānandā (S) (F) 1. pleasing others. 3. a prominent holy river (*M. Bh.*).

Aparṇā (S) (F) 1. without leaves. 3. another name for Pārvatī who undertook a penance in order to obtain Śiva as her consort and during the process gave up eating everything including leaves.

Apayā (S) (F) **1.** going away; milkless; waterless. **3.** a tributary of the river Sarasvatī (*Bhāgavata*).

Apekṣitā (S) (F) **1.** expected. **2.** desired; wanted; required; looked for.

Apsarā (S) (F) **1.** moving in the water of the clouds. **3.** celestial nymphs born of the churning of the Ocean of Milk (*V. Rāmāyaṇa*), who dwell in Svarga, the heaven of Indra and visit the earth in different shapes (*A. Veda*).

Āptī (S) (F) **1.** fitness; fulfilment; completion. **2.** abundance; fortune.

Āpūraṇī (S) (F) **1.** one that fulfils. **2.** the silkcotton tree (*Bombax celba*).

Apūrvā (S) (F) **1.** unprecedented. **2.** incomparable; new; extraordinary.

Arā (S) (F) **1.** decorative. **3.** a daughter of sage Śukra (*U. Rāmāyaṇa*).

Araḍā (S) (F) **1.** languid. **3.** a tutelary goddess (*G's Ś. Kalpa*).

Ārādhanā (S) (F) worship; adoration; prayer.

Ārādhitā (S) (F) **1.** one who receives the devotion of others. **2.** worshipped.

Arajā (S) (F) **1.** dustless. **2.** clean; pure; virtuous. **3.** the daughter of Uśanas (*V. Rāmāyaṇa*); a daughter of ṛṣi Bhārgava (*V. Rāmāyaṇa*).

Aramatī (S) (F) **1.** piety and devotion conjoined. **3.** as a goddess who protects the worshippers of the gods.

Aranī (S) (F) **1.** turning round. **3.** removes darkness by sifting the fire; wood of the tree *Ficus religiosa* used for kindling fire.

Araṇyānī (S) (F) **1.** wilderness. **2.** desert; large forest. **3.** the goddess of wilderness (*Ṛg Veda*).

Ārātī (S) (F) **1.** offering prayer; ceremonial adoration with kindled lamps. **2.** sacred; spiritual; venerated.

Aravindinī (S) (F) **1.** an assemblage of lotuses. **2.** fragrant; beautiful; auspicious; dear to the gods.

Arćanā (S) (F) **1.** worship; homage paid to deities. **2.** respected; propitiated.

Arćis (S) (F) **1.** ray of light; flame. **2.** illuminating; enlightening. **3.** the wife of Kṛṣāśva and mother of Dhūmraketu (*Bhāgavata*).

Arćiśmatī (S) (F) **1.** flaming. **2.** brilliant; resplendant. **3.** a daughter of Aṅgiras (*M. Bh.*).

Ardhagaṅgā (S) (F) **1.** half the Gaṅgā. **2.** as half as the Gaṅgā. **3.** another name for the river Kāverī.

Arhaṇā (S) (F) **1.** worship. **2.** honoured; venerated.

Arhantikā (S) (F) **1.** one who worships. **2.** has shunned violence. **3.** a Buddhist nun (*B. Literature*).

Arihan (S) (F) killing enemies.

Ariktā (S) (F) **1.** not empty. **2.** fulfilled; satisfied; abundant.

Ariprā (S) (F) **1.** spotless. **2.** clear; faultless; virtuous; divine.

Ariṣṭā (S) (F) **1.** unhurt; safe; secure. **3.** a daughter of Dakṣa, wife of Kaśyapa, and the mother of the gandharvas (*M. Bh.*); another name for Durgā.

Arjā (S) (F) **1.** dustless. **2.** free from passion; pure; virtuous; divine. **3.** a daughter of Uśanas (*Bhāgavata*).

Arkasutā (S) (F) **1.** daughter of the sun. **3.** another name for the river Yamunā.

Arogā (S) (F) **1.** without disease. **3.** Dākṣāyāṇī in Vaidyanātha (*M. Purāṇa*).

Ārohī (S) (F) **1.** ascending. **2.** growing; evolving; positive; progressive.

Arpaṇā (S) (F) **1.** act of offering. **2.** auspicious; sacred; venerated.

Arpitā (S) (F) **1.** offered. **2.** fixed upon; delivered; entrusted; given back; surrendered.

Arthanā (S) (F) request; entreaty.

Artikā (S) (F) elder sister.

Arujā (S) (F) daughter of the sun; free from disease.

Arūkṣitā (S) (F) **1.** not dry. **2.** young; tender; soft; supple.

Arūkṣṇā (S) (F) **1.** not dry. **2.** soft; tender; young.

Aruṇā (S) (F) **1.** red. **2.** passionate; fecund; life giving. **3.** an apsarā daughter of Kaśyapa and Prādhā (*M. Bh.*); a tributary of the river Sarasvatī (*M. Bh.*); the Rosary Pea (*Abrus precatorius*); the Shoeflower (*Hibiscus rosa chinensis*); the Saffron plant (*Crocus sativus*); the Indian Madder Plant (*Rubia cordifolia*); *Aconitum heterophyllum*; *Sphaeranthus indicus*; *Alpinia galanga*.

Aruṇābhā (S) (F) **1.** the red glow of the sun. **2.** life giving; passionate; fecund.

Aruṇapriyā (S) (F) **1.** beloved of the dawn. **3.** an apsarā (*H. Purāṇa*).

Arundhatī (S) (F) **1.** fidelity. **3.** the morning star Alcor in the Great Bear personified as the wife of Vasiṣṭha and the daughter of Prajāpati Kardama and Devahutī, regarded as the epitome of wifely devotion and considered to sit in Brahmā's assembly (*M. Bh.*); one of the Pleiades (*P. Samhitā*); the daughter of Dakṣa, wife of Dharma and mother of the divisions of the earth (*H. Purāṇa*); another name for the supernatural faculty also called Kuṇḍalinī.

Aruṇī (S) (F) **1.** glowing red; ruddy; red cow; dawn; gold; ruby. **2.** passionate; fecund; precious; illuminating; sacred. **3.** Aruṇa as a female in Indra's assembly (*H. Purāṇa*).

Aruṇikā (S) (F) **1.** tawny red. **2.** life giving; passionate; bright.

Aruṇimā (S) (F) **1.** reddish glow. **2.** glow of the dawn which is considered sacred.

Arūpā (S) (F) **1.** without form. **2.** unbounded; immense; divine. **3.** a daughter of Dakṣa (*M. Bh.*).

Āruṣī (S) (F) **1.** kills. **2.** takes lives; killer. **3.** a daughter of Manu, wife of Ćyavana and the mother of Aurva (*M. Bh.*).

Aruṣī (S) (F) **1.** reddish. **2.** the dawn; flame; bright; fecund; illuminating; sacred; enlightening.

Arvantī (S) (F) mare; nymph.

Āryā (S) (F) **1.** honoured; noble; a lady. **2.** respected; worshipped. **3.** one of the 7 mothers present at the birth of Subrahmaṇya (*M. Bh.*); another name for Bhadrakālī.

Āryakī (S) (F) **1.** respected; honoured. **3.** another name for Durgā(*A. Purāṇa*).

Āryamaṅī (S) (F) **1.** jewel among noble ladies; belonging to the sun. **3.** another name for the river Yamunā.

Āryāṁbā (S) (F) **1.** mother of the respectable. **3.** mother of Śaṅkarāćārya.

Āśā (S) (F) **1.** wish; desire; space; region; a quarter of the heavens. **3.** hope personified as the wife of a vasu (*H. Parāṇa*); daughter-in-law of Manas (*P. Ćandrodaya*).

Āṣaḍhikā (S) (F) born in the month of Āṣaḍha.

Āśalī (S) (F) **1.** beloved of the world; friend of the heavens. **2.** liked by all.

Asaṅginī (S) (F) **1.** not attached. **2.** not bound; a whirlwind.

Aśani (S) (F) a flash of lightning; thunderbolt.

Āsāvarī (S) (F) **1.** celestial spirit. **3.** a raga.

Aśikā (S) (F) **1.** dagger. **2.** sharp and piercing.

Asiknī (S) (F) **1.** the dark one. **2.** the night. **3.** a river now known as Ćenāb (*M. Bh.*); a daughter of Prajāpati Vīraṇa, wife of Dakṣa and the mother of 60 girls who are the mothers of creation (*H. Purāṇa*).

Asira (S) (F) **1.** an arrow. **2.** a beam; a ray.

Āśīṣā (S) (F) **1.** blessed. **3.** hope personified as the daughter of Bhaga (*H. Purāṇa*).

Asitā (S) (F) **1.** not white; unbound. **2.** the dark one; the night. **3.** a daughter of Vīraṇa and wife of Dakśa (*H. Purāṇa*); an apsarā (*M. Bh.*); another name for the river Yamunā.

Aśmakī (S) (F) **1.** rocky. **2.** strong yet subtle. **3.** the wife of Prāćinvān of the Purū dynasty and mother of Saṁyāti (*M. Bh.*).

Aśmatī (S) (F) **1.** as hard as rock. **2.** strong; tough; unyielding.

Asmi (S) (F) am.

Aśnā (S) (F) **1.** eating a lot. **2.** voracious. **3.** daughter of Bali and mother of a 100 sons (*V. Purāṇa*).

Aśokā (S) (F) **1.** without sorrow; blossom of the Aśoka tree (*Saraca indica*). **3.** one of the 5 arrows of Kāmā (*V. Purāṇa*); a Jaina deity (*A. Koṣa*).

Aśokārī (S) (F) **1.** enemy of the Aśoka tree. **3.** the Kadamba tree (*Anthocephalus cadamba*).

Aśrī (S) (F) **1.** ill luck; ugliness. **3.** the opposing force of Lakṣmī personified as a goddess who when propitiated will take back luck.

Astā (S) (F) arrow; missile.

Aṣṭābhujā (S) (F) **1.** 8 armed. **3.** another name for Durgā.

Āsthā (S) (F) consideration; regard; care; confidence; hope; support; prop.

Asthūlā (S) (F) **1.** not fat. **2.** delicate; thin.

Asti (S) (F) **1.** existing. **2.** present; existence which cannot be denied; an important person. **3.** the daughter of King Jarāsandha of Magadha and wife of Kaṅsa (*M. Bh.*).

Āstīkamātā (S) (F) **1.** mother of Āstīka. **3.** another name for Manasā.

Astṛti (S) (F) invincibility.

Asurā (S) (F) **1.** incorporeal. **2.** spiritual; ghost; demon; spirit. **3.** a daughter of Kaśyapa and Prādhā (*M. Bh.*).

Aśvākiṇī (S) (F) **1.** obtained from the horse. **2.** strong; swift. **3.** the 1st lunar mansion (*A. Koṣa*).

Aśvatthā (S) (F) day of the full moon in the month of Āśvina.

Aśvavatī (S) (F) **1.** rich in horses. **3.** an apsarā (*V. Purāṇa*); a river (*M. Bh.*).

Aśvikā (S) (F) a little mare.

Aśvinī (S) (F) **1.** possessing horses. **2.** wealthy; a swift mover. **3.** the first of the 27 lunar mansions (*B. Samhitā*); the nymph who was the mother of the aśvins (*Ṛg Veda*); another name for a wife of the sun.

Atibalā (S) (F) **1.** very strong. **2.** a daughter of Dakṣa.

Atićaṇḍā (S) (F) **1.** very fierce. **3.** a minor and intense form of Durgā.

Ātikī (S) (F) **1.** overflowing; outdoing; marriageable; strolling about; heavy bodied. **3.** a wife of Uṣasti (*Ć.Upaniṣad*).

Atimodā (S) (F) **1.** very fragrant; immensely happy. **2.** the jasmine (*Jasminum arboreum*).

Atiraktā (S) (F) **1.** very red. **2.** passionate; fecund; all consuming; unblemished; sacred. **3.** one of the 7 tongues of Agni (*A. Purāṇa*).

Atiriyā (S) (F) **1.** very dear. **2.** loved; eagerly sought after; rare.

Ātmādhikā (S) (F) dearer than one's self.

Ātmajā (S) (F) **1.** daughter of the soul. **3.** another name for Pārvatī.

Ātmodbhavā (S) (F) **1.** born of the soul. **2.** a daughter.

Ātreyī (S) (F) **1.** receptacle of glory; crosses the three worlds; belonging to Atri. **3.** wife of King Ūru the son of Manu and the mother of Aṅga, Sumanas, Svāti, Kratu, Aṅgiras and Gaya (*A. Purāṇa*); daughter of sage Atri who married Aṅgiras the son of Agni and who later became the Paruṣṇī river (*Br. Purāṇa*); a river (*M. Bh.*).

Atyūhā (S) (F) **1.** that which is fragrant. **2.** the jasmine (*Jasminum villosum*).

Aućiti (S) (F) appropriateness; the soul of good poetry (*Kṣemendra's Oućityavićāraćarćā*).

Aurjitya (S) (F) energy; vigour; strength.

Auśīnarī (S) (F) **1.** belonging to the mountains. **3.** a Śūdra girl of Uśīnara from whom was born Kakṣivān by Sage Gautama (*M. Bh.*); the wife of Purūravas (*Vikramorvaśīyam*).

Auvvayar (S) (F) **1.** best among the best. **3.** a celebrated Tamil poetess who lived for 240 years.

Avabhā (S) (F) shining; brilliant.

Avajiti (S) (F) conquest; victory.

Avanati (S) (F) **1.** bowing down. **2.** humble; modest.

Avani (S) (F) **1.** on course. **2.** the bed of a river; the earth.

Avantī (S) (F) **1.** endless; modest. **3.** the city of Ujjaini which is one of the sacred cities of the Hindus (*M. Bh.*).

Āvantikā (S) (F) **1.** very modest; coming from Avanti. **3.** the daughter of Yaugandharāyaṇa (*M. Bh.*).

Avantīvatī (S) (F) 1. bowed down. 3. wife of Pālaka (*K. Sāgara*).

Avarā (S) (F) 1. inferior. 2. youngest. 3. another name for Pārvatī.

Avarajā (S) (F) younger sister.

Avataṅsā (S) (F) garland; ring shaped ornament; earring; crest.

Aviṣī (S) (F) 1. not poisonous; heaven; earth; river. 2. nectar-like; life giving.

Aviśyā (S) (F) 1. desire; ardour. 2. desirous; full of ardour.

Āyati (S) (F) 1. stretching the future; extending the lineage; a descendant. 2. posterity; majesty; dignity; restraint of mind. 3. a daughter of Mahāmeru, the wife of Dhātā and mother of Prāṇa (*V. Purāṇa*).

Ayodhikā (S) (F) 1. never quarrels. 2. of calm disposition; sedate; peace-loving.

Ayomukhī (S) (F) 1. iron faced. 3. a rākṣasī (*V. Rāmāyaṇa*).

Ayugū (S) (F) 1. without a companion. 2. the only daughter.

B

Bābhravī (S) (F) **1.** fire-clad; roaming about; victorious; carrying. **2.** omnipresent; descendant of sage Babhru. **3.** another name for Durgā.

Bābhru (S) (F) **1.** reddish brown cow. **3.** a wife of Yadu.

Babitā (S) (F) **1.** born in the first quarter of an astrological day. **2.** reference here to 'bava' or 'baba' as being that quarter.

Bachendrī (S) (F) the sense of speech; tongue.

Bādarāyaṇī (S) (F) new; young; pure; perfume.

Badarī (S) (F) the Jujube Tree (*Zizyphus jujuba*); a source of the Gaṅgā and the neighbouring hermitage of Nara and Nārāyaṇa (*H. Purāṇa*).

Badarīvāsā (S) (F) **1.** dwelling at Badarī. **3.** another name for Durgā.

Bāgeśrī (S) (F) **1.** prosperity; beauty. **3.** a rāga.

Bagulā (S) (F) **1.** crane. **3.** the crane headed village goddess now identified with Durgā.

Bahubhujā (S) (F) **1.** many armed. **3.** another name for Durgā.

Bahudā (S) (F) **1.** giving much. **3.** a river now known as Jhelum; a wife of Parīkṣit.

Bahudāmā (S) (F) **1.** suppressor of many. **2.** strong and powerful. **3.** a mother of Skanda's retinue (*Ś. Purāṇa*).

Bahudantī (S) (F) **1.** with many teeth; with large teeth; with whom many folk-tales are connected. **3.** the mother of Purandara (*H. Purāṇa*).

Bahugandhā (S) (F) **1.** strong scented; very fragrant. **3.** a bud of the Ćampaka tree (*Michelia champaka*); the jasmine (*Jasminum auriculatum*); sandalwood; musk.

Bahulā (S) (F) **1.** broad; ample; abundant; a cow; cardamoms (*Elettaria cardamomum*); indigo (*indicum*). **3.** a mother attending on Skanda (*M. Bh.*); the wife of Uttama who was the son of Uttānapāda (*Mā. Purāṇa*); a river of ancient India (*M. Bh.*); a digit of the moon.

Bahulī (S) (F) **1.** manifold; magnified; multiplied. **2.** one who has many facets. **3.** the full moon in the month of Kārttika (*Pāṇini*).

Bahulikā (S) (F) **1.** manifold; magnified; multiplied. **2.** a multifaceted personality. **3.** the Pleiades.

Bahumatī (S) (F) **1.** extremely knowledgeable. **2.** a scholar.

Bahupuṣpā (S) (F) **1.** has many flowers; decorated with many flowers; many blossomed. **2.** respected; venerated. **3.** *Erythrina indica.*

Bahuputrī (S) (F) **1.** with many sons. **3.** another name for Durgā whose blessings are invoked when praying for a son.

Bahuputrikā (S) (F) **1.** with many daughters. **3.** an attendant of Skanda (*M. Bh.*).

Bahuratnā (S) (F) rich in gems.

Bahurūpā (S) (F) **1.** with many forms. **3.** one of the 7 tongues of fire (*A. Koṣa*).

Bāhusuyaśā (S) (F) **1.** earning fame through the strength of her arms. **2.** famous for her valour. **3.** the wife of King Parīkṣit of the Kuru dynasty and the mother of Bhīmasena (*M. Bh.*).

Bahvīśvarā (S) (F) **1.** follower of many gods; god of many. **3.** a sacred place on the banks of the Narmadā river.

Bakā (S) (F) **1.** crane. **3.** the daughter of the demon Sumāli and maternal aunt of Rāvaṇa (*U. Rāmāyaṇa*).

Bakavatī (S) (F) **1.** with the qualities of a heron. **2.** very attentive; patient; watchful; cautious. **3.** a river (*R. Taraṅgiṇī*).

Bakerukā (S) (F) **1.** a small crane; a branch of a tree bent by the wind. **2.** cautious; clever; goal oriented.

Bakulā (S) (F) **1.** resembling a crane; the blossom of the Bakula tree (*Mimusops elengi*). **2.** very attentive; patient; watchful; circumspect.

Bakulamālā (S) (F) a garland of Bakula blossoms (*Mimusops elengi*).

Bakulī (S) (F) **1.** lady of the blossoms. **2.** nature. **3.** a rāgiṇī of rāga Bhairava.

Bakulikā (S) (F) small Bakula blossom (*Mimusops elengi*).

Bakulitā (S) (F) decorated with Bakula blossoms (*Mimusops elengi*).

Bālā (S) (F) **1.** girl; jasmine. **2.** young; newly risen; child. **3.** mother of Vāli and Sugrīva said to have been formed by the eye dust of Prajāpati (*V. Rāmāyaṇa*).

Balā (S) (F) **1.** force; power; energy. **3.** a daughter of Raudrāśva; a deity who executes the orders of the 17th Arhat of the present Avasarpiṇī.

Baladā (S) (F) **1.** bestower of strength. **3.** a daughter of Raudrāśva (*H. Purāṇa*).

Balajā (S) (F) **1.** born of power. **2.** Arabian jasmine (*Jasminum sambac*); a pretty woman; the earth. **3.** a river (*Brahma Purāṇa*).

Bālakundā (S) (F) **1.** a young flower. **2.** the jasmine (*Jasminum pubescens*).

Bālāmbikā (S) (F) **1.** a virgin who is worshipped as mother. **3.** a goddess worshipped by south Indian tāntrics and considered identical to Kanyākumarī.

Balanćitā (S) (F) **1.** strongly stretched; carried by power. **3.** Balarāma's lute.

Balandharā (S) (F) **1.** possessor of power. **3.** a daughter of the king of Kāśī the wife of Bhīmasena and mother of Sarvaśa (*M. Bh.*).

Balapramathanī (S) (F) **1.** destroyer of the proud; destroyer of power. **3.** a form of Durgā (*H. Ć. Ćintāmaṇi*).

Bālapuṣpikā (S) (F) **1.** the young blossom. **2.** the strong scented jasmine (*Jasminum auriculatum*).

Bālasandhyā (S) (F) **1.** early twilight. **2.** dawn.

Bālasarasvatī (S) (F) the goddess of knowledge.

Balavatī (S) (F) **1.** powerful; strong; daughter; small cardamoms. **3.** the pious daughter of sage Kaṇva (*P. Purāṇa*).

Balavikarṇikā (S) (F) **1.** possessed with the rays of power. **3.** a form of Durgā (*H. Ć. Ćintāmaṇi*).

Balinī (S) (F) powerful; the constellation of Aśvinī.

Balotkaṭā (S) (F) **1.** with a frightening power. **2.** very powerful. **3.** mother of Skanda's retinue (*Sk. Purāṇa*).

Bāṇagaṅgā (S) (F) **1.** Gaṅgā like an arrow. **2.** a fast moving river. **3.** a river flowing past Someśa said to have been produced byRāvaṇa's cleaving a mountain with an arrow (*V. Purāṇa*).

Banaśrī (S) (F) beauty of the forest.

Bāṇasutā (S) (F) **1.** daughter of Bāṇa. **3.** the wife of Aniruddha (*Bhāgavata*).

Bandhamoćinī (S) (F) **1.** releasing from bonds. **3.** a yoginī (*K. Sāgara*).

Bandhinī (S) (F) **1.** who binds; bound. **2.** imprisoned; bond.

Bandhumatī (S) (F) **1.** with many brothers. **3.** an attendant of Vāsavadattā the wife of Udayana.

Bandhupriyā (S) (F) dear to friends and relations.

Bandhurā (S) (F) wavy rounded; lovely; charming.

Bānsurī (S) (F) flute.

Barhayitā (S) (F) as beautiful as the eye on a peacock-feather.

Barhidhvajā (S) (F) **1.** peacock-bannered. **2.** symbolized by a peacock; surrounded by peacocks. **3.** another name for Durgā.

Barhiṇā (S) (F) adorned with peacock-feathers.

Barhiṣa (S) (F) **1.** sacred Kuśā grass (*Desmostachya bipinnata*); ether; water; fire; sacrifice; light; splendour. **2.** the Kuśā grass is considered to be sacred because it serves as a seat for the gods; sacred; illuminating; renowned; respected; glorious. **3.** a son of Bṛhadrāja.

Barhiṣmatī (S) (F) **1.** blazing; provided with sacred grass. **2.** pure; pious; sacred; ambitious; a worshipper. **3.** a wife of Priyavrata, daughter of Viśvakarman and the mother of Uttama, Tāmasa and Raivata (*Bhāgavata*).

Basantī (S) (F) **1.** of the spring. **2.** the yellow colour associated with spring and stands for life; excitement and creation.

Bekurī (S) (F) **1.** playing a musical instrument. **2.** an apsarā.

Belā (S) (F) the jasmine creeper (*Jasminum sambac*); wave; time.

Bhadrā (S) (F) **1.** fair; good; beautiful; fortunate; prosperous; happy; gentle. **2.** gracious; blessed; auspicious; a cow. **3.** the 2nd, 7th and 12th days of the lunar fortnight (*P. Samhitā*); a form of Durgā (*T. Śāstra*); a form of goddess known as the Dākṣāyaṇī and considered to reside in Bhadreśvara (*V. Purāṇa*); a Buddhist deity (*A. Koṣa*); a vidyādharī (*V. Rāmāyaṇa*); a daughter of Surabhi (*V. Rāmāyaṇa*); the wife of Vaiśravaṇa (*M. Bh.*); a daughter of Soma and wife of Utathya (*V. Rāmāyaṇa*); a daughter of Raudrāśva and Ghṛtāćī (*H. Purana*); a daughter of Śrutakīrti and wife of Kṛṣṇa (*Bhāgavata*); a river of ancient India (*V. Purāṇa*); the daughter of King Kakṣivāna and the wife of King Vyuṣitāśva of the Purū dynasty (*M. Bh.*); a wife of Kubera (*M. Bh.*); the daughter of the king of Viśāla and wife of Śiśupāla (*M. Bh.*); a wife of Vasudeva (*H. Purāṇa*); a daughter of the king of Kāśi and wife of a grandson of King Sagara (*Br. Purāṇa*); a daughter of Meru and wife of King Āgnidhra (*Bhāgavata*); one of the 4 branches of the celestial Gaṅgā (*A. Koṣa*); a daughter of Rohiṇī (*Bhāgavata*); a wife of Garuḍa (*V. Purāṇa*); a daughter of Meru and wife of Bhadrāśva (*Bhāgavata*); another name for Subhadrā, the sister of Kṛṣṇa, the celestial Gaṅgā and gold.

Bhadrabhūṣaṇā (S) (F) **1.** precious ornament. **3.** a goddess.

Bhadrakālī (S) (F) **1.** goddess of welfare; destroyer of ignorance. **3.** a mother attending to Skanda (*Sk. purāṇa*);a form of Durgā (*Bhāgavata*).

Bhadrakarṇikā (S) (F) **1.** wearing beautiful earrings. **2.** listening only to pious talks. **3.** a form of goddess known as Dākṣāyaṇī who is considered to reside in Gokarṇa (*D. Bhāgavata*).

Bhadramanā (S) (F) **1.** kind-hearted; noble-minded. **3.** a daughter of Kaśyapa and Krodhavaśā (*V. āmāyaṇa*).

Bhadramanas (S) (F) **1.** noble minded; kindhearted. **3.** the mother of Airāvata (*M. Bh.*).

Bhadramātā (S) (F) **1.** beautiful mother. **3.** daughter of Kaśyapa and Krodhavaśā.

Bhadramukhī (S) (F) with a beautiful face.

Bhadrarūpā (S) (F) beautiful.

Bhadraṣaṣṭhī (S) (F) **1.** praising good. **3.** a form of Durgā.

Bhadrasomā (S) (F) **1.** as noble and beautiful as the moon. **3.** a river in Uttarakuru (*Mā. Purāṇa*); another name for the Gaṅgā.

Bhadrasvapnā (S) (F) seeing good dreams.

Bhadravallī (S) (F) **1.** a beautiful vine. **2.** the Arabian jasmine (*Jasminum sambac*)

Bhadrāvatī (S) (F) **1.** noble in character. **3.** a daughter of Kṛṣṇa (*Bhāgavata*); a wife of Madhu (*M. Bh.*)

Bhadrikā (S) (F) **1.** a noble woman. **2.** beautiful; meritorious; virtuous; auspicious; an amulet.

Bhagadā (S) (F) **1.** bestower of wealth and happiness. **3.** an attendant of Skanda (*M. Bh.*)

Bhagānandā (S) (F) **1.** bestower of happiness; enjoyer of fortune. **3.** a mother of Skanda's retinue (*M. Bh.*)

Bhāgavantī (S) (F) shareholder; fortunate.

Bhagavatī (S) (F) **1.** universal self and nature conjoined; creator. **3.** a goddess who is a personification of universal self and nature conjoined; another name for Lakṣmī.

Bhāgīrathī (S) (F) **1.** of Bhagīratha. **3.** another name for the Gaṅgā.

Bhāgyā (S) (F) fate; destiny; fortune; luck; happiness.

Bhāgyalakṣmī (S) (F) **1.** goddess of fortune. **3.** another name for Lakṣmī.

Bhāgyaśrī (S) (F) **1.** goddess of fortune. **3.** another name for Lakṣmī.

Bhaimā (S) (F) **1.** descendant of Bhīma. **2.** daughter of a fearsome warrior; the 11th day in the light half of the month of Māgha. **3.** another name for Damayantī.

Bhainā (S) (F) large Grey Babbler Bird; not afraid.

Bhairavī (S) (F) **1.** terrible; consort of Bhairava. **3.** a terrifying form of Kālī (*D. Bhāgavatā*); a rāga; one of the 8 Ambās or forms of Devī (*A. Koṣa*); a rāgiṇī; another name for Nivṛti.

Bhakti (S) (F) **1.** devotion. **2.** love; trust; homage; piety. **3.** a goddess or devi of Draviḍadeśa and the mother of Jñāna and Vairāgya (*Bhāgavata*).

Bhālesvarī (S) (F) goddess of forehead.

Bhallī (S) (F) **1.** a kind of arrow; a small spear. **2.** sharp; piercing and reaching its mark.

Bhāmā (S) (F) **1.** passionate; has splendour. **2.** charming; beautiful; famous; loving. **3.** a wife of Kṛṣṇa (*Bhāgavata*).

Bhāminī (S) (F) **1.** shining; radiant. **2.** beautiful; glorious; renowned passionate. **3.** the wife of King Avikṣit of Vaiśālī and the mother of Marutta (*Bhā. Purāṇa*).

Bhānavi (S) (F) **1.** descendant of the sun; shining like the sun. **2.** sacred; illuminating; glorious; enlightening. **3.** a river crossed by Rāma and Lakṣmaṇa (*V. Rāmāyaṇa*); another name for the Yamunā river.

Bhandanā (S) (F) applause; praise; sunrays.

Bhānū (S) (F) **1.** appearance; light. **2.** beautiful; glorious; virtuous; enlightened. **3.** a daughter of Dakṣa, wife of Dharma or Manu and the mother of Bhānu and Āditya (*V. Purāṇa*); the mother of Devarṣabha (*Bhāgavata*); a daughter of Kṛṣṇa (*V. Purāṇa*); mother of Śakuni.

Bhānujā (S) (F) **1.** daughter of the sun. **3.** another name for the Yamunā river.

Bhānumatī (S) (F) **1.** luminous; as intelligent as the sun. **2.** glorious; famous; enlightening; beautiful. **3.** the wife of Duryodhana (*M. Bh.*); a daughter of Bhānu and wife of Sahadeva (*M. Bh.*); a daughter of Kṛtavīrya, wife of King Ahamyāti and the mother of Sārvabhauma (*H. Purāṇa*); an extremely beautiful daughter of Aṅgiras (*M. Bh.*); a daughter of Vikramāditya (*A. Koṣa*); mother of Śaṁkara.

Bhānupriyā (S) (F) beloved of the sun.

Bhānuśrī (S) (F) as glorious as the sun.

Bhāradvajī (S) (F) **1.** belonging to Bharadvāja; with speed and strength. **3.** a river mentioned in the Purāṇas (*M. Bh.*).

Bharaṇī (S) (F) **1.** one who fulfils. **3.** the 2nd constellation with 3 stars.

Bharatā (S) (F) **1.** immersed in pleasures; well maintained. **3.** a daughter of Agni Bharata (*M. Bh.*); an apsarā (*V. Purāṇa*).

Bhāratī (S) (F) **1.** descendant of Bharata; well maintained; belonging to India; speech. **2.** articulate; meritorious; virtuous. **3.** a goddess identified with Sarasvatī (*Ṛg Veda*); a famous Purāṇic river from which fire is considered to have originated (*V. Purāṇa*).

Bhāravā (S) (F) **1.** a pleasing sound; moving with a steady speed; sacred basil (*Ocimum sanctum*) around which females move in singing the *Samīhagāna*, or a song sung in chorus thus resulting in the emanation of a melodious sound. **2.** pleasing; quick reflexes; agile and flexible.

Bhārgavī (S) (F) **1.** descendant of Bhṛgu; Śukra's daughter. **2.** radiant; charming; glorious; beautiful. **3.** another name for Devayānī, Lakṣmī and Pārvatī.

Bhārū (S) (F) **1.** heavy. **2.** takes up responsibilities. **3.** a daughter of Dakṣa and Vīraṇī and consort of the viśvadevas (*Ś. Purāṇa*).

Bhāsī (S) (F) **1.** illusory; transluscent; of the nature of light; bright; lustrous. **3.** a daughter of Tāmrā and mother of vultures (*H. Purāṇa*); a daughter of Prādhā (*M. Bh.*).

Bhāsvatī (S) (F) **1.** luminous. **2.** splendid; shining. **3.** the city of the sun (*K. Sāgara*); a river of ancient India (*Nirukta*); another name of the dawn.

Bhātī (S) (F) **1.** lovely. **2.** liked by all; perceptible; luminous; light; splendour; evidence; perception; knowledge.

Bhaṭṭārikā (S) (F) **1.** noble lady. **2.** sacred; virtuous; venerated; a tutelary deity. **3.** another name for Durgā.

Bhaṭṭinī (S) (F) noble lady.

Bhaulī (S) (F) **1.** full of feeling. **2.** humane; compassionate. **3.** a rāga.

Bhaumā (S) (F) **1.** of the earth. **2.** firm; unwavering; fecund. **3.** daughter of Satyabhāmā (*Bhā. Purāṇa*).

Bhavadā (S) (F) **1.** giving life. **3.** a mother attending on Skanda (*M. Bh.*).

Bhāvajā (S) (F) **1.** born of the heart. **2.** beautiful; sincere; compassionate; sentimental.

Bhāvanā (S) (F) **1.** feeling. **2.** fancy; thought; meditation; conception; imagination.

Bhāvaṅgamā (S) (F) **1.** touching the heart. **2.** charming; sincere; emotional.

Bhāvāṅganā (S) (F) **1.** embraced by Śiva; the consort of Śiva. **3.** another name for Pārvatī.

Bhavānī (S) (F) **1.** consort of Bhava. **3.** Pārvatī in her pacific and amiable form; a devī of the Śakti cult (*H. Purāṇa*).

Bhavanikā (S) (F) living in a castle.

Bhavantī (S) (F) **1.** now; existent; becoming. **2.** charming; new; a virtuous wife.

Bhavapuṣpā (S) (F) **1.** flowers offered to Śiva; with a flower-like heart. **2.** with a tender, compassionate heart. **3.** the blossoms of dhaturā, ćameli, etc. which are offered as an oblation to Śiva.

Bhavātmajā (S) (F) **1.** daughter of Śiva. **3.** another name for Manasā.

Bhāvikī (S) (F) emotional; sentimental.

Bhāvikī (S) (F) **1.** real. **2.** natural; full of feeling.

Bhāvinī (S) (F) **1.** inducing emotions. **2.** noble; beautiful; illustrious; sensitive; loving. **3.** an attendant of Skanda (*M. Bh.*).

Bhavitrā (S) (F) **1.** manifested. **2.** the earth as the manifest form of nature.

Bhāvukā (S) (F) **1.** happy; productive; prosperous; with a taste for the beautiful. **3.** a demon.

Bhavyā (S) (F) **1.** magnificent. **2.** good; beautiful; calm; tranquil; worthy. **3.** another name for Pārvatī.

Bhavyakīrti (S) (F) **1.** with magnificent fame. **2.** very wise.

Bhayā (S) (F) **1.** fear. **3.** a demoness who is the sister of Kāla, the wife of Heti the son of Brahmā and the mother of Vidyutkeśa (*V. Purāṇa*); the daughter of Anarta and Nikṛti (*H. Purāṇa*).

Bhayaṅkarī (S) (F) **1.** terrifying. **3.** a follower of Skanda (*M. Bh.*).

Bhedī (S) (F) **1.** one who gives out secrets; that which pierces. **3.** an attendant of Skanda (*M. Bh.*).

Bherisvatā (S) (F) **1.** with a musical instrument. **2.** a musician. **3.** an attendant of Skanda (*M. Bh.*).

Bherundā (S) (F) **1.** formidable; terrible. **3.** an intense, fear inducing form of Kālī; a yakṣiṇī (*A. Koṣa*).

Bhīmā (S) (F) **1.** terrible; powerful; tremendous; immense; whip. **3.** a form of Durgā (*H. Purāṇa*); an apsarā (*V. Rāmāyaṇa*).

Bhīmikā (S) (F) **1.** terrible. **3.** a goddess.

Bhīmārikā (S) (F) **1.** enemy of the terrible. **2.** powerful; fearless. **3.** a daughter of Kṛṣṇa and Satyabhāmā (*Bhāgavata*).

Bhīṣmasū (S) (F) **1.** mother of Bhīṣma. **3.** another name for Gaṅgā.

Bhogadā (S) (F) **1.** bestower of worldly pleasures. **2.** grants enjoyment and happiness. **3.** a tutelary goddess of the Piṅgalas (*T. Śāstra*).

Bhogavatī (S) (F) **1.** curving. **2.** a female serpent (*M. Bh.*) **3.** a mother attending on Skanda (*Sk. Purāṇa*); the city of serpents in the subterranean region (*M. Bh.*); the river Gaṅgā in Pātāla (*M. Bh.*).

Bhogyā (S) (F) **1.** worthy of being enjoyed. **2.** an object of enjoyment; a precious stone; money; corn grain.

Bhojā (S) (F) **1.** bestowing enjoyment. **2.** beautiful; liberal. **3.** a princess of the Bhojas (*Bhā. Purāṇa*); an exquisite woman of Sauvīra abducted by Sātyakī and then married to him (*Bhā. Purāṇa*); the wife of Vīravrata (*H. Purāṇa*).

Bhomirā (S) (F) **1.** originating from the earth. **2.** the coral; fecund; life-giving; tolerant.

Bhrājī (S) (F) **1.** lustre. **2.** sheen; splendour; fame; glory.

Bhramarāmbā (S) (F) **1.** the bee-mother. **3.** another name for Pārvatī who was incarnated in the form of a bee to slay an asura (*D. Saptaśati*).

Bhrāmarī (S) (F) **1.** dancing around; belonging to a bee; a form of kinetic energy; a magnet or lodestone. **3.** a yoginī or female attendant of Durgā (*D. Saptaśati*); a rākṣasi of Kaśyapa's family who was slain by Gaṇeśa (*M. Bh.*); another name for Durgā.

Bhrāmarikā (S) (F) **1.** wandering in all directions; honey of the large black bee. **2.** a spinning top.

Bhramī (S) (F) **1.** whirlpool; whirlwind. **3.** a daughter of Śiśumāra and wife of Dhruva (*Bhā. Purāṇa*); *Enhydra fluctuans.*

Bhṛngarī (S) (F) **1.** as black as bee; as bright as fire. **2.** cloves; gold.

Bhudevī (S) (F) **1.** the goddess of the earth. **3.** another name for Pṛthvī.

Bhūmayī (S) (F) **1.** full of existence. **2.** produced from the earth. **3.** another name for Ćhāyā the wife of the sun (*H. Purāṇa*).

Bhūmi (S) (F) **1.** earth. **2.** of existence; receptacle of existence; object; soil. **3.** the earth personified as a goddess who was the daughter of Brahmā and the wife of Mahāviṣṇu (*V. Purāṇa*); the daughter of Śiśumāra, wife of Dhruva and mother of Kalpa and Vatsala (*Bhāgavata*); the wife of King Bhūmipati (*M. Bh.*).

Bhūmijā (S) (F) **1.** born of the earth. **3.** another name for Sītā.

Bhūputrī (S) (F) **1.** daughter of the earth. **3.** another name for Sītā.

Bhūratna (S) (F) jewel of the earth.

Bhūṣā (S) (F) **1.** ornament; decoration; one who wears many ornaments. **2.** one who is an embellishment; precious; much loved; wealthy.

Bhūtā (S) (F) **1.** present; existing; true, real, past. **3.** the 14th day of the dark half of the lunar month; a wife of Bhṛgu.

Bhūtadamanī (S) (F) **1.** one who slays ghosts. **3.** one of the 9 Śaktis of Śiva (*H. Purāṇa*).

Bhūti (S) (F) **1.** existence; wellbeing; prosperity. **2.** wealth; might; power; ashes. **3.** the wife of Rući and mother of Manu Bhautya (*H. Purāṇa*).

Bhuvā (S) (F) fire; the earth.

Bhuvanā (S) (F) **1.** omnipresent; the earth. **3.** Bṛhaspati's sister, wife of Prabhāsa one of the 8 vasus and the mother of Viśvakarmā (*Br. Purāṇa*).

Bhuvanamatī (S) (F) **1.** owner of the world. **2.** princess.

Bhuvanamātṛ (S) (F) **1.** mother of the earth. **3.** another name for Durgā.

Bhuvanapāvanī (S) (F) **1.** one who makes the earth sacred. **3.** another name for the holy Gaṅgā.

Bhuvaneśānī (S) (F) mistress of the earth.

Bhuvaneśī (S) (F) **1.** goddess of the earth. 3. a goddess (*D. Bhāgavata*).

Bhuvis (S) (F) heaven.

Biḍālākṣa (S) (F) **1.** cat eyed. **3.** a rākṣasī.

Bidālikā (S) (F) **1.** young cat. **2.** a kitten.

Bījahāriṇī (S) (F) **1.** taking away seed. **3.** a daughter of Duḥsaha.

Bījākṣarā (S) (F) **1.** the seed alphabet; Om. **2.** the first syllable of a mantra; the atomic alphabet; profound; omnipotent.

Bījāñjalī (S) (F) **1.** a handful of seed. **2.** fecund; life-giving.

Bijlī (S) (F) **1.** lightning. **2.** bright; glorious; illuminating; enlightening.

Bilvapattrikā (S) (F) 1. leaf of the bilva tree. 3. a form of goddess known as the Dākṣāyāṇī who resides at the temple of Bilvaka (*D. Bhāgavata*).

Bimbā (S) (F) 1. disc of the sun or the moon; image; mirror. 2. that which reflects; a preceptor. 3. mother of King Bimbisāra; the wife of King Bālāditya of Kāśmira (*R. Taraṅgiṇī*).

Bimbī (S) (F) 1. as glorious as the sun or the moon; the fruit of the *Momordica monodelpha* plant; *Coccinia indica*. 3. the mother of King Bimbisāra (*B. Literature*).

Bimbinī (S) (F) the pupil of the eye.

Biṇā (S) (F) 1. lute. 2. melodious; harmonious.

Bindiyā (S) (F) 1. a small dot. 3. reference here to a small dot that married Hindu women wear on their forehead as an embellishment and a sign of auspiciousness.

Bindu (S) (F) a point; mark; symbol; drop; pearl; truth; alphabet; origin; which connotes; subtle; immeasurable; absolute; divine; the Brahman.

Bindumālinī (S) (F) 1. wearing a garland of pearls. 3. a rāga.

Bindumatī (S) (F) 1. learned; knower of the Absolute. 2. wise; illumined; enlightened; has attained mokṣa or salvation. 3. a wife of Marīci (*Bhāgavata*); a daughter of Śasābindu and wife of Māndhātṛ (*H. Purāṇa*); the wife of King Māndhātā and the mother of Pūrukutṣa and Mućukunda (*Bhāgavata*).

Bindurekhā (S) (F) 1. a line of dots; averse. 2. a poetic composition. 3. a daughter of Ćaṇḍavarman (*K. Sāgara*).

Binītā (S) (F) humble.

Bisālā (S) (F) 1. sprout. 2. bud; young shoot; a child.

Bisāvatī (S) (F) 1. abounding in lotus-fibre. 2. garbed in lotuses; fragrant; sacred; auspicious.

Bisinī (S) (F) 1. a collection of lotus flowers. 2. beautiful; fragrant; auspicious; famous; venerated; dear to the gods.

Bodhanā (S) (F) 1. the awakening; the arousing; the enlightening; the inspiring; the intellect. 2. knowledge. 3. the awakening of Durgā; a festival on the 9th day of the dark half of the month Bhadra.

Bodhi (S) (F) 1. perfect knowledge; wisdom; enlightenment. 3. the knowledge by which one becomes a Buddha or Jina in the Buddhist and Jaina religions respectively; the Bodhi tree (*Fiats religiosa*); meditating under which Gautama Buddha attained spiritual enlightenment and which since has been called the tree of wisdom.

Bodhinī (S) (F) 1. intellect. 2. awakens; knowledge; understanding; perception; wis-dom; enlightenment.

Brahmāmbikā (S) (F) mother of the Absolute; mother; the Absolute.

Brahmanadī (S) (F) 1. river of Brahmā. 3. another name for the river Sarasvatī which originated from the Kamandalu of Brahmā.

Brāhmaṇī (S) (F) 1. consort of Brahmā. 2. intelligent; wise; enlightened; venerated; sacred. 3. another name for Sarasvatī.

Brahmāṇī (S) (F) 1. consort of Brahmā. 2. the personified female energy or Śakti of Brahmā; perfume. 3. a river; another name for Durgā.

Brahmāñjali (S) (F) 1. to pray with cupped hands. 2. venerated; one who venerates; to join the hands while repeating the Vedas.

Brahmaputrā (S) (F) 1. daughter of Brahmā. 3. a river rising from the Tibet side of the Himālayas and falling with the Gaṅgā into the Bay of Bengal; Bulb bearing Yam (*Discorea bulbifera*).

Brahmavṛnda (S) (F) 1. an assembly of divine beings. 3. the city of Brahmā.

Brāhmī (S) (F) 1. holy. 2. the Śakti of Brahmā. 3. the feminine energy of Brahmā personified as Śakti and regarded as one of the 8 divine mothers of creation; the wife of Dhruva and mother of Kalpa; another name for Sarasvatī, Śatarūpā, Durgā and the constellation Rohiṇī; *Enhydra fluctuanes*.

Brahmiṣṭhā (S) (F) **1.** the highest form of the Absolute. **3.** another name for Durgā.

Bṛhadambālikā (S) (F) **1.** a stout mother. **2.** strong; voluptuous; courageous. **3.** an attendant of Skanda (*M. Bh.*).

Bṛhadbhāṣā (S) (F) **1.** has great splendour. **3.** a daughter of Sūrya and wife of Agni Bhānu (*M. Bh.*).

Bṛhaddhvani (S) (F) **1.** makes a lot of noise. **3.** a king of the family of Bharata (*Bhāgavata*).

Bṛhaddivā (S) (F) **1.** highly illuminated; celestial. **2.** bright; radiant; enlightened. **3.** a god-dess (*A. Brāhmaṇa*).

Bṛhadsenī (S) (F) **1.** mighty leader; has a large army. **3.** Damayantī's nurse (*Nalopākhyāna*).

Bṛhaddyuti (S) (F) **1.** highly luminous; intensely brilliant. **2.** great light; radiance.

Bṛhanmatī (S) (F) possesses a lot; immensely intellectual.

Bṛhantā (S) (F) **1.** destroyer of the powerful. **2.** strong; great. **3.** one of the 7 mothers of Skanda (*M. Bh.*).

Bṛhatī (S) (F) **1.** heaven and earth (*A. Koṣa*). **2.** speech; large; strong; reservoir; a Vedic metre. **3.** the lute of Nārada (*A. Koṣa*); the mother of Manu Ćākṣuṣa and wife of Ṛpu (*H. Purāṇa*); one of the 7 horses of the sun (*V. Purāṇa*).

Bṛhatkukṣi (S) (F) **1.** large bellied. **3.** a yoginī.

Bṛndā (S) (F) **1.** surrounded by many; the sacred basil (*Ocimum sanctum*). **3.** another name for Rādhā who was always surrounded by many friends.

Bṛjabālā (S) (F) **1.** daughter of nature. **2.** daughter of Bṛja. **3.** another name for Rādhā.

Bṛjalatā (S) (F) **1.** creeper of Bṛja. **3.** a kind of creeper that grows in Bṛja.

Budbudā (S) (F) **1.** bubble. **2.** an ornament resembling a bubble (*M. Bh.*). **3.** an apsarā.

Buddhakapālinī (S) (F) **1.** with an enlightened mind. **2.** wise; enlightened; venerated; one who has attained mokṣa or salvation. **3.** one of the 6 goddesses of magic (*D. Sāstra*).

Buddhi (S) (F) **1.** intelligence; intellect. **2.** judgement; reason. **3.** intelligence personified as a daughter of Dakṣa and wife of Dharma and mother of Bodha (*M. Bh.*) **3.** a wife of Gaṇeśa (*Purāṇas*).

Buddhidevī (S) (F) goddess of wisdom.

Buddhikāmā (S) (F) **1.** desirous of acquiring wisdom. **3.** a mother attending Skanda (*M. Bh.*).

Buddhikārī (S) (F) **1.** bestower of wisdom. **3.** another name for Sarasvatī.

Buddhimatikā (S) (F) intelligent; wise.

Bulā (S) (F) a nose-ring.

C

Ćahanā (S) (F) desire; affection.

Ćaitalī (S) (F) belonging to the mind; with a sharp memory.

Ćaitrī (S) (F) **1.** born in spring. **2.** as beautiful, tender and fresh as a new blossom; ever-happy.

Ćakorī (S) (F) **1.** shining; content. **2.** the female Greek partridge (*Perdix rufa*); fabled to subsist on moonbeams.

Ćakrākārā (S) (F) **1.** disc shaped. **2.** circular. **3.** another name for the earth.

Ćakramardikā (S) (F) **1.** destroyer of the disc. **3.** wife of Lilāditya (*R. Taraṅgiṇī*).

Ćakranemi (S) (F) **1.** felly of a wheel. **2.** disc; ring; thunderbolt; responsible for progress. **3.** a mother in Skanda's retinue (*M. Bh.*).

Ćakreśvarī (S) (F) **1.** goddess of the discus. **3.** a vidyādevī.

Ćakṣaṇī (S) (F) soothing to the eyes; illuminating.

Ćakṣurvardhanikā (S) (F) **1.** refreshing the eyes. **2.** beautiful; charming. **3.** a river which flows through Śaka Island (*M. Bh.*).

Ćākṣuṣī (S) (F) **1.** preceptor; seer. **2.** the faculty of perceiving everything in the 3 worlds (*M. Bh.*).

Ćalā (S) (F) **1.** shaking; fickle; lightning. **2.** that which is moving; a sprout; quicksilver; perfume. **3.** the incarnation of goddess Lakṣmī as a mare on the banks of the river Sarasvatī who regained her form after delivering a son who came to be known as Ekavīra the founder of the Hehaya kingdom (*D. Bhāgavata*); the tree *Altingia excelsa*.

Ćalamā (S) (F) **1.** ever moving goddess. **3.** goddess Pārvatī who is the personification of kinetic energy.

Ćallalamma (Telugu) (F) **1.** goddess of butter-milk. **3.** a goddess worshipped in the villages of South India.

Ćamalammā (Telugu) (F) **1.** the goddess of the downtrodden. **3.** the Telugu representation of Kālī.

Ćamelī (S) (F) a jasmine flower (*Jasminum grandifloum*).

Ćampā (S) (F) soothing; a flower of the Ćampakā tree (*Michelia champaka*).

Ćampākali (S) (F) **1.** a bud of the Ćampakā tree (*Michelia champaka*). **2.** tender; young; fragrant; much liked.

Ćampakavatī (S) (F) **1.** owner of Ćampaka trees; blooms eternally. **2.** fragrant; much liked; fecund; life-giving. **3.** a forest in Magadha (*Hitopadśa*).

Ćampāmālinī (S) (F) a garland of Ćampā flowers (*Michelia champaka*).

Ćampikā (S) (F) **1.** little Champā flower. **3.** a daughter of Bhūrikīrtī and wife of Kuśa.

Ćāmuṇḍā (S) (F) **1.** slayer of Ćaṇḍa and Muṇḍa. **2.** Ćaṇḍa and Muṇḍa conjoined. **3.** a terrific form of Durgā who, as goddess Kālī sprang from the forehead of goddess Ambikā to destroy the asuras Ćaṇḍa and Muṇḍa (*D. Bhāgavata*).

Ćāmuṇḍeśvarī (S) (F) **1.** the goddess Ćāmuṇḍī. **3.** a form of Durgā.

Ćamūrudṛṣ (S) (F) antelope eyed.

Ćanalakṣmī (S) (F) **1.** goddess of delight and satisfaction. **3.** another name for Lakṣmī.

Ćanasyā (S) (F) delighting.

Ćañćalā (S) (F) **1.** fickle; restless; moving constantly. **2.** lightning; a river. **3.** another name for Lakṣmī.

Ćañćalākṣī (S) (F) **1.** with restless playful eyes. **3.** a vidyādhara girl who cursed Rāvaṇa to die (*V. Rāmāyaṇa*).

Ćaṇḍā (S) (F) **1.** passionate; angry; wrathful. **3.** a female attendant of Durgā (*Brah. Purāṇa*); the wife of Uddālaka (*J. Bhārata*); Chaṇḍā/Chaṇḍī is a tutelary deity of Bengal and Mysore (*H. Purāṇa*); an attendant of the 12th Arhat of the present Avasarpiṇī (*He. Koṣa*); another name for Durgā; Cocklebur (*Xanthium strumarium*).

Ćaṇḍaghaṇṭā (S) (F) **1.** with passionate bells. **3.** another name for Durgā.

Ćandakiraṇa (S) (F) **1.** moonlight. **2.** fair; luminous; soothing.

Caṇḍālikā (S) (F) **1.** of a low caste. **3.** another name for Durgā.

Ćaṇḍālinī (S) (F) **1.** glorious; destroyer of Ćaṇḍa. **3.** a tāntric goddess (*T. Śāstra*).

Ćaṇḍamuṇḍā (S) (F) **1.** slayer of Caṇḍa and Muṇḍa. **3.** another name for Durgā.

Ćandanā (S) (F) **1.** sandalwood (*Pterocarpus santalinus*). **2.** fragrant; cool; soothing and auspicious **3.** a river (*V. Purāṇa*); saffron (*Crocus sativus*); *Ichnocarpus fnitescens.*

Ćaṇḍanāyikā (S) (F) **1.** slayer of Ćaṇḍa. **3.** a minor form of Durgā.

Ćāndanī (S) (F) **1.** moonlight; silver. **2.** fair; cool; luminous; soothing.

Ćandanīkā (S) (F) a small sandalwood tree (*Pterocarpus santalinus*).

Ćaṇḍarudrikā (S) (F) **1.** the glorious fierce goddess. **3.** mystical knowledge acquired by worship of the 8 forms of Durgā (*D. Bhāgavata*).

Ćaṇḍarūpā (S) (F) **1.** terrible in form. **3.** a goddess (*Brah. Purāṇa*).

Ćaṇḍavatā (S) (F) **1.** violent; passionate. **2.** warm. **3.** one of the 8 forms of Durgā (*D. Bhāgavata*).

Ćaṇḍavatī (S) (F) **1.** violent; passionate. **3.** a minor form of Durgā (*Brah. Purāṇa*).

Ćaṇḍi (S) (F) **1.** the passionate and angry. **3.** wife of Uddālaka; another name for Durgā.

Ćaṇḍikā (S) (F) **1.** slayer of Ćaṇḍa; fierce woman. **3.** a terrifying form of Pārvatī, who is worshipped under the name of Ćandikādevī and whose idol has twenty hands (*D. Bhāgavata*).

Ćaṇḍīkusumā (S) (F) **1.** the flower of a passionate woman. **3.** the Red Oleander (*Nerium odorum*).

Ćaṇḍogrā (S) (F) **1.** fierce and angry. **3.** a minor form of Durgā (*Brah. Purāṇa*).

Ćandrabālā (S) (F) **1.** daughter of the moon. **2.** a girl as beautiful as the moon; Cardamom (*Elettaria cardamomum*).

Ćandrabhāgā (S) (F) **1.** a piece of the moon. **3.** the river now called Ćenab (*M. Bh.*).

Ćandrabindu (S) (F) crescent moon.

Ćandradārā (S) (F) **1.** wives of the moon. **3.** 27 of Dakṣa's daughters married to Ćandra or the moon and considered to be the 27 lunar mansions.

Ćandragaurī (S) (F) **1.** as fair as the moon. **2.** extremely fair; tranquil; soothing.

Ćandragolikā (S) (F) moonlight.

Ćandrahāsā (S) (F) **1.** with a beautiful smile. **3.** a yoginī.

Ćandrajā (S) (F) **1.** daughter of the moon. **2.** a moonbeam.

Ćandrakalā (S) (F) **1.** l/16th of the moon's disc. **2.** the segments of the moon. **3.** each segment or crescent of the moon is personified as a goddess (*K. Sāgara*).

Ćandrakalī (S) (F) **1.** a digit of the moon. **2.** progressive.

Ćandrakāntā (S) (F) **1.** as lovely as the moon; beloved of the moon. **2.** moonstone; night; moonlight. **3.** another name for Rohiṇī, the consort of the moon.

Ćandrakānti (S) (F) **1.** as brilliant as the moon. **2.** silver; moonlight. **3.** the 9th day of the waxing moon (*J. Śāstra*).

Candralekha (S) (F) **1.** a digit of the moon. **3.** a daughter of Suśravas.

Ćandrālī (S) (F) moonbeam.

Ćandramā (S) (F) moonbeam.

Ćandramālā (S) (F) **1.** garland of the moon. **2.** the aura of the moon; of dazzling beauty. **3.** a river (*M. Bh.*).

Ćandramallikā (S) (F) **1.** queen of the moon. **3.** another name for Rohiṇī, the consort of the moon; *Crysanthemum coronarium.*

Ćandramasī (S) (F) **1.** lunar. **3.** the constellation Mṛgaśiras; the wife of Bṛhaspati (*H. Purāṇa*).

Ćandramatī (S) (F) **1.** as beautiful as the moon. **2.** with an intellect as bright as the moon. **3.** the wife of King Hariśćandra (*M. Bh.*).

Ćandramukhā (S) (F) 1. moonfaced. 2. beautiful. 3. a yakṣī considered to live in the Bakula tree (*Mimusops elengi*).

Ćandramukhī (S) (F) as beautiful as the moon.

Ćandrāṇi (S) (F) 1. wife of the moon. 3. another name for Rohiṇī, consort of the moon.

Ćandraprabhā (S) (F) 1. moonlight. 3. a female gandharva (*K. Sāgara*); the mother of Somaprabhā (*Ć. Ćarita*).

Ćandraśilā (S) (F) 1. stone of the moon. 2. cool; sedate; soothing and tranquil. 3. the moonstone.

Ćandraśrī (S) (F) 1. divine moon. 2. fair; beautiful; charming; soothing; tranquil.

Ćandraśubhra (S) (F) 1. illumined by the moon. 2. as fair as the moon.

Ćandrāsitā (S) (F) 1. pale white moon; cooled by the moon; a day in the bright half of the month. 3. an attendant of Skanda (*M. Bh.*).

Ćandratārā (S) (F) 1. the moon and the stars conjoined. 2. eye catching.

Ćandravadanā (S) (F) moon faced.

Ćandrāvalī (S) (F) 1. moon like. 3. a gopī and friend of Rādhā the beloved of Kṛṣṇa (*V. Purāṇa*); a yoginī.

Ćandravalli (S) (F) 1. vine of the moon. 3. the Mādhavī creeper (*Hiplage madoblata*).

Ćandravasā (S) (F) 1. one whose abode is the moon. 2. peaceful; tranquil. 3. a river (*Bhā. Purāṇa*).

Ćandrāvatī (S) (F) 1. lit by the moon. 2. brilliant. 3. the daughter of Sunābha the asura and the wife of Gadā (*H. Purāṇa*); a wife of King Hariśćandra in his previous birth (*Rāmāyaṇa*); a wife of King Dharmasena (*V. Pañćaviṅśatika*); the daughter of King Ćandragupta (*K. Sāgara*).

Ćāndrī (S) (F) 1. moonlight. 2. fair; cool; soothing. 3. *Psoralea corylifolia*.

Ćandrikā (S) (F) 1. moonlight. 2. fair; illuminating; cool; soothing; the Mallikā creeper (*Jasminum sambac*); Garden cress (*Lepidum sativm*); Fenugreek (*Trigonella foenum-graecum*); Cardamom (*Elletaria cardamomum*); *Rauwolfia serpentina*. 3. another name for the Ćandrabhāgā river; another name for Dākṣāyaṇī.

Ćandrikāmbuja (S) (F) 1. lotus of the night. 2. the night lotus (*Nelumbium speciosum*).

Ćandrimā (S) (F) moonlight.

Ćandrupā (S) (F) 1. with the form of the moon. 2. as beautiful as the moon.

Ćapalā (S) (F) 1. fickle; swift; wavering. 2. lightning. 3. another name for Lakṣmī.

Ćarćikā (S) (F) 1. repeating a word; smeared with unguents. 2. fragrant; inviting. 3. a tutelary goddess (*H. Ć. Ćintāmaṇi*); another name for Durgā.

Caraṇī (S) (F) 1. wandering from place to place; a wanderer. 2. a bird.

Ćarṇapūrṇa (S) (F) 1. full moon. 2. fair; beautiful; soothing; tranquil.

Ćarṣaṇi (S) (F) 1. active; agile; swift. 2. intelligence; moonlight; saffron. 3. Aryaman's daughters by Mātṛkā and the progenitors of the human race (*H. Purāṇa*); the wife of Varuṇa and the mother of Bhṛgu (*Var. Purāṇa*); the wife of Kubera (*V. Rāmayaṇa*).

Ćārubālā (S) (F) a beautiful girl.

Ćārūćitrā (S) (F) beautiful picture; one with a beautiful form.

Ćārudarśanā (S) (F) beautiful in appearance.

Ćārudhārā (S) (F) 1. beautiful. 3. another name for Indra's consort Śaći.

Ćaruḍhī (S) (F) 1. with an auspicious mind. 3. a mountain near Mahāmeru (*D. Bhāgavata*).

Ćārulatā (S) (F) beautiful vine.

Ćārulоćanā (S) (F) with beautiful eyes.

Ćārumatī (S) (F) 1. with an auspicious intellect. 2. intelligent; wise; enlightened. 3. the daughter of Kṛṣṇa and Rukmiṇī (*H. Purāṇa*).

Ćārunetrā (S) (F) 1. with beautiful eyes. 3. an apsarā in the court of Kubera (*M. Bh.*).

Ćāruśilā (S) (F) beautiful jewel.

Ćārutamā (S) (F) most beautiful.

Ćāruvāki (S) (F) **1.** sweet tongued. **3.** the wife of King Aśoka.

Ćaruvāṅgī (S) (F) **1.** with splendid limbs. **3.** a daughter of Kuśambha and the wife of King Bhadraśreṇya (*Br. Purāṇa*).

Ćāruveṇi (S) (F) **1.** a beautiful braid. **3.** a river (*M. Bh.*).

Ćāruvī (S) (F) **1.** splendour; splendid (*R. Taraṅginī*). **3.** another name for Kubera's wife Bhadrā.

Ćārvāṅgī (S) (F) **1.** with a beautiful body. **3.** a daughter of Kuśamba and wife of King Bhadraśrenya (*Bh. Purāṇa*).

Ćaturikā (S) (F) clever; skilful.

Ćatuṣkarṇī (S) (F) **1.** 4 eared. **3.** a mother in Skanda's retinue (*M. Bh.*).

Ćatuṣpathā (S) (F) **1.** living on a crossroad. **3.** an attendant of Skanda (*M. Bh.*).

Ćatvaravāsinī (S) (F) **1.** living on a crossroad. **3.** a mother and attendant of Skanda (*M. Bh.*).

Ćelanā (S) (F) **1.** of the nature of consiousness. **3.** a daughter of King Ćetaka of Vaiśāli and the wife of King Śreṇika (*P. Purāṇa*).

Ćeṣṭā (S) (F) **1.** effort; endeavour. **2.** motion; movement.

Ćetakī (S) (F) **1.** sentient. **3.** Spanish Jasmine (*Jasminum grandiflorum*); Black Myrobalan (*Terminalia chebula*).

Ćetanā (S) (F) **1.** intelligence. **2.** consciousness; mind; knowledge; sense; vitality; life; wisdom; understanding.

Ćhandā (S) (F) moon.

Ćhandodevī (S) (F) **1.** goddess of the metre. **3.** another name for Gāyatrī.

Ćhatramukhā (S) (F) **1.** umbrella faced. **2.** many faced. **3.** a nāga (*K. Vyūha*).

Ćhavi (S) (F) image; reflection; beauty; splendour; a ray of light.

Ćhavillākara (S) (F) **1.** of handsome appearance. **3.** a historian of Kāśmira (*R. Taraṅgiṇī*).

Ćhāyā (S) (F) **1.** shade; shadow. **2.** colour; lustre; beauty; resemblance; line; reflection. **3.** the daughter of Viśvakarmā (*V. Purāṇa*); a substitute wife of Sūrya and mother of Manu, Yama and Yamī, Sāvarṇi, Śani and Tāpanī (*H. Purāṇa*); a form of Durgā known as Kātyāyani (*A. Koṣa*); a rāga.

Ćhāyāgrāhī (S) (F) **1.** catching the image. **2.** mirror. **3.** a rākṣasi who was killed by Hanumān (*V. Rāmāyaṇa*).

Ćhinnamastā (S) (F) **1.** beheaded. **2.** she of the split skulls. **3.** a tāntric form of Durgā who is depicted as headless (*T. Śāstra*).

Ćinnintammā (Telugu) (F) village goddess regarded as the head of the household.

Ćintā (S) (F) consideration; thought.

Ćitaparā (S) (F) **1.** beyond the power of thought. **2.** incogitable; indescribable. **3.** another name for Kāmākṣī.

Ćitrā (S) (F) **1.** beautiful; wonderful; conspicuous. **2.** picture; anything bright that strikes the eye; ornament; constellation; sky; painting; heaven; worldly illusion. **3.** an apsarā (*M. Bh.*); a daughter of Gada; a river; the 14th lunar mansion; another name for Subhadrā.

Ćitra (S) (F) **1.** picture; conspicuous. **2.** excellent; distinguished; various; bright. **3.** son of Dhṛtarāṣṭra (*M. Bh.*); a king of elephants with whom Subrahmaṇya played (*M. Bh.*); warriors of the Kauravas (*M. Bh.*); a hero of the Ćedi kingdom who fought on the side of the Pāṇḍavas (*M. Bh.*); a gandharva; a Dravida king (*P. Purāṇa*); the herb *Cucumis trigonus*; Ceylon Leadwort (*Plumbago zeylanica*); Aśoka tree (*Saraca indica*).

Ćitrai (Tamil) (F) **1.** the spring. **2.** the month of April.

Ćitrajyotī (S) (F) **1.** wonderfully glorious. **2.** shining brilliantly.

Ćitrakeṣī (S) (F) **1.** having wonderful hair. **3.** an apsarā and consort of King Vatsa (*Bhāgavata*).

Ćitralatā (S) (F) **1.** wonderful vine. **3.** an apsarā (*B. Rāmāyaṇa*); Indian Madder (*Rubia cordifolia*).

Ćitralekhā (S) (F) **1.** beautiful outline; picture. **2.** portrait; digit of the moon. **3.** an apsarā who danced at the assembly of the Pāṇḍavas (*M. Bh.*); a companion of Uṣā the daughter of the demon Bāṇa (*Bhāgavata*); a daughter of Kumbhāṇḍa (*Bhāgavata*).

Ćitrālī (S) (F) a wonderful lady; friend of the strange.

Ćitramāyā (S) (F) worldly illusion; strange manifestation.

Ćitramayī (S) (F) **1.** full of wonders. **2.** like a picture.

Ćitrāṅgadā (S) (F) **1.** with wonderful limbs. **2.** with bejewelled arms. **3.** an apsarā (*M. Bh.*); a wife of Arjuna who was the daughter of King Ćitravāhana of Manālur and the mother of Babhruvāhana (*M. Bh.*); a daughter of Viśvakarmā (*M. Bh.*).

Ćitrāṅgī (S) (F) **1.** with a vareigated body. **2.** with a charming body. **3.** the daughter of King Bhadraśreṇya of the Hehayas and the wife of Durmada (*M. Bh.*); Indian Madder (*Rubia cordifolia*).

Ćitrapuṣpī (S) (F) **1.** variegated blossom. **3.** the *Hibiscus cannabinus.*

Ćitrarathī (S) (F) **1.** with a bright chariot. **3.** a form of Durgā.

Ćitraratī (S) (F) granter of excellent gifts.

Ćitrarekhā (S) (F) **1.** picture; a wonderful line. **3.** an apsarā who was skilled in the art of painting (*A. Veda*); a daughter of Kuṣmāṇḍa (*Bhāgavata*).

Ćitrasenā (S) (F) **1.** with a bright spear. **3.** an apsarā who danced in the court of Kubera (*M. Bh.*); a mother in Skanda's retinue (*M. Bh*); a river (*M. Bh.*).

Ćitraśilā (S) (F) **1.** of strange character; stony. **3.** a Purāṇic river (*M. Bh.*).

Ćitraśrī (S) (F) with divine beauty.

Ćitravāhā (S) (F) **1.** with an extraordinary current. **3.** a river of ancient India (*M. Bh.*).

Ćitravalayā (S) (F) **1.** with a painted bracelet. **3.** a goddess mentioned in the *Brahma Purāṇa.*

Ćitrvatī (S) (F) **1.** decorated. **3.** a daughter of Kṛṣṇa (*H. Purāṇa*).

Ćitriṇī (S) (F) **1.** endowed with marks of excellence. **2.** brightly ornamented; with various talents.

Ćitritā (S) (F) **1.** variegated; painted. **2.** decorated; decorated with ornaments.

Ćittā (S) (F) thoughtful; intellectual; spiritual.

Ćitti (S) (F) **1.** thought. **2.** devotion; thinking; understanding. **3.** the wife of Atharvan and (*Bhāgavata*); mother of Dadhyać (*Bh. Purāṇa*).

Ćityadyotā (S) (F) **1.** brightness conceived by imagination; enlightening the mind. **3.** a class of deities (*D. Bhāgavata*).

Ćūḍābhikṣuṇī (S) (F) **1.** a female ascetic who has a crest on the head; best among the ascetics. **3.** a Buddhist goddess (*B. Literature*).

Ćūḍakā (S) (F) **1.** forming the crest. **3.** an apsarā.

Ćūḍālā (S) (F) **1.** with a lock of hair on the crown of the head. **3.** the saintly wife of King Śikhidhvaja (*Yogavāśiṣṭha*).

Ćumbā (S) (F) **1.** kiss. **2.** adorable person.

Ćumban (S) (F) **1.** kiss. **2.** adorable person.

Ćunnī (S) (F) a small ruby.

D

Dadhijā (S) (F) **1.** daughter of milk; born of curd. **3.** the goddess Lakṣmī who is considered to be the daughter of the sea and born from the Ocean of Milk.

Dadhinadī (S) (F) **1.** river of curd. **3.** a river of ancient India (*M. Bh.*).

Dahadahā (S) (F) **1.** blazing; destroying enemies. **3.** a mother in Skanda's retinue (*M. Bh.*).

Dahanapriyā (S) (F) **1.** beloved of fire. **3.** the wife of Agni (*H. Koṣa*).

Dahanolkā (S) (F) firebrand.

Daityasenā (S) (F) **1.** one who has an army of demons. **3.** a daughter of Prajāpati, the sister of Devasenā and the wife of the asura Keśi (*M. Bh.*).

Dākinī (S) (F) **1.** witch. **3.** a female magician attendant of Kālī (*Brah. Purāṇa*).

Dakṣakanyā (S) (F) **1.** an able daughter. **3.** daughter of Dakṣa; another name for Durgā.

Dakṣāyaṇī (S) (F) **1.** coming from Dakṣa. **2.** gold; golden ornament; daughter of a perfect being. **3.** any daughter of Dakṣa; another name for the goddess Durgā.

Dākṣāyaṇinyā (S) (F) **1.** obtained from Dakṣa. **2.** gold; golden ornament; daughter of a perfect being. **3.** the Dākṣāyāṇī Aditi (*Mā. Purāṇa*).

Dakṣeyu (S) (F) **1.** striving for perfection; perfect. **3.** a daughter of Dakṣa and the mother of parrots (*V. Purāṇa*).

Dakṣiṇā (S) (F) **1.** a donation to an officiating priest or god. **2.** fit; able; righthanded; towards the south; a prolific cow. **3.** the daughter of Rući and Ākūti, the wife of Yajñapuruṣa (*V. Purāṇa*); the mother of a class of devas called the Yamas, as also of Phaladā — the god who awards the fruit of all actions, and reborn later as Suśilā a friend of Rādhā (*M. Bh.*); an idol of Durgā with its right side prominent (*D. Purāṇa*); the wife of Suyajña, the mother of Suyama and a previous incarnation of Lakṣmī (*Bhā. Purāṇa*).

Dakṣiṇakālika (S) (F) **1.** protectress of the south. **3.** a form of Durgā worshipped by the tāntrics (*T. Śastra*).

Dalajā (S) (F) **1.** produced from petals. **2.** honey.

Dalakoṣā (S) (F) treasure of petals; the jasmine flower.

Dāmā (S) (F) **1.** one who suppresses. **2.** wealthy; self-restrained. **3.** an attendant of Skanda (*M. Bh.*).

Damasvaśrī (S) (F) **1.** Dama's sister. **3.** another name for Damayantī.

Damayantī (S) (F) **1.** subduing men; self-restrained. **3.** the daughter of King Bhīma of Vidarbha, the wife of King Nala, considered to be the most noble of Indian heroines (*Nalopākhyāna*); a daughter of Pramloća; a king of jasmine.

Dānandadā (S) (F) **1.** donates generously. **3.** an apsarā or gāndharvī (*K. Vyūha*).

Danāyus (S) (F) **1.** suppressed. **3.** a daughter of Dakṣa; the wife of Kaśyapa and mother of Bala, Vikṣara, Vīra and Vrata (*M. Bh.*).

Daṇḍagaurī (S) (F) **1.** goddess of punishment. **3.** an apsarā (*M. Bh.*).

Dantā (S) (F) **1.** tamed; mild; having teeth. **3.** an apsarā (*M. Bh.*).

Dāntī (S) (F) patience; self restraint.

Danu (S) (F) **1.** noisy; high-pitched. **2.** growler. **3.** a daughter of Dakṣa, the wife of Kaśyapa and the mother of the 100 dānavas (*M. Bh.*).

Darpaṇikā (S) (F) a small mirror.

Darśanī (S) (F) **1.** worth looking at. **3.** another name for goddess Durgā.

Darśanojjvalā (S) (F) **1.** of brilliant aspect; fair to look at. **2.** the Jasmine.

Darśataśrī (S) (F) of noticeable beauty.

Darśayāminī (S) (F) a night that is worth seeing; night of the new moon.

Daśaharā (S) (F) **1.** eliminator of 10; destroyer of 10. **2.** taking away 10 sins. **3.** another name for the Gaṅgā.

Daśamālīka (S) (F) with 10 garlands.

Dāśanandinī (S) (F) **1.** daughter of a fisherman. **3.** another name for atyavatī.

Dāśeyī (S) (F) **1.** fisherman's daughter. 3. another name for Satyavatī.

Dāsī (S) (F) **1.** servant; devotee. 3. an important river of ancient India (*M. Bh.*); the *Leea aequata* shrub.

Dasrasū (S) (F) **1.** mother of the aśvins. 3. another name for Sañjñā.

Dattādevī (S) (F) **1.** goddess of gifts. 3. the wife of Samudragupta and mother of Ćandragupta II.

Datti (S) (F) a gift.

Dayā (S) (F) **1.** compassion; sympathy; pity. **3.** compassion personified as the daughter of Dakṣa and mother of Abhaya (*Bhā. Purāṇa*).

Dāyādī (S) (F) to whom the inheritance is given; daughter; heiress.

Dayānvitā (S) (F) surrounded by mercy; full of mercy.

Dayāvatī (S) (F) full of mercy.

Dayitā (S) (F) worthy of compassion; beloved; cherished; dear.

Dehinī (S) (F) **1.** of the body. 2. corporeal; bearer of a body. 3. another name for the earth.

Deśakārī (S) (F) **1.** done by country. 3. a rāgiṇī.

Deśapālī (S) (F) **1.** protected by the country. **2.** belonging to the country; a native. **3.** a rāga.

Deśnā (S) (F) gift; offering.

Deśtrī (S) (F) **1.** pointer; indicator. 3. an apsarā (*Ṛg Veda*).

Devabālā (S) (F) **1.** daughter of the gods. **3.** Jelly Leaf (*Sida rhombofolia*).

Devadattā (S) (F) **1.** given by the gods. 3. the mother of Gautama Buddha's cousin Devadatta (*B. Literature*).

Devadhānī (S) (F) **1.** divine abode. 3. Indra's city (*Bh. Purāṇa*)

Devagarbhā (S) (F) **1.** the womb of the gods. **2.** divine child. **3.** a river of ancient India (*Bhā. Purāṇa*).

Devagirī (S) (F) **1.** divine knowledge. **3.** a rāgiṇī.

Devago (S) (F) **1.** divine protectress. 3. a form of Śakti (*T. Śāstra*).

Devahūti (S) (F) **1.** invocation of the gods. **3.** a daughter of Manu Svāyambhuva, wife of Prajāpati Kardama, and the mother of Kapila (*Bh. Purāṇa*).

Devajāmi (S) (F) sister of the gods.

Devajayā (S) (F) wife of the gods.

Devakāñćanā (S) (F) **1.** divine gold. **3.** the tree *Bauhinea purpurea.*

Devakanyā (S) (F) celestial maiden.

Devakī (S) (F) **1.** divine; glorious; pious. **3.** the daughter of Devaka, wife of Vasudeva, the mother of Kṛṣṇa and the reincarnation of Aditī the wife of Kaśyapa (*Bhāgavata*).

Devakirī (S) (F) **1.** tongue of the gods. **3.** a rāginī in music regarded as the wife of Megharāja.

Devakrī (S) (F) **1.** myth. 3. a rāga.

Devakulyā (S) (F) **1.** divine pitcher; belonging to the gods. **3.** another name for the holy Gaṅgā, the river of the gods personified as the daughter of Pūrṇiman and the granddaughter of Marīći (*Bhāgavata*); the wife of Udgītha (*Bhā. Purāṇa*).

Devakusuma (S) (F) divine flower; cloves.

Devalā (S) (F) **1.** attached to the gods; music personified. **3.** the daughter of Āhuka and sister of Dhṛti and Ugrasena (*Bhā. Purāṇa*); a rāginī.

Devalatā (S) (F) **1.** divine vine. **2.** the Double jasmine (*Jasminum sambac*).

Devalekhā (S) (F) a divine line; with a divine outline; a celestial beauty.

Devamālā (S) (F) **1.** divine garland. **3.** an apsarā (*M. Bh.*).

Devamaṇī (S) (F) jewel of the gods.

Devamatī (S) (F) **1.** godly minded. **2.** meritorious; virtuous; venerated.

Devamātrā (S) (F) **1.** equivalent to a god. **3.** a mother in Skanda's retinue (*M. Bh.*).

Devamātṛ (S) (F) **1.** mother of the gods. **3.** another name for Dākṣāyāṇī (*H. Purāṇa*).

Devamāyī (S) (F) divine illusion.

Devamitrā (S) (F) **1.** friend of the gods. **3.** a mother in Skanda's retinue (*M. Bh.*).

Devanadī (S) (F) **1.** river of the gods. **3.** a river personified as a deity in Varuṇa's court (*M. Bh.*); another name for the Gaṇgā.

Devanandā (S) (F) **1.** joy of the gods. **3.** an apsarā (*S. Dvātriṅśika*).

Devaṅganā (S) (F) divine woman.

Devapratimā (S) (F) image of the gods; an idol.

Devārādhanā (S) (F) worship of the gods.

Devarakṣitā (S) (F) **1.** protected by the gods. **3.** a daughter of Devaka and sister of Devakī, the mother of Kṛṣṇa.

Devaraktadanṣi (S) (F) **1.** favoured by gods. **3.** a rāgiṇī.

Devarati (S) (F) **1.** delight of the gods. **3.** an apsarā (*K. Sāgara*).

Devarūpā (S) (F) **1.** of divine form. **3.** an apsarā (*K. Sāgara*).

Devasenā (S) (F) **1.** with an army of gods. **3.** a daughter of Prajāpati Dakṣa and wife of Subrahmaṇya (*M. Bh.*).

Devasmita (S) (F) **1.** with a divine smile. **3.** a heroine of *Kathāsaritsāgara*.

Devaśrī (S) (F) **1.** divine goddess. **3.** another name for Lakṣmī.

Devavaćanā (S) (F) **1.** with divine speech. **3.** a gandharvī (*M. Bh.*).

Devavāṇi (S) (F) divine voice.

Devavarṇinī (S) (F) **1.** describer of the gods. **3.** a daughter of Bharadvāja (*Rāmāyaṇa*); the wife of Viśravas and mother of Kubera (*Rāmāyaṇa*).

Devavatī (S) (F) **1.** owned by the gods. **3.** the daughter of the gandharva Maṇimaya; wife of the rākṣasa Sukeśa and mother of Mālyavān, Sumāli and Māli (*U. Rāmāyaṇa*); the daughter of the daitya Mandaramāli (*Rāmāyaṇa*).

Devavīti (S) (F) **1.** enjoyment for the gods. **2.** pleasing the gods. **3.** a daughter of Meru and wife of Ketumāla, the son of Agnidhra (*Bhā. Purāṇa*).

Devayānī (S) (F) **1.** chariot of the gods. **2.** one invested with divine power; divine affluence. **3.** a daughter of Śukrāćārya and Ūrjasvatī, the wife of Yayāti and mother of Yadu and Turvasu (*H. Purāṇa*); a wife of Skanda.

Devayoṣā (S) (F) the wife of a god.

Deveśī (S) (F) **1.** chief of the goddesses. **3.** another name for Durgā.

Devī (S) (F) **1.** divine; deity; goddess; queen; lady. **3.** the ultimate sāttvika force respon-sible for the creation of the worlds, who appears in various forms of which the 5 main are Durgā, Lakṣmī, Sarasvatī, Sāvitrī and Rādhā, the 6 partial forms are Gaṅgā, Tulasī, Manasādevī, Devasenā, Maṅgalāćaṇḍikā, Bhūmī, the Anśalakāladevis are also parts of this ultimate sāttvika force or Mahādevī, she is known by 108 names; a nymph beloved of the sun (*A. Koṣa*); the mother of the 18th Arhat of the present Avasarpiṇī (*H. Koṣa*); *Bryonopsis laciniosa*; *Cucumis trigonos*; Black myrobalan (*Terminalia chebula*); Velvet Leaf (*Cissampelos pareira*); *Clematis triloba*; *Desmodium gangeticum*; Common Flax (*Linum usitatissimum*).

Devikā (S) (F) **1.** minor deity; minor goddess. **2.** god like. **3.** a class of goddess of an inferior order—Aṇumatī, Rākā, Sinīvālī, Kuhū and Dhātṛ; the daughter of Śaibya king Govāsana, the wife of Yudhiṣṭhira and mother of Yaudheya (*M. Bh.*); Ash coloured Fleabane (*Vemonia cinerea*).

Devikādevī (S) (F) **1.** invested with divine quantities. **3.** a wife of Yudhiṣṭhira and mother of Yaudheya (*M. Bh.*); a river (*M. Bh.*).

Devikī (S) (F) derived from the goddess.

Devinā (S) (F) resembling a goddess.

Devīśī (S) (F) **1.** chief of the goddesses. **3.** another name for Durgā and Devakī, the mother of Kṛṣṇa.

Dhamadhamā (S) (F) **1.** making a noise. **2.** a blowhorn. **3.** an attendant of Skanda (*M. Bh.*).

Dhamanī (S) (F) **1.** pipe; tube. **3.** wife of Hrāda and mother of Vātāpi and Ilvala.

Dhanadā (S) (F) **1.** wealth bestowing. **2.** prize giving; giving booty or treasure (*Ṛg Veda*). **3.** a mother in Skanda's retinue (*Sk. Purāṇa*); a tāntric deity (*T. Śāstra*).

Dhanalakṣmī (S) (F) **1.** the goddess of wealth. **3.** another name for goddess Lakṣmī.

Dhanandadā (S) (F) **1.** granting wealth. **3.** a Buddhist deity.

Dhanaśrī (S) (F) **1.** goddess of wealth. **3.** a rāgiṇī.

Dhanavatī (S) (F) containing wealth.

Dhaneśvarī (S) (F) **1.** goddess of wealth. **3.** another name for the wife of Kubera.

Dhaniṣṭhā (S) (F) **1.** residing in wealth; extremely wealthy. **3.** a constellation.

Dhanuhastā (S) (F) **1.** with a bow in hand. **2.** archer. **3.** an attendant of the ultimate sāttvika force which is personified as Devī.

Dhanuṣmatī (S) (F) **1.** armed with a bow. **3.** the tutelary deity in the family of Vyāgh-rapāda (*Brahma Purāṇa*).

Dhanvanyā (S) (F) treasure of the jungle; an oasis.

Dhanyā (S) (F) **1.** virtuous. **2.** good; bestowing wealth. **3.** Dhruva's wife (*V. Purāṇa*).

Dhanyamālā (S) (F) **1.** auspicious garland. **2.** virtuous; meritorious. **3.** the foster mother of Atikāya.

Dharā (S) (F) **1.** bearer; supporter. **2.** the earth; a mass of gold. **3.** one of the 8 forms of Sarasvatī (*Purāṇas*); a wife of Kaśyapa (*H. Purāṇa*); the wife of the vasu named Droṇa (*V. Purāṇa*); another name for the earth.

Dhāraṇī (S) (F) **1.** holding; bearing possessing. **2.** a mystical verse used to assuage pain (*A. Veda*). **3.** a daughter of Svadhā (*D. Bh. Purāṇa*); the wife of Agnimitra (*M. Bh./Rāmāyaṇa*); the earth personified as the wife of Dhruva (*M. Bh./Rāmāyaṇa*).

Dharaṇisutā (S) (F) **1.** daughter of the earth. **3.** another name for Sītā, the consort of Rāma.

Dharmābhimukhā (S) (F) **1.** turned towards religion. **2.** religious; virtuous. **3.** an apsarā (*K. Vyuha*).

Dharmadravī (S) (F) **1.** with virtuous waters. **3.** another name for the Gaṅgā.

Dharmavratā (S) (F) **1.** acting according to Dharma. **3.** a daughter of Dharma and Dharmavatī and wife of sage Marīći (*V. Purāṇa*).

Dharmiṇī (S) (F) **1.** religious; virtuous; pious. **2.** a kind of perfume.

Dhātreyikā (S) (F) **1.** supporter; nurse; confidante. **3.** a maid of Draupadī (*M. Bh.*).

Dhenā (S) (F) **1.** milch cow. **2.** any beverage made of milk. **3.** the wife of Bṛhaspati (*T. Āraṇyaka*).

Dhenū (S) (F) **1.** cow. **3.** the earth as a life supporting cow; the feminine gender of any species.

Dhenukā (S) (F) **1.** milch cow. **3.** the wife of Kīrtimat the son of Aṅgiras (*V. Purāṇa*); a celestial river (*V. Purāṇa*).

Dhenumatī (S) (F) **1.** possessing the earth. **2.** that which yields nourishment. **3.** the wife of Devadyumna (*Bhāgavata*); another name for the river Gomatī.

Dhīlatī (S) (F) daughter.

Dhīṣaṇā (S) (F) **1.** Soma vessel. **2.** knowledge; intelligence; speech; praise; hymn; goddesses. **3.** The goddess of abundance and the divine guardian of the sacred fire (*Ṛg Veda*); the wife of Havirdhāna, daughter of Agni (*H. Purāṇa*) and the mother of Śukra, Gaya, Vraja, Ajina and Prāćinabarhis (*V. Purāṇa*); the wife of Kṛṣāśva and mother of Vedaśira, Devala, Vāyuna and Manu (*Bhāgavata*).

Dhītā (S) (F) bird-born; a daughter.

Dhīti (S) (F) **1.** thought; idea. **3.** wisdom; reflection; intention; devotion; prayer.

Dhṛtadevā (S) (F) **1.** goddess of constancy. **3.** a daughter of King Devaka, the wife of Vasudeva, and mother of Vipṛṣṭha (*Bhāgavata*).

Dhṛtadevī (S) (F) **1.** goddess of constancy. **3.** a daughter of Devala.

Dhṛtarāṣṭrī (S) (F) **1.** supporter of the nation. **3.** a daughter of Kaśyapa and Tāmrā and mother of Kraunćī, Bhāsī,

Śyeṇī, Dhṛtarāṣṭrī and Śukī (*V. Rāmāyaṇa*) and the mother of swans, geese and other waterbirds (*B. Jatakas*).

Dhṛtavatī (S) (F) **1.** steady; calm. **3.** a river (*M. Bh.*).

Dhṛti (S) (F) **1.** firmness. **2.** resolution; constancy; will; command; satisfaction; joy; resolution. **3.** personified as the daughter of Dakṣa who was the wife of Dharma and mother of Niyama (*V. Purāṇa*); a goddess who is the wife of Kapila (*Purāṇas*); one of the 16 digits of the moon (*V. Purāṇa*); the wife of Rudra Manu (*V. Purāṇa*).

Dhṛtimatī (S) (F) **1.** steadfast; resolute. **3.** a river of ancient India (*M. Bh.*).

Dhruvadevī (S) (F) **1.** goddess of the poles. **2.** a stable goddess; unshakeable; firm. **3.** the wife of Ćandragupta (*A. Koṣa*).

Dhruvaratnā (S) (F) **1.** imperishable jewel. **3.** a mother attending on Skanda (*M. Bh.*).

Dhūlikā (S) (F) pollen of flowers.

Dhūmalekhā (S) (F) **1.** line of smoke. **2.** one who is dark in visage. **3.** a daughter of a yakṣa (*K. Sāgara*).

Dhūmapāla (S) (F) **1.** protector of vapour. **3.** a river (*M. Bh.*).

Dhūminī (S) (F) **1.** smoky. **2.** one dark in visage. **3.** the wife of King Ajamīḍha and the mother of Ṛkṣa (*M. Bh.*).

Dhūmorṇā (S) (F) **1.** smoke covered. **2.** fire; that which is sacred; all consuming; life giving. **3.** the wife of Yama (*M. Bh.*); the wife of sage Mārkaṇḍeya (*M. Bh.*).

Dhūmrā (S) (F) **1.** smoky. **2.** vaporous. **3.** a daughter of Dakṣa who was the wife of Dharma and the mother of Dhruva and Dhara (*M. Bh.*); another name for Durgā.

Dhūmravarṇa (S) (F) **1.** smoke coloured. **3.** one of the 7 tongues of Agni.

Dhūśulyā (S) (F) **1.** soil coloured. **2.** muddy. **3.** a river of ancient India (*M. Bh.*).

Dhutī (S) (F) **1.** splendour; light; lustre. **2.** majesty. **3.** the goddess who protected Arjuna (*M. Bh.*).

Dhvajavatī (S) (F) **1.** decorated with banners. **2.** a queen. **3.** a divine attendant of a Bodhisattva (*L. Vistara*); the daughter of sage Harimedhās who lived in the sky as an attendant of the sun (*M. Bh.*).

Diddā (S) (F) **1.** eyeball. **3.** a celebrated princess of Kaśmira (*R. Taraṅgiṇī*).

Didhi (S) (F) firmness; stability; brightness.

Dīdhīti (S) (F) firm; stable; devotion; inspiration; religious reflection.

Dīdivī (S) (F) **1.** shining; bright; risen as a star. **3.** another name for Bṛhaspati.

Didyudyuta (S) (F) **1.** shining; missile. **3.** thunderbolt of Indra (*Ṛg Veda*); an apsarā.

Digaṅganā (S) (F) **1.** maiden of the quarter. **3.** quarter of the sky identified as a young virgin (*Bhāgavata*).

Dikkanyā (S) (F) **1.** maiden of a quarter. **3.** quarter of the sky deified as a young virgin (*B. Śatakam*).

Dīkṣā (S) (F) **1.** initiation. **2.** consecration; dedication. **3.** initiation personified as the wife of Soma, Rudra, Ugra and Rudra Vāmadeva (*Purāṇas*).

Dimbeśvarī (S) (F) **1.** goddess of creation. **3.** another name for Durgā.

Dinakarātmajā (S) (F) **1.** daughter of Dinakara. **3.** the river Yamunā who is considered to be the daughter of the sun.

Dinaprabhā (S) (F) day's splendour; the sunshine.

Dīpā (S) (F) illuminated; that which illuminates; enlightens.

Dipakalikā (S) (F) the flame of a lamp.

Dīpākṣī (S) (F) bright-eyed.

Dīpālī (S) (F) a row of lights.

Dīpamālā (S) (F) **1.** garland of lights. **2.** a row of lights.

Dīpana (S) (F) **1.** illuminating; passion. **2.** that which kindles, in flames. **3.** an attendant of Devī (*T. Śāstra*); Fetid Cassia (*Cassia occidentalis*).

Dīpanī (S) (F) **1.** exciting; animating; stimulating; illuminating. **2.** a tonic. **3.** Lovage (*Carum copticum*).

Dīpāñjalī (S) (F) a lamp for praying; a lamp held in the palm which is waved around the idol at the time of worship.

Dīpāvalī (S) (F) a row of lights.

Dīpavatī (S) (F) **1.** containing lights. **3.** a mythical river (*K. Purāṇa*).

Dīpikā (S) (F) **1.** a small lamp. **2.** light; lamp; lantern; moonlight. **3.** a rāgiṇī; Fire plant (*Plumbago rosea*).

Diprā (S) (F) radiant; flaming; shining.

Dīpśikhā (S) (F) the flame of a lamp.

Dīptī (S) (F) brightness; light; illuminating; enlightening.

Dīrghajihvā (S) (F) **1.** long tongued. **3.** a rākṣasi; (*M. Bh./Rāmāyaṇa*); a mother in Skanda's retinue (*M. Bh.*).

Dīrghikā (S) (F) **1.** a tall girl; an oblong lake. **3.** a daughter of Viśvākarman (*Purāṇas*).

Diśā (S) (F) region; direction; the point of the compass.

Diṣṭi (S) (F) direction; good fortune; happiness; auspicious juncture.

Diti (S) (F) **1.** glow. **2.** brightness; light; splendour; beauty. **3.** a daughter of Dakṣa; the wife of Kaśyapa and the mother of the daityas (*M. Bh.*) and the maruts (*V. Purāṇa*).

Divijā (S) (F) born of the sky; heaven born; celestial; a goddess.

Divolkā (S) (F) **1.** fallen from the sky. **2.** a meteor.

Divyā (S) (F) **1.** divine; celestial; heavenly; charming; beautiful. **3.** an apsarā (*Ṛg Veda*); asparagus race mosus; Barley (*Hordeum vulgare*); Indian Pennywort (*Hydrocotyle asiatica*); Black Myrobalan (*Tenninalia Chebula*).

Divyadevī (S) (F) divine goddess.

Divyagandhā (S) (F) **1.** with divine fragrance **3.** *Amomum subulatum*; Jew's Mallow (*Corchorus olitorius*).

Divyājyotī (S) (F) divine light.

Divyākṛti (S) (F) of divine form; beautiful.

Divyanārī (S) (F) **1.** celestial maiden. **2.** an apsarā.

Divyāṅganā (S) (F) celestial woman; apsarā.

Divyāstrī (S) (F) celestial woman; an apsarā.

Divyayamunā (S) (F) **1.** the divine Yamunā. **3.** a river in Kāmarūpa (*M. Bh.*).

Doṣā (S) (F) **1.** night. **2.** full of shortcomings. **3.** night personified as the wife of Puṣpārṇa and the mother of Pradoṣa, Niśitha and Vyuṣṭa (*Bhāgavata*).

Draupadī (S) (F) **1.** daughter of Drupada. **3.** another name for Kṛṣṇā who was the wife of the Pāṇḍu princes.

Dṛḍhamatī (S) (F) strong willed; resolute.

Dṛgbhū (S) (F) **1.** eye born. **2.** thunderbolt; the sun.

Driḍhā (S) (F) **1.** firm. **2.** fixed; stronghold; fortress. **3.** a Buddhist goddess.

Droṇā (S) (F) **1.** saviour of society. **3.** the daughter of Siṁhahanu (*B. Ćarita*).

Dṛṣadvatī (S) (F) **1.** stone like. **2.** that which is hard, firm, resolute. **3.** a river flowing into the Sarasvatī (*Ṛg Veda*); the mother of Aṣṭaka and wife of Viśvāmitra (*H. Purāṇa*); the mother of Pratardana (*H. Purāṇa*); the wife of Divodaśa (*H. Purāṇa*); the wife of Nṛpa and mother of Śibi Auśinara (*H. Purāṇa*); the mother of Prasenajit (*H. Purāṇa*); another name for Durgā.

Dṛśīkā (S) (F) good looking.

Druhī (S) (F) daughter.

Druti (S) (F) **1.** softened. **3.** the wife of Nakṣa and mother of Gaya (*Bhāgavata*).

Dulā (S) (F) **1.** shaking. **3.** one of the 7 kṛttikās (*T. Samhitā*).

Dulārī (S) (F) loveable.

Dulī (S) (F) a female tortoise.

Dumatī (S) (F) **1.** with bright intellect. **3.** a river (*A. Koṣa*).

Dundhā (S) (F) **1.** roaring; noisy; boisterous. **3.** a rākṣasi (*M. Bh.*).

Dundubhī (S) (F) **1.** born of a kettledrum; a throw of dice. **3.** a gandharvi (*M. Bh.*).

Durdharā (S) (F) **1.** difficult to withstand. **2.** irresistible; insatiable; difficult. **3.** Ćandragupta's wife (*H. Purāṇa*).

Dūrepaśyā (S) (F) **1.** farsighted. **3.** an apsarā (*M. Bh.*).

Durgā (S) (F) **1.** difficult to approach; the inaccessible or terrifying goddess. **3.** goddess of the universe worshipped in 64 different forms of which Pārvatī the daughter of Himavān and wife of Śiva is one (*T. Ārāṇyaka*).

Durgatināśinī (S) (F) **1.** eliminating distress. **3.** another name for Durgā.

Durgavatī (S) (F) **1.** owning a fort. **3.** a queen of Jabalpura.

Durgī (S) (F) **1.** one who lives in a fort. **3.** another name for Durgā.

Durgilā (S) (F) owning a fort.

Dūritārī (S) (F) **1.** enemy of sin. **3.** a Jaina goddess (*J. Koṣa*).

Duruktī (S) (F) **1.** harsh speech. **3.** harsh speech personified as the daughter of Krodha and Hinsā and the wife of Kali (*Bhāgavata*).

Dūrvā (S) (F) **1.** Panic grass (*Panicum dactylon*). **3.** wife of Dhṛṣtaketu.

Dūrvāksī (S) (F) **1.** ruining dūrvā grass (*Panicum dactylon*). **3.** wife of Vṛka.

Dūṣaṇa (S) (F) **1.** full of vices. **3.** the wife of Bhavana and mother of Tvaṣṭri (*Bhāgavata*).

Dusśalā (S) (F) **1.** difficult to praise. **3.** princes Dusśalā considered to be peerless, was the only daughter of Dhṛtarāṣṭra and Gāndhārī and the wife of King Jayadratha of Sindhū (*M. Bh.*).

Dvāparā (S) (F) **1.** born in the epoch of Dvāpara. **3.** a friend of Kāli (*M. Bh.*).

Dvārakā (S) (F) **1.** with many gates. **3.** Kṛṣṇa's capital on the west coast of Gujarāt supposed to have been submerged by the sea.

Dyotanā (S) (F) **1.** illuminating. **2.** enlightening; shining.

Dyotani (S) (F) brightness; splendour.

Dyudhunī (S) (F) heavenly Gaṅgā; the Ākāśagaṅgā or the Milky Way.

Dyukṣā (S) (F) of heaven; celestial.

Dyumayī (S) (F) **1.** full of brightness. **3.** a daughter of Tvaṣṭṛ and the wife of Sūrya.

Dyumnahūtī (S) (F) inspired invocation.

Dyuvadhū (S) (F) celestial woman; an apsarā.

E

Edhā (S) (F) prosperity; happiness.

Egattalā (Tamil) (F) the non-Aryan tutelary goddess of Madrās.

Ekā (S) (F) **1.** one and only. **2.** alone; peerless; matchless; firm; unique. **3.** another name for Durgā.

Ekabhakti (S) (F) the worship of one deity.

Ekaćandra (S) (F) **1.** the only moon. **2.** the best one. **3.** a mother in the retinue of Skanda (*M. Bh.*).

Ekāćāriṇī (S) (F) a woman devoted to a single man; obedient; a loyal chaste woman.

Ekadhanā (S) (F) **1.** a portion of wealth, **2.** one who has a portion of wealth.

Ekaja (S) (F) born alone; the only child.

Ekajatā (S) (F) **1.** with a single twisted lock of hair. **3.** a tāntric goddess; a rākṣasi in the castle of Rāvaṇa.

Ekākini (S) (F) lonely; alone.

Ekamatī (S) (F) concentrated.

Ekamukha (S) (F) **1.** single faced; with one mouth. **2.** the best kind of Rudrākṣaphala or the fruit of the Rudrākṣa tree (*Guazuma ulmifolia*) which is considered extremely auspicious.

Ekānaṅśā (S) (F) **1.** new moon. **3.** another name for Subhadrā, the wife of Arjuṇa and the sister of Kṛṣṇa and for Durgā.

Ekānaṅgā (S) (F) **1.** lover. **3.** the daughter of Yaśodā and foster sister of Kṛṣṇa (*Bhāgavata*).

Ekaṅgikā (S) (F) **1.** made of sandalwood. **2.** fair; frequent; auspicious; dear to the gods.

Ekāntā (S) (F) lovely, devoted to one.

Ekāntikā (S) (F) devoted to one aim.

Ekantin (S) (F) **1.** devoted to one object. **3.** another name for Siva and Viṣṇu.

Ekaparṇā (S) (F) **1.** single leafed; living on a single leaf. **3.** the daughter of Himavāna and Menā, the sister of Durgā, Aparṇā and Ekapātalā and the wife of sage Devala (*H. Purāṇa*).

Ekapātalā (S) (F) **1.** living on a single leaf. **3.** the daughter of Himavāna and Menā; the sister of goddess Durgā and the wife of sage Jaigiśavyā (*H. Purāṇa*).

Ekāṣṭakā (S) (F) **1.** a collection of 8. **2.** the time for consecration; the 8th day after the full moon in the month of Māgha (January-February). **3.** a Vedic deity who was the wife of Prajāpati and mother of Indra and Soma (*Ś. Brāhmaṇa*).

Ekavaktrā (S) (F) **1.** one faced. **3.** a mother of Skanda (*M. Bh.*).

Ekāvalī (S) (F) **1.** a string of pearls. **3.** the daughter of King Raibhya and Rukmarekhā and wife of Ekavīra (*Bhi. Purāṇa*).

Ekavīrā (S) (F) **1.** outstandingly brave. **3.** a daughter of Śiva (*M. Bh.*).

Ekiśā (S) (F) one goddess; the primal goddess.

Ekṣikā (S) (F) eye.

Elā (F) **1.** born of Ila; the earth. **3.** cardamom; the cardamom creeper (*Elettaria cardamomum*).

Elokṣī (S) (F) with hair as thick as the cardamom creeper.

Eṇākṣi (S) (F) doe eyed.

Eṇī (S) (F) a deer; spotted; a flowing stream.

Eṇīpadā (S) (F) with deer like feet; that which is fleet footed.

Eraka (S) (F) **1.** a hard grass. **3.** a grass which turned into a club when plucked by Kṛṣṇa; a nāga of the Kaurava family (*M. Bh.*).

Eśā (S) (F) wish; desire; aim.

Eṣaṇikā (S) (F) fulfilling desire; a goldsmith's balance.

Etā (S) (F) shining; flowing.

Etahā (S) (F) shining.

Etī (S) (F) arrival.

G

Gabhasti (S) (F) **1.** ray; light. **2.** moonbeam; sunbeam. **3.** another name for Svāhā the wife of Agni.

Gadādevī (S) (F) **1.** mace lady. **3.** Viṣṇu's mace personified as a beautiful woman.

Gaganadīpikā (S) (F) **1.** lamp of the sky. **3.** another name for the sun.

Gaganakuṇḍā (S) (F) **1.** pool of the sky. **2.** *Jasminum pubescent.*

Gaganāṅganā (S) (F) **1.** celestial damsel. **3.** an apsarā (*Purāṇas*).

Gaganasindhu (S) (F) **1.** ocean of the sky. **3.** another name for the Ākāśagaṅgā or celestial Gaṅgā.

Gajagāminī (S) (F) with a gait as graceful as an elephant.

Gajagatī (S) (F) a gait as graceful as an elephant.

Gajalakṣmī (S) (F) Lakṣmī who is as graceful as an elephant.

Gajamuktā (S) (F) pearl found on the foreheads of elephants, snakes and crocodiles.

Gajrā (S) (F) garland of flowers.

Gamati (S) (F) with a flexible mind.

Gambhārī (S) (F) **1.** sky reaching. **2.** the Gumhar tree (*Gmelina arborea*).

Gambhīrikā (S) (F) **1.** deep. **3.** a river.

Gamin (S) (F) with a graceful gait.

Gaṇā (S) (F) **1.** assembly; troop. **3.** a female attendant of Skanda (*M. Bh.*).

Gaṇanāyikā (S) (F) **1.** consort of the lord of the gaṇas. **3.** another name for goddess Pārvatī and Gaṇeśanī.

Gaṇapatīhṛdayā (S) (F) **1.** the heart of Gaṇapati. **3.** a Buddhist tāntric elephantheaded goddess (*B. Literature*).

Gaṇarupā (S) (F) **1.** of the form of gaṇas. **3.** a flower of the Madār tree (*Erythrina suberosa*) which is offered to Śiva.

Gaṇavatī (S) (F) **1.** followed by attendants. **3.** the mother of Divodāsa.

Gaṇḍā (S) (F) **1.** knot; a cheek. **3.** a servant of the Saptaṛṣis or the 7 Seers (*M. Bh.*).

Gaṇḍakī (S) (F) **1.** obstacle. **3.** a north Indian river flowing into the Gaṅgā (*M. Bh.*).

Gandhā (S) (F) fragrant.

Gandhajā (S) (F) consisting of fragrant perfume.

Gandhalatā (S) (F) **1.** fragrant creeper. **3.** another name for the Priyaṅgu creeper (*Aglaia odorotissima*).

Gandhāli (S) (F) **1.** perfumed. **3.** *Paederia foetida.*

Gandhālikā, Gandhakālī (S) (F) **1.** fragrant. **3.** an apsarā; another name for goddess Pārvatī and Satyavatī, the mother of Vyāsa.

Gandhamadanī (S) (F) **1.** intoxicating fragrance. **3.** the tree *Caesaria esculenta.*

Gandhamohinī (S) (F) with an enchanting fragrance; the bud of the Ćampaka tree (*Michelia ćampaka*).

Gandhaphalī (S) (F) **1.** with fragrant fruit. **3.** another name for the Priyaṅgu creeper (*Aglaia odorotissima*).

Gandhapuṣpam (S) (F) **1.** fragrance and flowers conjoined; collective name for the flowers and sandalwood offered at worship. **3.** Aśoka tree (*Saraca indica*); *Pandanus odoratissimus.*

Gāndhārī (S) (F) **1.** from Gāndhāra. **3.** the daughter of King Subala of Gāndhāra, the wife of King Dhṛtarāṣṭra and mother of the 100 Kauravas (*M. Bh.*); the wife of King Ajamīḍha of the Purū dynasty (*M. Bh.*); a vidyādevī (*M. Bh.*); a rāgiṇī.

Gandhārikā (S) (F) **1.** preparing perfume. **3.** the herb *Hedychium spicatum.*

Gandharvasenā (S) (F) **1.** army of gandharvas. **3.** the daughter of the gandharva Dhanavāhana who lived on Mount Kailāśa (*M. Bh.*).

Gandharvavatī (S) (F) **1.** one who is as learned in the arts as the gandharvas. **3.** the queen of Kāmarupa or Assam (*M. Bh.*).

Gāndharvī (S) (F) **1.** speech of a gandharva. **3.** the granddaughter of sage Kaśyapa and Krodhavaśā, the daughter of Surabhī and the mother of horses (*M. Bh.*); another name for Durgā; a seductive water-nymph who haunts the banks of rivers (*T. Śāstra*).

Gandhavadhu (S) (F) **1.** fragrant maiden. **3.** *Hedychium spicatum.*

Gandhavajrā (S) (F) **1.** with a perfumed thunderbolt. **3.** a goddess.

Gandhavalli (S) (F) 1. fragrant creeper. **3.** the Jelly Leaf (*Sida rhombofolia*).

Gandhavāruṇī (S) (F) **1.** with perfumed juice. **3.** *Alpinia galanga.*

Gandhavatī (S) (F) **1.** sweetly scented. **2.** wine. **3.** the earth; the city of Vāyu situated on Mount Mahāmeru; another name for Satyavati.

Gāndhinī (S) (F) **1.** fragrant. **3.** another name for Pṛthvī; *Caesaria esculenta.*

Gandhotamā (S) (F) **1.** the best fragrance. **3.** another name for wine.

Gāndinī (S) (F) **1.** one who gives a cow daily. **3.** the daughter of the king of Kāsī, the wife of Śvaphalka, the mother of Akrūra and known for donating one cow to the Brāhmins every day.

Gaṇeśagītā (S) (F) **1.** song of Gaṇeśa. **3.** a work of the Gāṇapatyas which is an inter-pretation of the *Bhāgavata* in which Gaṇeśa's name is substituted for Kṛṣṇa as the Supreme Deity.

Gaṇeśanī (S) (F) **1.** consort of Gaṇesa. **3.** the Śakti or female form of energy of Gaṇeśa, personified as his consort.

Gaṅgā (S) (F) **1.** the swift flowing. **3.** the holy Gaṅgā river which washes away the sins of people, is personified as a goddess, the consort of Śiva, and the mother of Kārttikeya, was brought down from the heavens by King Bhagīratha in the form of a river that originated from Viṣṇu's feet and coursing through Śiva's hair flowed from the heavens to the earth, where she became the wife of King Śāntanu and the mother of Bhīṣma (*M. Bh.*).

Gaṅgāhṛday (S) (F) the heart of the Gaṅgā; a sacred place near Kurukṣetra.

Gaṅgāṅginī (S) (F) daughter of Gaṅgā.

Gāṅgī (S) (F) **1.** of Gaṅgā; like the Gaṅgā; as sacred as the Gaṅgā river. **3.** another name for Durgā.

Gāṅgikā (S) like the Gaṅgā; one who is as pure, sacred and pious as the Gaṅgā river.

Gaṅgotrī (S) (F) **1.** the mouth of the Gaṅgā river. **3.** a place held sacred by the Hindus.

Gaṅgu (S) (F) **1.** where Gaṅgā flows. **2.** alluvial land. **3.** a tutelary lunar goddess.

Gaṇikā (S) (F) **1.** female elephant. **3.** Common White Jasmine (*Jasminum officianale*).

Gaṇikārikā (S) (F) **1.** made by the gaṇas. **3.** the creeper *Oxystelma esculentum.*

Gañjan (S) (F) surpassing; excelling; conquering.

Gañmānya (S) (F) distinguished; honoured; respected.

Gannikā (S) (F) **1.** counted of value. **3.** the Jasmine blossom (*Jasminum officianale*).

Garbhagṛha (S) (F) **1.** the inner house. **2.** the inner sanctum of a temple which enshrines the main deity and is regarded as the container of the seed.

Gārgī (S) (F) **1.** churn; a vessel for holding water. **3.** a Brahmavādinī or learned woman born in the Garga family (*M. Bh.*).

Garimā (S) (F) **1.** grace; divinity; greatness; sublimity. **3.** one of the 8 siddhis acquired by yoga.

Garvarī (S) (F) **1.** haughty. **3.** another name for Durgā.

Gati (S) (F) **1.** power of understanding; speed. **2.** gait. **3.** motion personified as a daughter of Kardama and Devahūtī and wife of Pulaha (*Bhāgavata*).

Gāthikā (S) (F) song.

Gātravatī (S) (F) **1.** with a handsome body. **3.** a daughter of Kṛṣṇa and Lakṣmanā.

Gaurāṅgī (S) (F) **1.** fair; cow coloured. **3.** Cardomum (*Elettaria cardamomum*).

Gaurī (S) (F) **1.** cow coloured; fair. **2.** that which is yellow; fair; brilliant;

beautiful; the Mallikā creeper (*Jasminum sambac*); the Sacred Basil plant (*Ocimum sanctum*). **3.** the consort of Varuṇa (*M. Bh.*); a female attendant of Pārvatī (*M. Bh.*); a river of ancient India (*M. Bh.*); another name for the earth and Pārvatī.

Gaurīkā (S) (F) **1.** like Gauri. **3.** another name for Śiva.

Gautamī (S) (F) **1.** dispeller of darkness. **3.** the teachings of Gautama Buddha; another name for the rivers Godāvarī and Gomatī, goddess Durgā, and Kṛpi the wife of Droṇa.

Gavah (S) (F) **1.** the moving ones. **2.** the stars of heaven.

Gāyanti (S) (F) **1.** of Gaya. **3.** wife of King Gaya the royal sage.

Gāyantikā (S) (F) **1.** singing. **3.** a Himalayan cave.

Gāyatrī (S) (F) **1.** 3 phased verse. **2.** a collection of 38-lettered Anuṣṭupa hymns; a Vedic mantra; a hymn to the sun. **3.** one of the 7 horses of the sun; another name for Sarasvatī the consort of Brahmā and the mother of the Vedas; Black Cateehu tree (*Acacia catechu*).

Gāyatriṇī (S) (F) one who sings hymns of the *Sāma Veda*.

Geṣṇā (S) (F) singer.

Ghanajñānī (S) (F) **1.** deeply wise; profoundly wise. **3.** another name for Durgā.

Ghanāñjanī (S) (F) **1.** with collyrium as black as the clouds. **3.** another name for Durgā.

Ghanāvallī, Ghanavallikā (S) (F) **1.** creeper of the clouds. **2.** lightning.

Ghaṇṭa (S) (F) **1.** bell. **2.** objects used in Hindu rituals especially for Śiva (*Ś. Purāṇa*). **3.** a Brāhmin of the Vasiṣṭha family who helped Indrayumna (*Rāmāyaṇa*).

Ghoṣā (S) (F) **1.** noisy; resounding. **2.** a proclamation; fame. **3.** an ascetic daughter of King Kakṣīvān famed for her knowledge of the *Ṛg Veda*; the climber *Luffa echinata*.

Ghoṣavatī (S) (F) **1.** resounding. **2.** resonant. **3.** the famous viṇā or lute of the emperor Udayana (*K. Sāgara*).

Ghoṣiṇī (S) (F) **1.** famed; proclaimed; noisy. **3.** the female attendants of Rudra (*Sk. Purāṇa*).

Ghṛtāćī (S) (F) **1.** abounding in clarified butter; full of water. **3.** a beautiful apsarā who was the mother of Śuka by Vyāsa, Droṇāćārya by sage Bharadvāja and a 100 daughters by sage Kuśanābha (*M. Bh.*); *Amomum subulatum*.

Ghṛtavatī (S) (F) **1.** composed of clarified butter. **3.** a river of ancient India (*M. Bh.*).

Ghugharī (S) (F) bracelet of jingling bells.

Ghūrṇikā (S) (F) **1.** one who whirls. **3.** the foster mother of Devayānī the daughter of Śukra (*M. Bh.*).

Gīra (S) (F) **1.** speech; voice; language; word; song; vedic hymn. **3.** another name for Sarasvatī.

Gīradevī (S) (F) **1.** the goddess of speech. **2.** one who is learned; wise. **3.** another name for the goddess Sarasvatī.

Giribhū (S) (F) **1.** originating from the mountain. **3.** another name for the holy Gaṅgā and Pārvatī.

Girigaṅgā (S) (F) Gaṅgā that comes from the mountains.

Girijā (S) (F) **1.** daughter of the mountain. **3.** Black myrobalan tree (*Terminalia chebula*); *Bauhinia vareigata* tree; the Cotton Teal bird (*Nettopus coromandelianus*); another name for Pārvatī the daughter of Himāvana and Menā and the consort of Śiva.

Girijambā (S) (F) **1.** daughter of the mountain. **3.** another name for Pārvatī.

Girikā (S) (F) **1.** summit of a mountain. **3.** the daughter of the river Śaktimatī and the wife of Uparićara and the wife of Vasu (*M. Bh.*).

Girikarṇī (S) (F) **1.** lotus of the mountain. **3.** a lotus (*A. Koṣa*).

Girikarṇikā (S) (F) **1.** having mountains for seed vessels. **2.** the earth. **3.** the Arabian Manna plant (*Alhagi camelorum*); the Blue Pea (*Clitoria tematea*); the Wild Guava (*Careya arborea*).

Girimallikā (S) (F) creeper of the mountain; a flower (*Wrightia antidysenterica*).

Girinandinī (S) (F) **1.** daughter of the mountain. **3.** another name for Pārvatī and Gaṅgā.

Girindramohinī (S) (F) **1.** beloved of the lord of the mountain. **3.** another name for Pārvatī.

Giriśā (S) (F) **1.** lady of the mountains. **3.** another name for Pārvatī.

Girīṣmā (S) (F) summer.

Girisutā (S) (F) **1.** daughter of the mountain. **3.** another name for Pārvatī.

Gīrni (S) (F) praise; celebrity.

Gītā (S) (F) **1.** song; lyric; poem. **3.** a religious book of the Hindus consisting of a sermon given by Kṛṣṇa to Arjuna during the war of Mahābhārata.

Gītālī (S) (F) lover of song.

Gītāñjalī (S) (F) devotional offering of a hymn.

Gītāśrī (S) (F) the divine Gītā.

Gīti (S) (F) song.

Gītikā (S) (F) a short song.

Go (S) (F) **1.** cow; bull; ox; bullock. **2.** ray, thunderbolt; moon; sun; heaven. **3.** a wife of sage Pulastya and mother of Vaiśravaṇa (*M. Bh.*); a daughter of Kakutstha and wife of Yayāti; another name for Gaurī.

Godāvarī (S) (F) **1.** granting water. **2.** that which bestows prosperity. **3.** a river in south India which originates from Brahmagiri in Nāsik and by bathing in which one attains the kingdom of Vāsukī (*Kādambarī*).

Godbikā (S) (F) Sītā's lizard (*Sitana ponticeriana*); emblem of the goddess Gaurī.

Gojā (S) (F) born amidst rays; born of milk; born in the earth.

Gokarṇā (S) (F) **1.** cow eared. **3.** the mother of Karṇa's serpent missile Aśvasena (*M. Bh.*).

Gokirātikā (S) (F) **1.** grating sound. **3.** the Sārikā (*Paradisca tristis*) or Indian Myna bird (*A. Koṣa*).

Golā (S) (F) **1.** circle; sphere; celestial globe. **3.** another name for goddess Durgā and the river Godāvarī.

Gomadhī (S) (F) **1.** wealthy in cows. **3.** another name for river Gomatī.

Gomatī (S) (F) **1.** rich in cattle; milky. **3.** a river personified as a goddess supposed to be the incarnation of Kauśikī the sister of Viśvāmitra and the wife of sage Ṛćīka (*Sk. Purāṇa*).

Gomeda (S) (F) **1.** one who respects cows. **2.** the beryl; a gem brought from the Himālayas and the river Indus which is used to purify water.

Gopabālā (S) (F) daughter of a cowherd.

Gopajā (S) (F) daughter of a cowherd.

Gopālī (S) (F) **1.** protector of cows. **2.** a cowherdess. **3.** an apsarā who danced for Arjuna (*M. Bh.*); a follower of Skanda (*M. Bh.*); *Ichnocarpus frutescens*; the Monkeybread tree (*Adansonia digitata*); another name for Rādhā.

Goparasā (S) (F) made of the water of the earth; nourished by the earth.

Gopī (S) (F) **1.** herdswoman. **3.** milkmaid and friend of Kṛṣṇa; *Ichnocarpus frutescens.*

Gopikā (S) (F) **1.** herdswoman. **2.** one who protects the herd. **3.** another name for Rādhā.

Gormā (S) (F) **1.** worth considering. **3.** another name for Pārvatī.

Goroćanā (S) (F) **1.** yellow pigment. **3.** a beautiful and virtuous woman.

Grāmakālī (S) (F) **1.** the Kāli of the village. **3.** the protective deity of the village and forest and in the same class as the nāgas.

Grāmaṇī (S) (F) ladies of the village; a class of 12 celestial beings who attend in pairs to Sūrya and Śiva (*H. Purāṇa*).

Gṛhadevī (S) (F) **1.** goddess of the household. **3.** a rākṣasī who protects the house.

Gṛhakanyā (S) (F) **1.** daughter of the house. **3.** Aloe (*Aloe vera*).

Gṛhalakṣmī (S) (F) the Lakṣmī of the house; the guardian goddess of a house who is invoked for prosperity and happiness.

Gṛhiṇī (S) (F) **1.** mistress of the house. **3.** Asfoetida (*Ferula narthex*); *Fagonia cretka.*

Guḍapuṣpa (S) (F) **1.** sweet flower. **3.** *Bassia latifolia.*

Guḍiyā (S) (F) doll.

Guhapriyā (S) (F) **1.** liking secret places. **3.** Indra's daughter.

Guhyakālī (S) (F) **1.** the mysterious Kālī. **3.** a form of Durgā.

Guhyeśvarī (S) (F) **1.** mystic deity. **3.** another name for Prajña the female energy of the Ādibuddha.

Gulāl (S) (F) auspicious powder.

Gulikā (S) (F) ball; anything round; a pearl.

Gulmiṇī (S) (F) clustering; a creeper.

Guṇajā (S) (F) **1.** daughter of virtue. **3.** the Priyaṅgu creeper (*Aglaia odoratissima*).

Guṇakali (S) (F) **1.** possessing virtues. **3.** a rāgiṇī of rāga Malkaus.

Guṇalakṣmī (S) (F) Lakṣmī the virtuous.

Guṇasundarī (S) (F) **1.** made beautiful with virtues. **3.** another name for the Supreme Being.

Guṇāvarā (S) (F) **1.** better in qualities. **2.** one who is meritorious; virtuous. **3.** an apsarā who danced for Arjuna (*M. Bh.*).

Guṇavatī (S) (F) **1.** virtuous. **3.** the mother of Mandodarī (*V. Rāmāyaṇa*); the wife of Sāmba the son of Kṛṣṇa; a river of ancient India; the mother of Divodāsa (*M. Bh.*).

Guṇavinā (S) (F) virtuous.

Guṅćā (S) (F) blossom; flowerbud.

Guṅćakā (S) (F) bunch of flowers.

Guṇḍū (Tamil) (F) plump; round; circle.

Guṇitā (S) (F) proficient; virtuous.

Guñjan (S) (F) humming; a cluster of blossoms.

Guṇṇikā (S) (F) well woven; a garland, a necklace.

Gupti (S) (F) preserving; protecting.

Gurnikā (S) (F) **1.** wife of a preceptor. **3.** a companion of Devayānī.

Gūrti (S) (F) approval; praise.

Gurućaraṇa (S) (F) at the feet of the guru.

Gurudā (S) (F) given by the guru.

Gurudéva (S) (F) the divine guru.

Gurudīpa (S) (F) lamp of the guru.

Gurumīta (S) (F) friend of the guru.

Gurumukha (S) (F) face of the preceptor; facing the preceptor; one who follows the guru; in the image of the guru.

Gurunāma (S) (F) name of the guru.

Guruprasāda (S) (F) the blessing of the guru.

Guruśaraṇa (S) (F) in the guru's protection.

Guruvaćana (S) (F) word or promise of the guru.

Guruvīra (S) (F) a warrior of the guru.

Guṭikā (S) (F) small ball; a pearl; a cocoon of the silkworm.

H

Haimā (S) (F) **1.** of the snow; golden. **3.** another name for Pārvatī and Gaṅgā.

Haimavatī (S) (F) **1.** one who has snow. **3.** a wife of Viśvāmitra (*M. Bh.*); a wife of Kṛṣṇa who cremated herself with him when he died (*M. Bh.*); a wife of Kauśika (*M. Bh.*); another name for Pārvatī as the daughter of Himavān; another name for the river Śatadru; Black Myrobalan (*Terminalia chebula*); *Berberis asiatica.*

Haimī (S) (F) **1.** golden. **3.** *Hedychium spicatum.*

Hairaṇyavatī (S) (F) **1.** possessing gold. **3.** a river that flows along a Purāṇic region known as Hiraṇmāya (*M. Bh.*).

Hākinī (S) (F) female demon like the Dākini.

Halā (S) (F) **1.** a female friend. **3.** another name for the earth, liquor and water.

Halimā (S) (F) **1.** full of poison. **3.** a Saptamatṛ of Skanda (*M. Bh.*).

Halipriyā (S) (F) **1.** beloved of Viṣṇu. **3.** the Kadamba tree (*Anthocephalus cadamba*).

Hansaćūḍa **1.** the crest of the swan. **3.** a yakṣa who worships Kubera in his assembly (*M. Bh.*).

Hansagāminī (S) (F) **1.** as graceful as a swan. **3.** another name for Brahmāṇī the consort of Brahmā.

Hansanāḍinī (S) (F) chattering like a swan; a woman with a slender waist; large hips; a gait as graceful as an elephant's and the voice of a cuckoo.

Hansanandinī (S) (F) daughter of a swan.

Hansapādā (S) (F) **1.** the foot of the swan. **3.** an apsarā (*V. Purāṇa*).

Hansapadikā (S) (F) **1.** with the feet of the Hansa. **3.** the first wife of Duṣyanta.

Hansaveṇī (S) (F) **1.** with a braid like a swan. **2.** with a beautiful braid. **3.** another name for Sarasvatī, the goddess of learning.

Hansī (S) (F) **1.** swan. **3.** a daughter of Bhāgiratha and wife of sage Kautsa (*M. Bh.*).

Hansikā (S) (F) **1.** swan. **3.** a daughter of Surabhī who is said to support the southern region.

Hansinī (S) (F) swan; goose.

Haramālā (S) (F) garland of Śiva.

Harapriyā (S) (F) **1.** beloved of Śiva. **3.** another name for Pārvatī.

Haraśekharā (S) (F) **1.** the crest of Śiva. **3.** another name for the river Gaṅgā.

Haraśṛngārā (S) (F) **1.** ornament of Śiva. **3.** a rāgiṇī; the tree *Nyctantes arbortristes.*

Hārāvalī (S) (F) garland of pearls.

Harī (S) (F) **1.** fawn-coloured; reddish brown; tawny. **3.** name of the mother of monkeys (*M. Bh.*).

Haribālā (S) (F) daughter of Viṣṇu.

Haribhadrā (S) (F) **1.** tawny and beautiful; a beautiful golden colour; as beautiful, auspicious and praiseworthy as Viṣṇu. **3.** a daughter of Kaśyapa and Krodhā, the wife of sage Pulaha and the mother of monkeys.

Harigaṅgā (S) (F) **1.** the Gaṅgā of Viṣṇu. **3.** the river Gaṅgā which flows from the foot of Viṣṇu.

Harijaṭā (S) (F) **1.** fire haired. **3.** a rākṣasa woman who guarded Sītā in the Aśoka grove (*V. Rāmāyaṇa*).

Harikāntā (S) (F) **1.** dear to Viṣṇu. **3.** another name for Lakṣmī.

Harilina (S) (F) engrossed and merged in Viṣṇu.

Harimālā (S) (F) garland of Viṣṇu.

Hariṇākṣī (S) (F) doe eyed.

Hariṇī (S) (F) **1.** gazelle; doe; green; Yellow Jasmine (*Jasminum humile*); a golden image. **3.** an apsarā; a yakṣinī; one of the 4 kinds of beautiful women; the mother of Viṣṇu; the daughter of Hiraṇyakaśipu and wife of the asura Viśvapati (*M. Bh.*); Indian Madder (*Rubia cordifolia*).

Harinmaṇī (S) (F) **1.** green gem. **2.** the emerald.

Haripiṇḍā (S) (F) **1.** with the limbs of Viṣṇu; lion limbed. **3.** a female attendant of Skanda (*M. Bh.*).

Hariprita (S) (F) beloved of Viṣṇu.

Haripriyā (S) (F) **1.** dear to Viṣṇu. **3.** another name for Lakṣmī, the earth, Tulasī or the Sacred Basil plant (*Ocimum sanctum*) and the Kadamba tree (*Anthocephalus cadamba*); *Gloriosa superba* creeper; Khuskhus Grass (*Vetiveria zizanioides*); *Pentapetes phoenicea*; *Wedelia calendulacea.*

Harisiddi (S) (F) **1.** achieving Hari; the proof of Hari; acquiring the supernatural powers of Hari. **3.** a goddess.

Hariśrāvā (S) (F) **1.** praising Hari. **3.** a river (*M. Bh.*).

Hariśrī (S) (F) beautifully golden; blessed with Soma.

Haritālikā (S) (F) **1.** bringer of greenery; goddess of fertility. **3.** 4th day of the bright half of the month of Bhādra (August-September) personified as a goddess of pleasure.

Harīti (S) (F) **1.** tawny; verdant; green. **3.** the goddess of Rājagṛha and mother of the yakṣas (*K. Sāgara*).

Harivallabha (S) (F) **1.** beloved of Viṣṇu. **3.** another name for Lakṣmī and Tulasī or the Sacred Basil plant (*Ocimum sanctum*); Shoeflower (*Hibiscus rosa chinensis*); *Pterospermum suberifolium.*

Harmyā (S) (F) house; palace; mansion.

Harośit (S) (F) very happy; joyful.

Harṣalā (S) (F) glad.

Harṣamaya (S) whose essence is joy.

Harṣavīṇā (S) (F) a lute that delights.

Harṣī (S) (F) happy; joyful.

Harṣitā (S) (F) full of joy.

Harṣumatī (S) (F) filled with joy.

Hasantī (S) (F) **1.** one that delights. **3.** the Mallikā Jasmine (*Jasminum sambac*).

Hāsavatī (S) (F) **1.** full of laughter. **3.** a tantra deity.

Hasikā (S) (F) abloom; smiling; causing laughter.

Hāsinī (S) (F) **1.** delightful. **3.** an apsara of Alakāpuri who danced in Kubera's assembly (*M. Bh.*).

Hasrā (S) (F) **1.** laughing woman. **3.** an apsarā (*Ṛg Veda*).

Hastakamalā (S) (F) **1.** with lotus in hand. **3.** another name for Lakṣmī.

Hastisomā (S) (F) **1.** ambrosia handed. **3.** a river mentioned frequently in the Purāṇas.

Hasumatī (S) (F) always laughing.

Hātāki (S) (F) a river formed by the conjoining of Śiva and Pārvatī.

Haṭhavilāsinī (S) (F) **1.** one who enjoys according to her own desire. **3.** another name for Pārvatī.

Havirbhū (S) (F) **1.** a place of sacrifice. **3.** a daughter of Devahutī and Kardama who married sage Pulatsya and was the mother of Agastya and Viśravas (*Bhāgavata*).

Havirdhānī (S) (F) **1.** whose wealth is the oblation. **3.** another name for the cow Kāmadheṅu.

Haviṣmatī (S) (F) **1.** offering in sacrifices. **3.** a daughter of Aṅgiras (*M. Bh.*).

Havyavāhinī (S) (F) **1.** oblation bearer. **3.** the tutelary deity of the Kapila family.

Hayamukhī (S) (F) **1.** horse faced. **3.** a rākṣasī.

Hayānanā (S) (F) **1.** horse faced. **3.** a yoginī.

Hāyatī (S) (F) flame.

Hayi (S) (F) wish; desire.

Hélā (S) (F) moonlight; without any difficulty; ease; passion; coquetry.

Hemā (S) (F) **1.** golden; the earth. **2.** handsome. **3.** an apsarā wife of Maya (*H. Purāṇa*); a river.

Hemabhā (S) (F) **1.** looking like gold. **3.** the palace of Rukmiṇī.

Hemākṣi (S) (F) golden eyed.

Hemalatā (S) (F) **1.** golden vine. **3.** the Yellow Jasmine (*Jasminum humile*).

Hemamalā (S) (F) **1.** golden garland. **3.** one of Yama's wives.

Hemāmālinī (S) (F) garlanded with gold.

Hemāmbikā (S) (F) **1.** golden mother. **3.** a form of Durgā whose shrine is at Pālaghat.

Hemāṅgadā (A) (F) **1.** golden bracelet. 3. an apsarā (*M. Bh.*).

Hemāṅginī (S) (F) golden bodied.

Hemāni (S) (F) **1.** made of gold. **2.** as precious as gold. **3.** another name for Pārvatī, the consort of Śiva.

Hemantī (S) (F) of winter.

Hemaprabhā (S) (F) golden light.

Hemapuṣpakā (S) (F) **1.** with golden flowers. **3.** the flower of the Ćampaka tree (*Michelia champaka*); the Yellow Jasmine (*Jasminum humile*).

Hemapuṣpikā (S) (F) **1.** with small golden flowers. **3.** the Yellow Jasmine (*Jasminum humile*).

Hemarāginī (S) (F) **1.** coloured gold. 3. Turmeric (*Curcuma longa*).

Hemavarṇā (H) (F) golden complexioned.

Hemavatī (S) (F) **1.** possessing gold. 3. the Prickly Poppy (*Argemone mexicana*); another name for Pārvatī.

Hemāvatī (S) (F) **1.** possessing gold. **2.** a mountain stream. **3.** another name for Pārvatī.

Hemayūthikā (S) (F) **1.** gold woven. 3. the Yellow Jasmine (*Jasminum humile*).

Herambā (S) (F) **1.** consort of Ganeśa the boastful. **3.** another name for Gaṇeśaṇi.

Hiḍimbā (S) (F) **1.** instigator. **3.** a wife of the Pāṇḍava prince Bhīma and the mother of Ghaṭotkaća (*M. Bh.*).

Hijjalā (S) (F) **1.** well wisher of water. **3.** a goddess of the Indian Oak tree (*Barringtonia acutangula*).

Hilmoćikā (S) (F) **1.** destroyer of sins. 3. *Enhydra fluctuans.*

Himā (S) (F) **1.** snow. **2.** winter; night. **3.** an apsarā who lives in the mountains (*A. Veda/V. Samhitā*).

Himajā (S) (F) **1.** daughter of snow; daughter of Himavāna. **3.** another name for Pārvatī; Black Myrobalan (*Terminalia chebula*; *Hedychium spicatum*).

Himānī (S) (F) **1.** glacier; snow; avalanche. **3.** another name for Pārvatī.

Himaraśmi (S) (F) **1.** white light; cool rayed. **3.** moonlight; moon.

Himaśailajā (S) (F) **1.** born of Himālaya; born of snow. **3.** another name for Pārvatī.

Himaśveta (S) (F) as white as snow.

Himasutā (S) (F) **1.** daughter of snow; daughter of Himavāna. **2.** fair; peaceful; calm. **3.** another name for Pārvatī.

Hinā (S) (F) fragrance; the Myrtle vine (*Lawsonia inermis*) commonly known as mehndi.

Hingulājā (S) (F) **1.** of vermilion. **3.** a goddess.

Hinsā (S) (F) injury personified as the wife of Adharma and daughter of Lobha and Niṣkṛti.

Hīrā (S) (F) **1.** diamond. 3. another name for Lakṣmī.

Hiraṇyā (S) (F) **1.** golden. **3.** one of the 7 tongues of fire.

Hiraṇyabindu (S) (F) **1.** golden spot. **2.** fire; a sacred pool near the Himālayas a dip in which is considered to wash away all sins.

Hiraṇyadā (S) (F) **1.** giving gold. **3.** another name for the earth.

Hiraṇyavakśā (S) (F) **1.** chest of gold. **3.** the earth personified as the goddess Vasundharā who conceals the treasures of the world in her bosom (*A. Veda*).

Hiyā (S) (F) heart.

Hlādinī (S) (F) **1.** lightning. **3.** the thunderbolt of Indra; a river which is a tributary of the Gaṅgā; the tree *Boswellia serrata.*

Holikā (S) (F) **1.** lighting the ceremonial fire. **3.** a sister of Hiraṇyakaśipu (*Bhāgavata*).

Hotrā (S) (F) **1.** invocation. **2.** invocation which is used in ritual. **3.** one of Agni's wives (*Ṛg Veda/A. Veda*).

Hradā (S) (F) lake; pond.

Hradinī (S) (F) **1.** pond like. **2.** very happy. **3.** a tributary of the Gaṅgā which flows eastwards.

Hṛdayagandhā (S) (F) **1.** fragrance of the heart. **2.** love; kindness; affection. **3.** Spanish Jasmine (*Jasminum grandiflorum*); the Woodapple tree (*Aegle marmelos*).

Hṛdvilāsinī (S) (F) **1.** diverting the heart. **3.** Turmeric (*Curcuma longa*).

Hṛī (S) (F) **1.** modesty. **3.** shyness personified as a daughter of Dakṣa and wife of Dharmā; one of the 16 daughters of Svāyambhuva Manu and Śatarūpā and a worshipper of Brahmā in his assembly (*Bhāgavata*).

Humbādevī (S) (F) goddess of jubilation.

Huṁkārā (S) (F) **1.** roaring. **3.** a yoginī.

Hutapriyā (S) (F) **1.** beloved of fire. **3.** another name for Svāhā, the wife of Agni.

I

Ibha (S) (F) elephant; the number 8.

Ibhī (S) (F) female elephant.

Iććhā (S) (F) desire; ambition; aim.

Iććhāvatī (S) (F) one who desires.

Iḍā (S) (F) **1.** this moment. **2.** intelligence; insight; the earth as the primal giver of food. **3.** the daughter of Vāyu who was the wife of Dhruva and mother of Utkala (*Bhāgavata*); a daughter of Manu Vaivasvata (*T. Samhitā*).

Iḍaviḍa/Ilavilā/Ilibila (S) (F) **1.** knower of libation; having insight. **2.** scholar; praise. **3.** the daughter of the royal sage Tṛṇabindu and Alambuṣā, wife of Viśravas and the mother of Kubera (*V. Parāṇa*).

Iḍīka (S) (F) **1.** belonging to Iḍa. **3.** another name for Pṛthvī or the earth.

Iḍitri (S) (F) one who praises.

Ihā (S) (F) wish; desire; effort; activity.

Ihitā (S) (F) desired.

Ijyā (S) (F) sacrifice; image; gift; donation; worship.

Ikṣa (S) (F) sight.

Ikṣeṇya (S) (F) deserving to be seen.

Ikṣita (S) (F) visible; seen.

Ikṣu (S) (F) **1.** sweetness. **2.** Sugarcane (*Saccharum officinarum*).

Ikṣudā (S) (F) **1.** granting wishes; bringing sweetness. **3.** a river (*M. Bh.*).

Ikṣugandhā (S) (F) **1.** smelling as sweet as sugarcane; that which is fragrant. **3.** *Saccharum spontaneum.*

Ikṣulā (S) (F) **1.** bringer of sweetness; granting wishes. **2.** one of the prongs of Śiva's trident (*Ś. Purāṇa*). **3.** a holy river (*M. Bh.*).

Ikṣulatā (S) (F) creeper of sweetness.

Ikṣumatī/Ikṣumālinī/Ikṣumālavī (F) **1.** one who has sugarcane; one who is sweet. **3.** a river which flowed near Kurukṣetra and was inhabited by the serpent lord Takṣaka (*M. Bh.*).

Ikṣuvāri (S) (F) **1.** sugarcane juice; the sea of syrup. **3.** one of the 7 seas of the world (*A. Koṣa*).

Ilā (S) (F) **1.** earth; speech; prayer; refreshment; recreation; vital spirit; offering; stream of praise. **2.** mother; teacher; priestess. **3.** a daughter of Manu Vaivasvata and Śraddhā, the sister of Ikṣvāku, the wife of Budha and the mother of Purūravas (*Bhāgavata*); the goddess of the earth who, with Sarasvatī and Mahī, forms the trinity which bestows delight; a river which pays homage to Kārttikeya (*M. Bh.*); a daughter of Dakṣa and wife of Kaśyapa; a wife of Vasudeva; a wife of the rudra Ṛtadhvaja; another name for Durgā.

Ilābilā (S) (F) the praised one; protector of the earth; the 5 stars on the head of the constellation Orion.

Ilākṣi (S) (F) eye of the earth; the axis of the earth; centre of the earth.

Ilīkā (S) (F) small earth; diminutive form of earth.

Ilikā (S) (F) of earth; transitory; corporeal.

Ilinā (S) (F) **1.** possessing high intelligence. **3.** a daughter of Medhātithi (*H. Purāṇa*); Yama's daughter (*V. Purāṇa*).

Ilīśā, Ileśā (S) (F) queen of the earth.

Ilvakā/Ilvika (S) (F) **1.** protector of the earth. **3.** the 5 stars at the head of the constellation Orion (*J. Śāstra*).

Inākṣi (S) (F) sharp eyed.

Indalī (S) (F) to attain power.

Indirā (S) (F) **1.** bestower of prosperity; bestower of power; powerful. **3.** another name for Lakṣmī.

Indīvaraprabhā (S) (F) **1.** the light of the blue lotus. **3.** a daughter of sage Kaṇva (*M. Bh.*).

Indīvariṇī (S) (F) a collection of blue lotuses.

Indrabālā (S) (F) daughter of Indra.

Indrabhā (S) (F) light of Indra.

Indrabhaginī (S) (F) **1.** sister of Indra. **3.** another name for Pārvatī.

Indrabhattārikā (S) (F) honoured by Indra.

Indradevī (S) (F) 1. as sacred as Indra. 3. a wife of King Meghavāhana.

Indrahūti (S) (F) invocation of Indra.

Indrākṣi (S) (F) 1. eyes like Indra. 3. a tutelary goddess.

Indramohinī (S) (F) 1. one to whom Indra is attracted. 3. an apsarā in Indra's court (*M. Bh.*).

Indrāṇī (S) (F) 1. consort of Indra. 3. the female form of Indra's energy personified as the daughter of Pulomān, the consort of Indra, the mother of Jayanta and Jayantī, also called Śaći and Aindrī and considered the epitome of beauty and voluptuousness (*A. Veda/Sk. Purāṇa*); *Amomum subulatum.*

Indranīlikā (S) (F) as blue as Indra.

Indrapurohitā (S) (F) 1. the priest of Indra. 3. the asterism Puṣya.

Indraśakti (S) (F) 1. the energy of Indra. 3. the feminine form of Indra's energy personified as his consort Indrāṇī.

Indrasenā (S) (F) 1. the army of Indra; the best warrior. 3. Draupadī in her previous incarnation (*M. Bh.*); a daughter of King Nala and Damayantī (*S. Samhitā*); a princess of Aṅga who married sage Ṛṣyaśṛṅga (*M. Bh.*).

Indratā (S) (F) the power and dignity of Indra.

Indrāyaṇī (S) (F) 1. wife of Indra. 3. the feminine form of Indra's energy, personified as his consort Śaći (*Sk. Purāṇa*).

Indu (S) (F) 1. a bright drop. 3. the moon; Soma; camphor (*Cinnamonun camphora*).

Indubhavā (S) (F) 1. coming from the moon. 3. a river.

Indujā (S) (F) 1. daughter of the moon. 3. another name for the river Narmadā.

Indukakṣā (S) (F) the radiating circle of the moon; the orbit of the moon.

Indukalā (S) (F) a digit of the moon.

Indukalikā (S) (F) a small piece of the moon; the Indian Screwpine (*Pandanus odoratissimus*).

Indukamalā (S) (F) 1. the blossom of the moon like lotus. 2. the blossom of the white lotus (*Nelumbium speciosum*).

Indukāntā (S) (F) 1. beloved of the moon. 2. night.

Indulekhā (S) (F) 1. a digit of the moon. 3. the 2nd day after the new moon.

Indumatī (S) (F) 1. the full moon; full of the moon. 2. fair; tranquil; soothing; healing. 3. the daughter of King Ćandrasena of Siṁhala and Guṇavātī who was the wife of Aja and sister of King Bhoja (*Raghuvanśa*); the mother of Nahuṣa (*Bhāgavata*); the wife of Raghu (*V. Rāmāyaṇa*); a river.

Induratna (S) (F) 1. jewel of the moon. 2. the pearl.

Induvadanā (S) (F) with a moon like face; with a beautiful face.

Inikā (S) (F) little earth.

Ipsā (S) (F) desire; wish.

Ipsitā (S) (F) wished for; desired.

Irā (S) (F) 1. speech; the earth; refreshment; nourishment; water. 3. a daughter of Dakṣa, a wife of sage Kaśyapa and the mother of grass (*A. Purāṇa*); an attendant of Kubera (*M. Bh.*); an apsarā (*M. Bh.*); another name for Sarasvatī.

Irajā (S) (F) daughter of the wind; primal water.

Irāmā (S) (F) 1. happiness of the earth. 3. a river that sage Mārkaṇḍeya is supposed to have seen in the stomach of the child Kṛṣṇa (*M. Bh.*).

Irāvatī (S) (F) 1. full of water or milk. 2. clouds. 3. the granddaughter of sage Kaśyapa, the daughter of Kadru and the wife of King Parīkṣita (*V. Rāmāyaṇa*); a river (*M. Bh.*); another name for Durgā as the consort of Rudra (*Bh. Purāṇa*); a daughter of Suśravas.

Irijayā (S) (F) victorious wind.

Irikā (S) (F) a diminutive form of earth.

Īśā (S) (F) faculty; power; dominion.

Īṣā (S) (F) 1. pole of a plough. 3. another name for Durgā.

Īśāṇā (S) (F) **1.** sovereign. **3.** another name for Durgā.

Īśanī (S) (F) **1.** ruling; possessing. **3.** the wood from the Śami tree (*Prosopis spicigera*) which, when rubbed, produces fire; another name for Durgā.

Īśānikā (S) (F) belonging to the north-east.

Īśī (S) (F) **1.** goddess. **3.** another name for Durgā.

Iṣikā (S) (F) a painter's brush; the pen used for writing auspicious things.

Iśitā (S) (F) **1.** desired. **2.** superiority; greatness. **3.** one of the 8 attributes of Śiva (*M. Bh.*).

Iṣṭā (S) (F) that which is worshipped through a sacrifice; the Śami tree (*Prosopis spicigera*).

Iṣṭara (S) (F) that which is desired more; dearer.

Iṣṭu (S) (F) wish; desire.

Iṣukā (S) (F) **1.** arrow like; arrow. **3.** an apsarā (*M. Bh.*).

Īśvarāgitā (S) (F) **1.** song of the lord. **3.** the 1st 11 chapters of the *Kurma Purāṇa* which are devoted to Śiva as the supreme deity.

Īśvarakāntā (S) (F) **1.** beloved of the gods. **3.** another name for Durgā.

Īśvarī (S) (F) **1.** best among the divine. **2.** consort of Īśvara. **3.** *Rauwolfia serpentina*; *momordica balsamina*; *Bryonopsis laciniosa*; another name for Pārvatī the consort of Īśvara or Śiva.

Itarā (S) (F) **1.** another. **3.** the mother of Aitareya.

Itkila (S) (F) full of fragrance; perfume.

Iya (S) (F) pervading.

J

Jabākusuma (S) (F) **1.** flower of meditation; flower of barley. **2.** beloved of Kṛṣṇa; the shoeflower (*Hibiscus rosa sinensis*).

Jabālā (S) (F) **1.** possessing a herd of goats; a young cowherdess. **3.** the mother of sage Satyakāmā (*M. Bh.*).

Jagadambā (S) (F) **1.** mother of the world. **3.** a form of Durgā (*D. Bh. Purāṇa*).

Jagadambikā (S) (F) **1.** little mother of the universe. **3.** a form of Durgā (*D. Bh. Purāṇa*).

Jagadgaurī (S) (F) **1.** fairest of the universe. **3.** another name for Manasā Devī and Pārvatī.

Jagadhātrī (S) (F) **1.** sustainer of the universe. **3.** another name for Pārvatī and Sarasvatī.

Jaganmātā (S) (F) **1.** mother of the world. **3.** another name for Durgā and Lakṣmī.

Jagatgaurī (S) (F) **1.** beauty of the world. **3.** another name for Manasā.

Jagatī (S) (F) **1.** of the universe; heaven and hell conjoined. **3.** a Vedic metre (*Ṛg Veda*); another name for the earth.

Jagavī (S) (F) born of the world.

Jāgṛti (S) (F) awakening.

Jāhnavī (S) (F) **1.** ear born. **3.** the daughter of Jahnu (*Bhāgavata*); another name for the river Gaṅgā.

Jaidurgā (S) (F) **1.** Durgā the victorious. **3.** a form of Durgā (*T. Śāstra*).

Jaijaivantī (S) (F) **1.** full of victory. **2.** a song of victory. **3.** a rāga.

Jailekhā (S) (F) **1.** a record of victory. **2.** has been victorious many times.

Jaimālā (S) (F) garland of victory.

Jaimān (S) (F) victorious.

Jaiprabhā (S) (F) the light of victory.

Jaipriyā (S) (F) **1.** beloved of victory. **3.** an attendant of Skanda (*M. Bh.*).

Jaiśīlā (S) (F) **1.** character of victory. **2.** one to whom victory comes habitually.

Jaisudhā (S) (F) nectar of victory; the sweet taste of victory.

Jaitvatī (S) (F) **1.** bearer of victory. **2.** victorious. **3.** a daughter of Uśinara.

Jaivāhinī (S) (F) **1.** victorious army; an army of victors. **3.** Indra's wife.

Jaivantī (S) (F) long lived; being victorious.

Jaivatī (S) (F) **1.** being victorious. **2.** winning.

Jalā (S) (F) **1.** full of water. **3.** a tributary of the Yamunā river (*M. Bh.*).

Jalabālā (S) (F) **1.** maiden of water; daughter of the water. **2.** nymph. **3.** another name for Lakṣmī .

Jalabālikā (S) (F) **1.** maiden of water; daughter of the waters. **2.** lightning as the daughter of cloud.

Jaladevatā (S) (F) god of water; goddess of water.

Jaladhijā (S) (F) **1.** daughter of the ocean. **3.** another name for Lakṣmī.

Jalahāsinī (S) (F) **1.** smile of water. **3.** a wife of Kṛṣṇa (*Bhāgavata*).

Jalaja (S) (F) **1.** born of water. **2.** the lotus (*Nelumbium speciosum*). **3.** Sweet Flag (*Acorus calamus*); another name for Lakṣmī.

Jalajākṣī (S) (F) lotus eyed.

Jalajātā (S) (F) **1.** born of the water. **2.** a lotus (*Nelumbium speciosum*).

Jalajinī (S) (F) a group of lotuses.

Jalakānta (S) (F) **1.** beloved of water. **2.** the ocean; the wind.

Jalakusumā (S) (F) **1.** flower of water. **2.** the lotus (*Nelumbium speciosum*).

Jalalatā (S) (F) creeper of water; a wave; a watervine.

Jalāmbikā (S) (F) **1.** mother of water. **2.** a well.

Jalandhamā (S) (F) **1.** water blower. **3.** a daughter of Kṛṣṇa (*Bhā. Purāṇa*).

Jalandharā (S) (F) **1.** water bearer. **3.** a daughter of Kāśirāja and the sister of Duryodhana's wife Bhānumatī (*M. Bh.*).

Jalanīlī (S) (F) **1.** as blue as water. **2.** a water nymph.

Jalapadmā (S) (F) Water Lotus (*Nelumbium speciosum*).

Jalapriyā (S) (F) **1.** dear to water. **3.** the Ćātaka bird; another name for Dākṣāyāṇī.

Jalapuṣpā (S) (F) Water Lily (*Nymphaea alba*).

Jalarākṣasī (S) (F) **1.** demon of the waters. **3.** a rākṣasī who tried to swallow Hanumān; a mother of nāgas.

Jalārṇavā (S) (F) ocean of water.

Jalavālikā (S) (F) **1.** encircled by water. **2.** lightning.

Jalelā (S) (F) **1.** goddess of water. **3.** a mother attending on Skanda (*M.Bh*).

Jallatā (S) (F) **1.** a streak of water. **2.** a wave.

Jāmā (S) (F) daughter.

Jambālini (S) (F) **1.** maiden of water. **3.** a river (*A. Koṣa*).

Jambhalā (S) (F) **1.** yawning. **3.** a rākṣasi by meditating on whom women became pregnant (*A. Koṣa*).

Jambhālikā (S) (F) yawning; a song.

Jambu (S) (F) **1.** Roseapple tree (*Eugenia jambolana*); an island covered on 3 sides by the ocean (i.e. Bhārata or India) which stands on the southern side of Mahāmeru mountain and bears flowers and fruit throughout the year. **3.** a fabulous river flowing down from Mount Meru which is formed by the juice of the Jambu tree that stands on the top (*M. Bh.*).

Jambukā (S) (F) **1.** a seedless grape. **3.** an attendant of Durgā (*M. Bh.*).

Jambumatī (S) (F) **1.** rich in Jambu trees. **3.** an apsarā.

Jambūnadī (S) (F) **1.** the Jambu river. **3.** one of the 7 arms of the celestial Gaṅgā (*M. Bh.*).

Jambuvadinī (S) (F) **1.** Jambu faced. **3.** a goddess who lives on the banks of the Jambu river and bestows health, wealth, happiness and a long life (*T. Śāstra*).

Jamī (S) (F) **1.** consort of Yama. **3.** the consort of the lord of death, who is the goddess of femininity and maternity (*T. Śāstra*).

Jāmī (S) (F) **1.** daughter-in-law. **3.** an apsarā.

Jamunā (S) (F) **1.** of Yama. **3.** another name for the river Yamunā personified as the sister of Yama (*G. Purāṇa*).

Janabālikā (S) (F) **1.** daughter of the people; very bright. **2.** lightning.

Jānakī (S) (F) **1.** daughter of Janaka. **3.** another name for Sītā.

Janamohinī (S) (F) infatuating men.

Janapadī (S) (F) **1.** living place of people. **3.** an apsarā who was the consort of Śaradvān and the mother of Kṛpa and Kṛpī (*M. Bh.*).

Janaśrutī (S) (F) folklore.

Janeṣṭhā (S) (F) **1.** desired by men. **3.** the Spanish jasmine (*Jasminum grandiflorum*).

Jāngulī (S) (F) **1.** with knowledge of poisons. **3.** the Buddhist deity who is a version of the goddess Manasā (*S. Puṇḍarīka*); another name for Durgā.

Janhitā (S) (F) one who thinks of the welfare of men.

Jantumatī (S) (F) **1.** full of living beings; the one who conceives. **3.** the earth.

Janujā (S) (F) born; a daughter.

Japā (S) (F) **1.** repetition of the names of the deities. **2.** recitation of god's name on a rosary. **3.** the Shoe flower (*Hibiscus rosa chinensis*).

Jarā (S) (F) **1.** old age. **2.** Gṛhadevī or goddess of the household. **3.** the rākṣasī wife of the King Bṛhadratha of Magadha and mother of Jarāsandha (*M. Bh.*); a rākṣasī.

Jaratkarū (S) (F) **1.** wearing out the body. **3.** another name for Manasā the goddess who was the daughter of Kaśyapa and was incarnated as the sister of Vāsuki, the wife of sage Jaratkaru and the mother of Āstika (*Brahma Purāṇa*).

Jarāyu (S) (F) **1.** viviparous. **3.** an attendant of Skanda (*M. Bh.*).

Jaritā (S) (F) **1.** old; decayed. **3.** a Sarṅgikā bird who had 4 sons by ṛṣi Mandapāla.

Jarjarānanā (S) (F) **1.** old faced. **2.** with a wrinkled face. **3.** a mother in Skanda's retinue (*M. Bh.*).

Jārul (S) (F) queen of flowers; the Crepe Myrtle (*Lagerstroemia indica*).

Jasalinā (S) (F) abode of fame.

Jasarānī (S) (F) queen of fame.

Jaṭālikā (S) (F) **1.** with twisted hair. **3.** a mother in Skanda's retinue (*M. Bh.*).

Jātarūpa (S) (F) beautiful; brilliant; golden.

Jatī (S) (F) **1.** birth. **3.** Spanish Jasmine (*Jasminum grandiflorum*); the Malati creeper (*Hiptage madoblata*).

Jaṭilā (S) (F) **1.** complex; having twisted hair. **3.** a woman skilled in Vedic knowledge who was born in the dynasty of Gautama (*M. Bh.*).

Jātūkarṇā (S) (F) **1.** with patient ears. 3. Bhavabhūti's mother (*Kaṇvādi*).

Jāvitrī (S) (F) spice; mace (*Myristica fragrans*).

Jayā (S) (F) **1.** victory; victorious. **3.** Pārvatī who was the daughter of Dakṣa and the wife of Śiva (*M. Purāṇa*); a daughter of the hermit Gautama (*Bhāgavata*); a handmaiden of Durgā who was the wife of the gaṇa Puṣpadanta (*K. Sāgara*); the mother of the 12th Arhat of the present Avasarpiṇī (*He. Koṣa*); a maid of Pārvatī who was the daughter of the prajāpati Kṛṣāśva (*M. Bh.*); a tutelary deity (*Brahmā Purāṇa*); a Śakti (*Ś. Purāṇa*); a yoginī (*He. Koṣa*).

Jayadevī (S) (F) **1.** goddess of victory. **3.** a Buddhist deity.

Jayalakṣmī (S) (F) goddess of victory.

Jayalalitā (S) (F) **1.** as beautiful as victory. **3.** the goddess of victory; the fickle Lakṣmī.

Jayanā (S) (F) **1.** bestower of victory. **2.** the armour for cavalry. **3.** a daughter of Indra (*A. Koṣa*).

Jayanandinī (S) (F) **1.** daughter of victory. **3.** daughter of Lakṣmī.

Jayanī (S) (F) **1.** one who brings victory. **3.** a daughter of Indra (*A. Koṣa*).

Jayantī (S) (F) **1.** victorious in the end. **2.** a flag. **3.** a daughter of Indra and the wife of Śukra (*A. Koṣa*); the wife of King Ṛṣabha and the mother of 300 children (*Bhāgavata*); a yoginī; Kṛṣṇa's birthnight (*H. Purāṇa*); a river (*M. Bh.*); *Curcuma longa*; another name for Durgā and Dākṣāyāṇī.

Jayaśrī (S) (F) **1.** goddess of victory. **3.** a nāga virgin (*K. Vyūha*); a sword (*R. Taraṅgiṇī*).

Jayatsenā (S) (F) **1.** with victorious armies. **3.** a mother in Skanda's retinue (*M. Bh.*).

Jayitā (S) (F) victorious.

Jayitri (S) (F) victorious.

Jetaśrī (S) (F) **1.** goddess of gains. **3.** a rāga.

Jhālā (S) (F) a girl; the heat of the sun.

Jhambāri (S) (F) **1.** enemy of darkness. **3.** fire; Indra's thunderbolt; another name for Indra.

Jhaṅkāriṇī (S) (F) **1.** producing a tinkling sound. **2.** a bell; a woman wearing anklets. **3.** another name for Durgā and the Gaṅgā.

Jharnā (S) (F) **1.** flowing down. **2.** spring; fountain; a streamlet.

Jhaṣodari (S) (F) **1.** feeding on fish. **2.** a fisherwoman. **3.** another name for Satyavatī.

Jhaṣudharū (S) (F) **1.** catching fish. **2.** a fisherwoman. **3.** another name for Satyavatī.

Jhaṭā (S) (F) daughter; fighter; girl; splendour; brilliance.

Jhaṭalikā (S) (F) light; lustre; splendour.

Jhaṭi (S) (F) **1.** glittering; shining; producing glitter. **2.** the White jasmine (*Jasminum pubescens*).

Jhillikā (S) (F) light; moth; sunshine.

Jhilmil (S) (F) sparkling.

Jhūmarī (S) (F) **1.** ornament of the forehead. **3.** a rāgiṇī.

Jighatsu (S) (F) **1.** hungry. **3.** a demon (*A. Veda*).

Jigīṣā (S) (F) desire to be victorious.

Jījābāi (S) (F) **1.** victorious woman. **3.** Śivāji's mother.

Jitavatī (S) (F) **1.** one who has acquired victory; best among women. **3.** a daughter of King Uśīnara who was considered the most beautiful woman in the world (*M. Bh.*).

Jitī (S) (F) obtaining victory.

Jitvarī (S) (F) **1.** best among the victorious. **3.** another name for the city of Benaras.

Jityā (S) (F) victorious.

Jīvantikā (S) (F) **1.** bestower of long life. **2.** *Tinospora corolifolia.*

Jīvapuṣpā (S) (F) flower of life.

Jīvikā (S) (F) **1.** the source of life. **2.** water; occupation.

Jñānavatī (S) (F) endowed with knowledge.

Jogū (S) (F) praising.

Joṣā (S) (F) woman.

Jośikā (S) (F) cluster of buds; a young woman.

Jośyā (S) (F) delightful.

Jūhī(S) (F) jasmine flower (*Jasminum pubescens*).

Jūrṇī (S) (F) firebrand; glowing fire's blaze.

Juṣṭi (S) (F) love; service.

Jutikā (S) (F) a kind of camphor.

Jvālā (S) (F) **1.** flame. **2.** blaze; light; torchglow; shine. **3.** a daughter of Takṣaka, the wife of King Ṛkṣa and the mother of Matīnara (*M. Bh.*); the wife of King Nīladhvaja who made Gaṅgā curse Arjuna (*M. Bh.*).

Jvālāmukhā (S) (F) **1.** flame faced. **3.** a tutelary deity of Lomaśa's family located in the hills of north east Punjab (*T. Śastra*).

Jvalanā (S) (F) **1.** flaming; shining. **3.** a daughter of Takṣaka and wife of Ṛćeyu (*H. Purāṇa*).

Jvālantaśikharā (S) (F) **1.** flame tufted. **3.** a gandharva virgin (*K. Vyūha*).

Jvālitā (S) (F) lighted; blazing; shining; flaming.

Jvālitrī (S) (F) lighted; shining; flaming.

Jyesṭhā (S) (F) **1.** eldest sister. **3.** the 18th lunar mansion of 3 stars (*T. Brāhmaṇa*); a deity of inauspicious things considered the elder sister of Lakṣmī because she preceded Lakṣmī from the Ocean of Milk (*P. Purāṇa*); a star considered to bring luck (*V's B. Samhitā*); a yoginī or fierce village goddess (*D. Bh. Purāṇa*); another name for Gaṅgā.

Jyeṣṭhilā (S) (F) **1.** elder. **2.** superior; greater. **3.** a river that lives in the palace of Varuṇa (*M. Bh.*).

Jyotā (S) (F) the brilliant one.

Jyotī (S) (F) **1.** brilliant; flame like. **2.** the light of the sun; dawn; fire; lightning; brightness of the sky; light of heaven; light as a divine principle of life and source of intelligence; Fenugreek (*Trigonella foenum-graecum*).

Jyotiranikā (S) (F) with a shining face.

Jyotirhastā (S) (F) **1.** fire handed. **3.** another name for Durgā.

Jyotirlekhā (S) (F) **1.** a line of light. **2.** studded with rows of stars. **3.** a daughter of a yakṣa (*K. Sāgara*)

Jyotiṣmatī (S) (F) luminous; brilliant; shining; celestial; belonging to the world of light; Intellect tree (*Celastrus paniculate*); Black Liquorice (*Cardiospenrmum halicacabum*)

Jyotsnā (S) (F) **1.** moonlight. **2.** a moonlit night; light; splendour. **3.** one of Brahmā's bodies; one of the 16 digits of the moon; another name for Durgā; the annual *Trichosanthes cucumerina.*

Jyotsnākalī (S) (F) **1.** a piece of the moon; moonlight. **3.** the daughter of the moon and wife of Varuṇa's son Puṣkara; the 2nd daughter of Ćandra who married the Sun (*M. Bh.*).

Jyotsnī (S) (F) a moonlit night.

K

Kāberī (S) (F) **1.** full of water. **2.** harlot; courtesan. **3.** a river in south India.

Kabūtarī (S) (F) pigeon.

Kadalī (S) (F) **1.** the banana tree (*Musa sapientum*). **3.** the sacred river on the banks of which Rāma lived (*V. Rāmāyaṇa*).

Kadalīgarbhā (S) (F) **1.** born from a plantain tree. **3.** the daughter of sage Maṅkaṇaka and the wife of King Dṛdhavarman (*K. Sāgara*).

Kadambā (S) (F) group; cloud; the Kadambā tree (*Adina cordifolia*).

Kādambakī (S) (F) flowers of Kadambā (*Adina cordifolia*); to transform into flowers of the Kadambā.

Kādambarī (S) (F) **1.** coming from the Kadambā tree (*Adina cordifolia*). **2.** female cuckoo; wine distilled from the flowers of the Kadambā tree. **3.** a river in Jambudvīpa (*A. Koṣa*); a Sanskṛt work by Bāṇabhaṭṭa (*Kādambarī*); a daughter of Ćitraratha and Madirā (*Kādambarī*); the heroine of the prose romance by this name composed by Bāṇa; another name for Sarasvatī.

Kādambinī (S) (F) **1.** a garland of clouds. **3.** a daughter of Takṣaka.

Kadhapriyā (S) (F) ever loved; ever friendly.

Kadru (S) (F) **1.** tawny; brown. **2.** a Soma vessel; the earth in a personified form. **3.** a daughter of Dakṣa, wife of Kaśyapa and the mother of serpents (*M. Bh.*)

Kāhalā (S) (F) **1.** mischievous. **2.** a young woman; a kind of musical instrument. **3.** an apsarā (*M. Bh.*); Varuṇa's wife.

Kāhinī (S) (F) mischievous; young.

Kaikasī (S) (F) **1.** growing plants in water. **2.** grows in water; vertebra; rib. **3.** the daughter of Sumāli and Ketumatī, the wife of Viśravas and the mother of Rāvaṇa, Kumbhakaraṇa and Vibhīṣana (*V. Rāmāyaṇa*).

Kaikeyī (S) (F) **1.** princess of the Kekayas. **3.** a wife of King Daśaratha of Ayodhyā and the mother of Bharata (*V. Rāmāyaṇa*); the wife of King Ajamīdha of the Purū dynasty (*M. Bh.*); another name for Sudeṣṇa the wife of the king of Virāṭa.

Kaileśvarī (S) (F) **1.** goddess of water. **2.** the family goddess. **3.** another name for Durgā.

Kairavī (S) (F) moonlight.

Kairaviṇī (S) (F) water born; the White Lotus plant (*Nelumbium speciosum*).

Kājal (S) (F) kohl; collyrium.

Kajjalī (S) (F) collyrium.

Kajrī (S) (F) collyrium coloured; cloud like; a folksong of Uttar Pradesh sung in the monsoon.

Kākalī (S) (F) voice of the cuckoo; a musical instrument.

Kākalikā (S) (F) **1.** with a low and sweet voice. **3.** an apsarā (*V. Purāṇa*).

Kākāsyā (S) (F) **1.** crow faced. **3.** a Buddhist goddess.

Kākati (S) (F) **1.** cawing like a crow. **3.** a tutelary goddess form of Durgā (*T. Śāstra*).

Kākī (S) (F) **1.** female crow. **3.** one of the 7 mothers of Skanda (*M. Bh.*); the original mother of crows personified as a daughter of Kaśyapa and Tāmrā (*H. Purāṇa*).

Kākinī (S) (F) **1.** a small coin equal to 20 cowries. **3.** a goddess (*T. Śāstra*).

Kakṣī (S) (F) of jungle; perfume; fragrant earth.

Kakṣivatasutā (S) (F) **1.** daughter of Kakṣivant. **3.** a female sage Ghoṣā daughter of sage Kakṣivant and sister of Bhadra (*Ṛg Veda*).

Kakubha (S) (F) **1.** peak; summit; quarter of the heavens; splendour; beauty. **2.** a wreath of ćampaka flowers (*Michelia champaka*). **3.** a rāgiṇī (*Kavyādarśa*).

Kakuda (S) (F) **1.** summit. **2.** symbol of royalty. **3.** a daughter of Dakṣa and wife of Dharma (*T. Samhitā*).

Kakudmi (S) (F) **1.** mountain daughter. **3.** a river (*P. Purāṇa*); another name for Revatī the wife of Balarāma.

Kalā (S) (F) **1.** a small point; a digit of the moon; art; an atom. **2.** a small part of anything; skill; ingenuity. **3.** a daughter of Devahūti, the wife of Marīći and the mother of Kaśyapa and Pūrṇimā (*Bhāgavata*); a daughter of Dakṣa (*M. Purāṇa*).

Kalahapriyā (S) (F) **1.** quarrelsome. **3.** a prostitute who attained svarga by observing the Kārttikavrata (*P. Purāṇa*).

Kālakā (S) (F) **1.** blue; black. **2.** pupil of the eye; a female crow; flawed gold; fragrant earth. **3.** an attendant of Skanda (*M. Bh.*); the daughter of Dakṣa and mother of the Kālakeyas (*D. Bh. Purāṇa*); an attendant of the 4th Arhat (*J.S. Koṣa*); a vidyādharī (*K. Sāgara*); a river (*M. Bh.*); another name for Durgā.

Kālakanyā (S) (F) daughter of time; daughter of death.

Kālakarṇī (S) (F) **1.** black eared. **3.** a yoginī; another name for Lakṣmī.

Kalamālī (S) (F) dispelling darkness; splendid; sparkling.

Kalāndikā (S) (F) bestower of art and/ or skills; wisdom; intelligence.

Kālañjarī (S) (F) **1.** dwelling in the Kālanjara mountain. **3.** another name for Pārvatī.

Kalāpinī (S) (F) as blue as the peacock's tail; the night.

Kālarātri (S) (F) **1.** dark night; night of death. **3.** the devī presiding over the night on the eve of death (*M. Bh./ Rāmāyaṇa*).

Kalāvatī (S) (F) **1.** with digits; moonlight. **2.** well versed in the 64 arts. **3.** a daughter of the king of Kāśī and wife of King Daśārha of Mathura (*M. Bh.*); a tāntric ceremony in which Durgā enters the body of the novice (*T. Śāstra*); the lute of the gandharva Tumburu (*A. Koṣa*); a daughter of apsarā Alambuṣa (*K. Sāgara*); a rāga.

Kalaviṅkā (S) (F) a sparrow (*Passer indicus*); the Indian cuckoo (*Cuculus scolopaceus*).

Kalehikā (S) (F) **1.** black sandalwood. **3.** an attendant of Skanda (*M. Bh.*).

Kalī (S) (F) bud.

Kālī (S) (F) **1.** blackness; destroyer of time. **2.** night; a succession of black clouds. **3.** goddess Durgā in her terrible form representing eternal time, both giving life and taking it and worshipped as the tutelary deity of Bengal (*D. Bh. Purāṇa*); the daughter of Dakṣa and the mother of the asuras (*M. Bh.*); one of the 16 vidyādevīs; one of the 7 tongues of fire (*M. Upaniṣad*); a sister of Yama (*H. Purāṇa*); a wife of Bhīma (*Bhāgavata*); a river *Bhāgavata*); a Śakti (*M. Bh.*); another name for Satyavatī, the mother of Vyāsa; Bedda Nut (*Terminalia belerica*).

Kālikā (S) (F) **1.** dark blue; black. **2.** a flaw in gold; a multitude of clouds; fog; a kind of fragrant earth. **3.** mother of Skanda's retinue (*M. Bh.*); an attendant of the 4th Arhat (*J.S. Koṣa*); a vidyādharī (*K. Sāgara*); a kinnarī (*M. Bh.*); another name for Durgā.

Kalikā (S) (F) **1.** 1/16th of the moon; bud. **2.** progressive; tender; fragrant; the herb *Tephrosia purpurea*.

Kalīkaṇṭha (S) (F) **1.** with a pleasing voice. **2.** dove; the Indian cuckoo (*Cuculus scolopaceus*). **3.** an apsarā (*B. Rāmāyaṇa*).

Kālimā (S) (F) blackness; darkness; the mother Kāli.

Kalindakanyā (S) (F) **1.** daughter of Kalinda.**3.** another name for the river Yamunā.

Kālindī (S) (F) **1.** belonging to Kalinda; the Yamunā river which begins its journey from Mount Kalinda. **3.** a wife of Asita and mother of Sagara; a wife of Kṛṣṇa (*Bhāgavata*); Wild Guava (*Careya arborea*).

Kalinī (S) (F) **1.** carrier of blossoms; pea plant; pulse. **2.** a watermelon; a vessel; red flowers. **3.** a daughter of Sūrya; a wife of Kṛṣṇa (*Bhā. Purāṇa*); the wife of Asita and mother of Sagara; another name for the river Yamunā.

Kalivināśinī (S) (F) **1.** one who destroys the Kaliyuga. **3.** a goddess (*Br. Purāṇa*).

Kalli (S) (F) ornament for the wrist.

Kallolinī (S) (F) **1.** always happy. **2.** a surging stream; a river. **3.** a river (*V. Rāmāyaṇa*).

Kalmāṣī (S) (F) **1.** having black spots. **2.** speckled; variegated. **3.** the cow of Jamadagni that grants all desires (*Purāṇas*); another name for the Yamunā river.

Kalmeṣikā (S) (F) variegated.

Kalpalatā (S) (F) **1.** a wish granting creeper. **3.**a creeper of Indra's paradise that grants all wishes.

Kalpanā (S) (F) imagination; doing; decoration; composition; idea.

Kalpataru (S) (F) **1.** a wish granting tree. **3.** one of the 5 trees of Paradise that fulfils all desires (*Pañćatantra*).

Kalpavatī (S) (F) competent.

Kalya (S) (F) **1.** praise; eulogy. **3.** another name for the mother of Vyāsa.

Kalyāṇavatī (S) (F) **1.** full of virtue. **3.** a princess (*K. Sāgara*).

Kalyāṇī (S) (F) **1.** beneficial. **2.** lucky; excellent; propitious; a sacred cow. **3.** a follower of Skanda (*M. Bh.*); a rāgiṇī; Dākṣāyāṇī in Malaya (*M. Bh.*); another name for Pārvatī; Indian Senna (*Cassia augustifolia*); *Teramnus labialis.*

Kamā (S) (F) beauty; radiance; loveliness.

Kāmā (S) (F) **1.** desired; loved. **3.** a daughter of Pṛthūśravas and the wife of King Ayutanāyi (*M. Bh.*).

Kāmāćārī (S) (F) **1.** following one's own desires. **2.** unrestrained. **3.** a mother of Skanda's retinue (*M. Bh.*).

Kāmaćārini (S) (F) **1.** moving at will. **3.** Dākṣāyaṇī in Mount Mandāra.

Kāmadā (S) (F) **1.** granting desires. **3.** a follower of Skanda (*M. Bh.*).

Kāmadhenu (S) (F) **1.** the desire granting cow. **3.** the mythical cow of Vasiṣṭha which satisfies all desires (*Brah. Purāṇa*); the mother of cattle (*K. Sāgara*).

Kāmaduhā (S) (F) **1.** which grants desires. **3.** a mythical cow that grants all desires (*Brah. Purāṇa*); a river flowing from Mount Kumuda (*V. Samhitā*).

Kāmadyū (S) (F) **1.** granter of wishes. **3.** the daughter of Purumitra and wife of Vimada (*Ṛg Veda*).

Kāmakalā (S) (F) **1.** the art of love. **3.** another name for Rati.

Kāmakāntā (S) (F) beloved of Kāma; the jasmine (*Jasminum sambac*).

Kāmākhya (S) (F) **1.** giver of desires. **3.** another name for Durgā.

Kāmākṣī (S) (F) **1.** with voluptuous eyes. **3.** a tantric goddess (*T. Śastra*); another name for Durgā; Indian Bead (*Canna indica*).

Kamalā (S) (F) **1.** born of a lotus. **2.** spring; desirous; beautiful; excellent; wealth. **3.** another name for Lakṣmī; the mother of Prahlāda (*P. Purāṇa*); a follower of Skanda (*M. Bh.*); the daughter of Reṇu; wife of Jayāpīḍa (*R. Taraṅgiṇī*); another name for Dākṣāyāṇī.

Kamalādevi (S) (F) **1.** lady of the lotus. **3.** the wife of King Lalitāditya and mother of King Kuvalayāpīda (*M. Bh.*).

Kamalākṣī (S) (F) **1.** lotus eyed. **3.** a mother in Skanda's retinue (*M. Bh.*).

Kamalalakṣmī (S) (F) Lakṣmī of the lotus.

Kamalālayā (S) (F) **1.** abiding in a lotus. **3.** another name for Lakṣmī.

Kamalaloćanā (S) (F) lotus eyed.

Kamalanayanī (S) (F) lotus eyed.

Kāmalatā (S) (F) creeper of love; sensuous; exotic; exquisite.

Kamalekṣaṇā (S) (F) lotus eyed.

Kamalī (S) (F) a collection of lotuses; water; the sārasa crane (*Grus antigone*).

Kāmāli (S) (F) **1.** full of desire. **2.** extremely passionate. **3.** another name for Reṇukā.

Kamalīkā (S) (F) a small lotus.

Kamalinī (S) (F) **1.** lotus plant; a collection of lotuses. **2.** beautiful; fragrant; auspicious; dear to the gods.

Kāmanā (S) (F) desire.

Kāmāndakā (S) (F) **1.** with bound desires. **3.** a Buddhist priestess (*B. Literature*).

Kāmāndaki (S) (F) with bound desires.

Kāmarekhā (S) (F) line of love.

Kāmasenā (S) (F) **1.** warrior of love. **3.** wife of Nidhipati.

Kāmasū (S) (F) **1.** gratifying wishes. **3.** another name for Rukmiṇī.

Kāmāyakā (S) (F) **1.** desired abode. **3.** the forest in which the Pāṇḍavas stayed for the 12 years of their exile (*M. Bh.*).

Kāmāyanī (S) (F) **1.** the mirror of love. **3.** Jayaśankara Prasad's work which contains 125,000 couplets.

Kāmbojinī (S) (F) **1.** she-elephant. **3.** an attendant of the Devī.

Kāmeśvari (S) (F) **1.** consort of Kāmeśvara. **3.** another name for Pārvatī and Rati.

Kāminī (S) (F) **1.** desirable. **2.** beautiful; loving; *Berberis asiatica.*

Kāmitā (S) (F) desired; wished for.

Kāmmā (S) (F) lovable.

Kāmodī (S) (F) **1.** that which excites. **2.** a musical note that excites. **3.** a rāgiṇī of the Dīpaka rāga; a goddess who, upon its churning, emerged out of the Ocean of Milk.

Kamrā (S) (F) **1.** desirable; beautiful. **2.** loving.

Kāmuka (S) (F) **1.** desired. **3.** Madhāvi Creeper (*Hiptage madoblata*).

Kāmunā (S) (F) desired; the flower *Hedchium ellipticum.*

Kāmyā (S) (F) **1.** beautiful; desirable; amiable; striving. **3.** a celestial woman.

Kaṇā (S) (F) atom; small; sand.

Kanā (S) (F) girl; maid; eye.

Kaṇakā (S) (F) **1.** born of sand. **3.** another name for Sītā.

Kanakakuṇḍalā (S) (F) **1.** wearing golden earrings. **3.** the mother of the yakṣa Harikeśa (*M. Bh.*).

Kanakalatā (S) (F) a golden vine.

Kanakamañjarī (S) (F) golden blossom.

Kanakāmbarā (S) (F) clad in gold; golden; a flower (*Crossandra infundibuliformis*).

Kanakamudrā (S) (F) golden ring; gold coin.

Kanakaprabhā (S) (F) **1.** with the lustre of gold; as bright as gold. **2.** *Bauhinia variegata*; *Jasminum bignoniaceum.*

Kanakarekhā (S) (F) **1.** a line of gold. **3.** the daughter of the king of Kanakapurī (*K. Sāgara*).

Kanakasundarī (S) (F) as beautiful as gold.

Kanakavāhinī (S) (F) **1.** golden stream. **3.** a river (*R. Taraṅgiṇī*).

Kanakāvalī (S) (F) golden chain.

Kanakavallī (S) (F) golden creeper.

Kanakvaraṇa (S) (N) **1.** of golden colour. **3.** a king supposed to have been the former incarnation of Sākyamuni (*M. Bh.*).

Kanakavatī (S) (F) **1.** possessing gold. **2.** golden. **3.** a follower of Skanda (*M. Bh.*).

Kanakvī (S) (F) a small kite.

Kaṇam (S) (F) the black soiled earth; sand.

Kānana (S) (F) **1.** forest. **2.** grove. **3.** the mouth of Brahmā.

Kānanabālā (S) (F) forest maiden.

Kāñcanābhā (S) (F) golden splendour.

Kāñcanagaurī (S) (F) **1.** as fair as gold. **3.** another name for Pārvatī.

Kāñcanākṣī (S) (F) **1.** golden eyed. **3.** a river which flows through Naimiṣāraṇya and is a part of the river Sarasvatī (*M. Bh.*).

Kāñcanamālā (S) (F) **1.** garland of gold. **3.** an attendant of Vāsavadattā; the wife of Udayana; the daughter of Kṛkin and the wife of Aśoka's son Kuṇāla (*K. Vyūha*); an apsarā.

Kāñcanaprabhā (S) (F) **1.** as bright as gold. **3.** a vidyādhara princess (*K. Sāgara*).

Kañcapi (S) (F) **1.** connoisseur of glory. **3.** the lute of Sarasvatī (*Purāṇas*).

Kāñcī (S) (F) **1.** shining. **2.** waistband with bells. **3.** a pilgrimage centre in South India.

Kandalā (S) (F) the flower of the Kandalī tree (*Rhizophora mucronata*); deer; lotus seed; a flag; a banner.

Kandalīkusuma (S) (F) the flower of the Kandalī tree (*Rhizophora mucronata*).

Kandarā (S) (F) **1.** lute. **2.** cave; hollow. **3.** a mother of Skanda's retinue (*M. Bh.*).

Kandarpā (S) (F) **1.** inflamer. **3.** a divine woman attending on the 15th Arhat (*J.S. Koṣa*).

Kandarpabālā (S) (F) daughter of Kāma, the inflamer.

Kandarpamātṛ (S) (F) **1.** mother of Kāma. **3.** another name for Lakṣmī.

Kandharā (S) (F) water bearer; a cloud.

Kandiri (S) (F) root like; the Sensitive Plant (*Mimosa pudica*).

Kāṇḍulā (S) (F) **1.** itching. **2.** an itching in various bodily parts which induces sexual desires. **3.** a rāgiṇī.

Kaṇḍūti (S) (F) **1.** sexual desire. **3.** a follower of Skanda (*M. Bh.*).

Kaṅgana (S) (F) a bracelet.

Kanī (S) (F) girl.

Kaṇīci (S) (F) creeper with blossoms.

Kaṇīkā (S) (F) an atom; small; diminutive.

Kanikā (S) (F) girl.

Kanīna (S) (F) youthful; the pupil of the eye; the little finger.

Kaniṣṭhā (S) (F) the little finger; the youngest.

Kanitā (S) (F) iris of the eye.

Kañjarī (S) (F) musical instrument; a bird.

Kañjira (S) (F) tambourine.

Kaṅkā (S) (F) **1.** scent of the lotus. **3.** a daughter of Ugrasena and sister of Kaṅka (*Bhāgavata/V. Purāṇa*).

Kaṅkālinī (S) (F) **1.** with a necklace of bones. **3.** another name for Durgā.

Kaṅkaṇā (S) (F) **1.** a bracelet. **2.** an ornament; a crest. **3.** a mother in the retinue of Skanda (*M. Bh.*).

Kaṅkaṇikā (S) (F) a small bell; a tinkling ornament.

Kāṅkṣā (S) (F) wish; desire; inclination.

Kāṅkṣiṇī (S) (F) one who desires.

Kannakī (S) (F) **1.** chaste and devoted wife. **3.** another name for Sītā.

Kannikā (S) (F) maiden.

Kaṅsavatī (S) (F) **1.** made of metal. **3.** the sister of Kaṇsa.

Kāntā (S) (F) beloved; perfume; the earth.

Kānti (S) (F) **1.** glory; beauty; wish; decoration; a digit of the moon. **3.** another name for Lakṣmī; Garden Pea (*Pisum sativum*).

Kānupriyā (S) (F) beloved of Kṛṣṇa.

Kaṇvasutā (S) (F) **1.** daughter of Kaṇva. **3.** another name for Śakuntalā.

Kanyā (S) (F) **1.** daughter; maiden. **3.** the zodiac sign of Virgo; *Aloe vera*; Bulb bearing Yam (*Dioscorea bulbifera*); *Capparis sepiaria*; another name for Durgā.

Kanyakā (S) (F) **1.** the smallest; girl; maiden; daughter; the virgin goddess. **3.** the zodiac constellation Virgo; another name for Durgā.

Kanyākumārī (S) (F) **1.** the eternal virgin. **3.** the daughter of Dakṣa (*M. Bh.*); a devotee of Śiva who sat in meditation on the southernmost shore of India and in whose memory a pilgrimage centre has been established there (*Purāṇas*); the child that escaped from Kaṅsa at the time of Kṛṣṇa's birth (*P. Purāṇa*); *Amomum subulatum*; another name for Durgā.

Kanyalā (S) (F) girl.

Kanyanā (S) (F) maiden; girl.

Kanyāratna (S) (F) a gem of a girl.

Kāpalamālā (S) (F) **1.** with a garland of skulls. **3.** an attendant of Devī.

Kapālinī (S) (F) **1.** consort of Kapālī. **3.** another name for Durgā.

Kapardikā (S) (F) a small shell (*Cypraea moneta*).

Kapardinī (S) (F) **1.** whose hair is braided like a cowrie shell. **3.** a goddess (*Brahma Purāṇa*).

Kaphinī (S) (F) **1.** phlegmatic. **3.** a river.

Kāpī(S) (F) **1.** of Kṛṣṇa. **3.** a river *(M.Bh.)*

Kapilā **1.** monkey coloured. **2.** a brown cow; perfume; tawny. **3.** a fabulous cow of Indra celebrated in the Purāṇas (*M. Bh.*); a daughter of Dakṣa and wife of Kaśyapa (*M. Bh.*); the mother of Panćāśikha (*M. Bh.*); the consort of Puṇḍarīka an elephant of a quarter (*A. Koṣa*); a holy place of Kurukṣetrā (*M. Bh.*); a river of ancient India (*M. Bh.*); the Śīśam tree (*Dalbergia sissoo*).

Kapiladhārā (S) (F) **1.** with brown waves. **2.** muddy. **3.** another name for the Gaṅgā.

Kapilī (S) (F) **1.** with tawny waves. **3.** a river in modern Nowgong which is in Assam.

Kapiñjalā (S) (F) **1.** with brown water. **2.** Francoline partridge. **3.** a river of ancient India (*M. Bh.*).

Kapisā (S) (F) **1.** monkey coloured. **2.** brown; reddish. **3.** the mother of the Piśāćas; a river (*M. Bh.*).

Karabhorū (S) (F) one whose thighs resemble the trunk of an elephant.

Karālā (S) (F) **1.** terrible; opening; wide; tearing. **2.** formidable. **3.** one of the 7 tongues of Agni; another name for Durgā.

Karālī (S) (F) **1.** the terrible. **3.** Durgā in her destructive form.

Karālī (S) (F) **1.** frightening. **2.** destructive; fear inducing. **3.** one of Agni's 7 tongues of fire (*M. Upaniṣad*).

Karālikā (S) (F) **1.** that which tears. **2.** sword. **3.** another name for Durgā.

Karambhā (S) (F) **1.** mixed. **2.** fennel; *foeniculum vulgare*; *Asparagus racemosus*. **3.** a princess of Kaliṅga, the wife of King Akrodhana of the Purū dynasty and the mother of Devātithi (*M. Bh.*); *Aglaia odoratissima*; *Capparis zeylanica*.

Karañjanilayā (S) (F) **1.** wind of the Karañja tree (*Pongamia glabra*). **3.** the daughter of Dakṣa, the wife of Kaśyapa, the mother of all trees and who is believed to stay in the Karañja tree (*M. Bh.*); another name for Analā.

Karavirī (S) (F) **1.** strong armed. **2.** a good cow; the oleander flower (*Nerium odorum*). **3.** another name for Aditī.

Karburī (S) (F) **1.** golden; lioness; tigress. **3.** another name for Durgā.

Kareṇumatī (S) (F) **1.** like a female elephant. **3.** the daughter of King Śiśupāla of Ćedi, the wife of Nakula and the mother of Niramitra (*M. Bh.*).

Kārikā (S) (F) a collection of verses on philosophy.

Kariśmā (S) (F) miracle.

Karīśṇī (S) (F) goddess of elephants; goddess of wealth.

Karkarī (S) (F) a lute.

Karmanāśā (S) (F) **1.** one who destroys fate or action. **2.** one who destroys the merit of works. **3.** river between Kāśī and Vihāra (*Bh. Purāṇa*).

Karmiṣṭhā (S) (F) extremely diligent.

Karṇadhārā (S) (F) **1.** having large ears. **3.** an apsarā (*K. Vyūha*).

Karṇamotī (S) (F) **1.** pearls of the ear. **3.** Pārvatī with pearls in her ears; Durgā in her form as Ćāmuṇḍa (*T. Sastra*).

Karṇapiśāćī (S) (F) **1.** witch of the ear. **3.** a tantric goddess who, when properly invoked is considered to whisper the future of people in the ear of her devotees (*J. Śāstra*).

Karṇapravaraṇā (S) (F) **1.** one who whispers in the ears. **3.** a follower of Skanda (*M. Bh.*).

Karṇapūra (S) (F) **1.** that which fulfils the ears. **2.** ornament of flowers worn round the ears; a blue lotus flower (*Nymphaea stellata*). 3. the father of Kavićandra and the author of *Alamkāra Kaustubha*.

Karṇī (S) (F) **1.** with ears. **2.** a good listener. **3.** Kaṇsa's mother (*Bhāgavata*).

Karṇikā (S) (F) **1.** creeper. **2.** heart of a lotus; earring. **3.** an apsarā who sang and danced at the birth celebrations of Arjuna (*M. Bh.*); *Rosa alba*; *Crysanthemum indicum*.

Kārpanī (S) (F) gladness.

Karpūratilakā (S) (F) **1.** one who applies camphor on the forehead. **3.** another name for Jayā, a friend of Durgā.

Karpūrī (S) (F) scented with camphor.

Karṣṇā (S) (F) **1.** black. **2.** belonging to the dark half of the month; that which belongs to Kṛṣṇa.

Kārttikī (S) (F) **1.** the full moon night in the Kārttika month. **2.** pious; holy.

Karuṇā (S) (F) **1.** compassion. **2.** tenderness; mercy.

Karuṇāmallī (S) (F) **1.** the vine of compassion. **3.** the jasmine (*Jasminum sambac*).

Kāruṇyā (S) (F) merciful; compassionate; praiseworthy.

Karvarī (S) (F) **1.** variegated. **2.** tigress; night. **3.** another name for Durgā.

Kaśerū (S) (F) **1.** backbone. **2.** the root of the grass (*Scirpus kysoor*). **3.** one of the 9 divisions of Bhāratavarṣa; the beautiful daughter of Prajāpati Tvaṣṭṛ who married Kṛṣṇa (*M. Bh.*).

Kāśī (S) (F) **1.** shining; splendid; a clenched hand. **3.** an old and most sacred pilgrimage centre of India which has the famous Viśvanātha temple whose Śivaliṅga is considered to have been installed by Brahmā (*Rāmāyaṇa*); a prince of the family of Bharata who was the son of Suhotra and grandfather of Dhanvantari (*H. Purāṇa*); a son of Kaviprajāpati (*M. Bh.*); the wife of Sudeva and the mother of Supārśva; another name for the sun.

Kāśivara (S) (F) **1.** lord of Kāśī. **3.** another name for Śiva.

Kāṣṭhā (S) (F) **1.** the path of the wind; top; summit; cardinal point; a quarter of the world; a 16th of the moon; form; appearance; water; the sun. **3.** a daughter of Dakṣa, the wife of Kaśyapa and the mother of the solidungulous quadripeds (*Bhā. Purāṇa*).

Kastūrī (S) (F) scented with musk.

Kasturīgandhī (S) (F) **1.** fragrant with musk. **3.** another name for Kālī and Satyavatī.

Kasturīkā (S) (F) musk.

Kāsū (S) (F) spear; lance; light; lustre; understanding.

Kāśvī (S) (F) shining; beautiful.

Kaśyapī (S) (F) **1.** belonging to Kaśyapa. **3.** another name for the earth which was given as a gift to Kaśyapa by Paraśurāma.

Kātyāyanī (S) (F) **1.** dressed in red. **3.** a wife of Yājñavalkya (*Rāmāyaṇa*); another name for Pārvatī.

Kaukulikā (S) (F) **1.** belonging to the universe. **2.** one who considers the universe as his family. **3.** a mother of Skanda (*M. Bh.*).

Kaumarī (S) (F) **1.** the virgin. **2.** a rāgiṇī. **3.** another name for Pārvatī as the virgin god-dess and the consort of Kārttikeya.

Kaumudī (S) (F) **1.** moonlight personified as the wife of Candra; festivity. **3.** full moon day in the month of Kārttika.

Kausalā (S) (F) **1.** from Kosala. **3.** a wife of Kṛṣṇa.

Kauśalikā (S) (F) **1.** present. **2.** offering.

Kausalya (S) (F) **1.** skill; welfare; cleverness; from Kosala. **3.** a wife of King Daśaratha and mother of Rāma (*V. Rāmāyaṇa*); the wife of the king of Kāśī and mother of Ambā, Ambikā, Ambālikā (*M. Bh.*); the wife of a Yādava king and mother of Keśin (*D. Bhāgavata*); the wife of King Janaka of Mithilā (*V. Rāmāyaṇa*); mother of Dhriṭarāṣṭra and Pāṇḍu; wife of Purū and mother of Janamejaya (*M. Bh.*).

Kauśikā (S) (F) **1.** drinking vessel; silk. **2.** receptacle; cup. **3.** a goddess sprung from the body of Pārvatī (*H. Purāṇa*).

Kauśikī (S) (F) **1.** sheathed; hidden; silken; covered. **3.** Viśvāmitra's sister Satyavatī who turned into the Gomatī river beside which stood the hermitage of Viśvāmitra and which is now known as the Kosi and falls in Bihar (*H. Purāṇa*); another name for Durgā.

Kauṭiryā (S) (F) **1.** living in a hut. **3.** another name for Durgā.

Kautukā (S) (F) causing curiosity or admiration; giving pleasure.

Kāvalī (S) (F) bangle.

Kāverī (S) (F) **1.** full of water; a courtesan; turmeric. **3.** a daughter of

Yuvanāśva and wife of Jahnu changed into a holy river of south India and whose devī is a worshipper of Varuṇa (*Sk. Purāṇa*); a rāga; *Curcuma longa.*

Kavikā (S) (F) poetess.

Kavitā (S) (F) poem.

Kāvyamātā (S) (F) **1.** mother of the poet; mother of the physician. **2.** mother of an intel-ligent one. **3.** the mother of Śukra the preceptor of the daityas (*V. Purāṇa*).

Kayādhū (S) (F) **1.** removing illusion. **2.** bestowing wisdom. **3.** a wife of Hiraṇyakaśipu and the mother of Prahlāda (*Bhā. Purāṇa*).

Kekayī (S) (F) **1.** princess of the Kekaya tribe. **3.** wife of Daśaratha and mother of Bharata.

Kelakā (S) (F) **1.** playful; sportive; knower of arts. **2.** a dancer; a musician; a dancer who dances on the edge of a sword.

Kelikilā (S) (F) **1.** sport; amusement. **3.** another name for Rati.

Kenātī (S) (F) **1.** surpassing all. **3.** another name for Rati, the wife of Kāma.

Kesarini (S) (F) saffron coloured; a lioness.

Keśayantrī (S) (F) **1.** long haired. **3.** a mother in Skanda's retinue (*M. Bh.*).

Keśikā (S) (F) **1.** long haired. **3.** the mother of Jahnu (*V. Purāṇa*); *Asparagus racemosus.*

Keśini (S) (F) **1.** long haired. **3.** an apsarā who was the daughter of Kaśyapa and Prādhā and the mother of Hanumān (*M. Bh.*); the wife of King Ajamīḍha and mother of Jahnu, Vraja and Rupinā (*A. Purāṇa*); the wife of Sudhanvā the son of Aṅgiras (*M. Bh.*); a wife of King Sagara and the mother of Asamañjas (*V. Rāmāyaṇa*); the wife of Viśravas (*Bhā. Purāṇa*); a servant of Pārvatī (*A. Koṣa*); a maid of Damayantī (*Nalopākhyāna*); another name for Durgā.

Ketakī (S) (F) **1.** golden. **3.** the Ketakī flower (*Pandanus odoratissimus*) worn on Śiva's head.

Ketumatī (S) (F) **1.** endowed with brightness. **3.** the wife of Sumālin and the mother of Prahasta a minister in Rāvaṇa's court (*V. Rāmāyaṇa*).

Kevalī (S) (F) **1.** one who has attained the absolute. **3.** a Jaina who has achieved pure, absolute knowledge (*J. Literature*).

Kevikā (S) (F) flower of the *Pandanus odoratissimus.*

Keyūradharā (S) (F) **1.** one who wears an armlet. **3.** an apsarā (*K. Vyuha*).

Keyūrin (S) (F) with an armlet.

Khaḍgahastā (S) (F) **1.** sword-handed. **3.** an attendant of Devī.

Khadirikā (S) (F) **1.** the Lājvantī creeper (*Mimosa pudica*). **3.** another name for Indra and the moon.

Khagaṅgā (S) (F) the celestial Gaṅgā.

Khalā (S) (F) **1.** mischievous. **3.** a daughter of Raudrāśva.

Khalu (S) (F) **1.** indeed; verily; **3.** a river of ancient India (*M. Bh.*).

Khanḍakhanḍā (S) (F) **1.** found in pieces. **3.** a female attendant of Skanda (*M. Bh.*).

Khanḍinī (S) (F) **1.** made of parts; having continents. **3.** the earth.

Khapagā (S) (F) **1.** stream of the heavens. **3.** another name for the Gaṅgā.

Kharajaṅghā (S) (F) **1.** solid shanked; strong thighed. **3.** a mother in the retinue of Skanda (*M. Bh.*).

Kharakarṇī (S) (F) **1.** ass eared. **3.** a mother of the retinue of Skanda (*M. Bh.*).

Kharapuṣpā (S) (F) pungent flower; a sharp leaved variety of ocimum.

Kharī (S) (F) **1.** mule. **3.** a mother of the retinue of Skanda (*M. Bh.*).

Kharikā (S) (F) powered musk.

Kharjūrī (S) (F) reaching the skies; the Wild Date tree (*Phoenix sylvestris*).

Khaśā (S) (F) **1.** pervading the air. **2.** a kind of perfume. **3.** a wife of Kaśyapa (*V. Purāṇa*) and mother of the yakṣas and rākṣasas.

Khatū (S) (F) an ornament worn on the wrist or ankle.

Khelī (S) (F) **1.** moving in the sky. **2.** arrow; bird; sun; song; hymn.

Khullanā (S) (F) **1.** small. **3.** a tutelary deity of Bengal (*T. Śāstra*).

Khyāti (S) (F) **1.** declaration; view; perception; idea; knowledge; celebrity; glory; hymn of praise. **3.** a daughter of Dakṣa, the wife of Bhṛgu and the mother of Dāta, Vidhātā and Lakṣmī (*A. Purāṇa*); a daughter of King Kuru and Āgneyi (*V. Purāṇa*); one of the 9 daughters of Kardama and Devahūtī (*D. Bh. Purāṇa*); another name for Lakṣmī.

Kiki (S) (F) Bluejay (*Coracias garrulus*).

Kilāla (S) (F) **1.** nectar; wine. **3.** a sweet heavenly drink akin to Amṛta (*A. Veda*).

Kīli (S) (F) **1.** parrot. **3.** a parrot said to be the offspring of Kaśyapa and Śuki (*Rāmāyaṇa*)

Kiṁnarī (S) (F) **1.** female singer. **3.** a singer in Indra's court (*V. Rāmāyaṇa*).

Kimpunā (S) (F) **1.** small and pious. **3.** a river in Devaloka which worships Varuṇa (*M. Bh.*).

Kiṁśuka (S) (F) **1.** a very small parrot; which parrot? **3.** the parrot shaped; odourless blossoms of *Butea frondosa*; Intellect Tree (*Celastrus paniculata*).

Kiñjalā (S) (F) brook.

Kiṅkiṇā (S) (F) **1.** a small bell. **3.** a tāntric goddess.

Kiraṇamayī (S) (F) full of rays.

Kirātī (S) (F) **1.** from the mountain. **3.** another name for Pārvatī and the Gaṅgā.

Kirmī (S) (F) an image of gold.

Kīrti (S) (F) **1.** fame; renown; glory. **3.** a daughter of Śuka the son of Vyāsa and Pīvari and the wife of prince Aṇu the son of King Brahmadatta (*D. Bhāgavata*); a daughter of Dakṣa and Prasūti and a wife of Dharma (*V. Purāṇa*); the goddess of fame and reputation (*M. Bh.*).

Kīrtida (S) (F) **1.** one who bestows fame. **3.** Rādhā's mother (*Bhā. Purāṇa*).

Kīrtimālinī (S) (F) **1.** garlanded with fame. **3.** an attendant of Skanda (*Sk. Purāṇa*).

Kiśorī (S) (F) maiden; adolescent.

Kiyā (S) (F) the cooing of a bird.

Kokā (S) (F) **1.** cuckoo; Ruddy Shelduck (*Anas casarca*); Wild Date tree (*Phoenix sylvestris*). **3.** an attendant of Skanda (*M. Bh.*); the earlier name of the river Śoṇa (*Ś. Brāhmaṇa*); another name for Viṣṇu.

Kokilādevī (S) (F) **1.** goddess of the cuckoo. **2.** with a sweet sound. **3.** a goddess (*T. Śastra*).

Kolambī (S) (F) Śiva's lute.

Koṅkaṇā (S) (F) **1.** living on the western shores. **3.** the mother of Paraśurāma (*A. Koṣa*).

Kośin (S) (F) bud; the mango tree (*Mangifera indica*).

Koṭarā (S) (F) **1.** hollow of a tree. **3.** an attendant of Skanda (*M. Bh.*); the mother of Bāṇa (*Bhā. Purāṇa*); another name for Durgā.

Koṭiśrī (S) (F) **1.** goddess of millions. **3.** another name for Durgā.

Koṭisthā (S) (F) **1.** goddess of millions. **3.** tutelary deity of the Ćyavana family (*Br. Purāṇa*).

Koṭṭeśvarī (S) (F) **1.** goddess of the fort. **3.** another name for Durgā.

Krāntī (S) (F) **1.** revolution; the sun's course; surpassing. **2.** going; proceeding; overcoming.

Krauñćī (S) (F) **1.** curlew; snipe; heron. **3.** a daughter of Kaśyapa and Tāmṛā and the mother of curlews (*V. Rāmāyaṇa*).

Kṛti (S) (F) **1.** action; creation. **3.** a wife of Saṁhrāda and mother of Panćajana (*Bh. Purāṇa*).

Kriyā (S) (F) **1.** performance; work; action. **3.** religious action personified as a daughter of Dakṣa and wife of Dharma (*M. Bh.*); or as a daughter of Kardama and wife of Kratu (*Bh. Purāṇa*).

Kṛmī (S) (F) **1.** silkworm; ant; lacinsect. **3.** a wife of Uśīnara and mother of Kṛmi (*H. Purāṇa*); a river (*M. Bh.*).

Kroḍakāntā (S) (F) **1.** dear to Saturn. **3.** another name for the earth.

Krodhā (S) (F) **1.** angry. **3.** passion personified as a child of Lobha and Nikṛti (*V. Purāṇa*); a daughter of Dakṣa and wife of Kaśyapa (*M. Bh.*); a dānava (*M. Bh.*).

Krodhanā (S) (F) **1.** an angry woman; bad tempered. **2.** a passionate woman; vixen. **3.** a mother in Skanda's retinue (*M. Bh.*); a yoginī; another name for Durgā.

Krodhavaśā (S) (F) **1.** the power of passion. **2.** passionate. **3.** a daughter of Dakṣa and wife of Kaśyapa whose asura children guarded the lotus lake of Kubera (*M. Bh.*).

Krośaṇā (S) (F) **1.** crying. **3.** a mother in Skanda's retinue (*M. Bh.*).

Kroṣṭukī (S) (F) **1.** jackal. **3.** a daughter of Krodhavaśā and mother of the yellow apes (*M. Bh.*).

Kṛpā (S) (F) compassion; favour; kindness; pity.

Kṛpī (S) (F) **1.** beautiful. **3.** the daughter of sage Śaradvata and apsarā Janapadī, the sister of Kṛpa, the wife of Droṇa and the mother of Aśvatthāman (*M. Bh.*).

Kṛśaṇa (S) (F) pearl; gold; form; shape.

Kṛśāṅgā (S) (F) **1.** slender. **2.** bean bodied; **3.** an apsarā; another name for the Priyaṅgu creeper; *Aglaia odoratissima*; *Capparis zeylanica.*

Kṛśāṅgī (S) (F) **1.** slender. **3.** an apsarā.

Kṛṣi (S) (F) ploughing; the cultivation of the soil personified; the earth.

Kṛṣṇā (S) (F) **1.** dark; night. **2.** pupil of the eye; a dark blossomed and dark blossomed plant; a kind of perfume. **3.** the daughter of King Drupada who married the 5 Pāṇḍava brothers and was known as Draupadī or Pāñćālī (*M. Bh.*); a river in South India (*Bhā. Purāṇa*); a female attendant of Skanda (*M. Bh.*); one of the 7 tongues of Agni (*A. Purāṇa*); a yoginī; another name for Durgā.

Kṛṣṇakarṇī (S) (F) **1.** black eared. **3.** a female attendant of Skanda (*M. Bh.*).

Kṛṣṇan (S) (F) **1.** blackness. **2.** lead; the centre of the pupil of the eye.

Kṛṣṇāṅgī (S) (F) **1.** black bodied. **2.** a kind of parrot. **3.** an apsarā (*V. Purāṇa*).

Kṛṣṇapiṅgā (S) (F) **1.** dark brown. **3.** another name for Durgā.

Kṛṣṇavallī (S) (F) **1.** dark leaved. **3.** another name for Tulasī (*Ocimum sanctum*); *Ichnocarpus frutescens.*

Kṛṣṇavarṇā (S) (F) **1.** black. **3.** an attendant of Skanda(*M. Bh.*).

Kṛṣṇaveṇī (S) (F) **1.** with dark blue braids. **3.** a river in South India from where Agni is supposed to have emerged (*M. Bh.*).

Kṛṣṇī (S) (F) dark night.

Kṛtadyuti (S) (F) **1.** with accomplished glory. **3.** a queen of King Ćitraketu (*Bhāgavata*).

Kṛtamālā (S) (F) **1.** one who makes garlands. **3.** the river in which Mahāviṣṇu appeared as a fish (*Bhā. Purāṇa*).

Kṛtasthalā (S) (F) **1.** abode of action. **3.** an apsarā.

Kṛtī (S) (F) **1.** accomplishment; creation. **2.** magic; enchantment; making; performing; the act of doing. **3.** the wife of Saṁhrāda and mother of Pañćajana (*Bhā. Purāṇa*).

Kṛtsnakarā (S) (F) **1.** one who does all. **2.** a perfect performer. **3.** an apsarā (*K. Vyuha*).

Kṛttikā (S) (F) **1.** covered with stars. **3.** the Pleiades constellation which is made of 6 stars with Agni as its regent and these 6 stars or Kṛttikās are supposed to have been nymphs who became the nurses of Kārttikeya (*Sk. Purāṇa*) who then merged to form the Kṛttika stars of Pleiades.

Kṛttivāśasā (S) (F) **1.** covered with skin. **3.** another name for Durgā.

Kṛtvī (S) (F) **1.** accomplished. **3.** the daughter of sage Śuka, the wife of Anuha of the Ajamīḍha family and the mother of Brahmadatta (*H. Purāṇa*).

Kṛtyā (S) (F) 1. action. 2. achievement; right; proper; magical rites. 3. female deity; a rākṣasi (*M. Bh.*); a river (*M. Bh.*).

Kṛtyakā (S) (F) 1. full of achievements. 3. an enchantress who is the cause of destruction worshipped by Tāntrikas (*T. Śāstra*).

Krumu (S) (F) 1. zigzag. 3. a river mentioned in the *Ṛg Veda* and which is now Kurum a tributary of the Indus.

Krūrā (S) (F) 1. cruel; pitiless. 3. a wife of Kaśyapa, and mother of the asuras, she is also known as Krodhā (*M. Bh.*).

Krūradantī (S) (F) 1. with cruel teeth. 2. one who chews/exterminates everything; goddess of destruction. 3. another name for Durgā.

Kṣā (S) (F) 1. earth. 2. that which is patient; enduring; hearing.

Kṣamā (S) (F) 1. of earth; patience; the number one. 2. mercy. 3. patience personified as a daughter of Dakṣa, wife of Pulaha and the mother of Kardama, Urvarīyān and Sahiṣṇu (*V. Purāṇa*); another name for Durgā and the earth.

Kṣamāmatī (S) (F) with a merciful mind.

Kṣamāvatī (S) (F) 1. one who is compassionate; enduring; forbearing; tame. 3. the wife of Nidhipati (*M. Bh.*).

Kṣamyā (S) (F) of the earth; terrestrial.

Kṣaṇadā (S) (F) 1. bestower of moments; bestower of leisure. 2. one who bestows life; night; water.

Kṣānti (S) (F) 1. forbearance; patience. 2. endurance; indulgence; the state of saintly abstraction. 3. a river (*V. Purāṇa*).

Kṣapā (S) (F) night.

Kṣatriyāṇī (S) (F) wife of a noble warrior.

Kṣemā (S) (F) 1. safety; security; welfare; peace. 2. tranquillity; bliss; final emancipation. 3. an apsarā (*M. Bh.*); another name for Durgā.

Kṣemāgirī (S) (F) 1. mountain of security. 2. that which is full of security. 3. another name for goddess Bhadrakālī.

Kṣemaṁkarā (S) (F) 1. conferring peace and prosperity. 3. another name for Durgā.

Kṣemaṅkarī (S) (F) 1. conferring peace; security; happiness. 3. another name for Durgā.

Kṣemyā (S) (F) 1. goddess of welfare. 3. another name for Durgā.

Kṣiprā (S) (F) 1. fast. 3. a river in Ujjain (*M. Bh.*).

Kṣīrābdhija (S) (F) 1. born of the Ocean of Milk. 2. amṛta or any other precious objects produced at the churning of the Ocean of Milk. 3. another name for Lakṣmī.

Kṣīrajā (S) (F) 1. born of milk. 3. another name for Lakāmī.

Kṣīrasāgarā (S) (F) the sea of milk.

Ksīravatī (S) (F) 1. made of milk. 3. a river (*M. Bh.*).

Kṣīrīn (S) (F) 1. milky; with plenty of milk. 3. a tree from which milk flows unceasingly and from which we get cloth, ornaments, etc. (*M. Bh.*); Prickly Poppy (*Argemone mexicana*).

Kṣīrodijā (S) (F) 1. produced from the Ocean of Milk. 3. another name for Lakṣmī.

Kṣitāditī (S) (F) 1. the Aditī of the earth. 3. another name for Devakī the mother of Kṛṣṇa.

Kṣiti (S) (F) abode; dwelling; habitation; the earth; settlements; colonies; soil of the earth; races of men.

Kṣitibhū (S) (F) 1. born of the earth. 3. another name for Sītā.

Kṣitijā (S) (F) 1. born of the earth. 3. another name for Sītā.

Kṣityāditī (S) (F) 1. the Aditī of the earth. 3. another name for Devakī the mother of Kṛṣṇa (*Bhā. Purāṇa*).

Kṣoṇā (S) (F) 1. immovable. 3. another name for the earth.

Kṣoṇī (S) (F) 1. immovable; stable. 3. the earth.

Kṣubhā (S) (F) 1. weapon. 3. the deity which presides over punishment.

Kṣumā (S) (F) **1.** arrow. **2.** Common Flax (*Linum usitatissimum*).

Kṣūnu (S) (F) fire.

Kubhināsā (S) (F) **1.** jar nosed. **2.** one with extremely wide nostrils. **3.** a wife of the gandharva Aṅgāraparṇa (*M. Bh.*); a rākṣasī and mother of Lavaṇa (*V. Rāmāyaṇa*).

Kubjā (S) (F) **1.** hunch backed. **3.** a widow who was incarnated as Tilottamā the apsarā (*Bhā. Purāṇa*).

Kuḍāyikā (S) (F) **1.** one who lives under the earth. **3.** a rāga.

Kuhārīta (S) (F) the song of the Kokila or Indian Cuckoo (*Cuculus scolopaceus*).

Kuhāvatī (S) (F) **1.** one who owns the Zizyphus tree (*Zizyphus jujuba*); bearer of a song. **3.** another name for Durgā.

Kuhū (S) (F) **1.** the cry of the Kokila or Indian Cuckoo (*Cuculus scolopaceus*). **3.** the new moon night personified as the daughter of Aṅgiras and Śraddhā (*V. Purāṇa*).

Kujā (S) (F) **1.** daughter of the earth. **3.** another name for Durgā, Sītā and the horizon.

Kukkuṭikā (S) (F) **1.** hen. **3.** a female attendant of Skanda (*M. Bh.*).

Kukṣijā (S) (F) **1.** born from the womb. **3.** a daughter of Priyavrata and Kāmyā (*M. Bh.*).

Kukubhā (S) (F) female personification of music or rāgiṇīs.

Kuladevī (S) (F) **1.** the family goddess. **3.** another name for Durgā.

Kulambā (S) (F) deity of the family.

Kulampunā (S) (F) **1.** one who makes the family pious. **2.** the virtue of the family. **3.** a river that ought to be remembered daily (*M. Bh.*).

Kulanārī (S) (F) **1.** a woman of a good family. **2.** one who is virtuous.

Kulāṅganā (S) (F) highborn woman.

Kulasundarī (S) (F) **1.** maiden of the family. **3.** a deity (*Br. Purāṇa*).

Kuleśvarī (S) (F) **1.** family goddess. **3.** another name for Durgā.

Kulyā (S) (F) **1.** virtuous. **2.** well born; presiding over a river as a deity.

Kumāradevī (S) (F) **1.** goddess of children. **3.** a Lićchavi princess who was the wife of Ćandragupta I.

Kumārī (S) (F) **1.** daughter; maiden; the Jasmine (*Jasminum pubescens*); gold. **3.** a princess of the Kekaya kingdom who was the wife of the Purū King Bhīmasena and the mother of Pratiśravas (*M. Bh.*); the wife of the serpent Dhanañjaya (*M. Bh.*); a daughter of Vasudeva and Rohiṇī (*Bhā. Purāṇa*); the central part of the universe (*V's. B. Samhitā*); a river of ancient India (*M. Bh.*); another name for Durgā, Dākṣāyaṇī, Sītā and the Śyāmā bird (*Copsychus malabaricus indicus*); *Aloe vera*; *Crysanthemum indicum*; *Rosa alba*.

Kumārikā (S) (F) **1.** virgin; girl; the Jasmine (*Jasminum sambac*). **3.** another name for Durgā and Sītā.

Kumbhamātā (S) (F) **1.** goddess of pots. **3.** tutelary goddess of a village represented by a pot.

Kumbharī (S) (F) **1.** enemy of Aquarius; destroyer of pitchers; one who hates the harlots. **3.** a form of Durgā (*A. Koṣa*).

Kumbhayonī (S) (F) **1.** pot born. **3.** an apsarā (*M. Bh.*).

Kumbhikā (S) (F) **1.** a small waterjar. **3.** a mother of Skanda's retinue (*M. Bh.*); Water lettuce (*Pistia stratiotes*); *Ochrocarpos longifolius*.

Kumbhināḍī (S) (F) **1.** one who sounds like a pitcher. **3.** a daughter of the rākṣasa Sumāli and Ketumatī (*M. Bh.*).

Kumbhināśi (S) (F) **1.** one who feeds on poison. **2.** venomous. **3.** a daughter of Viśvavasu and Analā and the mother of Lavaṇāsura by the rākṣasa Madhu (*V. Rāmāyaṇa*); the wife of the gandharva Aṅgāraparṇa (*M. Bh.*).

Kumbhinī (S) (F) **1.** shaped like a jar. **3.** another name for the earth.

Kumkum (S) (F) saffron (*Crocus Sativus*); red; pollen; red sandalwood paste applied on the forehead.

Kumudapuṣpā (S) (F) **1.** white water lily. **3.** a gandharvī.

Kumudasundarī (S) (F) as beautiful as the white water lily (*Nymphaea alba*).

Kumudavatī (S) (F) **1.** abounding in water lilies. **3.** the daughter of the serpent king Kumuda, the wife of Kuśa and the mother of Atithi (*Bhā. Purāṇa*); the wife of the Kirāta King Vimarṣaṇa (*Ś. Purāṇa*); the wife of Pradyumna (*Bhā. Purāṇa*).

Kumudikā (S) (F) one who bears or wears water lilies.

Kumudinī (S) (F) an assemblage of white water lilies.

Kunālikā (S) (F) the Indian Cuckoo (*Cuculus scolopaceus*).

Kuṇḍalī (S) (F) **1.** round; circle. **3.** a child of Garuḍa (*M. Bh.*); a son of Dhṛtarāṣṭra (*M. Bh.*); a river (*M. Bh.*).

Kuṇḍalinī (S) (F) **1.** decorated with earrings. **3.** a Śakti or form of Durgā; *Tinospora cordifolia.*

Kundamālā (S) (F) a garland of Jasmine flowers.

Kundanikā (S) (F) jasmine.

Kundarikā (S) (F) **1.** olibanum; the plant *Boswellia thurifera.* **3.** a female attendant of Skanda (*M. Bh.*).

Kuṇḍavāsinī (S) (F) **1.** living in a pitcher. **3.** Gautama's tutelary deity (*B. Purāṇa*).

Kundinī (S) (F) an assemblage of jasmines.

Kuñjā (S) (F) bower; arbour; shrub or jungle.

Kuñjalatā (S) (F) forest creeper.

Kuñjikā (S) (F) **1.** belonging to the bower. **3.** Nutmeg flower (*Nigella sativa*).

Kunśī (S) (F) shining.

Kuntala (S) (F) plough; spear; perfume; barley; a lock of hair; *Pavonia odorata.*

Kuntī (S) (F) **1.** spear; lance. **3.** the sister of Kṛṣṇa's father, the daughter of King Śūrasena, foster daughter of Śūrasena's nephew Kuntibhoja, wife of King Pāṇḍu, the mother of the Pāṇḍavas and the supposed in-carnation of Siddhi (*M. Bh.*); a rākṣasī; a river (*V. Purāṇa*).

Kuraṅgākṣī (S) (F) fawn eyed; beautiful.

Kuraṅgī (S) (F) **1.** spot in the moon; deer. **3.** a daughter of Prasenajit (*K. Sāgara*).

Kūrdanā (S) (F) the full moon day in the month of Ćaitra; a festival held in honour of Kāma.

Kurīra (S) (F) ornament of the head.

Kuśadhārā (S) (F) **1.** with sharp waves. **3.** a river of ancient India (*M. Bh.*).

Kūṣmāṇḍinī (S) (F) **1.** born from a pumpkin. **3.** a goddess (*H. Purāṇa*).

Kuśodakā (S) (F) **1.** water purified by kuśā. **3.** Dākṣāyāṇī in Kuśādvīpa.

Kusumā (S) (F) **1.** flower like. **2.** a blossom; Ringworm Plant (*Cassia obtusifolia*); Yellow Champaka (*Michelia champaka*).

Kusumaćandra (S) (F) moon among flowers; the kuṁkuma or the saffron flower.

Kusumalatā (S) (F) a blossoming creeper.

Kusumāñjali (S) (F) an offering of flowers.

Kusumāvatī (S) (F) **1.** with flowers. **3.** another name for Pāṭaliputra.

Kusumitā (S) (F) decorated with flowers; made of flowers.

Kusummayā (S) (F) consisting of flowers.

Kuthodarī (S) (F) **1.** wealthy; with a large stomach. **3.** a daughter of Nikumbha (*K. Purāṇa*).

Kuṭilā (S) (F) **1.** curved.**2.** curled; bent; flowing in curved lines. **3.** a river.

Kuvalayadhṛs (S) (F) **1.** blue lotus eyed. **2.** with beautiful eyes.

Kuvalayavatī (S) (F) **1.** possessing Blue Lotuses (*Nymphaea stellata*). **3.** a princess (*K. Sāgara*).

Kuvalayiṇī (S) (F) abounding in water lilies.

Kuvalayitā (S) (F) decorated with water lilies.

Kuvarānī (S) (F) **1.** lady of the lotuses. **2.** princess.

Kuvīrā (S) (F) **1.** warrior of the earth; brave woman. **3.** a river (*M. Bh.*).

L

Lābukī (S) (F) a kind of lute.

Laghupuṣpā (S) (F) delicate flower; flower of the Kadamba tree (*Anthocephalus indicus*).

Laghuvī (S) (F) delicate; small.

Laharī (S) (F) wave.

Lajjā (S) (F) **1.** modesty. **3.** a daughter of Dakṣa and the wife of Dharmā and mother of Vinaya (*V. Purāṇa*).

Lajjakā (S) (F) modest; the Wild Cotton tree (*Gossypium stocksii*).

Lajjanā (S) (F) modest; the Wild Cotton tree (*Gossypium stocksii*).

Lajjāsīlā (S) (F) of modest character.

Lajjāvantī (S) (F) shy; modest; the Touch-me-not plant (*Mimosa pudica*).

Lajjāvatī (S) (F) full of modesty.

Lajjitā (S) (F) coy; modest; bashful.

Lākinī (S) (F) **1.** one who takes and gives. **3.** a tāntric goddess.

Lākṣā (S) (F) lac; a red dye used by women of ancient India for feet and lips; the lac plant; lac obtained from cochineal.

Lākṣakī (S) (F) **1.** relating to or made of/or dyed with lac. **3.** another name for Sītā.

Lakṣamaṇā (S) (F) **1.** with auspicious marks; accomplisher of target. **3.** a wife of Kṛṣṇa (*M. Bh.*); a daughter of Duryodhana; an apsarā; a Buddhist Devī; the mother of the 8th Arhat of the present Avasarpiṇī; another name for Sumitrā, a wife of Daśaratha and the mother of Lakṣmaṇa.

Lakṣitā (S) (F) seen; beheld; marked; distinguished.

Lakṣmī (S) (F) **1.** fortune; prosperity; success; beauty; splendour; lustre; charm; the wife of a hero; pearl; turmeric. **3.** the consort of Mahāviṣṇu, the goddess of fortune, prosperity and success, depicted as emerging front a lotus standing in the Ocean of Milk and the more prominent of her incarnations on the earth include Tulasī, Rādhā, Sītā and Vedavatī (*D. Bh. Purāṇa*); the daughter of Dakṣa and wife of Dharma (*M. Bh.*); a digit of the moon; *Curcuma longa*; *Prosopis spicigera*; *Aphanamixis polystachya*.

Lakṣmīgṛha (S) (F) **1.** the home of Lakṣmī. **2.** the Red Lotus plant (*Nymphaea rubra*).

Lalantikā (S) (F) a long necklace.

Lālātī (S) (F) forehead.

Lalāṭikā (S) (F) an ornament of the forehead.

Lālimā (S) (F) **1.** reddish glow; redness. **2.** aurora; blush; roseate; beautiful; lovely; charming; an ornament for the forehead; the best of its kind; sign; banner; symbol.

Lalita (S) (F) **1.** lovely; desirable; pleasing; soft; gentle; graceful; wanton; voluptuous; sporting. **3.** a rāga.

Lalitā/Lalithā (S) (F) **1.** woman; lovely; desirable. **2.** a woman. **3.** the Fairy Bluebird (*Irena puella*); a rāga; a form of Durgā; a river; a gopī.

Lalitakā (S) (F) **1.** favourite daughter. **3.** an ancient holy Tīrtha of Brahmā (*M. Bh.*).

Lalitalocanā (S) (F) **1.** with beautiful eyes. **3.** a daughter of the vidyādhara Vāmadatta (*K. Sāgara*).

Lalitāṅgī (S) (F) with a beautiful body.

Lalitasyā (S) (F) loveliness; charm; grace.

Lāllī (S) (F) blush; radiance; prestige; sweetness.

Lālukā (S) (F) necklace.

Lambā (S) (F) **1.** great; large; spacious; tall; pendulous. **3.** a daughter of Dakṣa and Asiknī and the wife of Dharma (*H. Purāṇa*); a mother attending Skanda (*M. Bh.*); another name for Durgā and Lakṣmī.

Lambakeśaka (S) (F) **1.** long haired. **3.** a sage (*G. Sutra*).

Lambapayodharā (S) (F) **1.** large breasted. **3.** a mother of Skanda (*M. Bh.*).

Lambinī (S) (F) **1.** hanging down. **3.** a mother of Skanda (*M. Bh.*).

Lambodarī (S) (F) **1.** consort of Lambodara. **3.** another name for Gaṇeśanī.

Lambūṣā (S) (F) **1.** a hanging ornament. **2.** a necklace of 7 strings.

Laṅgapriyā (S) (F) **1.** adorable. **3.** the Kadambā tree (*Anthrocephalus indicus*).

Lāṅgali (S) (F) **1.** the plough carrier. **3.** a celebrated Purāṇic river which worships Varuṇa in the form of a goddess (*M. Bh.*).

Lāṅgaliśā (S) (F) **1.** the pole of the plough. **3.** another name for Durgā.

Laṅghati (S) (F) **1.** flowing with speed. **3.** a celebrated Purāṇic river which worships Varuṇa in the form of a goddess who sits in his court (*M. Bh.*).

Laṅkālakṣmī (S) (F) **1.** the goddess of Laṅkā. **3.** the goddess of Laṅkā who was the incarnation of Vijayalakṣmī or the goddess of victory and was released from her curse by Hanumān (*K. Rāmāyaṇa*).

Laṅkiṇī (S) (F) **1.** belonging to Laṅkā. **3.** the tutelary goddess of Laṅkā (*V. Rāmāyaṇa*).

Lapitā (S) (F) **1.** spoken; speech; voice. **3.** the wife of sage Mandapāla (*M. Bh.*).

Lasā (S) (F) saffron; turmeric.

Latā (S) (F) **1.** vine; a string of pearls; a slender woman; the Madhavi creeper (*Hiptage madoblata*); the Priyaṅgu creeper. **3.** an apsarā who was set free from a curse by Arjuna (*M. Bh.*); a daughter of Meru and wife of Ilāvṛta (*Bh. Purāṇa*).

Laṭabhā (S) (F) handsome; beautiful.

Latāmaṇi (S) (F) coral.

Latikā (S) (F) ornament of the forehead; the vermilion dot on the forehead; a string of pearls; a small creeper.

Laṭkan (S) (F) an ornament of the hair; lace; the Lorikeet bird (*Loriculus vernalis*).

Lauheyī (S) (F) **1.** copper coloured. **3.** an apsarā.

Lavalī (S) (F) **1.** a vine. **2.** Custard apple (*Annona reticulate*).

Lavalīkā (S) (F) a tiny vine.

Lavalīna (S) (F) devoted; engrossed.

Lavaṇā (S) (F) lustrous; beautiful.

Lavaṅgalatā (S) (F) beautiful creeper; the clove vine (*Limonia scandens*).

Lavaṅgi (S) (F) **1.** of the clove plant. **3.** an apsarā.

Lāvaṇyā, Laboṇyā (S) (F) lustrous; beautiful.

Lāvaṇyalakṣmī (S) (F) goddess of beauty.

Lāvaṇyamayī (S) (F) consisting of beauty; full of charm.

Lekhā (S) (F) **1.** line. **2.** lightning; streak; a figure; a mark; the crescent moon; the crest; horizon.

Lelāyamānā (S) (F) **1.** flickering. **3.** one of the 7 tongues of fire (*M. Upaniṣad*).

Lepākṣī (S) (F) with painted eyes.

Libnī (S) (F) a manuscript of the gods.

Libujā (S) (F) vine.

Līlā (S) (F) **1.** play; pleasure; amusement; ease; beauty; charm; grace; play of universal energy. **3.** a yoginī.

Līlāvati (S) (F) **1.** playful; beautiful; graceful; charming. **3.** the wife of the demon Maya; a well-known work by Bhāskarāćārya, the wife of King Dhruvasandhi of Kosala (*Bh. Purāṇa*); the wife of Avīkṣita; another name for Durgā.

Līnā (S) (F) **1.** absorbed; united with. **2.** merged; engrossed.

Lingadhāriṇī (S) (F) **1.** wearing the badge of Śiva. **3.** Dākṣāyāṇi in Naimiṣa.

Lipi (S) (F) alphabet; manuscript; document; anointing; writing.

Lipikā (S) (F) **1.** alphabet; manuscript. **2.** writing; anointing.

Lоćanā (S) (F) **1.** eye.**2.** illuminating; brightening. **3.** a Buddhist goddess (*B. Literature*).

Lohakārī (S) (F) **1.** blacksmith. **3.** a tāntric goddess (*T. Śastra*).

Lohamuktikā (S) (F) a red pearl.

Lohitā (S) (F) **1.** red. **2.** ruby. **3.** one of 7 tongues of fire (*G. Sūtra*).

Lohitākṣī (S) (F) **1.** red eyed. **3.** a follower of Skanda(*M. Bh.*).

Lohitamukti (S) (F) ruby.

Lohitārāṇī (S) (F) **1.** red crossing. **3.** an ancient river of Purāṇic fame (*M. Bh.*).

Lohitāyanī (S) (F) **1.** red. **3.** the daughter of Lohitārānī and a foster mother of Subrahmaṇya (*M. Bh.*).

Lohitikā (S) (F) the ruby.

Lohityā (S) (F) **1.** rice. **3.** the Purāṇic name for the river Brahmaputra (*V's B. Samhitā*), whose goddess is a devotee of Varuṇa and sits in his court (*H. Purāṇa*); an apsara.

Lokajananī (M) (F) **1.** mother of the world. **3.** another name for Lakṣmī.

Lokāloka (S) (F) **1.** glory of the world; one who enlightens the people. **3.** a mythical golden mountain that surrounds the earth and acts as a boundary to the 3 worlds (*A. Veda*).

Lokamātrī (S) (F) **1.** mother of the world. **3.** another name for Lakṣmī.

Lokavya (S) (F) one who deserves heaven.

Lolā (S) (F) **1.** fickle; vibrating; changing; beautiful. **2.** lightning. **3.** the mother of the daitya Madhu; a yoginī; another name for Lakṣmī and Dākṣāyāṇī in Utpalavartaka.

Lolitā (S) (F) agitated; tremulous; fickle.

Lopāmudrā (S) (F) **1.** with an imperceptible form. **3.** the daughter of the king of Vidarbha, the wife of sage Agastya, the embodiment of wifely devotion and the supposed authoress of a part of the *Ṛg Veda.*

Lotikā (S) (F) **1.** Sorrel (*Oxalis pussilla*). **2.** light reddish-brown.

Lumbikā (S) (F) a kind of musical instrument.

Lumbinī (S) (F) **1.** grove. **3.** the grove where Buddha was born (*B. Literature*).

M

Madālambe 1. dependant upon intoxication. 2. excited; inspired; arrogant. 3. the mother of Bāsava the bull.

Madālasā (S) (F) 1. lazy with intoxication. 2. languid; indolent. 3. the daughter of the gandharva Viśvavasu and the wife of Kuvalayāśva (*Purāṇas*); the daughter of the rākṣasa Bhramaraketu; a vidyādharī and wife of Ćampaka (*D. Bh. Purāṇa*); the wife of King Ṛtadhvaja of Kāśī and the mother of Alarka.

Madanalekhā (S) (F) 1. a love letter; a sequence of love. 3. the daughter of King Pratāpamukha of Varāṇasī (*K. Sāgara*).

Madanamañćūkā (S) (F) 1. erotically aroused. 3. a daughter of Madanavega and Kaliṅgasenā (*K. Sāgara*).

Madanamañjarī (S) (F) 1. bud of love. 3. a daughter of the yakṣa prince Dundubhi (*K. Sāgara*).

Madanarekhā (S) (F) 1. the path of Kāma. 3. the mother of Vikramāditya (*S. Dvātriṇśikā*).

Madanī (S) (F) vine; musk.

Madanikā (S) (F) 1. aroused; excited. 3. an apsarā who was the daughter of Menakā (*K. Sāgara*).

Madayantī (S) (F) 1. exciting. 3. the wife of King Kalmāṣapāda (*M. Bh.*); Arabian Jasmine (*Jasminum sambac*); another name for Durgā.

Madayantikā (S) (F) 1. exciting. 2. the Arabian Jasmine (*Jasminum sambac*).

Madayatī (S) (F) 1. exciting; Arabian Jasmine (*Jasminum sambac*). 3. the wife of Mitrasaha (*K. Sāgara*).

Mādhavā (S) (F) 1. full of intoxication; verdal. 2. relate to the spring; exotic; exciting. 3. an apsarā sent by Indra to destroy the meditation of Viṣṇu (*Bhā. Purāṇa*).

Mādhavapriyā (S) (F) 1. beloved of Mādhava. 3. another name for Rādhā.

Mādhavaśrī (S) (F) vernal beauty.

Mādhavī (S) (F) 1. sweet; intoxicating drink; the date flower; honey-sugar; Sacred Basil (*Ocimum sanctum*); a woman of the race of Madhu. 3. the Dākṣāyāṇī in Śriśaila (*M. Bh.*); the daughter of King Yayāti (*M. Bh.*); a follower of Skanda (*M. Bh.*); a rāgiṇī; Fennel (*Foeniculum capillaceum*); *Hiptage madoblata*; another name for Durgā and Subhadrā.

Mādhavīlatā (S) (F) spring creeper; *Hiptage madoblata*; *Gaertnera racemosa.*

Madhu (S) (F) anything sweet; mead; Soma; honey; butter; nectar; sugar; water.

Madhubālā (S) (F) sweet maiden.

Madhudhārā (S) (F) stream of honey.

Madhudīpa 1. lamp of spring. 3. another name for Kāma.

Madhudivā (S) (F) 1. excited by honey; inspired by wine; excited by the spring. 3. a sacred river (*M. Bh.*).

Madhugandhikā (S) (F) sweet smelling.

Madhujā (S) (F) 1. made of honey. 2. a honeycomb; the earth.

Madhukaśā (S) (F) 1. whip of sweetness; dew. 3. the whip used by the aśvins to sweeten the Soma juice; the daughter of the maruts who could bestow immortality (*Ṛg Veda*).

Madhukulyā (S) (F) 1. a stream of honey. 3. a river in Kuśa dvīpa (*Bhā. Purāṇa*).

Madhukumbhā (S) (F) 1. pitcher of honey. 3. a mother attending on Skanda (*M. Bh.*).

Madhūlikā (S) (F) 1. sweetness. 2. a kind of bee; citron; liquorice; Black Mustard (*Brassica nigra*). 3. a follower of Skanda (*M. Bh.*); *Clematis triloba.*

Madhumādhavi (S) (F) a spring flower abounding in honey.

Madhumallī (S) (F) the vine of spring; the Mālati blossom (*Jasminum grandiflorum*).

Madhumatī (S) (F) 1. rich in honey; intoxicated by the spring. 2. sweet; pleasant; agreeable. 3. the daughter of the asura Madhu and the wife of

Haryaśva (*H. Purāṇa*); an attendant of Lakṣmī (*Pañćatantra*); a river (*H. Purāṇa*).

Madhumītā (S) (F) sweet friend.

Madhupratikā (S) (F) with a sweet mouth; having the qualities of a yoginī.

Madhupuṣpā (S) (F) a spring flower; rain.

Madhurākṣī (S) (F) beautiful eyed.

Madhurasvarā (S) (F) **1.** sweet voiced. **3.** an apsarā (*M. Bh.*).

Mādhurī (S) (F) **1.** sweetness; loveliness; charm. **2.** mead; wine; treacle; syrup; the double Jasmine blossom (*Jasminum sambac*); *Fennel* (*Foeniculum capillaceum*); a kind of musical instrument.

Madhurīlatā (S) (F) vine of sweetness.

Madhurimā (S) (F) sweetness; charm; comeliness.

Madhuṛtu (S) (F) spring season.

Madhuśrī (S) (F) **1.** the beauty of spring. **3.** one of the 2 queens of spring (*K. Granthāvali*).

Madhuvāhini (S) (F) **1.** carrying sweetness. **3.** a river (*M. Bh.*).

Madhuvantī (S) (F) **1.** endowed with nectar.

Madhuvatī (S) (F) with an intoxicating beauty.

Madhuvidyā (S) (F) **1.** sweet knowledge. **2.** a mystical lore of the devas.

Madhuvratā (S) (F) **1.** fasting for spring; absorbed in sweetness. **2.** the queen bee.

Mādhvāćārya **1.** preceptor of the Mādhva doctrine. **3.** the author of *Sarvadar-śanasamgraha* and founder of a Vaiṣṇava sect.

Madhvijā (S) (F) **1.** born of honey. **2.** an intoxicating drink.

Madirā (S) (F) **1.** intoxicating; nectar; wine; spirituous liquor. **3.** one of the 7 wives of Vasudeva (*M. Bh.*); the mother of Kādambarī; another name for the wife of Varuṇa and the goddess of wine (*V. Purāṇa*); another name for Durgā (*H. Purāṇa*).

Madirāvatī (S) (F) with intoxicating beauty.

Madirekṣaṇā (S) (F) with intoxicating eyes.

Madrā (S) (F) **1.** belonging to the Madra dynasty. **3.** a wife of sage Atri and the mother of Soma (*Br. Purāṇa*); a daughter of Raudrāśva (*H. Purāṇa*).

Madravatī (S) (F) **1.** princess of the Madras. **3.** the wife of Parīkṣit and mother of Janamejaya (*M. Bh.*); the 2nd wife of Pāṇḍu and the mother of Nakula and Sahadeva (*M. Bh.*); the wife of Sahadeva (*M. Bh.*); the wife of Kroṣṭu; a wife of Kṛṣṇa (*Bhā. Purāṇa*).

Mādrī (S) (F) **1.** a princess of Madra. **3.** *Aconitum heterophyllum*; a wife of Pāṇḍu and mother of Nakula and Sahadeva; (*M. Bh.*); a wife of Kroṣṭa; a wife of Kṛṣṇa (*H. Purāṇa*).

Māgadhī (S) (F) of Magadha; Common White Jasmine (*jasminum officianale*); a river (*V. Rāmāyaṇa*).

Maghā (S) (F) **1.** gift; reward; wealth. **3.** the 10th Nakṣatra or constellation, regarded as a wife of the moon (*A. Veda*); the wife of Śiva (*M. Bh.*).

Māghī (S) (F) giving gifts; the day of the full moon in the month of Māgha (December/January/February).

Māghoni (S) (F) liberality; the east.

Māghyā (S) (F) born in the month of Māgha; the blossom of Jasmine (*Jasminum pubescens*).

Maguṇḍī (S) (F) **1.** female magician. **3.** a mythical being whose daughters are female demons (*A. Veda*).

Māhā (S) (F) great; cow.

Mahābhāgā (S) (F) **1.** highly fortunate; pure; holy. **3.** the Dākṣāyaṇī in Mahālaya.

Mahābhaṭṭārikā (S) (F) **1.** great warrior. **3.** another name for Durgā.

Mahābhīmā (S) (F) **1.** very powerful. **3.** another name for Pārvatī.

Mahābhogā (S) (F) **1.** causing great enjoyment. **3.** another name for Durgā.

Mahābuddhi (S) (F) **1.** extremely intelligent. **3.** an asura (*K. Sāgara*).

Mahāćaṇḍā (S) (F) **1.** very fierce. **3.** an attendant of Durgā; another name for a form of Durgā known as Ćāmuṇḍā.

Mahāćūḍā (S) (F) **1.** great crested. **3.** a mother attending on Skanda.

Mahādevā (S) (F) **1.** the great deity. **3.** a daughter of Devaka (*V. Purāṇa*).

Mahādevī (S) (F) **1.** the great deity; the chief wife of a king; the consort of Mahādeva. **3.** the Dākṣāyāṇī in the Śālagrāma (*A. Koṣa*); another name for Pārvatī (*M. Bh.*); another name for Lakṣmī (*M. Bh.*).

Mahādyotā (S) (F) **1.** extremely shiny. **2.** glorious. **3.** a tāntric goddess (*B. Literature*).

Mahāgaṅgā (S) (F) the great Gaṅgā.

Mahāgaurī (S) (F) **1.** the great Gaurī. **3.** one of the 9 forms of Durgā (*D. Purāṇa*); a prominent river in India (*M. Bh.*).

Mahāghoṣā (S) (F) **1.** loud sounding. **3.** a tāntric deity (*B. Literature*).

Mahājavā (S) (F) **1.** extremely fast; fleet flooted. **3.** a mother attending on Skanda (*M. Bh.*).

Mahājayā (S) (F) **1.** extremely victorious. **3.** another name for Durgā.

Mahājñānagītā (S) (F) **1.** singer of the great knowledge. **3.** a tāntric deity.

Mahājñānavatī (S) (F) **1.** great possessor of knowledge. **3.** another name for Manasā.

Mahājñānayutā (S) (F) **1.** great possesser unbounded knowledge. **3.** another name for Manasā.

Mahājuṣakā (S) (F) a celestial flower.

Mahākalā (S) (F) the night of the new moon.

Mahākālī (S) (F) **1.** consort of Mahākāla. **3.** goddess Durgā in her terrifying form (*M. Bh.*); a goddess who executed the commands of the 5th Arhat of the present Avasarpiṇī (*J.S. Koṣa*); one of the 16 Jaina vidyādevis (*J.S. Koṣa*); one of Durgā's attendants (*D. Purāṇa*).

Mahākāntā (S) (F) **1.** very pleasing. **3.** another name for the earth.

Mahākarṇī (S) (F) **1.** large eared. **3.** a follower of Skanda (*M. Bh.*).

Mahākāśī (S) (F) **1.** of the great sky. **3.** a tutelary goddess of the Mātaṅgajas.

Mahākrūrā (S) (F) **1.** extremely cruel. **3.** a yoginī (*T. Śastra*).

Mahālakṣmī (S) (F) **1.** the great Lakṣmī. **3.** in actuality Mahālakṣmī is the Śakti or feminine energy of Nārāyaṇa but is sometimes identified with Durgā or Sarasvatī; Dākṣāyaṇī in Karavīra (*K. Sāgara*).

Mahālīlāsarasvatī (S) (F) **1.** the ever sporting goddess. **3.** a form of the goddess Tārā (*T. Śastra*).

Mahallikā (S) (F) **1.** a female attendant. **3.** a daughter of Prahlāda (*Bhā. Purāṇa*).

Mahāmānasī (S) (F) **1.** with a noble intellect. **3.** a Jaina goddess (*J.S. Koṣa*).

Mahāmānasikā (S) (F) **1.** high minded. **2.** noble; virtuous. **3.** one of the 16 Jaina vidyādevīs (*J.S. Koṣa*).

Mahāmantrā (S) (F) **1.** a great spell. **3.** a Buddhist goddess.

Mahāmantrānusāriṇī (S) (F) **1.** follower of the great spell. **3.** one of the 5 Buddhist tutelary goddesses (*B. Literature*).

Mahāmārī (S) (F) **1.** great destroyer. **3.** a form of Durgā.

Mahāmatī (S) (F) **1.** great intellect. **3.** a particular lunar day personified as a daughter of Aṅgiras (*M. Bh.*).

Mahāmātṛ (S) (F) **1.** the great mother. **3.** each deity of a class of deities who are a personification of the Śakti or female energy of Śiva.

Mahāmayūrī (S) (F) the great peahen said to protect against poison; one of the 5 amulets and one of the 5 tutelary goddesses of the Buddhists.

Mahamedhā (S) (F) **1.** great intelligence. **3.** another name for Durgā.

Mahāmohā (S) (F) **1.** great infatuation. **3.** another name for Durgā.

Mahānadī (S) (F) **1.** a great river. **3.** a river of Bengal; another name for the Gaṅgā.

Mahāniśā (S) (F) **1.** the greatest of the nights. **3.** another name for Durgā.

Mahāprabhā (S) (F) **1.** of great splendour. **3.** another name for the river Narmadā.

Mahāprajāpatī (S) (F) **1.** great lord of life and creatures. **3.** the foster mother and aunt of Buddha and the 1st woman to embrace his doctrines.

Mahāpratisarā (S) (F) **1.** greatly expanded. **2.** a great leader. **3.** one of the 5 Buddhist tutelary goddesses.

Mahāpuṇyā (S) (F) **1.** extremely auspicious. **2.** very purifying; very good; beautiful. **3.** a river.

Mahārakṣā (S) (F) **1.** great saviour; goddess of protection. **3.** one of the 5 Buddhist tutelary goddesses.

Mahārānī (S) (F) great queen.

Mahāraudrī (S) (F) **1.** consort of Rudra. **3.** a form of Durgā (*H. Ć. Ćintāmaṇi*).

Mahārukhā (S) (F) of pleasing appearance.

Mahāsādhvī (S) (F) **1.** supremely chaste woman. **3.** another name for Sītā.

Mahāsahasrapramardini (S) (F) **1.** destroyer of 1000 greats. **3.** one of the 5 Buddhist tutelary goddesses (*B. Literature*).

Mahāsetāvatī (S) (F) **1.** extremely fair complexioned. **2.** very beautiful. **3.** one of the 5 Buddhist tutelary goddesses.

Mahāsmṛti (S) (F) **1.** great tradition. **3.** another name for Durgā.

Mahāśrī (S) (F) **1.** the great divinity. **3.** a Buddhist goddess; another name for Lakṣmī.

Mahāsudhā (S) (F) the great nectar.

Mahāśuklā (S) (F) **1.** extremely white. **2.** eternally pure; eternally white. **3.** another name for Sarasvatī.

Mahāsundarī (S) (F) **1.** supreme beauty. **3.** another name for the tantric goddess Tārā.

Mahāśvetā (S) (F) **1.** very white. **3.** a consort of the sun; the earth goddess; another name for Durgā and Sarasvatī.

Mahātattvā (S) (F) **1.** the great principle. **2.** the intellect. **3.** one of Durgā's attendants (*A. Koṣa*).

Mahatī (S) (F) **1.** greatness. **3.** Nārada's lute (*Bhāgavata*).

Mahattārī (S) (F) **1.** great star. **3.** a form of the Buddhist goddess Tārā.

Mahāvalli (S) (F) **1.** the great creeper. **2.** the Mādhavi creeper (*Hiptage madoblata*).

Mahāvāṇī (S) (F) **1.** the great speech. **2.** transcendent word. **3.** another name for Sarasvatī.

Mahāvegā (S) (F) **1.** moving swiftly. **3.** a mother attending on Skanda (*M. Bh.*).

Mahāvibhūti (S) (F) **1.** great might; great splendour. **3.** another name for Lakṣmī.

Mahāvidyā (S) (F) **1.** great knowledge; great science or art. **3.** another name for Lakṣmī.

Mahāvidyeśvarī (S) (F) **1.** goddess of great knowledge. **3.** a form of Durgā (*A. Koṣa*).

Mahāyakṣī (S) (F) **1.** expert in illusionary magic. **3.** a tāntric deity (*T. Śāstra*).

Mahāyaśas (S) (F) **1.** very famous. **3.** a mother in Skanda's retinue (*M. Bh.*).

Mahelikā (S) (F) woman.

Mahendrāṇī (S) (F) consort of Mahendra.

Maheśanī (S) (F) **1.** great lady; consort of Maheśa. **3.** another name for Pārvatī.

Maheśvarī (S) (F) **1.** great goddess. **3.** Dākṣāyāṇī in Mahākāla (*M. Bh.*); another name for Durgā; a river.

Mahī (S) (F) **1.** great world; earth; heaven and earth conjoined. **3.** a divine being associated with Iḍā and Sarasvatī (*Ṛg Veda*); a river (*M. Bh.*); the number 1.

Mahikā (S) (F) dew; frost.

Mahimā (S) (F) **1.** greatness; majesty; glory. **2.** might; power.

Mahīputrī (S) (F) **1.** daughter of the earth. **3.** another name for Sītā.

Mahiṣadā (S) (F) **1.** master of the earth; given by the buffalo. **3.** a follower of Skanda (*M. Bh.*).

Mahiṣaghnī (S) (F) **1.** slayer of the demon Mahiṣa. **3.** another name for Durgā.

Mahiṣamardinī (S) (F) **1.** crusher of Mahiṣa. **3.** another name for Durgā.

Mahiṣānanā (S) (F) **1.** buffalo faced. **3.** a follower of Skanda (*M. Bh.*).

Mahiṣī (S) (F) **1.** queen; consort; of high rank; female buffalo. **3.** the 15th day of the light half of the month Taiśa; another name for the Gaṅgā.

Mahiṣmatī (S) (F) **1.** rich in buffaloes. **3.** a particular lunar day personified by a daughter of Aṅgiras (*M. Bh.*).

Mahīsutī (S) (F) **1.** daughter of the earth. **3.** another name for Sītā.

Mahitā (S) (F) **1.** flowing on the earth; greatness. **3.** a river (*Bhā. Purāṇa*).

Mahīyā (S) (F) happiness; exultation.

Mahodarī (S) (F) **1.** big bellied. **3.** an attendant of Durgā (*K. Sāgara*); a daughter of Maya (*V. Purāṇa*).

Maholkā (S) (F) great firebrand; great meteor.

Mahotpala (S) (F) **1.** the great lotus. **2.** Indian Lotus (*Nelumbium nucifera*). **3.** Dākṣāyaṇī in Kamalākśa.

Mahulī (S) (F) **1.** enchanting voice. **3.** a rāga.

Mahuratā (S) (F) **1.** moment; instant. **3.** a daughter of Dakṣa, the wife of Dharma, and the mother of all auspicious moments of time (*H. Purāṇa*).

Mainā (S) (F) intelligence; the Common Indian Starling (*Stumus vulgaris*).

Maithilī (S) (F) **1.** of Mithilā. **3.** another name for Sītā.

Maitrāyaṇī (S) (F) **1.** of Mitra; friendly. **3.** the mother of Pūrṇa.

Maitreyī (S) (F) **1.** friendly. **3.** the wife of sage Yājñavalkya who was one of the most learned and virtuous women in ancient India.

Maitrī (S) (F) **1.** friendship; benevolence; goodwill. **3.** goodwill personified as the daughter of Dakṣa and Prasūti, the wife of Dharma and the mother of Abhaya (*Bhā. Purāṇa*); an Upaniṣad (*M. Upaniṣad*).

Makarandikā (S) (F) **1.** nectar like; a metre in music. **3.** a daughter of a vidyādhara (*K. Sāgara*).

Makarī (S) (F) **1.** she crocodile. **3.** a river of Purāṇic fame (*M. Bh.*).

Mākī (S) (F) heaven and earth conjoined.

Makṣīkā (S) (F) bee.

Mālā (S) (F) **1.** necklace; rosary; garland; wreath; row; line; streaks. **3.** a river (*M. Bh.*).

Maladā (S) (F) **1.** that which brings fortune. **3.** a wife of sage Atri (*Br. Purāṇa*).

Mālādevī (S) (F) **1.** goddess of garlands. **3.** a form of Lakṣmī worshipped in Jabalpur.

Mālādharī (S) (F) **1.** wreathed; garlanded. **3.** a rākṣasī (*B. Literature*).

Malahā (S) (F) **1.** destroying dirt. **3.** a daughter of Raudrāśva (*H. Purāṇa*).

Mālāsikā (S) (F) **1.** garlanded. **3.** a rāgiṇī.

Mālaśrī (S) (F) **1.** beautiful garland. **3.** a rāga.

Mālatī (S) (F) **1.** Spanish Jasmine (*Jasminum grandiflorium*); bud; blossom; maid; virgin; moonlight; night; Velvet Leaf (*Cissampelos pareira*); *Hiptage madoblata*. **3.** a river.

Mālatikā (S) (F) **1.** made of Jasmine. **3.** a mother attending on Skanda (*M. Bh.*).

Mālatimālā (S) (F) a garland of Jasmine blossoms.

Mālāvatī (S) (F) **1.** garlanded. **2.** crowned. **3.** the wife of Kuśadhvaja; the wife of Upabarhaṇa.

Mālavi (S) (F) **1.** princess of the Mālavas. **3.** the wife of King Aśvapati of Madra and progenitress of the Mālavas (*M. Bh.*); a rāgiṇī.

Mālavikā (S) (F) **1.** of Mālava; *Ipomoea turpethum*. **3.** the heroine of a drama by Kālidāsa (*A. Koṣa*).

Malayagandhinī (S) (F) **1.** scented with sandalwood. **3.** a companion of Umā (*A. Koṣa*); a vidyādharī (*A. Koṣa*).

Malayavāsinī (S) (F) **1.** dwelling on the Malaya mountains. **3.** another name for Durgā.

Malayavatī (S) (F) very fragrant.

Mālikā (S) (F) the mogra or double jasmine; daughter; necklace; intoxicating drink; *Hibiscus mutabilis.*

Mālinī (S) (F) **1.** fragrant; sweet smelling; Spanish Jasmine (*Jasminum grandiflorum*); a female gardener. **3.** a rākṣasī and mother of Vibhīṣaṇa by Viśravas (*M. Bh.*); name assumed by Draupadī in the court of Virāṭa (*M. Bh.*); the daughter of Sukaru and wife of Śvetakarṇa (*H. Purāṇa*); the wife of Priyavrata (*H. Purāṇa*); the wife of Prasenajit (*B. Literature*); an apsarā (*M. Bh.*); wife of Rući and mother of Manu Raućya (*Mā. Purāṇa*); one of the 7 Mātris of Skanda (*M. Bh.*); an attendant of Durgā; another name for Durgā and the Gaṅgā.

Mallārī (S) (F) **1.** enemy of wrestlers. **3.** a rāgiṇī.

Malligandhī (S) (F) smelling like jasmine.

Mallikā (S) (F) Arabian Jasmine (*Jasminum sambac*); queen; garland; necklace; daughter.

Malūka (S) (F) the Sacred Basil (*Ocimum sanctum*).

Mālyavatī (S) (F) **1.** crowned with garlands. **3.** a river (*V. Rāmāyaṇa*).

Māmalladevi (S) (F) **1.** goddess of warriors. **3.** the mother of Śrīharṣa.

Māmamī (S) (F) **1.** mine. **3.** a Buddhist devī.

Mamatā (S) (F) **1.** sense of ownership; motherly love. **3.** the wife of Litathya, sister-in-law of Bṛhaspati and mother of sage Bharadvāja (*M. Bh.*); the wife of Utathya; mother of sage Dīrghatamas (*Ṛg Veda*).

Māmukhi (S) (F) **1.** face less. **3.** a Buddhist devī.

Mānadā (S) (F) **1.** giving honour. **3.** a digit of the moon.

Managarvā (S) (F) **1.** with a proud mind. **2.** full of pride. **3.** an apsarā who was reborn as the monkey Añjanā and became the mother of Hanumān (*V. Rāmāyaṇa*).

Manajña/Manojña (S) (F) princess; pleasing; agreeable; beautiful; charming.

Manākā (S) (F) **1.** according to the mind. **2.** a loving woman; a female elephant; the rosary bead; Elephant's Ears (*Alocasia indica*).

Manmathā (S) (F) **1.** destroying the mind. **2.** agitating; suffusing with love. **3.** another name for Dākṣāyāṇī.

Manamohinī (S) (F) attracting the heart.

Mananyā (S) (F) deserving praise.

Manaprīti (S) (F) **1.** dear to the heart. **2.** delight; gladness.

Manasā (S) (F) **1.** conceived in the mind. **2.** mental power; mind; heart. **3.** a goddess who is the daughter of Kaśyapa, sister of Anantanāga, wife of Jaratkaru, mother of Āstīka, the protector of men from serpents and is the tutelary deity of snakes and fertility(*K. Vyūha*); a kinnarī.

Manasā (S) (F) intention.

Manasādevī (S) (F) **1.** goddess of mental powers. **3.** a devī born of the mind of Kaśyapa who was also known as Jaratkarū (*K. Vyūha*).

Mānasī (S) (F) **1.** mental or spiritual adoration. **3.** a kinnarī; a vidyādevī.

Manasiddhī (S) (F) **1.** control of the mind; one who attains all desires. **3.** a goddess (*V. D. Ćaritam*).

Manastokā (S) (F) **1.** mental satisfaction. **2.** mentally satisfied. **3.** another name for Durgā.

Manasvī (S) (F) **1.** that which controls the mind. **2.** intelligence; high mindedness; one with a sound mind.

Manasvinī (S) (F) **1.** one who controls the mind. **2.** noble; proud; high minded; virtuous. **3.** a daughter of Dakṣa, wife of Dharma and the mother of Ćandra (*M. Bh.*); the wife of Mṛkandu; *Momordica balsamina*; another name for Durgā.

Manavarā (S) (F) pleasant to the mind.

Mānāvī (S) (F) **1.** wife of Manu; daughter of man. **3.** a goddess executing the demands of the 11th Arhat of the present Avasarpiṇī; a prominent river of ancient India (*M. Bh.*); a vidyādevī; *Jasminum auriculatum.*

Māṇavikā (S) (F) damsel; maiden.

Manāyī (S) (F) Manu's wife.

Mandā (S) (F) **1.** slow; pot; vessel; inkstand. **3.** a digit of the moon (*A. Koṣa*); another name for Dākṣāyaṇī.

Mandākinī (S) (F) **1.** that which moves slowly; the Milky Way. **3.** a branch of the Gaṅgā which flows through Kedāranātha (*M. Bh.*); a holy river which flows near the Ćitrakūṭa mountain (*M. Bh.*); a Purāṇic river arising from the Kedāra mountains (*M. Bh.*); one of the 2 wives of Viśravas and the mother of Kubera (*P. Purāṇa*); the celestial Gaṅgā (*M. Bh.*); Kubera's park (*M. Bh.*).

Mandanā (S) (F) gay; cheerful.

Mandarā (S) (F) **1.** slow. **2.** large; firm. **3.** a wife of Viṣvakarmā and the mother of Nala the monkey (*V. Rāmāyaṇa*).

Mandaradevī (S) (F) **1.** coming from Mount Mandāra. **3.** a sister of Mandāradeva (*K. Sāgara*); another name for Durgā.

Mandāralakṣmī (S) (F) **1.** goddess of the Indian Coral tree (*Erythrina indica*). **3.** the wife of King Siṁhadhvaja (*K. Sāgara*).

Mandāramālā (S) (F) **1.** a garland of coral flowers. **3.** an apsarā who was the daughter of Vasu (*K. Sāgara*).

Mandarāvatī (S) (F) bearer of coral flowers.

Mandārikā (S) (F) the Indian Coral tree (*Erythrina indica*).

Mandavāhinī (S) (F) **1.** gently flowing. **3.** a river (*M. Bh.*).

Māṇḍavī (S) (F) **1.** able administrator. **3.** Dākṣāyaṇī in Māṇḍavya (*M. Bh.*); a daughter of Kuṣadhvaja, the wife of Bharata, the mother of Śūrasena and Subāhu and the cousin of Sītā (*U. Rāmāyaṇa*).

Māṇḍavikā (S) (F) of administration; of people.

Māndhārī (S) (F) bearer of honour.

Mandirā (S) (F) of temple; a slow sound; sacred; venerated; melodious; metallic cymbals producing a musical sound.

Maṇḍitṛ (S) (F) **1.** that which adorns. **2.** an ornament.

Mandodarī (S) (F) **1.** narrow waisted; one who can digest secrets. **3.** an incarnation of the apsarā Madhurā, the daughter of Maya, the favourite wife of Rāvaṇa, the mother of Meghanā, Atikāya and Akṣakumāra (*V. Rāmāyaṇa*) and regarded as one of the 5 chaste women; a mother attending on Skanda (*D. Bh. Purāṇa*); a princess of Siṁhala and wife of King Ćārudeṣṇa of Madra (*D. Bh. Purāṇa*).

Mandrā (S) (F) pleasant; agreeable; charming; low voiced.

Mangalā (S) (F) **1.** auspicious; lucky. **2.** a faithful wife; Couch Grass (*Cynodon dactylon*); the white and blue flowering Dūrvā grass (*Panicum dactylon*); the Karañja blossom (*Pongamia glabra*); Spanish Jasmine (*Jasminum grandiflorum*). **3.** the mother of the 5th Arhat of the present Avasarpiṇī (*J.S. Koṣa*); another name for Umā, Durgā and the Dākṣāyaṇī as worshipped in Gayā.

Maṅgalaćaṇḍī (S) (F) **1.** goddess of welfare. **3.** a form of Durgā (*A. Koṣa*).

Mangalaćaṇḍikā (S) (F) **1.** goddess of welfare. **3.** a tutelary deity of the Vedas who is a form of Durgā and worshipped by Paramaśiva (*D. Bhāgavata*).

Mangalāvatī (S) (F) **1.** bestowed with luck. **3.** a daughter of Tumburu (*K. Sāgara*).

Maṅgalī (S) (F) **1.** auspicious. **2.** scented with jasmine.

Maṅgalyā (S) (F) **1.** auspicious. **2.** Sandalwood (*Santalum album*); Wood Apple (*Ferronia elephantum*); *Prosopis spicigera*; *Aglaia odoratissima.* **3.** another name for Durgā.

Maṅgammā (S) (F) **1.** enticing heart. **2.** beautiful; that which charms the heart.

Maṇibhūmi (S) (F) a mine of pearls.

Maṇićūḍā (S) (F) **1.** jewel crested. **3.** a kiṇnarī (*K. Vyūha*).

Maṇidhāriṇī (S) (F) **1.** bearer of jewels. **2.** bejewelled; ornamented. **3.** a kinnarī.

Maṇijalā (S) (F) **1.** with crystal clear water. **3.** a river (*M. Bh.*).

Māṇikā (S) (F) **1.** of jewels. **2.** a particular weight.

Māṇikāmbā (S) (F) **1.** mother of jewels. **3.** the mother of Viṭṭhala.

Maṇikarṇikā (S) (F) **1.** jewelled earring. **3.** a daughter of Ćandraghoṣa; a sacred pool in Benaras (*R. Upaniṣad*).

Maṇikuṭṭikā (S) (F) **1.** inlaid with jewels. **3.** a follower of Skanda (*M. Bh.*).

Maṇimālā (S) (F) **1.** a necklace of jewels. **2.** beautiful; lustrous. **3.** another name for Lakṣmī.

Maṇimañjarī (S) (F) cluster of jewels.

Maṇingā (S) (F) **1.** treasure of jewels. **3.** a river.

Māninī (S) (F) **1.** resolute; self respecting. **3.** a daughter of Vidūrastha and wife of Rājyavardhana (*Mā. Purāṇa*); the daughter of sage Tṛṇabindu and the mother of Viśravas (*Mā. Purāṇa*); an apsarā (*V. Purāṇa*).

Maṇiprabhā (S) (F) **1.** splendour of a jewel. **3.** an apsarā (*K. Vyūha*).

Maṇiratna (S) (F) jewel.

Maṇirоćanī (S) (F) **1.** one who likes jewels. **3.** a kinnarī (*K. Vyūha*).

Manīṣā (S) (F) thought; reflection; consideration; wisdom; intelligence; conception; idea; prayer; hymn; desire; wish; request; reflection; intellect.

Maniṣī (S) (F) desired by heart.

Manīṣikā (S) (F) understanding; intelligence.

Maṇiśilā (S) (F) a jewelled stone.

Manīṣitā (S) (F) wisdom.

Maniṣka (S) (F) wisdom; intelligence.

Maṇisraj (S) (F) a garland of jewels.

Maniṣṭhakā (S) (F) the little finger.

Maṇīyā (S) (F) glass bead.

Mañjā (S) (F) a cluster of blossoms.

Mañjarī (S) (F) **1.** a cluster of blossoms. **2.** spring; stalk of a flower; a flowerbud; a shoot; a sprout; a sprig; blossom; vine; pearl; Mango tree (*Mangifera indica*).

Mañjarikā (S) (F) **1.** a small cluster of blossoms. **2.** a small pearl; the Tulasī plant.

Mañjī (S) (F) a cluster of blossoms.

Mañjimān (S) (F) **1.** bearer of blossoms. **2.** beauty; elegance.

Mañjirā (S) (F) **1.** anklet. **2.** an ornament for the foot. **3.** a river (*A. Koṣa*).

Mañju (S) (F) **1.** attracting the heart. **2.** beautiful; lovely; charming; pleasant; sweet.

Mañjugati (S) (F) **1.** having a graceful gait. **2.** the flamingo.

Manjughoṣā (S) (F) **1.** with a sweet sound. **3.** an apsarā (*A Koṣa*).

Mañjulā (S) (F) **1.** taking the heart. **2.** beautiful; pleasing; lovely; charming; a bower; an arbour; a spring. **3.** a river of Purāṇic fame (*M. Bh.*).

Mañjulatā (S) (F) vine of beauty.

Mañjulikā (S) (F) beautiful.

Mañjumatī (S) (F) **1.** with a lovely heart. **2.** loving; compassionate; humane.

Mañjunaśī (S) (F) **1.** connoisseur of beauty. **2.** a beautiful woman. **3.** the wife of Indra; another name for Durgā.

Manjuśrī (S) (F) **1.** divine beauty. **3.** another name for Lakṣmī.

Mañjutara (S) (F) most lovely.

Manobhāvanā (S) (F) **1.** feeling of the heart. **2.** sentiment; emotion.

Manodarī (S) (F) **1.** pleasing to the heart. **3.** the wife of Dārukāsura (*Ś. Purāṇa*).

Manogati (S) (F) **1.** the heart's course. **2.** wish; desire.

Manoharā (S) (F) **1.** winning the heart. **2.** that which steals the heart. **3.** the wife of the vasu Soma; an apsarā in the court of Kubera (*M. Bh.*); a kinnarī; wife of Dhara and mother of Śiśira (*H. Purāṇa*); Yellow Jasmine.

Manoharī (S) (F) **1.** that which steal the heart; Spanish Jasmine (*Jasmine grandiflorum*). **3.** the wife of Varćasvin and mother of Śiśira; an apsarā; a kinnarī.

Manohārikā (S) (F) one who steals the heart.

Manojavā (S) (F) **1.** with the speed of thought; born of the mind. **3.** one of the 7 tongues of Agni (*M. Upaniṣad*); a mother attending on Skanda (*M. Bh.*); a river (*V. Purāṇa*).

Manojñā (S) (F) **1.** agreeable to the mind. **2.** pleasant; charming; beautiful; a princess.

Manojvalā (S) (F) as fair as thought; *Jasminum auriculatum.*

Manokāmanā (S) (F) hearts desire.

Manomohinī (S) (F) attracting the heart.

Manoramā (S) (F) **1.** gratifying the mind. **2.** pleasing; beautiful; charming. **3.** the daughter of the vidyādhara Indīvara, the wife of Svāroćiṣa and the mother of Vijaya; an apsarā who was the daughter of Kaśyapa and Prādhā (*M. Bh.*); a branch of the Sarasvatī river (*M. Bh.*); the wife of King Dhruvasandhi of Kosala; a gandharvī; Musk Jasmine (*Jasminum pubescens*).

Manoritā (S) (F) **1.** of the mind. **2.** desire; wish.

Manotī (S) (F) **1.** daughter in mind. **2.** vow of offering to a deity.

Manovallabhā (S) (F) heart's beloved.

Manovatī (S) (F) **1.** desired by the mind. **3.** the daughter of the vidyādhara Ćitrāṅgada; the daughter of the asura Sumāya; the city of Brahmā on Mount Mahāmeru (*D. Bh. Purāṇa*); an apsarā.

Manovindā (S) (F) amusing to the mind.

Mantharā (S) (F) **1.** slow; broad; indolent; curved; crooked; an obstacle. **3.** the humpbacked slave of Kaikeyī who is sup-posed to have been an incarnation of the gāndharvī Dundubhī (*M. Bh.*); a daughter of Viroćana (*V. Rāmāyaṇa*).

Manthinī (S) (F) **1.** that which churns. **2.** a butter vat. **3.** a mother attending on Skanda (*M. Bh.*).

Mantikā (S) (F) **1.** thoughtful. **3.** an Upaniṣad.

Mantramālā (S) (F) **1.** a garland of hymns. **2.** a collection of prayers and magical verses. **3.** a river (*Ṛg Veda*).

Mantraṇā (S) (F) counsel; advice; deliberation.

Mantriṇī (S) (F) the queen of chess; the 12th lunar mansion.

Manū (S) (F) **1.** of the mind. **2.** desirable. **3.** an apsara born of Kaśyapa and Prādhā (*M. Bh.*).

Manujā (S) (F) **1.** daughter of man. **2.** woman.

Mānuṣī (S) (F) woman; humane.

Mānyā (S) (F) to be respected; worthy of honour.

Manyantī (S) (F) **1.** honourable. **3.** the daughter of Agni Manyu (*Bhā. Purāṇa*).

Mānyavatī (S) (F) **1.** honoured; esteemed. **3.** the daughter of Bhīmarāja and wife of Avīkṣit (*Mā. Purāṇa*).

Mārakkā (S) (F) **1.** death. **3.** the goddess Mariamma who is a form of Pārvatī.

Marālī (S) (F) female swan.

Marālikā (S) (F) small swan.

Mārdavā (S) (F) softness; kindness.

Mārgaṇapriyā (S) (F) **1.** lover of research; one who loves inquiry. **3.** a daughter of Kaśyapa and Prādhā (*M. Bh.*).

Mārgapālī (S) (F) **1.** protecting the roads. **3.** a goddess (*P. Purāṇa*).

Mārgavatī (S) (F) **1.** follower of the path; bearer of the path. **3.** the goddess of paths and the protector of travellers (*K. Sāgara*).

Māri (S) (F) **1.** of death; of love. **3.** a form of Durgā as the goddess of death.

Mariammā (S) (F) **1.** mother of death; mother of love. **3.** a form of Pārvatī (*G. Purāṇa*).

Mārīći (S) (F) **1.** ray of light. **3.** a Buddhist goddess; the wife of Parjañya (*V. Purāṇa*); an apsarā (*M. Bh.*).

Marīćikā (S) (F) mirage.

Māriṣā (S) (F) **1.** worthy; respectable. **3.** a nymph born of trees and moonlight (*V. Purāṇa*); the mother of Dakṣa (*H. Purāṇa*); the wife of Śūra (*Bhā. Purāṇa*); a river of Purāṇic fame (*M. Bh.*); a daughter of Kaṇḍu (*M. Bh.*).

Mārjani (S) (F) **1.** that which cleans. **2.** washing; purifying; a broom. **3.** an attendant of Durgā (*S. Koṣa*).

Mārjārakarṇī (S) (F) **1.** cat eared. **3.** another name for Ćāmuṇḍā.

Mārkaṇḍeyi (S) (F) **1.** winning over death. **3.** the wife of Rajas (*V. Purāṇa*).

Mārṣṭnī (S) (F) **1.** dwelling in cleanliness. **2.** washing; ablution; purification. **3.** the wife of Duḥsaha (*V. Purāṇa*).

Marudevī (S) (F) **1.** consort of Marudeva. **3.** a queen of Ayodhyā and mother of Jaina Tīrthaṅkara Ṛṣabhadeva (*J. Literature*).

Mārulā (S) (F) **1.** rock born; born due to the blessings of Śiva; a kind of duck. **3.** a poetess.

Maruṭā (S) (F) with a high forehead.

Mārutī (S) (F) consort of Marut; the northwest quarter; the constellation Svāti.

Maruttaruṇī (S) (F) **1.** wind virgin. **3.** a vidyādharī (*H. Purāṇa*).

Marutvān **1.** lord of the winds. **3.** another name for Indra.

Marutvatī (S) (F) **1.** attended by the maruts. **3.** a daughter of Dakṣa and wife of Dharma (*H. Purāṇa*).

Maryā (S) (F) mark; limit; boundary.

Maryādā (S) (F) **1.** containing clear marks. **2.** frontier; limit; boundary; rule of morality; propriety of conduct; a ring used as an amulet. **3.** wife of Devātithi (*M. Bh.*); wife of Arvāćīna (*M. Bh.*).

Māśī (S) (F) **1.** bean coloured. **2.** dark complexioned. **3.** the wife of Sūra.

Masmā (S) (F) **1.** not ink. **2.** fair complexioned. **3.** 2 princesses (*R. Taraṅgiṇī*).

Mātāli (S) (F) **1.** mother's friend. **3.** an attendant of Durgā.

Matallī (S) (F) anything excellent.

Matallikā (S) (F) anything excellent of its kind.

Mātaṅgī (S) (F) **1.** roaring at will; an elephant. **3.** the daughter of Krodhavaśā and Kaśyapa and the mother of elephants (*V. Rāmāyaṇa*); one of the 10 Mahāvidyās; the mother of Vasiṣṭha (*V. Rāmāyaṇa*); a form of Durgā (*A. Koṣa*).

Mataṅginī (S) (F) **1.** roaming at will. **3.** a daughter of Mandāra (*H. Purāṇa/ K. Sāgara*).

Mathurā (S) (F) **1.** the city of Mathurā. **3.** the birthplace of Kṛṣṇa.

Mati (S) (F) **1.** devotion; prayer; worship; hymn; thought; intention; wish; opinion; no-tion; perception; intelligence; memory. **3.** opinion personified as the daughter of Dakṣa and the wife of Soma or as the wife of Viveka or as the wife of Dharma (*M. Bh.*).

Matkulikā (S) (F) **1.** born in a family of drunkards. **3.** a follower of Skanda (*M. Bh.*).

Matkuṇikā (S) (F) **1.** insect; bug. **3.** a mother attending on Skanda (*H. Purāṇa*).

Mātṛ (S) (F) **1.** with true knowledge; mother. **2.** the earth; water. **3.** the personified energies of the principal deities; the Mātṛs who are closely connected with the worship of Śiva and were attendants to his son Skanda (*M. Bh.*); the 13 wives of Kaśyapa are also called Mātṛs (*M. Bh.*); another name for Durgā, Lakṣmī and Dākṣāyaṇī.

Mātṛkā (S) (F) **1.** divine mother. **3.** the wife of Aryaman (*Bhā. Purāṇa*).

Matsyā (S) (F) **1.** of a fish. **3.** another name for Satyavatī.

Matsyagandhā (S) (F) **1.** smelling like a fish. **3.** another name for Satyavatī.

Matsyanārī (S) (F) **1.** mermaid. **3.** another name for Satyavatī.

Matsyodarī (S) (F) **1.** born of a fish. **3.** another name for Satyavatī.

Maulimālikā (S) (F) a chaplet.

Maurvī (S) (F) **1.** girdle made of Mūrvā or bowstring hemp. **2.** a bowstring. **3.** a wife of Ghaṭotkaća.

Maurvikā (S) (F) bow string.

Māyā (S) (F) **1.** wealth; illusion. **2.** unreality; phantom; art; wisdom; compassion; sympathy. **3.** illusion sometimes identified with Durgā, sometimes regarded as a daughter of Anṛta and Nirṛti and the mother of Mṛtyu or as a daughter of Adharma (*Purāṇas*); the mother of Gautama Buddha (*B. Literature*); one of the 9 Śaktis of Viṣṇu (*Bhā. Purāṇa*); another name for Lakṣmī (*A. Koṣa*).

Māyādevī (S) (F) **1.** goddess of illusion; goddess of wealth. **3.** the mother of Gautama Buddha; the wife of Pradyumna (*V. Purāṇa*).

Māyārati (S) (F) **1.** Māyā and Rati combined. **2.** one who loves wealth. **3.** a wife of Pradyumna (*Bhā. Purāṇa*).

Māyāvatī (S) (F) **1.** with illusory powers. **3.** an incarnation of Rati and wife of Pradyumna (*H. Purāṇa*); the wife of a vidyādhara (*H. Purāṇa*).

Mayūrāṅkī (S) (F) with peacock marks; a jewel.

Māyūrī (S) (F) peahen.

Māyūrika (S) (F) **1.** with peacock feathers. **3.** a rāgiṇī; Bombay Hemp (*Hibiscus cannabinus*).

Medhā (S) (F) **1.** intelligence; wisdom; prudence. **3.** wisdom personified as the daughter of Dakṣa and Prasūti and the wife of Dharma (*V. Purāṇa*); a form of the Dākṣāyāṇī in Kāśmīra; a form of Sarasvatī; a sister of Agni (*A. Veda*).

Medhanī (S) (F) **1.** of intelligence. **3.** the consort of Brahmā.

Medhāvīkīrti (S) (F) with the fame of wisdom.

Medhavinī (S) (F) **1.** learned. **3.** a wife of Brahmā (*A. Veda*).

Medhyā (S) (F) **1.** full of sap; vigorous; mighty; strong; fresh; clean; pure; wise; intelligent. **3.** a holy place on the west coast; the river that flows through it is believed to be the place of origin of Agni (*M. Bh.*); Black Catechu tree (*Acacia catechu*); Intellect tree (*Celastrus paniculata*); *Prosopis spicigera.*

Medinī (S) (F) **1.** fertile. **2.** the earth. **3.** another name for the earth goddess.

Meghajā (S) (F) **1.** born of the clouds. **2.** water; a large pearl.

Meghakarṇā (S) (F) **1.** cloud eared. **3.** a mother in Skanda's retinue (*M. Bh.*).

Meghamālā (S) (F) **1.** a garland of clouds. **3.** a mother attending on Skanda (*H. Purāṇa*).

Meghamallārikā (S) (F) **1.** instigator of clouds. **3.** a rāga.

Meghamañjari (S) (F) cloud blossom.

Meghanā (S) (F) **1.** the rumbling of clouds. **2.** thunder.

Meghanādā (S) (F) **1.** with the sound of clouds. **2.** the thunder. **3.** a yoginī (*Bhā. Purāṇa*).

Megharaṅgikā (S) (F) **1.** cloud coloured. **2.** dark complexioned. **3.** a rāga.

Megharañjanī (S) (F) **1.** one who delights the clouds. **3.** a rāga.

Megharavā (S) (F) **1.** cloud noise. **2.** the thunder. **3.** a mother attending on Skanda (*M. Bh.*).

Megharekhā (S) (F) a row of clouds.

Meghaśvanā (S) (F) **1.** one who sounds like the clouds. **3.** a mother of Skanda (*M. Bh.*).

Meghavāhinī (S) (F) **1.** riding on a cloud. **3.** a mother of Skanda (*M. Bh.*).

Meghavalī (S) (F) a row of clouds.

Meghayantī (S) (F) **1.** one who makes the weather cloudy; one who is responsible for creating the clouds **3.** one of the 7 kṛttikās (*A. Veda*).

Mekalā (S) (F) **1.** knower of the self; of the ṛṣi Mekala; girdle. **3.** another name for the river Narmadā.

Mekhalā (S) (F) **1.** girdle. **2.** belt; the slope of a mountain; the line drawn around an altar. **3.** another name for the river Narmadā.

Menā (S) (F) **1.** intellect; speech; woman. **3.** the daughter of Mahāmeru and wife of Himavān (*V. Rāmāyaṇa*), who according to the *Viṣṇu Purāṇa* is the mind born daughter of Svadhā and the mother of Maināka, Gaṅgā and Pārvatī, according to the *Rāmāyaṇa*, the mother of Umā or Pārvatī and Gaṅgā both of which were married to Śiva, and according to the *Vāmana Purāṇa*, the mother of Rāgiṇī, Kuṭilā, Kālī or Umā and Sunābha ; an apsarā daughter of King Vṛṣṇāśva, the mother of Śakuntalā by sage Viśvāmitra and the mother of Pramadvarā by the gandharva Viśvavasu (*Ṛg Veda*).

Menajā (S) (F) **1.** daughter of Menā. **3.** another name for Pārvatī.

Menākā (S) (F) **1.** born of the mind; of the mountains; of woman. **3.** one of the 6 prominent celestial maidens and an apsarā of extraordinary beauty, the daughter of King Vṛṣṇāśva according to the *Ṛg Veda*, according to the *Viṣṇu Purāṇa*, the mind born daughter of Svadhā, mother of Maināka, Gaṅgā and Pārvatī, the mother of Śakuntalā by sage Viśvāmitra and the mother of Pramadvarā by the gandharva Viśvavasu.

Menākātmajā (S) (F) **1.** daughter of Menākā. **3.** another name for Pārvatī.

Menāvatī (S) (F) **1.** possessed with intellect. **3.** another name for Pārvatī.

Meni (S) (F) thunderbolt; speech.

Menitā (S) (F) wise; intelligent.

Merudevī (S) (F) **1.** goddess of the Meru mountain. **3.** one of the 9 daughters of Mahāmeru, wife of King Nābhi and the mother of Rṣabha who was an incarnation of Viṣṇu (*Bhā. Purāṇa*).

Meruprabhā (S) (F) **1.** shining like the Meru mountain; of great splendour. **2.** extremely charming.

Meruśrī (S) (F) **1.** loftiest among the beautiful. **2.** the most beautiful; with the beauty of Meru. **3.** a nāgakanyā (*K. Vyuha*).

Midhuṣī (S) (F) **1.** liberal; bountiful. **3.** Śakti or the feminine energy of Īśāṇa personified as his consort.

Mihikā (S) (F) mist; fog; snow.

Milikā (S) (F) desiring union.

Mīnā (S) (F) **1.** a gem; a goblet of wine; a fish; multi coloured glass; a stick. **3.** a daughter of Ūṣā, a wife of Kaśyapa and the mother of fish (*Purāṇas*); the zodiac sign of Pisces (*V. Rāmāyaṇa*).

Mīnākṣī (S) (F) **1.** fish eyed; a species of Dūrvā grass. **3.** a daughter of Kubera (*Bh. Parāṇa*); an incarnation of Pārvatī as the daughter of the Pāṇḍya king of Madurai; a yakṣiṇī.

Mīnāli (S) (F) **1.** fish catcher. **2.** a fisher-woman. **3.** another name for Satyavatī.

Mīnāti (S) (F) **1.** fish like. **2.** voluptuous; having a tendency towards fatness.

Mīra (S) (F) **1.** the ocean; the sea; limit; boundary. **3.** a renowned saint poetess and devotee of Kṛṣṇa.

Miśī (S) (F) Dill (*Anethum panmori*); a species of sugarcane; *Nardostachys jatamansi*.

Miśrakeśī (S) (F) **1.** with hair of mixed colours. **3.** a beautiful apsarā born of Kaśyapa and Prādhā, the wife of Raudrāśva and the mother of 10 sons (*M. Bh.*); the wife of King Vatsaka the brother of Vasudeva (*M. Bh.*).

Mītā (S) (F) one who has been measured and gauged; tried and tested; a friend.

Mitāli (S) (F) friendship.

Miṭhāī (H) (F) sweetmeat.

Mithyā (S) (F) **1.** false; wrong. **3.** untruth personified as the wife of Adharma (*K. Purāṇa*).

Mītī (S) (F) friend.

Mitrā (S) (F) **1.** friend. **2.** companion; associate. **3.** a queen of Hastināpura and mother of Jaina Tīrathaṅkara Arahātha (*J. S. Koṣa*); the mother of Maitreya and Maitreyī (*Bhā. Purāṇa*); a companion of Pārvatī (*M. Bh.*).

Mitravatī (S) (F) **1.** with friends. **3.** a daughter of Kṛṣṇa (*H. Purāṇa*).

Mitravindā (S) (F) **1.** possessor of companions. **3.** a princess of Avantī who was first cousin and wife of Kṛṣṇa (*Bhā. Purāṇa*); a river (*Bh. Purāṇa*).

Mituṣī (S) (F) with limited desires.

Modakī (S) (F) 1. pleasing; delighting. 2. a sweetmeat.

Modayantikā (S) (F) rejoicing; delighting; the Arabian Jasmine (*Jasminun sambac*).

Modinī (S) (F) 1. glad; cheerful. 3. *Jasminum Sambac.*

Mohanā (S) (F) 1. infatuating. 2. beautiful. 3. a wife of Sugrīva (*P. Purāṇa*).

Mohanī (S) (F) 1. infatuating. 2. charming. 3. one of the 9 Śaktis of Viṣṇu (*A. Koṣa*); an apsarā (*P. Ratra*); a rākṣasī (*A. Veda*).

Mohinī (S) (F) 1. fascinating; the jasmine blossom. 3. the female form assumed by Mahāviṣṇu during the war of the devas and the asuras for the Amṛta (*Bhā. Purāṇa*); a daughter of Rukmāṅgada (*V. Purāṇa*); an apsarā (*P. Rātra*).

Mohonā (S) (F) endearing.

Molinā (S) (F) a tree that grows from a root.

Monā (S) (F) alone.

Moraćandrikā (S) (F) 1. the moon of the peacock. 2. the moon like eye at the end of a peacock's tail.

Morikā (S) (F) peahen; postern gate.

Mornī (S) (F) peahen.

Mṛḍā (S) (F) 1. compassionate. 2. the earth; clay. 3. another name for Pārvatī.

Mṛḍānī (S) (F) 1. consort of Mṛḍa. 3. another name for Pārvatī.

Mṛdānta (S) (F) passing through a constellation.

Mṛdinī (S) (F) good earth; soil.

Mṛdu (S) (F) soft; delicate; tender; pliant; gentle; mild; a vine with red grapes; the Guava tree (*Psidium guyava*).

Mṛdukā (S) (F) 1. soft; tender. 3. an apsarā (*K. Vyuha*).

Mṛdvaṅgī (S) (F) soft bodied; delicate.

Mṛdvikā (S) (F) softness; gentleness; mildness; a vine; a bunch of red grapes (*Vitis vinifera*).

Mṛgākṣī (S) (F) 1. deer eyed. 2. Bitter Cucumber (*Citrullus colocynthis*); *Cucumis trigonos.*

Mṛgaloćanā (S) (F) doe eyed.

Mṛgamandā (S) (F) 1. moving like a fawn. 2. fleet footed. 3. a daughter of Kaśyapa who was the progenitress of lions (*M. Bh.*).

Mṛganayanā (S) (F) fawn eyed.

Mṛganetrā (S) (F) 1. fawn eyed. 2. born under the constellation Mṛga or Capricorn.

Mṛgāṅganā (S) (F) doe.

Mṛgāṅkalekhā (S) (F) 1. a line of the moon. 3. a daughter of the king of the vidyādharas (*K. Sāgara*).

Mṛgāṅkavatī (S) (F) 1. possessor of the moon. 3. the daughter of an ancient king called Śrībimbakī (*H. Purāṇa*).

Mṛgarājinī (S) (F) 1. lioness. 3. a gāndharvī.

Mṛgavatī (S) (F) 1. possessor of deer. 3. the mythical progenitress of antelopes and bears (*V. Rāmāyaṇa*); the Dākṣāyāṇī on the Yamuṇā (*K. Sāgara*).

Mṛgayā (S) (F) the chase personified as an attendant of Revanta.

Mṛgekṣaṇā (S) (F) deer eyed.

Mṛgī (S) (F) 1. doe. 3. the mother of deer, and the daughter of Kaśyapa and Tāmrā (*M. Bh.*).

Mṛgīśṇā (S) (F) doe eyed.

Mṛgottamā (S) (F) 1. the most beautiful deer. 2. the constellation Mṛgasiras.

Mṛkṣiṇī (S) (F) 1. tearing up. 2. a rain cloud; a torrent.

Mṛṇālī (S) (F) lotus stalk.

Mṛṇālikā (S) (F) a lotus root.

Mṛṇalinī (S) (F) 1. a collection of lotuses. 2. fragrant; tender; sacred; venerated; dear to the gods.

Mṛṣā (S) (F) 1. lie; falsehood. 3. the wife of Adharma and the mother of Dambha and Māyā (*Bhā. Purāṇa*).

Mṛṣaṇā (S) (F) **1.** deliberation. **2.** reflection; thought.

Mṛtsā (S) (F) good earth; fragrant soil.

Mṛtsnā (S) (F) **1.** good earth. **2.** excellent soil; fertile and fragrant earth.

Mṛttikā (S) (F) **1.** earth; clay. **2.** loam.

Mṛtyū (S) (F) **1.** death. **3.** the goddess of death born of Brahmā or Māyā (*M. Bh.*).

Mudā (S) (F) **1.** delight; happiness. **3.** joy personified as a daughter of Tuṣti (*Bhā. Purāṇa*).

Mudāvatī (S) (F) **1.** filled with joy. **3.** a daughter of King Vidūratha (*M. Bh.*).

Muditā (S) (F) **1.** happy; joyous; glad. **3.** the wife of the agni Saha (*M. Bh.*).

Mudī (S) (F) happy; moonshine.

Muditapuṣpā (S) (F) **1.** happy flower. **3.** a gandharvī (*K. Vyūha*).

Mudrā (S) (F) posture; sign; seal; signatory.

Mugdhā (S) (F) young; beautiful; innocent; artless; tender.

Mugdhākṣī (S) (F) fair eyed.

Mugdhavadhū (S) (F) young and lovely.

Muhūrtā (S) (F) **1.** moment; instant. **3.** a space of time personified as the daughter of Dakṣa, the wife of Dharma or Manu and the mother of the Muhūrtas (*H. Purāṇa*).

Mūkāmbikā (S) (F) **1.** the silent mother. **3.** a shrine of a form of Durgā in north Cannore on the Mālābar coast in which only the lower portion of the goddess head is depicted.

Mukhamaṇḍī (S) (F) **1.** having a filled mouth. **3.** a mother attending on Skanda (*H. Purāṇa*).

Mukhanivāsinī (S) (F) **1.** dwelling in the mouth. **3.** another name for Sarasvatī.

Mukhaśrī (S) (F) **1.** beautiful face. **2.** with a beautiful face.

Muktabandhanā (S) (F) **1.** released from bonds. **2.** the Arabian Jasmine (*Jasminum sambac*).

Muktābhā (S) (F) with a pearly lustre; the Double Jasmine (*Jasminum sambac*).

Muktabuddhī (S) (F) with an emancipated mind.

Muktālatā (S) (F) a string of pearls.

Muktāli (S) (F) pearl necklace.

Muktāmbarī (S) (F) **1.** freed of clothes; wearing clothes of pearls. **3.** a rāga.

Muktāvalī (S) (F) **1.** a pearl necklace. **3.** the wife of Ćandraketu (*K. Sāgara*).

Mukti (S) (F) **1.** liberation; freedom. **3.** freedom personified as the wife of Satya (*H. Purāṇa*).

Muktikā (S) (F) a pearl.

Mukulikā (S) (F) a small blossom; a low humming made to a put a child to sleep.

Mukundā (S) (F) **1.** a gem; one who liberates. **3.** the wife of ṛṣi Vāćaknavī (*Bhā. Purāṇa*).

Mukuṭā (S) (F) **1.** wearing a crown. **3.** a mother attending on Skanda (*M. Bh.*).

Mūlatanī (S) (F) **1.** the root bodied. **2.** the original body. **3.** another name for Gaurī.

Muṇḍāmālinī (S) (F) **1.** garlanded with heads. **3.** a form of Durgā (*Mā. Purāṇa*).

Mundarī (S) (F) ring.

Muṇḍī (S) (F) **1.** bald. **3.** a mother in Skanda's retinue (*M. Bh.*).

Munī (S) (F) **1.** ascetic; inspired. **3.** a daughter of Dakṣa and wife of Kaśyapa and mother of the yakṣas and gandharvas.

Munia (S) (F) a small girl.

Munilakṣmī (S) (F) **1.** the treasure of an ascetic. **2.** knowledge.

Munipuṣpakā (S) (F) **1.** the flower of ascetics. **2.** the blossom of *Agati grandiflora*.

Munivatī (S) (F) **1.** sage like. **3.** a kinnarī (*K. Vyuha*).

Murā (S) (F) **1.** merciless; a fragrant plant. **3.** the wife of Nanda and mother of Ćandragupta (*V. Purāṇa*).

Murajā (S) (F) **1.** a great drum (*M. Bh.*) **3.** Kubera's wife.

Muralī (S) (F) **1.** flute; pipe. **2.** melodious; harmonious; sweet; enchanting.

Muralikā (S) (F) a small flute.

Murandalā (S) (F) **1.** encompassing. **3.** a river of ancient India (*A. Koṣa*); another name for the Narmadā river.

Mūrdhanyā (S) (F) **1.** highest; preeminent. **3.** mother of Vedaśiras (*V. Purāṇa*).

Mūrjā (S) (F) **1.** born of bondage; born of destruction. **3.** a wife of Kubera (*M. Bh.*).

Mūrkhalikā (S) (F) an arrow in the form of a bird's heart.

Murmurā (S) (F) **1.** ember. **3.** a river from which Agni the lord of fire originated (*M. Bh.*).

Mūrti (S) (F) **1.** material form; idol; statue. **2.** embodiment; incarnation; image. **3.** a daughter of Dakṣa, wife of Dharma and the mother of Nara and Nārāyaṇa (*Bhā. Purāṇa*).

N

Nabhanū (S) (F) **1.** follower of the sky. **2.** one who moves towards the sky; a spring.

Nabhanyā (S) (F) **1.** springing forth from the heavens. **2.** ethereal; celestial; heavenly.

Nabhasarit (S) (F) **1.** sky river. **3.** the Ākāśgaṅgā or the celestial Gaṅgā, commonlyknown as the Milky Way.

Nabhaśćarī (S) (F) **1.** celestial; aerial. **2.** a god; a vidyādhara; bird; cloud; wind.

Nabhasindhu (S) (F) **1.** river of the sky. **2.** the Ākāśgaṅgā or the celestial Gaṅgā, commonly known as the Milky Way.

Nabhaśvātī (S) (F) **1.** born of the sky. **2.** lightning; thunder.

Nabhasvatī (S) (F) **1.** bearer of the sky; young. **2.** the wind. **3.** the wife of Antardhāna and the wife of Havirdhāna.

Nabhoreṇu (S) (F) **1.** sky dust. **2.** the mist.

Naḍantikā (S) (F) **1.** reed destroying. **3.** a river of ancient India (*V. Purāṇa*).

Nadvalā (S) (F) **1.** a quantity of reeds. **3.** a daughter of Prajāpati Vairāja and wife of Manu Ćākṣuṣa.

Nāgabhaginī (S) (F) **1.** sister of a snake. **3.** another name for Manasā.

Nāgamātṛ (S) (F) **1.** mother of serpents. **3.** another name for the goddess Manasā.

Nāgamitrā (S) (F) **1.** friend of the serpents. **3.** a Buddhist disciple of Rahulamitra of Nālandā; another name for Śiva.

Nāgammā (Tamil) (F) **1.** mother of snakes. **3.** a poetess.

Naganadī (S) (F) mountain river.

Naganāmana (S) (F) mark of a mountain; the Sacred Basil plant (*Ocimum sanctum*).

Naganandinī (S) (F) **1.** mountain born. **3.** another name for Pārvatī.

Nāganikā (S) (F) serpent maiden.

Nāgāñjanā (S) (F) elephant.

Nāgapuṣpikā (S) (F) flower of the mountains; the Yellow Jasmine (*Jasminum big-noniaceum*); *Crinum asiaticum.*

Nagariṇī (S) (F) civic; civilized; urban.

Nāgaśrī (S) (F) **1.** the wealth of the serpents. **3.** wife of King Dharmadatta of Kosala.

Nāgavīthī (S) (F) **1.** a row of serpents; the moon's path; the serpent's path. **3.** a daughter of Dharma and Yāmī (*V. Purāṇa*).

Nāgendrī (S) (F) **1.** daughter of the mountain lord; daughter of the serpent lord; daughter of the king of elephants; coming through the Himālayas. **3.** a river of ancient India (*S. Māhatmya*).

Nāgijā (S) (F) **1.** daughter of the serpent. **3.** the blossom of *Mesua roxburghii.*

Nāgilā (S) (F) best among serpents; best among elephants.

Naginā (S) (F) obtained from a mountain; jewel; gem.

Nāgnajitī (S) (F) **1.** one who conquers mendicants. **3.** the daughter of Nagnajit and a wife of Kṛṣṇa (*M. Bh.*).

Naidhruvā (S) (F) **1.** near perfection; nearing eternity. **3.** another name for Pārvatī.

Naikabāhū (S) (F) **1.** many armed. **3.** another name for Pārvatī.

Naimā (S) (F) **1.** belonging to one. **2.** striving for the absolute.

Naimloć**anī** (S) (F) **1.** with twinkling eyes. **3.** the city of Varuṇa situated on the western mountain Manasottara.

Nainikā (S) (F) pupil of the eye.

Nākanadī (S) (F) **1.** river of heaven. **3.** the Ākāśgaṅgā or the celestial Gaṅgā also known as the Milky Way.

Nākanārī (S) (F) **1.** heavenly woman. **2.** an apsarā.

Nākavanitā (S) (F) **1.** heavenly woman. **2.** an apsarā.

Nakṣatramālā (S) (F) **1.** a garland of stars. **2.** a necklace of 27 pearls.

Naktamukhā (S) (F) **1.** preface of the night. **2.** the evening.

Naktī (S) (F) night.

Nakulī (S) (F) **1.** a female mongoose; the *Salmalia malabarica*; Saffron (*Crocus sativus*). **3.** a wife of Śiva (*A. Koṣa*).

Naladā (S) (F) **1.** the nectar of a flower; Spikenard (*Nardostachys jatamans*). **3.** a daughter of Raudrāśva (*H. Purāṇa*); an apsarā (*A. Veda*).

Nālakinī (S) (F) **1.** a multitude of lotuses. **2.** a lotus lake.

Nalamī (S) (F) fragrant nectar; the lute of Śiva.

Nalapriyā (S) (F) **1.** beloved of King Nala. **3.** another name for Queen Damayantī.

Nalinī (S) (F) **1.** the Lotus (*Nelumbium speciosum*); Water Lily (*Nymphaea alba*); a multitude of lotuses. **2.** beautiful; fragrant; sacred; dear to the gods. **3.** a wife of Ajamīḍha and the mother of Nīla (*Bhā. Purāṇa*); a tributary of the Gaṅgā (*Bhā. Purāṇa*).

Namitā (S) (F) **1.** bowed; bent down. **2.** one who worships; a devotee; humble; modest; submissive.

Namratā (S) (F) **1.** bowing; humility; submissiveness; meekness. **2.** humble; modest; submissive.

Namyā (S) (F) **1.** to be bowed to; venerable. **2.** the night.

Nānakī (S) (F) sister of Nānaka.

Nandā (S) (F) **1.** delight; prosperity; happiness. **3.** felicity personified as a wife of Harṣa (*M. Bh.*); a daughter of Vibhīṣana; the mother of the 10th Arhat of the present Avasarpiṇī (*J.S. Koṣa*); a river flowing near Kubera's city Alakā (*Bh. Purāṇa*); the 6th day of the light half of the month (*V's B. Saṃhitā*); an apsarā (*H. Purāṇa*); another name for Durgā.

Nandādevī (S) (F) **1.** goddess of happiness. **3.** a lofty Himālayan peak.

Nandanā (S) (F) **1.** gladdening; a daughter. **3.** a divine garden of the gods (*M. Bh.*); Indra's paradise (*A. Veda*); another name for Durgā.

Nandanamālā (S) (F) **1.** garland of delight. **3.** a garland worn by Kṛṣṇa (*Bhā. Purāṇa*).

Nandantī (S) (F) **1.** delighting. **2.** a daughter.

Nandarānī (S) (F) **1.** the wife of Nanda. **3.** another name for Yaśodā.

Nandayantī (S) (F) bestowing joy.

Nandī (S) (F) **1.** happiness. **3.** joy personified as a daughter of heaven, the wife of Kāma and the mother of Harṣa (*Bhā. Purāṇa*); another name for Durgā (*D. Purāṇa*); the city of Indra.

Nandighoṣa **1.** the music of joy. **3.** Arjuna's chariot (*M. Bh.*).

Nandikā (S) (F) **1.** pleasure giving. **3.** Indra's pleasure ground.

Nandinī (S) (F) **1.** delightful; a daughter. **3.** a Mātṛ attending on Śiva (*M. Bh.*); a fabulous cow owned by Vasiṣṭha and was the mother of Surabhī (*M. Bh.*); another name for Durgā, Gaṅgā and the river Bāṇanāsa; Garden Cress (*Lepidum sativum*).

Nanditā (S) (F) one who pleases.

Narā (S) (F) **1.** woman. **3.** wife of Uśīnara and mother of Nara (*Agni Purāṇa*).

Naradattā (S) (F) **1.** given by man. **3.** a goddess executing the commands of the 20th Arhat of the present Avasarpiṇī (*L. Vistara*); one of the 16 vidyādevīs (*J.S. Koṣa*).

Narādhārā (S) (F) **1.** supporting men. **3.** another name for the earth.

Nārāyaṇi (S) (F) **1.** belonging to Nārāyaṇa, Viṣṇu or Kṛṣṇa. **3.** the army of Kṛṣṇa that was given to Duryodhana to fight the Mahābhārata war (*M. Bh.*); another name for Durgā, Lakṣmī, Gaṅgā and Gaṇḍakī; *Aspargus racemosus.*

Nārī (S) (F) **1.** woman. **3.** a daughter of Meru and wife of Agnīdhra's son Nābhi (*Bhā. Purāṇa*).

Nāristhā (S) (F) **1.** dear to a woman. **3.** the Arabian Jasmine (*Jasminum sambac*).

Narmadā (S) (F) **1.** pleasure giver. **3.** a river personified as the wife of Purukutsa, the mother of Trasadasyu, a reincarnation of Tapatī and daughter of the sun and depicted as a goddess who lives in the palace of Varuṇa (*Ś. Purāṇa*); a gandharvī (*V. Rāmāyaṇa*).

Narmadyuti (S) (F) bright with joy; happy; merry.

Nartakī (S) (F) dancer.

Nāsikā (S) (F) **1.** nostril. **3.** the mother of the 2 aśvins (*M. Bh.*).

Natā (S) (F) **1.** bowed; curved. **3.** daughter of Śuki and mother of Vinatā.

Nāṭakī (S) (F) **1.** dancer. **3.** the court of Indra (*A. Koṣa*).

Natī (S) (F) modesty; humility.

Nāṭikā (S) (F) **1.** consisting of dancers and/or actors. **3.** a rāgiṇī.

Naukarṇī (S) (F) **1.** the helm of a ship. **3.** a Mātṛ attending on Skanda (*M. Bh.*).

Navamallikā (S) (F) **1.** the new creeper; the Jasmine (*Jasminum sambac*). **3.** a daughter of King Dharmavardhana of Śrāvastī.

Navamī (S) (F) the 9th; the 9th day of a lunar half month.

Navāṅgi (S) (F) **1.** new body. **2.** with a fresh body; a refreshing and exquisite woman.

Navikā (S) (F) new; fresh; young.

Navīnā (S) (F) new; fresh; young.

Naviṣṭhi (S) (F) **1.** song of praise. **2.** a hymn.

Navīyā (S) (F) new; a young.

Nayajā (S) (F) daughter of wisdom.

Nayanā (S) (F) **1.** of eye. **2.** the pupil of the eye.

Nayanaprīti (S) (F) delighting the eye.

Nayanatārā (S) (F) **1.** star of one's eye. **2.** beloved; very dear to one.

Nayavatī (S) (F) **1.** bearer of prudence. **2.** one who is prudent.

Nehā (S) (F) **1.** loving. **2.** affectionate.

Netramatī (S) (F) **1.** having eyes. **2.** observant; with discriminatory powers; wise. **3.** a south Indian river.

Netravatī (S) (F) **1.** having eyes. **2.** observant; with discriminatory powers; wise. **3.** another name for Lakṣmī.

Nibhā (S) (F) resembling; like; similar.

Niboddhri (S) (F) knowing; wise.

Nićikā (S) (F) **1.** consisting of parts. **2.** consists of all parts; constitutes a whole; perfect; an excellent cow.

Nīćitā (S) (F) **1.** covered; full of; flowing down. **3.** a holy river of ancient India (*M. Bh.*); another name for the Gaṅgā.

Niddhā (S) (F) **1.** having a treasure; determined. **2.** giving; endeavouring.

Nidhyāna (S) (F) intuition; sight.

Nidhyāti (S) (F) meditation; reflection.

Nidī (S) (F) to shine upon; to bestow.

Nīhārikā (S) (F) **1.** misty. **3.** the Milky Way.

Nikṛti (S) (F) **1.** baseness; dishonesty; wickedness. **3.** one of the 8 vasus (*H. Purāṇa*); a daughter of Adharma and Lobha (*M. Bh.*).

Nikṣubhā (S) (F) **1.** not excitable. **3.** an apsarā consort of Sūrya and mother of men who married into the Bhoja family (*Bh. Purāṇa*).

Nīlā (S) (F) **1.** blue; the Indigo plant (*Indigofera tinctoria*). **3.** a daughter of Kaśyapa and Keśinī (*Br. Purāṇa*); a Gopikā who was a friend of Kṛṣṇa.

Nīlagandhikā (S) (F) the blue ruby.

Nīlagaṅgā (S) (F) **1.** blue river. **3.** a river with pure blue water and considered as pious as Gaṅgā.

Nīlākṣā (S) (F) blue eyed.

Nīlakuntalā (S) (F) **1.** blue earrings; with blue earrings; with a blue lock of hair. **3.** a friend of Durgā.

Nīlamaṇī (S) (F) blue gem; sapphire.

Nīlanīraja (S) (F) Blue Water lily (*Nymphaea alba*).

Nīlañjanā (S) (F) antimony; lightning.

Nīlāñjasā (S) (F) **1.** blue hued lightning. **3.** an apsarā.

Nīlavastrā (S) (F) **1.** blue clad. **3.** another name for Durgā.

Nīlī (S) (F) **1.** Indigo (*Indigofera tinctoria*); antimony. **3.** a goddess; the 2nd wife of King Ajamīḍha and the mother of Duṣyanta and Parameṣṭhī (*M. Bh.*); a rāgiṇī; a river (*M. Bh.*).

Nīlimā (S) (F) blue.

Nilimpikā (S) (F) little cow.

Nīlinī (S) (F) **1.** the Indigo plant (*Indigofera tinctoria*); a type of Convulvulus with blue blossoms. **3.** a wife of Śunaśśepa and mother of Śānti (*A. Purāṇā*).

Nimā (S) (F) **1.** to measure to adjust. **3.** the mother of Kabir.

Nimiṣā (S) (F) the twinkling of an eye.

Nimloćā (S) (F) **1.** the setting of the sun. **3.** an apsarā (*K. Sāgara*).

Nimruktī (S) (F) sunset.

Nīnā (S) (F) ornamented; slender.

Ninī (S) (F) to offer as sacrifice; to accomplish.

Nipā (S) (F) to guard; to watch over.

Nīrā (S) (F) consisting of water; juice; liquor.

Nīrajā (S) (F) **1.** water born. **2.** water lily; pearl.

Nīrajākṣī (S) (F) **1.** lotus eyed. **2.** beautiful.

Nīrājitā (S) (F) **1.** illuminated. **2.** shone upon consecrated.

Nirañjanā (S) (F) **1.** spotless. **2.** pure; the day of full moon. **3.** another name for Durgā.

Nirbha (S) (F) to shining forth; appearance; progress.

Nirbhāśitā (S) (F) illumined.

Nirguṇḍi (S) (F) the root of a lotus.

Nirikṣā (S) (F) unseen; not seen before; expectation; hope.

Nirjarī (S) (F) not becoming old; young; fresh; immortal; ambrosia.

Nirmārṣṭi (S) (F) **1.** washing; ablution. **3.** a wife of Dusśaha (*Ma. Purāṇa*).

Nirṛti (S) (F) **1.** calamity; evil; destruction. **3.** the wife of Adharma and mother of Bhaya, Mahābhaya and Antaka (*M. Bh.*).

Nīruvindhyā (S) (F) **1.** water from the Vindhya mountain. **3.** a river.

Nirvā (S) (F) blowing like wind; refreshing; exhilarating.

Nirvāṇī (S) (F) **1.** goddess of bliss. **3.** a deity who executes the commands of the 16th Arhat of the present Avasarpiṇī (*J.S. Koṣa*).

Niryūhā (S) (F) prominence; chaplet; crest; pinnacle; head.

Niśā (S) (F) **1.** night; vision; dream. **3.** a wife of Agni Bhānu (*M. Bh.*).

Niśādi (S) (F) twilight.

Niśājala (S) (F) **1.** water of the night. **2.** dew.

Nisamā (S) (F) matchless.

Niśāpuṣpa (S) (F) **1.** night flower. **3.** the White Water lily (*Nymphaea alba*).

Niśćalā (S) (F) **1.** immovable; fixed. **3.** another name for the earth.

Nisćirā (S) (F) **1.** coming forth; appearing. **3.** a river glorified in the Purāṇas.

Niśī (S) (F) exciting; strengthening.

Nisidh (S) (F) gift; oblation.

Niśītā (S) (F) night.

Niṣkā (S) (F) **1.** undeceitful; pure; honest. **2.** a golden ornament for the neck; a golden vessel. **3.** 6th of a pound of gold (*M. Smṛti*).

Niṣkuṭikā (S) (F) **1.** a pleasure grove near a house. **3.** a Mātṛ attending Skanda (*Sk. Purāṇa*).

Niṣṇā (S) (F) clever; skilful.

Niṣṭhā (S) (F) firmness; faith; determination; loyalty; fidelity; devotion.

Niṣṭigrī (S) (F) **1.** thundering and raining. **3.** Indra's mother (*K. Sāgara*).

Nītā (S) (F) led; guided; well behaved; modest; correct.

Nitambinī (S) (F) with beautiful hips.

Nithā (S) (F) carried; red; way; stratagem.

Nītikā (S) (F) moral person; a guide; a leader.

Nityā (S) (F) **1.** eternal. **2.** constant and indispensable. **3.** a tāntric Śakti; another name for Durgā and Manasā.

Nityaśrī (S) (F) with eternal beauty.

Nityasundarī (S) (F) eternally beautiful.

Nityayauvanā (S) (F) **1.** ever youthful. **3.** another name for Draupadī.

Nīva (S) (F) to become fat.

Niveditā (S) (F) offered to god.

Niyati (S) (F) **1.** fate; destiny; restraint; religious duty. **3.** the daughter of Meru and wife of Vidhātā, she was the mother of Prāṇa, and became a goddess after her death, she sits at Brahmā's court (*M. Bh.*); another name for Durgā (*D. Purāṇa*).

Niyutsā (S) (F) **1.** warrior. **3.** the wife of Praṣṭāva and mother of Vibhu (*M. Bh.*).

Nṛpāṅganā (S) (F) **1.** of a king. **2.** princess; queen.

Nukrī (S) (F) the bird, Indian Courser (*Cursorius coromandelicus*).

Nūpura (S) (F) **1.** ornament for the toes and ankles; anklet. **3.** a descendant of Ikṣvāku (*M. Bh.*).

Nūpurottamā (S) (F) **1.** with the best anklets. **2.** best dancer. **3.** a kinnarī (*H. Purāṇa*).

Nuti (S) (F) praise; worship; reverence.

Nyāyikā (S) (F) logician.

O

Odatī (S) (F) **1.** refreshing. **2.** the dawn.

Oghavatī (S) (F) **1.** possessing current. **2.** a stream that flows rapidly. **3.** daughter of King Oghavāna and wife of Sudarśana the son of Agni; one of the 7 Sarasvatī rivers of the world, Oghavatī was brought to the Kuruksetra and Bhīṣma lay on his bed of arrows at her banks (*M. Bh.*).

Ojasvī (S) (F) brave; bright; splendid.

Ojasvinī (S) (F) brave; bright; energetic; vigorous; shining; powerful.

Ojobalā (S) (F) **1.** having power. **3.** a deity of the Bodhi tree.

Om (S) (F) creation; development and destruction; essence of life; the sacred syllable which is the seed of all mantras; assent; so be it; the sound is a combination of 'A' which signifies Viṣṇu, 'U' for Śiva and 'M' signifying Brahmā, the sound is called 'Praṇava' (essence of life) or 'Brahman' (ultimate essence).

Omalā (F) bestower of the Om; the sacred word for the earth; bestower of birth, life and death; earth.

Omīśā (S) (F) goddess of the sacred syllable; goddess of birth, life and death.

Omkārā (S) (F) **1.** the syllable Om; an auspicious beginning. **3.** a Buddhist Śakti.

Omvatī (S) (F) possessing the power of the Om; sacred.

Oṣadhi (S) (F) **1.** light containing; medicine; herb; medicinal herbs. **3.** plants that possess a healing power (*Ṛg Veda*); a tutelary goddess whose shrine is at Uttarakuru (*Ma. Purāṇa*).

P

Padmā (S) (F) **1.** the lotus; hued one. **3.** the mother of Munisuvrata; a daughter of Bṛhadratha and wife of Kalki (*V. Purāṇa*); a devī (*D. Purāṇa*); another name for goddess Manasā and Lakṣmī.

Padmabālā (S) (F) daughter of the lotus.

Padmagṛhā (S) (F) **1.** lotus housed; living in a lotus. **3.** another name for Lakṣmī.

Padmajā (S) (F) **1.** born of a lotus. **3.** another name for Lakṣmī.

Padmakarā (S) (F) **1.** with a lotus in hand. **3.** another name for Śrī.

Padmalāñćanā (S) (F) **1.** marked by lotuses. **2.** surrounded by lotuses. **3.** another name for Lakṣmī, Sarasvatī and Tārā.

Padmālayā (S) (F) **1.** living in a lotus. **3.** another name for Lakṣmī.

Padmamālinī (S) (F) **1.** lotus garlanded. **3.** another name for Lakṣmī.

Padmamayī (S) (F) made of lotus flowers.

Padmanā (S) (F) **1.** lotus faced. **3.** another name for Lakṣmī and Sarasvatī.

Padmāñjalī (S) (F) an offering of lotuses.

Padmaprabhā (S) (F) **1.** with a light of the lotus. **2.** lotus coloured. **3.** a daughter of Mahādanṣtra (*K. Sāgara*).

Padmapriyā (S) (F) **1.** one who loves lotuses. **3.** another name for Manasā.

Padmarati (S) (F) lover of lotuses.

Padmarūpā (S) (F) **1.** with the beauty of a lotus. **3.** another name for Lakṣmī.

Padmasaugandhikā (S) (F) as fragrant as the lotus; abounding in lotuses.

Padmasnuṣā (S) (F) **1.** dwelling in the lotus. **3.** another name for Gaṅgā, Lakṣmī and Durgā.

Padmaśrī (S) (F) **1.** divine lotus; as beautiful as a lotus. **3.** a Bodhisattva (*B. Literature*).

Padmavarṇā (S) (F) **1.** lotus clothed; lotus coloured. **3.** another name for Lakṣmī.

Padmāvatī (S) (F) **1.** full of lotus flowers. **3.** a wife of Aśoka (*Bhā. Purāṇa*); a mother in Skanda's retinue (*M. Bh.*); a Jaina deity (*J.S. Koṣa*); a wife of King Śṛgāla (*H. Purāṇa*); a wife of Yudhiṣṭhira (*R. Taraṅgiṇī*); a wife of Jayadeva; a wife of Vīrabāhu; a river which is an incarnation of Mahālakṣmī; the wife of Emperor Udayana; a mother in Skanda's train (*M. Bh.*); a daughter of King Satyaketu of Vidarbha who was the wife of Ugrasena and the mother of Kaṅsa (*P. Purāṇa*); the queen of Rajagraha and mother of Jaina Tīrthaṅkara Munisuvrata; a Jaina deity; another name for Lakṣmī and Manasā.

Padminī (S) (F) lotus (*Nelumbium speciosum*); an assemblage of lotuses.

Padminīkā (S) (F) a multitude of lotuses.

Padmodbhavā (S) (F) **1.** sprung from a lotus. **3.** another name for Manasā.

Pahāḍī (S) (F) hillock; a rāgiṇī.

Pajasvati (S) (F) firm; strong; brilliant.

Pakṣālikā (S) (F) **1.** full of feathers. **3.** a mother attending on Skanda (*M. Bh.*).

Pakṣiṇī (S) (F) day of the full moon; a female bird.

Palaksī (S) (F) white.

Palālā (S) (F) **1.** a stalk; a straw. **3.** one of the 7 mothers of Skanda (*M. Bh.*).

Palāśinī (S) (F) **1.** covered with foliage. **3.** a river (*M. Bh.*).

Pālitā (S) (F) **1.** guarded; protected. **2.** cherished. **3.** a mother in Skanda's retinue (*M. Bh.*).

Pallavī (S) (F) sprouting; a young shoot.

Pallavikā (S) (F) resembling a blossom; a scarf.

Pañćaćūḍā (S) (F) **1.** 5 crested. **3.** an apsarā (*V. Rāmāyaṇa*).

Pañćaḍākinī (S) (F) **1.** the 5th ḍākini; with 5 deities of energy. **3.** an attendant of the devī (*D. Bh. Purāṇa*).

Pañćajanā (S) (F) **1.** bearer of 5 sons. **3.** a daughter of Viśvarūpa and wife of Bharata (*Bhā. Purāṇa*).

Pañćajanī (S) (F) **1.** made of 5 elements. **3.** a daughter of Viśvarupa and wife of Ṛṣabha, she was the mother of Sumati,

Rāṣṭrabhṛt, Sudarśana, Āvarana and Dhūmraketu (*Bhāgavata*).

Pāñćālī (S) (F) **1.** princess of the Pāñćālas. **2.** companion of 5; a doll. **3.** a rāga; another name for Draupadī.

Pāñćālikā (S) (F) princess of Pāñćāla; doll.

Pañćānanī (S) (F) **1.** consort of Pañćānana. **3.** another name for Durgā.

Pañćavaktrā (S) (F) **1.** 5 faced. **3.** another name for Durgā.

Pañćavallabhā (S) (F) **1.** loved by 5. **3.** another name for Draupadī.

Paṇḍā (S) (F) wisdom; knowledge; learning.

Pāndalameghā (S) (F) **1.** pale cloud. **3.** a nāga maid (*K. Vyuha*).

Pāṇḍarā (S) (F) **1.** pale. **2.** white; white yellow. **3.** a Buddhist Śakti or female energy; Jasmine blossom.

Pāṇḍurā (S) (F) **1.** yellow lady. **3.** a Buddhist deity (*G's Dharmaśāstra*).

Pāṇḍuraṅgā (S) (F) **1.** white coloured. **3.** a goddess.

Pāṇḍuśarmilā (S) (F) **1.** wife of the sons of Paṇḍu. **3.** another name for Draupadī.

Pāṇīhatā (S) (F) **1.** created by hand. **3.** a lake created by the gods for Gautama Buddha (*L. Vistara*).

Paniṣṭhi (S) (F) admiration; praise.

Pāñjari (S) (F) **1.** impression of full hand. **3.** another name for the Narmadā river.

Pankajākṣī (S) (F) lotus-eyed.

Paṅkajinī (S) (F) abounding in lotuses.

Pannā (S) (F) emerald.

Panū (S) (F) admiration.

Pāṇyā (S) (F) admired; astonishing; glorious; praiseworthy; excellent.

Pāpaghnī (S) (F) **1.** destroying sin. **3.** a river.

Paramā (S) (F) that which is transcendent; the perfect woman.

Paramāṅganā (S) (F) a supreme woman; an excellent or beautiful woman.

Paramātmikā (S) (F) possessing a supreme soul; the supreme; the highest; the greatest.

Parameśvarī (S) (F) **1.** supreme goddess. **3.** another name for Durgā.

Parapuṣṭā (S) (F) **1.** female cuckoo. **3.** a daughter of a king of Kauśāmbi (*K. Sāgara*).

Paraśuhastā (S) (F) **1.** with an axe in hand. **3.** an attendant of the devī (*Ś. Purāṇa*).

Pārāvatī (S) (F) **1.** coming from a distance. **2.** a song peculiar to cowherds. **3.** a river (*H. Purāṇa*).

Parighrā (S) (F) to cover with kisses.

Parimugdha (S) (F) bewitchingly lovely; extremely lovely.

Pariniṣṭhā (S) (F) dwelling at the top; highest point; complete knowledge; complete accomplishment.

Pariṇītā (S) (F) led around; complete; a married woman.

Paripūrnasahasraćandrāvati (S) (F) **1.** possessing a thousand moons; **3.** another name for Indra's wife.

Pariśobhitā (S) (F) **1.** adorned. **2.** beautiful. **3.** an apsarā and a gandharvī (*K. Sāgara*).

Parisraja (S) (F) a garland.

Parivīta (S) (F) **1.** extremely free; extremely liked; extremely useless. **3.** the bow of Brahmā (*Ṛg Veda*).

Paramāṅganā (S) (F) excellent woman.

Parṇāśā (S) (F) **1.** feeding on leaves. **2.** *Cedrela toona*. **3.** a river personified by an apsarā of Varuṇa's court (*M. Bh.*).

Parṇinī (S) (F) **1.** winged; plumed; leafy. **3.** an apsarā (*H. Purāṇa*).

Parokṣī (S) (F) beyond perception; mysterious; undiscernable.

Pārthivī (S) (F) **1.** daughter of the earth. **3.** another name for Sitā and Lakṣmī (*Bhā. Purāṇa*).

Pārul (S) (F) practical; beautiful; gracious.

Paruṣṇī (S) (F) **1.** violent; severe. **3.** a river now called Rāvi.

Parvadhi **1.** container of time periods. **3.** another name for the moon.

Parvaṇī (S) (F) the period of the change of the moon; day of the full moon.

Parvatarājakanyā (S) (F) **1.** daughter of the king of mountains. **3.** another name for Pārvatī.

Parvatavāsinī (S) (F) **1.** dwelling in mountains. **3.** another name for Durgā (*D. Bh. Purāṇa*).

Pārvatī (S) (F) **1.** of the mountains. **2.** mountain stream. **3.** the wife of Śiva who was the daughter of Himavata the king of the mountains and Menā, she is the reincarnation of Satī — an aspect of Mahāmāya or the eternal Śakti, she is known by different names and worshipped in different forms, the more prominent of which are Kālī; Gaurī, Umā, Īśvarī, Aparṇa, Ćaṇḍikā, Bhavānī, Durgā, Bhairavi, Ambikā, Dākṣāyaṇī, Girijā, Kātyāyānī, Rudrāṇī and Ćāmuṇḍā; Cashewnut (*Anacardium occidentale*); *Lannea grandis*; *Woodfordia fruticosa*; Common Flax (*Linum usitatissimum*).

Parviṇī (S) (F) festival; a holiday.

Pāśāinī (S) (F) **1.** controller of thirst. **3.** a river (*M. Bh.*).

Pastyā (S) (F) **1.** dwelling. **3.** a goddess of household affairs (*Ṛg Veda*).

Paśudā (S) (F) **1.** giver of cattle. **3.** a mother in Skanda's retinue (*M. Bh.*).

Pātalā (S) (F) 1. pale red. **2.** pink. **3.** a form of Durgā; a form of Dākṣāyaṇī; the trumpet flower (*Bignonia suaveolens*).

Pāṭalī (S) (F) **1.** the trumpet flower (*Bignonia suaveolens*). **3.** a daughter of King Mahendravarman.

Pataṅganā (S) (F) butterfly.

Patangī (S) (F) **1.** flying. **3.** a wife of Tārkṣa and mother of the flying animals.

Patangikā (S) (F) small bird; a little bee.

Paṭeśvarī (S) (F) **1.** goddess of clothes. **3.** another name for Durgā.

Pāthamañjarī (S) (F) **1.** decorating the path. **2.** one who makes the path easy. **3.** a rāgiṇī.

Pāthojinī (S) (F) a collection of lotus plants.

Pathyā (S) (F) **1.** of path; way; road. **3.** the goddess of travellers and paths (*K. Sāgara*); *Mimordica balsamina*; Black Myrobalan (*Terminalia chebula*).

Pātrī (S) (F) **1.** vessel. **2.** small furnace; competent; worthy; protector. **3.** another name for Durgā.

Paṭṭadevī (S) (F) **1.** turbaned woman. **2.** the main queen of a king.

Pattradevī (S) (F) **1.** plumed lady; lady of leaves. **3.** a Buddhist deity; another name for Dhanalakṣmī.

Pattralekhā (S) (F) decorated with lines of fragrant spices.

Pattrapuṣpā (S) (F) flowers and leaves conjoined; made up of flowers and leaves; the Sacred Basil plant (*Ocimum sanctum*).

Paṭumatī (S) (F) with a clever mind.

Paulomī (S) (F) **1.** daughter of Puloman. **3.** the wife of Indra; the wife of Bhṛgu (*Vā. Purāṇa*).

Pauralikā (S) (F) **1.** pleasant to citizens. **3.** a rāga.

Pauravī (S) (F) **1.** descended from Purū. **3.** a wife of Vasudeva (*Bhāgavata*); a wife of Yudhiṣthira and mother of Devaka (*Bhāgavata*); a rāga.

Paurṇamī (S) (F) day of full moon.

Pauśṭī (S) (F) **1.** strong; satisfied; voluptuous; **3.** the wife of King Purū and the mother of Pravīra, Iśvara and Raudrāśva (*M. Bh.*).

Pavākā (S) (F) **1.** purifier. **2.** storm; whirlwind.

Pāvakārćis (S) (F) a flash of fire.

Pāvakī (S) (F) **1.** purifying. **3.** the Vedic name of Sarasvatī; the wife of Agni (*M. Bh.*).

Pāvanī (S) (F) **1.** holy; pure; purifying. **2.** Sacred Basil (*Ocimum sanctum*); water; the Rudrākṣa seed. **3.** another name for the goddess Gaṅgā.

Pāvīrāvī (S) (F) daughter of lightning; thunder.

Pavitrā (S) (F) **1.** pure; holy; sacred; beneficient. **2.** Sacred Basil (*Ocimum sanctum*); Saffron; the Pippala tree. **3.** a river (*M. Bh.*).

Pavitravatī (S) (F) **1.** cleansing; purifying. **3.** a river (*Bhā. Furāṇa*).

Pāyala (S) (F) **1.** of the foot. **2.** anklet; strength.

Payodā (S) (F) **1.** giver of water; milk giver. **3.** a mother in Skanda's retinue (*M. Bh.*).

Payoṣṇī (S) (F) **1.** milky. **3.** a holy river starting from the Vindhya mountains (*M. Bh.*).

Pedari (S) (F) **1.** with a protruding stomach. **2.** grinder; coverer. **3.** a female deity (*J.S. Koṣa*).

Pelavā (S) (F) delicate; fine; soft; tender.

Perantālu (S) (F) goddess of virginity.

Peśanī (S) (F) well formed; beautiful.

Phalāhārī (S) (F) **1.** eating fruits. **3.** another name for Durgā.

Phalakāvana (S) (F) **1.** heavenly forest. **2.** a place that has been consecrated by the prayers and sacrifices of devotees. **3.** a forest sacred to Sarasvatī.

Phalakṛṣṇa (S) (F) **1.** with black fruit. **3.** the Caraunda plant (*Carissa carandas*) (*M. Bh.*).

Phalamdā (S) (F) **1.** giving fruit. **3.** a female gandharva (*H. Purāṇd*).

Phalavatī (S) (F) **1.** fruitful. **2.** successful. **3.** a twig of a thorn tree; a fruit bearing plant.

Phalinī (S) (F) **1.** fruitful. **3.** another name for the Priyaṅgu creeper; *Aglaia odoratissima*; Bottle Gourd (*Lagenaria vulgaris*).

Phalyā (S) (F) flower; bud.

Phaṇipriya (S) (F) **1.** beloved of the hooded ones. **2.** wind.

Phullāmbikā (S) (F) woman; a bloom; a woman in full bloom.

Phullanalini (S) (F) a lotus in full bloom.

Phullarā (S) (F) **1.** blooming woman; woman full of grace. **3.** the wife of Kālaketu (*Kau. Upaniṣad*).

Pcchilā (S) (F) **1.** slimy; slippery. **3.** a river of North India (*M. Bh.*).

Picuvaktrā (S) (F) **1.** with thick lips. **3.** a yoginī (*H. Koṣa*).

Pikī (S) (F) Indian Cuckoo (*Cuculus varius*).

Pikkā (S) (F) a weight approximately equal to the weight of 13 pearls; a string of 13 pearls.

Pīlā (S) (F) **1.** slopping. **3.** an apsarā.

Pīlak (S) (F) yellow coloured; Golden Oriole.

Pilpilā (S) (F) **1.** impelling again and again; inciting again and again. **3.** another name for Lakṣmī.

Pinākinī (S) (F) **1.** bow shaped; with the bow. **3.** a river (*H. Purāṇa*).

Piṇḍinī (S) (F) **1.** receiving oblations. **3.** an apsarā (*Bhā. Purāṇa*).

Piṅgā (S) (F) **1.** yellow. **2.** bowstring; yellow pigment; tawny; turmeric; saffron. **3.** another name for Durgā.

Piṅgākṣī (S) (F) **1.** tawny eyed. **3.** a deity presiding over the family; a mother in Skanda's retinue (*H. Purāṇa*).

Piṅgalā (S) (F) **1.** of yellow hue; golden; fiery; reddish brown. **3.** the elephant of the south quarter; another name for Lakṣmī.

Piṅgaleśvarī (S) (F) **1.** goddess of the Piṅgala state. **3.** a form of Dākṣāyaṇī (*A. Koṣa*).

Piñjalā (S) (F) **1.** confused. **3.** a river of Purāṇic fame (*M. Bh.*).

Piśācā (S) (F) **1.** of yellow colour; corpse like in appearance; a ghost. **3.** a daughter of Dakṣa and mother of the Piśācs (*V. Purāṇa*).

Piśunā (S) (F) **1.** informing against; betraying. **2.** saffron. **3.** a river described as the Mandākinī (*Rāmāyaṇa*).

Pītadipā (S) (F) **1.** yellow light; of yellow hue. **3.** a Buddhist deity.

Pītayūthī (S) (F) an assemblage of yellow; yellow jasmine.

Pītikā (S) (F) saffron; Yellow Jasmine (*Jasminum humile*); honey; turmeric.

Pīvanārī (S) (F) **1.** fat; strong; robust; voluptuous. **3.** the wife of Vedaśiras (*H. Purāṇa*); a princess of Vidarbha (*Mā. Purāṇa*).

Pīvarā (S) (F) **1.** fat; stout. **3.** a daughter of the gandharva Huhu (*K. Sāgara*).

Pīvarī (S) (F) **1.** fat. **3.** the wife of Śuka the son of Vyāsa and the mother of Kṛṣṇa, Gauraprabha, Bhūri, Devaśruta and Kīrti (*M. Purāṇa*).

Pīvatī (S) (F) 1. swelling; overflowing; exuberant; abounding; increasing. 2. acceptor of scripture. 3. a mind born daughter of Dharma who was the wife of Śuka and mother of goddess Kīrtimatī (*M. Bh.*).

Pīyūṣakaṇikā (S) (F) nectar drop.

Plakṣajātā (S) (F) 1. rising near the fig tree. 3. a tributary of the Gaṅgā believed to be an incarnation of Sarasvatī (*M. Bh.*).

Plakṣavatī (S) (F) 1. surrounded by fig trees. 3. a river (*M. Bh.*); another name for the Sarasvatī river.

Potrī (S) (F) 1. purifier. 3. another name for Durgā.

Potriratha (S) (F) 1. hog-vehicled. 3. a female divinity; another name for Māyā.

Prabhā (S) (F) 1. light; splendour; radiance. 3. light personified variously as the wife of the sun or as wife of Kalpa and mother of Prātar, Madhyam and Sāya or as a form of Durgā in the disc of the sun (*H. Purāṇa*); a devī in the court of Brahmā (*M. Bh.*); an apsarā (*M. Bh.*); a daughter of Svarbhānu who married Āyus and was the mother of Nahuṣa (*Br. Purāṇa*); a wife of King Puṣpārṇa (*Bhāgavata*).

Prabhadrā (S) (F) 1. very noble; very gentle; charming; beautiful. 3. the wife of Karṇa's son (*M. Bh.*).

Prabhātā (S) (F) 1. goddess of dawn. 3. a wife of Dharma and mother of the vasus Pratyūṣa and Prabhāsa (*M. Bh.*).

Prabhātī (S) (F) the song of the morning.

Prabhāvalī (S) (F) 1. shining. 2. graceful; radiant. 3. a rāga.

Prabhāvatī (S) (F) 1. luminous; radiant. 2. splendid. 3. the daughter of Vajranābha and wife of Pradyumna (*Bhā. Purāṇa*); the daughter of Suvīra and wife of Marutta (*M. Purāṇa*); the mother of the 19th Arhat 6f the present Avasarpinī (*J.S. Koṣa*); a wife of Sūrya; a mother in Skanda's retinue (*M. Bh.*); a wife of King Ćitraratha of Aṅga (*M. Bh.*); a Buddhist deity (*L. Vistara*); an apsarā (*V. Purāṇa*).

Prabhūti (S) (F) arisen; well being; welfare; success; riches.

Praćaṇḍikā (S) (F) 1. very fiery. 3. a form of Durgā (*D. Purāṇa*).

Praćaṇḍogrā (S) (F) 1. with a burning anger. 3. a yoginī (*D. Purāṇa*).

Praćayikā (S) (F) gatherer; one who gathers flowers.

Prāćikā (S) (F) 1. driving. 2. a female falcon.

Praćodikā (S) (F) 1. inflamer. 3. the daughter of Niyojikā and granddaughter of Duhsaha (*M. Purāṇa*).

Prādhā (S) (F) 1. extremely distinguished. 2. supreme; eminent. 3. a daughter of Dakṣa and mother of apsarās and gandharvas (*M. Bh.*).

Pradhānā (S) (F) 1. chief; most important; original; source; intellect; understanding. 3. a Śakti.

Pradhī (S) (F) great intelligence.

Pradīpikā (S) (F) one that illuminates; torch; a small lamp.

Pradīpti (S) (F) light; lustre; radiance.

Pradveśi (S) (F) 1. one who hates. 3. the wife of Dīrghatamas (*Ṛg Veda*).

Pragalbhā (S) (F) 1. bold; confident. 3. another name for Durgā.

Pragati (S) (F) progress.

Praghasā (S) (F) 1. devourer. 3. a mother in Skanda's retinue (*M. Bh.*); a rākṣasī (*V. Rāmāyaṇa*).

Prahasantī (S) (F) 1. laughing; smiling. 3. Jasmine (*Jasminum officianale*).

Prajāgarā (S) (F) 1. fully awake; attentive. 3. an apsarā (*M. Bh.*).

Prajaktā (S) (F) mother of the people; goddess of creation.

Prajāpatī (S) (F) 1. lord of the people; lord of creation. 3. the sister of Mahāmāyā and foster mother of Gautama Buddha (*B. Literature*).

Prajāvatī (S) (F) 1. having many children. 2. mother. 3. the wife of Priyavrata (*Bhā. Purāṇa*); a tutelary deity of the Sumantus (*Var. Purāṇa*).

Prajñā (S) (F) 1. wisdom; intelligence; knowledge; discrimination. 3. wisdom personified as the goddess of arts and eloquence; a form of Sarasvatī.

Prajvālā (S) (F) inflamed; flame; light.

Prakāśikā (S) (F) one who enlightens; one that illuminates; bright; shining; illuminating; brilliant; celebrated; renowned.

Prakāśinī (S) (F) throwing light; making visible.

Prakhyā (S) (F) look; appearance; brightness; splendour; renown; fame; celebrity.

Prakīrtī (S) (F) highly celebrated; very famous; renowned; celebration; declaration.

Prākṛtī (S) (F) 1. original; primary substance. 3. nature as the personified will of the Supreme Spirit (*Ṛg Veda*).

Prālambikā (S) (F) one that hangs down; golden necklace; a pearl ornament.

Pramā (S) (F) basis; foundation; true knowledge.

Pramadā (S) (F) 1. joyous enchanting; dissolute; mad; intoxicated. 2. handsome; woman. 3. the zodiac sign of Virgo.

Pramadvarā (S) (F) 1. inattentive; careless. 2. proud of one's beauty. 3. the daughter of Menakā and the gandharva Viśvavasu, she was the wife of Ruru and mother of Śunaka *(M. Bh.)*.

Pramandanī (S) (F) 1. with a swan's gait. 3. an apsarā (*A. Veda*).

Pamāthā (S) (F) 1. pain. 2. mare like. 3. the wife of Kṣupa and mother of Vīra (*M. Purāṇa*).

Pramatha (S) (F) 1. one who harasses; torments. 3. an attendant of Skanda given to him by Yama (*M. Bh.*); a class of attendants of Śiva; a son of Dhṛtarāṣṭra (*M. Bh.*).

Pramathinī (S) (F) 1. exciting; tormenting. 3. an apsarā (*M. Bh.*).

Pramikā (S) (F) 1. highest; best; greatest. 2. one who fulfils desires and thereby gives desired form to devotees by fulfilling their ambition.

Pramīlā (S) (F) 1. lassitude; enervation; exhaustion from indolence. 3. the leader of the Strirājya who married Arjuna (*M. Bh.*).

Pramitī (S) (F) right perception; wisdom; prudence.

Pramloċā (S) (F) 1. with shy eyes. 3. an apsarā who was the consort of sage Kaṇḍu.

Pramohinī (S) (F) 1. enticing; infatuating. 3. a gandharva maiden.

Prāṇatī (S) (F) bending; salutation; reverence; obeisance.

Prāṇavatī (S) (F) full of life; living; strong; powerful.

Praṇayinī (S) (F) beloved; worshipper; devotee.

Praṇayitā (S) (F) animated; kept alive.

Prāṇśvarī (S) (F) goddess of life; very dear in life; beloved.

Praṇītā (S) (F) 1. led forward; conducted; advanced; promoted; produced; performed; executed; finished; written; composed; established. 2. a cup used for sacrifices; holy water. 3. a river (*A. Koṣa*).

Praṇīti (S) (F) conduct; leading; guidance.

Prāñjalī (S) (F) upright; respectful; joining the hollowed open hands as a mark of respect.

Prapāṭikā (S) (F) 1. one who manifests. 2. multiplying into many forms. 3. young shoot or sprout.

Prāpti (S) (F) 1. achievement; advent; occurrence; arrival; discovery obtainment. 3. the wife of Śama who was a son of Dharma (*M, Bh.*); a daughter of Jarāsandha (*H. Purāṇa*); a wife of Kansa (*Bhāgavata*).

Prārthanā (S) (F) prayer.

Prāśā (S) (F) ardent desire.

Prāsahā (S) (F) 1. force; power. 2. powerful. 3. the wife of Indra.

Praśamī (S) (F) 1. calmed; tranquil. 3. an apsarā (*M. Bh.*).

Prasannā (S) (F) pleasing; propitiating.

Praśastā (S) (F) 1. praised; happy; consecrated. 2. clear; calm. 3. a holy river (*M. Bh.*).

Praśasti (S) (F) fame; praise; glorification.

Prasattī (S) (F) satisfaction; clearness; brightness; purity.

Prasavitrī (S) (F) 1. impeller; vivifier. 3. daughter of Suryā.

Prasiddhī (S) (F) fame; accomplishment; success; attainment.

Praśuci (S) (F) extremely pure.

Prasūtī (S) (F) **1.** coming forth; appearance. **2.** child; offspring. **3.** a daughter of Svāyambhuva Manu and the wife of Dakṣa (*D. Bh. Purāṇa*).

Prasvāpiṇī (S) (F) **1.** inducing to sleep. **2.** making others sleep. **3.** a daughter of Satrājit and wife of Kṛṣṇa (*Bhā. Purāṇa*).

Pratāpī (S) (F) **1.** brilliant; majestic; powerful; glorious. **3.** the wife of Pramatī and the mother of Ruru (*D. Bh. Purāṇa*).

Pratibhā (S) (F) image; light; splendour; appearance; intelligence; understanding; thought; idea; wit.

Pratibhāvatī (S) (F) full of understanding; splendid; bright; intelligent; bold; ready witted.

Pratīcyā (S) (F) **1.** from the west; with foresight. **3.** a wife of Pulastya (*M. Bh.*).

Pratijnā (S) (F) acknowledgement; agreement; promise; vow; declaration.

Prātīkā (S) (F) **1.** symbolic; an image; beautiful. **2.** the Chinese Rose (*Hibiscus rosa sinesis*).

Pratimā (S) (F) image; likeness; symbol; idol.

Pratirupā (S) (F) **1.** image; likeness; agreeable; beautiful. **3.** a daughter of Meru (*Bh. Purāṇa*).

Pratiśruti (S) (F) answer; promise; assent.

Pratiṣṭhā (S) (F) **1.** steadfastness; stability. **2.** base; foundation; support; preeminence; fame; celebrity. **3.** a mother in Skanda's retinue (*M. Bh.*).

Prātṛ (S) (F) **1.** dawn; morning. **3.** the daughter of Dhātṛ and Rākā (*Ṛg Veda*).

Pratyaṅgirā (S) (F) **1.** *Acacia sirissa.* **3.** a tāntric form of Durgā.

Pravā (S) (F) **1.** blowing forth. **3.** a daughter of Dakṣa (*Vā. Purāṇa*).

Pravarā (S) (F) **1.** best. **2.** best among women. **3.** a river of Purāṇic fame (*M. Bh.*).

Prekṣā (S) (F) beholding; seeing; viewing.

Premā (S) (F) beloved; love; affection; kindness.

Premalatā (S) (F) the vine of love.

Premāvatī (S) (F) full of love.

Preraṇā (S) (F) direction; command.

Preṣṭhā (S) (F) dearest; most beloved.

Prītī (S) (F) **1.** pleasure; joy; affection; love; satisfaction. **3.** joy personified as a daughter of Dakṣa and as one of the 2 wives of Kāma (*H. Purāṇa*); a digit of the moon (*K. Sāgara*); a wife of sage Pulastya and the mother of Dattoli (*V. Purāṇa*).

Prītījuṣā (S) (F) **1.** loving; beloved. **3.** the wife of Aniruddha (*M. Purāṇa*).

Priyā (S) (F) **1.** beloved; dear. **3.** a daughter of Dakṣa (V. *Purāṇa*); Arabian Jasmine (*Jasminum sambac*); Kadamba tree (*Anthocephalus cadamba*).

Priyadarśikā (S) (F) good looking.

Priyadarśinī (S) (F) dear to the sight.

Priyadattā (S) (F) **1.** given with love. **3.** a mystical name for the earth.

Priyakāriṇī (S) (F) **1.** doer of pleasing acts. **3.** the mother of Mahāvira (*J. S. Koṣa*).

Priyālā (S) (F) **1.** bestowing pleasure. **2.** a vine; a bunch of grapes; Butter tree (*Bassia latifolia*); Common Grape vine (*Vitis vinifera*).

Priyamdadā (S) (F) **1.** giving what is pleasant. **3.** a gandharvī.

Priyamukhā (S) (F) **1.** with a lovely face. **3.** a gandharvī.

Priyaśiṣyā (S) (F) **1.** beloved pupil. **3.** an apsarā (*M. Bh.*).

Priyavarccas (S) (F) **1.** one who loves strength. **3.** an apsarā of the court of Kubera (*Sk. Purāṇa*).

Pṛṣadvarā (S) (F) **1.** best among spotted antelopes. **3.** a daughter of Menakā and wife of Ruru (*K. Sāgara*).

Pṛśanī (S) (F) tender; gentle.

Pṛṣatī (S) (F) **1.** dappled cow. **3.** the daughter of Priśata(*A. Veda*).

Pṛśṇī (S) (F) **1.** dappled cow. **2.** the earth; cloud; milk; the starry sky; a ray of light. **3.** a mother of the maruts (*M. Bh.*); the wife of Savitṛ

(*Bh. Purāṇa*); the wife of King Sutapas who in a former birth was Devakī the mother of Kṛṣṇa (*Bhā. Purāṇa*).

Pṛṣṭi (S) (F) rib; a ray of light; touch.

Pṛthā (S) (F) 1. extended; enlarged; fat; voluptous; robust; stout. 3. a daughter of Sūra who was adopted by Kunti and became the wife of Pāṇḍu, she mothered Karna, Yudhiṣṭhira, Arjuna and Bhīma (*M. Bh.*).

Pṛthikā (S) (F) jasmine.

Pṛihukīrti (S) (F) 1. one whose fame has reached far. 3. a daughter of Śura (*H. Purāṇa*).

Pṛthuśiras (S) (F) 1. large headed. 3. a daughter of Puloman (*H. Purāṇa*).

Pṛthuvaktrā (S) (F) 1. wide mouthed. 3. a mother in Skanda's retinue (*M. Bh.*).

Pṛthuvastrā (S) (F) 1. with many clothes. 3. a mother in the Skanda's retinue (*M. Bh.*).

Pṛthvī (S) (F) 1. the broad and extended one. 2. the earth. 3. daughter of Pṛthu (*Ṛg Veda*); the queen of Benaras and mother of Jaina Tīrthaṅkara Supārśvanātha (*J.S. Koṣa*); *Amomum subulatum*; Nutmeg flower (*Nigella sativa*); Horse Purslane (*Trianthema port ulacastrum*).

Pūjā (S) (F) worship; honour; adoration; respect; reverence; veneration.

Pūjitā (S) (F) 1. honoured; adorned; worshipped. 2. goddess.

Pulindī (S) (F) 1. wild; mountaineer. 3. a rāga.

Pulomā (S) (F) 1. to be thrilled. 3. the daughter of the demon Vaiśvānara and wife of Bhṛgu (*H. Purāṇa*).

Pulomajā (S) (F) 1. daughter of Puloman. 3. another name for Indrāṇī.

Puṇḍarīkā (S) (F) 1. lotus like. 3. a daughter of Vasiṣṭha and wife of Prāṇa (*V. Purāṇa*); an apsarā (*M. Bh.*).

Puṇḍarīsrajā (S) (F) a garland of lotuses.

Punītā (S) (F) sacred; pious; holy.

Puñjikāsthalā (S) (F) 1. abode of hail. 3. an apsarā who was the maid of Bṛhaspati and was later reborn as Añjanā the mother of Hanumān (*V. Samhitā*).

Puṇyā (S) (F) 1. virtue; good work; meritorious act; purity. 2. holy basil. 3. a daughter of Kratu and Saṁnati (*V. Purāṇa*).

Puṇyajanī (S) (F) 1. meritorious. 3. the wife of Manibhadra who was an attendant of Śiva (*Br. Purāṇa*).

Puṇyaślokā (S) (F) 1. well spoken of. 3. another name for Sītā and Draupadī.

Puṇyavatī (S) (F) 1. full of virtues. 2. righteous; virtuous; honest; fortunate; happy; blessed; beautiful.

Puralā (S) (F) 1. abode of cities. 2. guardian of fortresses; protector of fortresses. 3. another name for Durgā.

Puramālinī (S) (F) 1. garlanded with castles. 2. one near which many cities are situated. 3. a river (*M. Bh.*).

Purandarā (S) (F) 1. destroyer of strong holds. 3. another name for Gaṅgā.

Purandhi (S) (F) 1. woman; liberality; munificence. 3. kindness shown by gods to men; personified as a goddess of abundance and liberality.

Pūraṇi (S) (F) 1. fulfilling; completing; satisfying. 3. one of the 2 wives of the deity Ayenār; another name for Durgā; Red Silk Cotton tree (*Bombax ceiba*).

Purañjanī (S) (F) understanding; intelligence.

Purāvatī (S) (F) 1. surrounded by cities; proceeding; going ahead. 3. a river (*M. Bh.*).

Puravī (S) (F) 1. eastern. 2. living; inviting. 3. a rāgiṇī.

Purlā (S) (F) 1. abode of cities. 3. another name for Durgā.

Pūrṇā (S) (F) 1. complete. 2. abundant; content. 3. a digit of the moon; a river (*V. Purāṇa*).

Pūrnāmṛtā (S) (F) 1. full of nectar. 3. a digit of the moon.

Pūrṇaśakti (S) (F) 1. perfect energy. 3. a form of Rādha (*Bhā. Purāṇa*).

Pūrṇimā (S) (F) the night or day of full moon.

Pūrṇodarā (S) (F) 1. with satiated appetite. 3. a deity (*A. Koṣa*).

Puruhutā (S) (F) **1.** invoked by many. **3.** a form of Dākṣāyaṇī (*M. Purāṇa*).

Purukṛpā (S) (F) **1.** abounding in mercy. **2.** compassionate.

Purupriyā (S) (F) dear to many.

Purūvī (S) (F) **1.** fulfiller. **2.** one that satiates; eastern. **3.** a rāgiṇī.

Pūrvābhirāmā (S) (F) **1.** ancient giver of pleasures. **3.** a river (*M. Bh.*).

Pūrvaćittī (S) (F) **1.** foreboding. **3.** an apsarā (*M. Bh.*).

Pūṣā (S) (F) **1.** nourishing; cherishing. **3.** a digit of the moon.

Pūṣanā (S) (F) **1.** nourisher; protector. **3.** a mother in Skanda's retinue (*M. Bh.*).

Pushṭi (S) (F) **1.** fatness; growth; increase; prosperity; comfort; opulence; fullness. **3.** the mother of Lobha (*Mā. Purāṇa*); a daughter of Dhruva (*V. Purāṇa*); a daughter of Paurṇamāsa; (*V. Purāṇa*); one of the 16 divine Matṛs; a digit of the moon (*Br. Purāṇa*); a wife of Gaṇeśa (*Br. Purāṇa*); form of Dākṣāyaṇī (*M. Purāṇa*); a form of Sarasvatī (*Br. Purāṇa*); the daughter of Dakṣa and Prasūti and the wife of Dharma (*V. Purāṇa*); a Śakti (*H.Ć Ćintāmaṇi*).

Puṣkarā (S) (F) **1.** lotus like. **3.** one of the 8 wives of Śiva.

Puṣkarasraj (S) (F) lotus wreath.

Puṣkarāvatī (S) (F) **1.** abounding in lotuses; consisting of lotuses. **3.** a form of Dākśāyaṇī (*M. Purāṇa*).

Puṣkariṇī (S) (F) **1.** lotus pond. **3.** the wife of Ćākṣuṣa and mother of Manu; the wife of Emperor Bhūmanyu (*M. Bh.*); the wife of King Ulmūka (*Bhā. Purāṇa*); another name for Viṣṇu.

Puṣpā (S) (F) **1.** flower like. **2.** flower; blossom.

Puṣpadantī (S) (F) **1.** flower toothed. **3.** a rākṣasī.

Puṣpajā (S) (F) **1.** born of a flower; daughter of flowers. **2.** nectar. **3.** a river rising in the Vindhya mountains (Mā. *Purāṇa*).

Puṣpajātī (S) (F) **1.** born of flowers. **3.** a river rising in the Malaya mountains (*V. Purāṇa*).

Puṣpamañjari (S) (F) flower blossom; the Blue Lotus (*Nelumbium Speciosum*).

Puṣpāṅganā (S) (F) flower bodied.

Puṣpāṅgī (S) (F) flower bodied.

Puṣpareṇu (S) (F) **1.** the dust of flowers. **2.** pollen.

Puṣpavallī (S) (F) flower vine.

Puṣpaveṇī (S) (F) **1.** garland or braid of flowers. **3.** a river (*M. Bh.*).

Puṣpendū (S) (F) the moon of flowers; the white lotus.

Puṣpī (S) (F) **1.** flower like. **2.** tender; soft; beautiful; fragrant; flower; blossom.

Puṣpotkaṭā (S) (F) **1.** bearing flowers. **3.** a rākṣasī, the mother of Rāvaṇa and Kumbhakarṇa (*M. Bh.*).

Pūtā (S) (F) **1.** purified; clear; bright. **2.** Durva grass. **3.** another name for Durgā.

Pūtanā (S) (F) **1.** blowing hard. **3.** a demon killed by infant Kṛṣṇa; a yoginī; an attendant of Skanda (*M. Bh.*).

Pūti (S) (F) purity.

Putrī (S) (F) daughter.

Putrikā (S) (F) doll; puppet; daughter; small statue.

R

Racanā (S) (F) 1. accomplishment; creation; production; literary work. 3. the wife of Tvaṣṭṛ *(Bhā. purāṇa)*.

Rādhā (S) (F) 1. full moon day in the month of Vaiśākha; prosperity; success; lightning. 3. the cowherdess who was the reincarnation of Lakṣmī as the daughter of Vṛṣabhānu and Kalāvatī of Gokula, the beloved of Kṛṣṇa and his mental power, is considered one of the 5 forces which help Viṣṇu in the process of creation (*Bhā. Purāṇa*); the foster mother of Karṇa and the wife of Adhiratha (*M. Bh.*); the 21st Nakṣatra of 4 stars (*Pañcatantra*).

Rādhanā (S) (F) speech.

Rādhanī (S) (F) worship.

Rādhikā (S) (F) 1. successful; prosperous. 3. another name for Rādhā.

Rāgā (S) (F) 1. the act of colouring; feeling; beauty; harmony; melody; loved of all beings; passionate. 3. a daughter of Bṛhaspati (*M. Bh.*); a daughter of Aṅgiras (*M. Bh.*); a mode of Indian classical music.

Rāgalatā (S) (F) 1. passion creeper. 3. another name for Rati.

Rāgamaya (S) (F) 1. red; full of passion; full of colour; full of love. 2. beloved; dear.

Rāgavatī (S) (F) 1. full of love; coloured; impassioned. 2. beloved.

Rāgiṇī (S) (F) 1. melody; attachment; love. 3. an apsarā who was the daughter of Himavān and elder sister of Pārvatī (*Mā. Purāṇa*); a form of Lakṣmī; a musical mode in Indian classical music.

Rāhuratna (S) (F) 1. jewel of Rāhu. 2. the hyacinth.

Rājādhidevī (S) (F) 1. goddess of the kings. 2. queen. 3. a daughter of the solar King Sūra and Māriṣā and the wife of King Jayasena of Avantī (*Bhāgavata*).

Rājakalā (S) (F) 1. a royal piece. 3. a digit of the moon.

Rājakanyā (S) (F) princess.

Rājakesarī (S) (F) shining gold; lion among kings.

Rājakumārī (S) (F) 1. daughter of a king. 2. princess.

Rājamahiṣī (S) (F) queen of a state.

Rājamaṇī (S) (F) crown jewel; royal gem.

Rajamukhī (S) (F) 1. with a shining silvery face. 3. an apsarā (*Sk. Purāṇa*).

Rajanī (S) (F) 1. the dark one. 2. night; turmeric; queen. 3. a holy river in ancient India (*M. Bh.*); the wife of Vivasvata and mother of Revata; an apsarā; another name for Durgā.

Rajanīgandhā (S) (F) 1. scented at night. 2. the tuberose (*Polianthes uberosa*).

Rajanīmukha (S) (F) 1. night faced. 2. the evening.

Rājanvatī (S) (F) 1. abode of kings. 3. another name for the earth.

Rājapuṣpā (S) (F) 1. royal flower. 3. the tree *Mesua roxburghii.*

Rājaśrī (S) (F) 1. royalty; grandeur. 3. a gandharvī.

Rājavi (S) (F) 1. royal bird. 2. the Blue Jay (*Coracias benghalensis*).

Rājeśvarī (S) (F) 1. goddess of a state. 2. princess.

Rājitā (S) (F) illuminated; resplendent; bright; brilliant.

Rājīvalocanā (S) (F) 1. lotus eyed; with eyes as blue as the blue lotus. 3. a daughter of King Jarāsandha (*Bhā. Purāṇa*).

Rājīviṇī (S) (F) a collection of blue lotuses.

Rājñī (S) (F) 1. queen. 3. the western quarter or that which contains the soul of the universe; the wife of the Sun.

Rājyadevī (S) (F) 1. goddess of state; royal woman. 3. the mother of Bāṇa.

Rājyalakṣmī (S) (F) 1. wealth of a state; royal Lakṣmī. 2. with the fortune and glory of a king.

Rājyaśrī (S) (F) 1. grace of the kingdom; goddess of the kingdom.

2. royal grace. 3. the sister of King Harṣa and the daughter of King Prabhākaravardhana.

Rājyavatī (S) (F) 1. possessing a kingdom. 2. princess.

Rākā (S) (F) the day of the full moon personified as a goddess who is his consort, she is the daughter of Aṅgiras and Smṛtī (*V. Purāṇa*); a rākṣasī who was the mother of Śūrpaṇakhā and Khara by sage Viśrāvas (*M. Bh.*); a daughter of Sumālin; daughter of Aṅgiras and Śraddhā; the wife of Dhātṛ and the mother of Prātṛ; a river (*Bh. Purāṇa*).

Rākāniśā (S) (F) the night of the full moon.

Rākiṇī (S) (F) 1. night. 3. a tāntra goddess.

Rakṣā (S) (F) 1. protection. 2. an amulet; a charm that protects.

Rakṣāmaṇī (S) (F) 1. a jewel of protection. 2. a jewel worn as an amulet against evil.

Rakṣaṇā (S) (F) protection; guarding.

Rakṣitā (S) (F) 1. protected. 3. an apsarā who was the daughter of Kaśyapa and Prādhā (*M. Bh.*).

Rakṣitṛ (S) (F) guardian; protector.

Rakṣovikṣobhinī (S) (F) 1. agitating rākṣasas, 3. a goddess.

Raktā (S) (F) 1. painted; red; beloved; dear; pleasant. 2. Rosary Pea (*Abrus precatorius*) 3. one of the 7 tongues of fire.

Raktahaṅsā (S) (F) 1. red swan; happy soul. 3. a rāgiṇī.

Raktakañćana (S) (F) 1. red gold. 2. *Bauhinia variegata.*

Raktakumuda (S) (F) Red Lotus (*Nymphaea rubra*).

Raktapa (S) (F) 1. blood drinking. 3. a Dākinī.

Raktapadma (S) (F) Red Lotus (*Nymphaea rubra*).

Raktapallava (S) (F) 1. red leaf; with red leaves. 2. the Aśoka tree (*Saraca indica*).

Raktapuṣpā (S) (F) 1. red flowered. 3. the pomegranate blossom; *Nerium odorum*; *Rottleria tinctoria*; *Bombax heptaphyllus*; *Hibiscus rosa sinensis.*

Rakti (S) (F) redness; pleasing; loveliness; affection; devotion.

Ramā (S) (F) 1. enchanting; beautiful; charming; vermilion; red earth; good luck; fortune; opulence; splendour. 3. the mother of the 9th Arhat of the present Avasarpiṇī; an apsarā; a daughter of Śaśidhvaja and wife of Kalki; another name for Mahālakṣmī; the Aśoka tree.

Ramādevī (S) (F) 1. goddess of beauty. 2. lovely woman. 3. the mother of Jayadeva.

Rāmagaṅgā (S) (F) 1. the Gaṅgā that pleases and refreshes. 3. a river.

Rāmakelī (S) (F) 1. sport of Lakṣmī. 3. a rāgiṇī.

Rāmakirī (S) (F) 1. of omnipresent nature. 2. all pervading. 3. a rāgiṇī.

Rāmakṛt (S) (F) 1. causing rest. 3. a rāga.

Rāmalā (S) (F) bestower of pleasure; lover.

Ramaṇā (S) (F) 1. enchanting; worthy of being loved. 2. charming; beloved. 3. Dākṣāyaṇī in Rāmatīrtha.

Ramaṇī (S) (F) 1. loving; delighting; pleasure; joy; sexual union; beautiful; charming. 3. a nāgakanyā (*R. Taraṅgiṇī*).

Ramaṇikā (S) (F) loving; pleasing; joyful; beautiful; charming.

Ramāpriyā (S) (F) 1. dear to Ramā. 2. lotus.

Ramātārā (S) (F) 1. the star of fortune; the best Lakṣmī. 3. the Sacred Basil plant.

Rāmāyaṇi (S) (F) the mirror of Rāma; one well versed in the *Rāmāyaṇa.*

Rambhā (S) (F) 1. lovable; pleasing; agreeable; staff; plantain (*Musa sapientum*); the lowing of the cow. 3. the daughter of Kaśyapa and Prādhā she was the wife of Nalakūbara considered the most beautiful of apsarās; the wife of Mayāsura (*Br. Purāṇa*); Dākṣāyaṇī in the Malaya mountains.

Rambhiṇī (S) (F) 1. the staff of a spear. 3. spear of the maruts (*Ṛg Veda*).

Rambhoru (S) (F) 1. with thighs like a plantain tree. 2. with lovely thighs; a beautiful woman. 3. another name for a beautiful woman.

Rāmeśvarī (S) (F) consort of Rāma.

Rāmilā (S) (F) bestower of pleasure; lover.

Ramyā (S) (F) 1. enchanting; enjoyable. 3. a daughter of Mount Meru (*Bh. Purāṇa*); another name for night; a river.

Ramyarūpā (S) (F) with a lovely form.

Rāṇā (S) (F) 1. murmuring. 3. a goddess.

Raṇadā (S) (F) making a sound; bestower of battles.

Raṇadurgā (S) (F) Durgā, as the goddess of battle.

Raṇajītā (S) (F) victorious in battle.

Raṇalakṣmī (S) (F) goddess of war; the fortunes of war.

Raṅgabhūti (S) (F) 1. born of love. 3. the night of full moon in the month of Āṣvina.

Raṅgadevatā (S) (F) 1. goddess of pleasure. 3. a goddess who presides over sports and diversions.

Raṅgajā (S) (F) vermilion; born of love.

Raṅgamāṇikya (S) (F) 1. coloured stone. 2. ruby.

Raṅganāyakī (S) (F) 1. beloved of Kṛṣṇa. 3. Rukmiṇī as consort of Kṛṣṇa.

Raṅgatī (S) (F) 1. coloured; loveable. 2. agreeable; excited; passionate. 3. a rāga.

Rangitā (S) (F) charmed; delighted; painted; coloured.

Raṅhitā (S) (F) swift; quick; rapid.

Rāṇī (S) (F) queen.

Rañjanā (S) (F) 1. pleasing; exciting; charming. 2. the *Nyctantes arbor tristis* tree; turmeric; saffron; perfume.

Rañjikā (S) (F) 1. one who pleases; exciting love; charming; pleasing. 2. Red Sandalwood (*Pterocarpus satalinus*).

Rañjinī (S) (F) 1. colouring; entertaining; delighting; amusing; pleasing; charming. 2. the *Nyctantes arbor tristis*; turmeric; saffron.

Rañjitā (S) (F) coloured; pleased; made happy; delighted.

Rāno (S) (F) a peacock's tail.

Rantū (S) (F) way; road; river.

Raṇvā (S) (F) pleasant; delightful; agreeable; lovely; joyous; gay.

Raṇvitā (S) (F) joyous; gay.

Raṇyā (S) (F) delectable; pleasant; war like.

Rasā (S) (F) 1. juice; water; nectar; essence; sentiment; taste; passion; milk; a chemical; quicksilver; the tongue; grapes; love; delight; charm; sentiment. 3. a mythological stream personified as a goddess of the *Ṛg Veda* and said to flow round the world; another name for the earth.

Rāsa (S) (F) 1. noise; sport; play; full of essence; full of sentiments. 3. the dance of Kṛṣṇa and the gopīs (*H. Purāṇa*).

Rasajñā (S) (F) 1. one who knows the sentiment. 2. knowledgeable about different arts. 3. another name for Gaṅgā.

Raśanā (S) (F) rope; cord; a ray of light; beam.

Rasanā (S) (F) 1. knower of taste. 2. tongue; taste; perception.

Rasanikā (S) (F) impassioned; full of feeling.

Rāsapriyā (S) (F) 1. fond of the Rāsa. 3. another name for a gopī.

Rasavantī (S) (F) delighting; charming; sentimental; emotional.

Rasavatī (S) (F) delighting; full of nectar; sentimental; emotional.

Rasikā (S) (F) with discrimination; aesthetic; sentimental; full of passion; passionate; tasteful; elegant.

Rasīśvari (S) (F) 1. goddess of the Rasa. 3. another name for Rādhā.

Raśmi (S) (F) 1. rope; cord; ray. 2. sunbeam; moonbeam.

Raśmikā (S) (F) a tiny ray of light.

Rāṣṭradevī (S) (F) 1. queen of the kingdom. 3. a wife of Ćitrabhānu.

Rāṣṭrī (S) (F) ruler.

Rasyā (S) (F) with essence; emotional; sentimental; full of feelings; juicy.

Rathaćitrā (S) (F) 1. like a multicoloured chariot. 3. a Purāṇic river (*Bhā. Purāṇa*).

Rathantarā (S) (F) 1. one who sits inside the chariot. 3. the daughter of Tansu.

Rathāntarī (S) (F) 1. dweller of the chariot. 3. a daughter of King Īlina and the mother of King Duṣyanta (*M. Bh.*).

Rathavīti (S) (F) 1. the horse of the carriage. 3. wife of Arćanānas.

Rathyā (S) (F) highway; crossroad; a group of chariots.

Rati (S) (F) 1. pleasure; enjoyment; desire; passion; love. 3. a daughter of Dakṣa and wife of Kāma (*M. Bh.*); an apsarā of Alakāpurī (*M. Bh.*); the wife of Vibhu and mother of Pṛthuseṇā (*Bhā. Purāṇa*); the 6th digit of the moon.

Ratikarā (S) (F) 1. causing pleasure. 3. an apsarā.

Ratimadā (S) (F) 1. intoxicated with love. 3. an apsarā (*K. Sāgara*).

Ratiprīti (S) (F) 1. love, pleasure and passion conjoined. 2. Rati and Prīti conjoined.

Ratnā (S) (F) jewel.

Ratnagarbhā (S) (F) 1. womb of jewels. 3. another name for the earth.

Ratnakalā (S) (F) piece of a jewel.

Ratnakūṭā (S) (F) 1. jewelled peak. 3. a wife of sage Atri (*P. Purāṇa*).

Ratnamālā (S) (F) 1. jewelled necklace. 3. a gandharvī.

Ratnamālāvatī (S) (F) 1. with a necklace of jewels. 3. an attendant of Rādhā (*Pañćatantra*).

Ratnamañjari (S) (F) 1. jewel blossom. 3. a vidyādharī.

Ratnāmbarī (S) (F) clad in jewels.

Ratnāṅgi (S) (F) with jewelled limbs.

Ratnapīṭhā (S) (F) 1. the seat of jewels. 3. a gandharvī (*K. Vyūha*).

Ratnaprabhā (S) (F) 1. the shine of jewels. 3. a nāga maiden (*K. Sāgara*); an apsarā; another name for the earth.

Ratnarāśī (S) (F) 1. collection of jewels. 3. another name for the sea.

Ratnarekhā (S) (F) 1. a line of jewels; ornamented; embellished. 2. very precious; very gracious.

Ratnasū (S) (F) 1. producing jewels. 2. the earth.

Ratnāvalī (S) (F) 1. a necklace of jewels. 3. a Sanskṛt play written by King Harṣavardhana.

Ratnavara (S) (F) 1. best among all precious things. 2. gold.

Ratnavatī (S) (F) 1. abounding in jewels. 3. another name for the earth.

Ratnolkā (S) (F) 1. jewelled meteor. 3. a tāntric deity.

Ratnottamā (S) (F) 1. best jewel. 3. a tāntric deity.

Rātri (S) (F) 1. night. 3. the sister of Uṣā and a divine mother.

Rātridevī (S) (F) goddess of the night; the presiding deity of the night.

Rātrikā (S) (F) night.

Ratū (S) (F) 1. truthful; true speech. 3. another name for the celestial Gaṅgā.

Ratujā (S) (F) daughter of truth.

Raudranetrā (S) (F) 1. fierce eyed. 3. a Buddhist goddess.

Raupya (S) (F) 1. made of silver; silvery. 3. a Purāṇic river of ancient India where the holy bath of sage Jamadagni was situated (*M. Bh.*).

Ravićandrikā (S) (F) 1. glory of sun. 2. moonlight. 3. a rāga.

Ravijā (S) (F) 1. born of the sun. 3. another name for Yamunā.

Ravipriya (S) (F) 1. beloved of the sun. 3. Dākṣayāṇī in Gaṅgadvāra.

Raviṣṭā (S) (F) 1. loved by the sun. 3. another name for the orange tree; *Polanisia Icosandra.*

Ṛbhyā (S) (F) worshipped.

Ṛćā (S) (F) the collected body of the Vedas; splendour; praise; hymn.

Ṛddhi (S) (F) 1. prosperity; success; wealth; abundance; supremacy; supernatural power. 3. a wife of Gaṇeśa; a wife of Kubera; Varuṇa's wife (*M. Bh.*); another name for Lakṣmī and Pārvatī.

Ṛddhimā (S) (F) full of prosperity; spring; love.

Ṛdū (S) (F) pleasant; soft; charming.

Rebhā (S) (F) singer of praise.

Reem (S) (F) hṛm, seed name of goddess Durgā, i.e. a mantra considered to be very potent in effecting riches.

Rejākṣī (S) (F) with eyes of fire; fiery eyes.

Rekhā (S) (F) **1.** line; streak. **3.** a servant of Bhānumatī the wife of Duryodhana (*M. Bh.*).

Reṇukā (S) (F) **1.** born of dust. **3.** the mother of sage Paraśurāma and wife of Jamadagni; a wife of Viśvāmitra (*H. Purāṇa*).

Reṇumatī (S) (F) **1.** with pollen. **3.** wife of Nakula and mother of Śatānīka.

Reśaman (S) (F) silk; soothing.

Revā (S) (F) **1.** one that moves; agile. **2.** swift; quick. **3.** the wife of Kāma; a rāga; another name for the river Narmadā and Kali.

Revatī (S) (F) **1.** prosperity; wealth. **2.** the 27th constellation of 32 stars; cow. **3.** the daughter of King Revata and the wife of Balarāma (*Bhāgavata*); the wife of King Vikramaśila's son and the mother of Manu Raivata the lord of the 5th Manvantara; the wife of Mitra (*Bh. Purāṇa*); a yoginī identified with Aditi; the 5th Nakṣatra; a rāgiṇī; a wife of Amṛtodana.

Rīṇā (S) (F) melted; dissolved.

Riṣṭā (S) (F) **1.** sword. **3.** another name for the mother of the apsarās.

Rīti (S) (F) motion; course; streak; stream; prosperity; remembrance; protection; auspiciousness.

Rītikā (S) (F) of a stream; brass.

Riyā (S) (F) one who sings; singer.

Ṛjuvani (S) (F) **1.** granting liberally. **3.** the earth.

Ṛkṣā (S) (F) **1.** female bear; the best; a star. **3.** the wife of solar dynasty King Ajamīdha (*M.Bh.*); a follower of Skanda (*M. Bh.*).

Ṛkṣambikā (S) (F) **1.** mother of the bears; mother of the stars. **3.** a follower of Skanda (*M. Bh.*).

Roćamānā (S) (F) **1.** consisting of light. **2.** shining; bright; splendid; agreeable. **3.** an attendant of Skanda (*M. Bh.*).

Roćanā (S) (F) **1.** bright; light; brightness. **2.** bright sky; handsome woman; beautiful; blossom of the Śālmali tree. **3.** the daughter of King Devaka and the wife of Vasudeva, she was the mother of Hema and Hemāngada (*Bhā. Purāṇa*); a grand daughter of Rukmin the king of Vidarbha and the wife of Aniruddha the grandson of Kṛṣṇa (*Bhā. Purāṇa*); Drumstick tree (*Moringa oleifera*); Sour Lime (*Citrus acida*); White Cotton tree (*Ceiba Pentadra*); Red Lotus (*Nymphaea rubra*); Indian Laburnum (*Cassia fistula*).

Roćanī (S) (F) delighting; agreeable.

Roći (S) (F) light; beam; ray.

Roćiras (S) (F) light; aura; glow.

Roćukā (S) (F) causing pleasure; one who gives pleasure; delighting.

Rodasī (S) (F) **1.** heaven and earth conjoined. **3.** a Vedic goddess who personifies lightning as the wife of Rudra and the mother of the maruts, she is considered immortal, heroic and the bestower of wealth (*Ṛg Veda*); the earth (*V. Rāmāyaṇa*).

Rodhasvatī (S) (F) **1.** with high embankments. **3.** a holy river in India (*Bhā. Purāṇa*).

Rohantī (S) (F) climbing; vine.

Rohī (S) (F) **1.** rising up; red. **2.** a doe.

Rohiṇī (S) (F) **1.** ascending; tall; increasing. **2.** the mother of all cows; the Sandalwood tree; red cow. **3.** the most beloved of all the 27 wives of the moon (*T. Samhitā*); the daughter of the agni called Manu and Niśā and the wife of Hiraṇyakaśipu (*M. Bh.*); the mother of sage Utathya; the constellation Tauri which has 5 stars one of which is Aldebaran; a wife of

Kṛṣṇa (*Bhā. Purāṇa*); the wife of Mahādeva (*Purāṇas*); one of the 16 vidyādevīs (*A. Koṣa*); a river between Kapilavastu and Kol (*V. Purāṇa*); a daughter of Dakṣa and Surabhi and mother of Vimalā, Anala and Kāmadhenu the celestial cow, she is the feminine counterpart of the rising sun personified as Rohita and is the divinity of cattle; a wife of Vasudeva and the mother of Balarāma (*M. Bh.*).

Rohitā (S) (F) **1.** red. **3.** daughter of Brahmā.

Romā (S) (F) full of hair.

Romaśā (S) (F) **1.** having thick hair; hairy. **3.** daughter of Bṛhaspati.

Romolā (S) (F) hairy; charming.

Ropanā (S) (F) causing to grow; healing.

Rośansā (S) (F) wish; desire.

Royinā (S) (F) rising; growing.

Ṛṣikulyā (S) (F) **1.** of the family of ṛṣis. **3.** a sacred river of the *Mahābhārata* (*M. Bh.*).

Ṛṣmā (S) (F) moonbeam.

Ṛṣvā (S) (F) elevated; high; great; noble.

Ṛtu (S) (F) any fixed time; period; fixed order; season.

Ṛtumbharā (S) (F) **1.** of divine truth; filled with season. **3.** another name for the earth.

Ṛtuśrī (S) (F) splendour of the seasons; queen of the seasons.

Ṛtusthalā (S) (F) **1.** abode of light; abode of seasons. **3.** an apsarā (*M. Bh.*).

Rućā (S) (F) light; splendour; brightness; desire; the voice of the Mynah.

Rući (S) (F) **1.** beauty; lustre; light; desire; taste; pleasure. **3.** an apsarā of Alakāpurī who danced at the cour of Kubera (*M. Bh.*); the wife of sage Devaśarman (*M. Bh.*).

Rućikā (S) (F) shining; of taste; desirable; ornament.

Rućirā (S) (F) desirable; charming; winsome; pleasing; dainty.

Rućitā (S) (F) bright; brilliant; delighted; glittering; sweet; dainty.

Rūdhī (S) (F) rise; ascent; birth; fame.

Rudrā (S) (F) **1.** crying; howling. **3.** consort of Śiva; a wife of Vasudeva (*Vā. Purāṇa*); a daughter of Raudrāśva (*V. Purāṇa*); another name for Pārvatī.

Ṛudrabhairavī (S) (F) **1.** angry and frightening. **3.** another name for Pārvatī.

Rudraćaṇḍi (S) (F) **1.** the roaring goddess. **3.** a form of Durgā.

Rudrakālī (S) (F) **1.** black and angry; roaring and deadly. **2.** roarer. **3.** a form of Durgā (*D. Purāṇa*).

Rudrakrīḍā (S) (F) pleasure ground of Rudra; display of Rudra.

Rudrāmbā (S) (F) **1.** the angry mother. **3.** Pārvatī the consort of Rudra.

Rudrāmbikā (S) (F) **1.** the angry mother. 1, the consort of Rudra. **3.** another name for Pārvatī.

Rudrāṇī (S) (F) **1.** wife of Rudra. **3.** the wife of Rudra; another name for Pārvatī.

Rudrapriyā (S) (F) **1.** dear to Rudra. **3.** another name for Pārvatī; Black Myrobalan (*Terminalia chebuld*).

Rudrapuṣpa (S) (F) red blossom; the China Rose (*Hibiscus rosa sinensis*).

Rudrasī (S) (F) Rudra like; red.

Rudrasundarī (S) (F) **1.** beloved of the terrible; beloved of Rudra. **3.** a form of Goddess Durgā.

Ruhā (S) (F) **1.** grown; risen; mounted. **3.** the daughter of Surasā (*M. Bh.*); Couch Grass (*Cynodon dactyton*).

Ruhānī (S) (F) of higher values; spiritual.

Rūhī (S) (F) ascending; of higher value; soul.

Ruhikā (S) (F) one that rises; longing; desire.

Rukmarekhā (S) (F) **1.** golden line. **3.** the wife of King Raibhya and the mother of Ekāvalī (*Bhā. Purāṇa*).

Rukmavatī (S) (F) **1.** possessing gold. **2.** golden; as beautiful as gold. **3.** the daughter of Rukmin and the wife of Pradyumna, she was the mother of Aniruddha (*Bhā. Purāṇa*).

Rukmiṇī (S) (F) **1.** the sister of Rukmin and the chief queen of Kṛṣṇa, she mothered Pradyumna and is supposed to have been an incarnation of Lakṣmī (*M. Bh.*). **3.** Dākṣāyāṇī in Dvārāvatī (*M. Bh.*).

Rumā (S) (F) **1.** salty; salt mine. **3.** a hymn of *Ṛg Veda* which is a favourite of Indra; a woman who sprang from the Ocean of Milk (*K. Rāmāyaṇa*); the daughter of the monkey Panasa and wife of Sugrīva (*V. Rāmāyaṇa*); a river.

Rūpā (S) (F) **1.** bearer of form. **2.** silver. **3.** a river (*V. Purāṇa*); another name for the earth.

Rūpālī (S) (F) excellent in form; beautiful.

Rūpamatī (S) (F) **1.** possessing beauty. **3.** a queen of Mandu who was the wife of Bāz Bahādur.

Rūpāṅgī (S) (F) with a beautiful body.

Rūpasī (S) (F) beautiful.

Rūpaśikhā (S) (F) **1.** crest of beauty; most beautiful. **3.** a daughter of the rākṣasa Agniśikha (*K. Sāgara*).

Rūpaśrī (S) (F) divinely beautiful.

Rūpavajrā (S) (F) **1.** with powerful beauty; one whose beauty strikes like a thunderbolt. **3.** a Buddhist goddess.

Rūpavatī (S) (F) **1.** possessed with beauty; beautiful. **3.** a river (*Bh. Purāṇa*).

Rūpavidyā (S) (F) **1.** form of knowledge. **3.** the figure of the 12 handed Devī in a sitting position.

Rūpeśvarī (S) (F) goddess of beauty.

Rūpikā (S) (F) possessing a form; figure; shape; appearance; coin of gold or silver.

Rūpiṇikā (S) (F) possessing a beautiful form; embodied; corporeal.

Ruṣabhānu (S) (F) **1.** the angry sun. **3.** the wife of the asura Hiraṇyākṣa (*Bhāgavata*).

Ruśamā (S) (F) **1.** angerless; calm. **3.** a learned priest of the Vedas and a protégé of Indra.

Rūsaṇā (S) (F) **1.** covering; adorning; decoration. **3.** a wife of Rudra.

Ruśatī (S) (F) white; fair in complexion.

S

Śabarā (S) (F) **1.** variegated; spotted; brindled. **3.** a yoginī.

Śabarī (S) (F) **1.** variegated; belonging to the Śabara tribe. **3.** a gandharvī who was changed into a forest woman and then saved by Rāma (*K. Rāmāyaṇa*).

Sābhramatī (S) (F) **1.** full of water; cloudy. **3.** a river flowing through Ahmedabad.

Saććandrikā (S) (F) splendid moonlight.

Śaćī (S) (F) **1.** might; aid; kindness; favour; grace; skill; dexterity. **3.** the daughter of Puloman and wife of Indra, one aspect of her was reborn as Draupadī (*M. Bh.*); the mother of Ćaitanya.

Śaćikā (S) (F) **1.** kind; graceful; skilled; dextrous. **3.** the wife of Indra.

Ṣaḍabhujā (S) (F) **1.** 6 armed. **3.** another name for Durgā.

Sadājyotī (S) (F) eternal lamp.

Sadākāntā (S) (F) **1.** always loved. **3.** a river in Purāṇic India (*M. Bh.*).

Sadāśiṣa (S) (F) a good blessing.

Sadāśivā (S) (F) **1.** always belonging to Śiva; always kind, happy and prosperous. **3.** another name for Durgā.

Sādhakā (S) (F) **1.** effective; efficient; productive; magical. **3.** another name for Durgā.

Sādhanā (S) (F) accomplishment; performance; worship; adoration.

Sādhikā (S) (F) **1.** accomplished; skilful; wor-shipper; efficient. **3.** another name for Durgā.

Sādhri (S) (F) conqueror.

Sādhumatī (S) (F) **1.** virtuous minded. **3.** a tāntra deity (*B. Literature*).

Sadhūmavarṇā (S) (F) **1.** enveloped in smoke. **3.** one of the 7 tongues of fire.

Sādhvī (S) (F) chaste; virtuous; faithful; honest; righteous; pious; noble; unerring; peaceful.

Sādhyā (S) (F) **1.** accomplishment; perfection. **3.** a daughter of Dakṣa and wife of Dharma and mother of the Sādhyas (*H. Purāṇa*).

Sadvatī (S) (F) **1.** righteous; truthful; pious. **3.** a daughter of Pulastya and wife of Agni.

Sāgarakukṣi (S) (F) **1.** living in the whirlpools of the oceans. **3.** a nāga maiden.

Sāgarāmbarā (S) (F) **1.** ocean clad. **2.** the earth.

Sāgaranemī (S) (F) **1.** encircled by the ocean. **2.** the earth.

Sāgarī (S) (F) of the ocean.

Sāgarikā (S) (F) of the ocean.

Sahā (S) (F) **1.** tolerant. **3.** an apsarā (*M. Bh.*); another name for the earth; *Aloe vera*; *Rosa alba*.

Sahadevī (S) (F) **1.** protected by the goddesses; mighty goddess. **3.** a daughter of Devaka and wife of Vasudeva (*H. Purāṇa*).

Sahajanyā (S) (F) **1.** produced together. **3.** an apsarā (*H. Purāṇa*).

Sahasrabhujā (S) (F) **1.** 1000 armed. **3.** another name for Durgā.

Sahelī (S) (F) a friend; attached with; small minaret.

Sahima (S) (F) with snow.

Sahitā (S) (F) **1.** being near. **3.** a river (*V. Purana*).

Sahitrā (S) (F) full of patience; enduring.

Sahurī (S) (F) **1.** full of heat; mighty; strong; victorious. **2.** the earth.

Śaibyā (S) (F) **1.** belonging to the Śibis. **3.** a wife of King Sagara who was also known as Keśinī; wife of King Dyumatsena of Śālva and mother of Satyavān; a wife of Kṛṣṇa (*M. Bh.*).

Śailā (S) (F) **1.** dwelling in the mountains. **3.** Pārvati's mother.

Śailajā (S) (F) **1.** daughter of the mountain. **3.** another name for Pārvatī.

Śailakanyā (S) (F) **1.** daughter of the mountain. **3.** another name for Pārvatī.

Śailaputrī (S) (F) **1.** daughter of a mountain. **3.** another name for Pārvatī.

Śailarājasutā (S) (F) 1. daughter of the king of mountains. 3. another name for Pārvatī and Gaṅgā.

Śailāsā (S) (F) 1. dweller of mountains. 3. another name for Pārvatī.

Śailendrajā (S) (F) 1. daughter of the mountain lord. 3. another name for the Gaṅgā.

Śailī (S) (F) carved in rock; style; custom; visage; habit.

Sairandhrī (S) (F) 1. maid. 2. a maid servant in the women's apartments. 3. Draupadī in King Virāṭa's court (*M. Bh.*).

Śaivī (S) (F) 1. prosperity; auspiciousness. 3. another name for the goddess Manasā.

Sajanī (S) (F) 1. a woman worth keeping company with. 2. sweetheart.

Śaka (S) power; might; help; aid; herb; vegetation.

Sakalasiddhi (S) (F) possessing all perfection.

Śākambharī (S) (F) 1. herb nourishing. 2. the tutelary goddess of vegetation. 3. another name for Durgā.

Śākinī (S) (F) 1. goddess of herbs; helpful; powerful. 3. another name for Pārvatī as the procurer of plants; an attendant of Durgā.

Śakrāṇi (S) (F) 1. consort of Śakra. 3. another name for Śaćī.

Śākrī (S) (F) 1. of Indra. 2. consort of Indra.

Sākṣī (S) (F) 1. with eyes. 2. witness.

Śakti (S) (F) 1. power; ability; strength; might; energy. 3. the energy of a deity personified as his wife, the 8 primary Śaktis are Indrāṇī, Vaiṣṇavī, Śāntā, Brahmāṇī, Kaumārī, Nārasiṅhī, Vārāhī, Māheśvarī also Ćāmuṇḍā and Ćaṇḍikā, another sect includes Kārttikī and Pradhānā, some sects count 50 different forms of the Śakti of Viṣṇu and 50 of Śiva, those counted as white Śaktis or those of a mild nature are Lakṣmī, Sarasvatī, Gaurī etc., the dark or fierce Śaktis includes Durgā, Kāli (*K. Sāgara*).

Śaktimatī (S) (F) powerful.

Śaktiyaśas (S) (F) 1. with powerful fame. 3. a vidyādharī.

Śakunī (S) (F) auspicious object; lucky omen.

Śakunikā (S) (F) 1. bird. 3. a mother in Skanda's retinue (*M. Bh.*).

Śakuntalā (S) (F) 1. bird; protected by birds. 3. the daughter of Menakā by Viśvāmitra, she was adopted by the sage Kaṇva, she married King Duṣyanta of the Lunar dynasty and became the mother of the Emperor Bharata.

Śakunti (S) (F) bird.

Śakuntikā (S) (F) a small bird.

Śalabhā (S) (F) 1. grasshopper. 3. the wife of sage Atri (*Br. Purāṇa*).

Śalabhī (S) (F) 1. grasshopper; locust. 3. a mother in Skanda's retinue (*M. Bh.*).

Śaladā (S) (F) 1. procurer of the spear. 3. a daughter of Raudrāśva.

Śalākā (S) (F) 1. small stick; a needle. 3. the wife of sage Dhanañjaya.

Sālakaṭāṅkaṭā (S) (F) 1. fire of the house. 3. a rākṣasī who was the daughter of Sandhyā the wife of Vidyutkeśa and the mother of Sukeśa (*V. Rāmāyaṇa*).

Salatā (S) (F) a plant yielding Soma juice.

Śālāvatī (S) (F) 1. owning a house; housewife; lady of the house. 3. a wife of Viśvāmitra (*H. Purāṇa*).

Sālikā (S) (F) flute.

Śalinā (S) (F) 1. courteous. 2. Fennel (*Foeniculum capillaceum*).

Śālīnī (S) (F) 1. with a fixed abode. 2. settled; established; domestic; shy; bashful; modest.

Śālmalī (S) (F) 1. garlanded with Sālmali trees. 3. a river of the lower regions; a Śakti of Viṣṇu.

Śālmālinī (S) (F) the Red Silkcotton tree (*Bombax celba*).

Salonī (H) (F) beautiful.

Samā (S) (F) of a peaceful nature; equanimity; similarity; a year.

Śamā (S) (F) 1. tranquil; peaceful; calm; lamp. 3. an apsarā.

Samadu (S) (F) daughter.

Samajyā (S) (F) fame; reputation.

Samākhyā (S) (F) name; fame; celebrity.

Samāli (S) (F) a collection of flowers; a nosegay.

Samana (S) quiet; calm; rich; affluent; abundant; universal.

Samangini (S) (F) 1. complete in all parts. 3. a deity of the Bodhi tree.

Śāmani (S) (F) tranquillity; peace.

Śamanī (S) (F) 1. the calming one. 2. night.

Samardhukā (S) (F) 1. prospering; succeeding. 2. daughter.

Samastī (S) (F) 1. all that is reaching; attaining; totality. 2. the universe.

Samatā (S) (F) equality; sameness; fairness; benevolence.

Samatā (S) (F) 1. equality. 2. peaceful.

Śāmbhavī (S) (F) 1. a kind of blue flowering sacred grass (*Cynodon dactylon*). 3. another name for Durgā.

Sambhogayakṣiṇī (S) (F) 1. deity of enjoyment. 3. a yoginī.

Śambhu (S) (F) 1. helpful; benevolent; kind. 3. the wife of Dhruva and mother of Ślișți and Bhavya (*V. Purāṇa*).

Śambhukāntā (S) (F) 1. wife of Śiva. 3. another name for Durgā.

Śambhupriyā (S) (F) 1. dear to Śiva. 3. another name for Durgā.

Sambhūtī (S) (F) 1. birth; origin; manifestation of might. 3. fitness personified as the daughter of Dakṣa and wife of Marīci (*Purāṇas*); a wife of Jayadratha and mother of Vijaya (*Bhāgavata*).

Sambuddhi (S) (F) perfect knowledge; perception.

Sameḍī (S) (F) 1. moving one. 3. a mother attending on Skanda (*M. Bh.*).

Samīcī (S) (F) 1. praise; eulogy. 2. a doe. 3. an apsarā.

Samīhā (S) (F) wish; desire.

Śamīkā (S) (F) 1. peaceful. 3. a daughter of Aurva and wife of Mandara (*G. Purāṇa*).

Śāmilī (S) (F) of the Śami tree (*Prosopis spicigera*); containing fire; chaplet; garland.

Śamirā (S) (F) a chameli flower.

Samiṣa (S) (F) dart; javelin.

Samitī (S) (F) 1. committee; senate; herd. 3. society personified as a daughter of Prajāpati.

Sammati (S) (F) 1. harmony; agreement; respect; homage; wish; desire; self knowledge; love; order. 3. a river (*V. Purāṇa*).

Śampā (S) (F) lightning.

Sampad (S) (F) perfection; attainment; success; accomplishment; blessing; glory; fate.

Sampāṅgi (S) (F) possessed with a balanced body.

Sampatpradā (S) (F) 1. bestowing fortune. 3. a form of Bhairavī.

Sampattī (S) (F) 1. prosperity; welfare; accomplishment; concord; being. 3. a form of Prākṛtī and wife of Iṣāṇa.

Samprīti (S) (F) complete satisfaction; joy, delight.

Sampriyā (S) (F) 1. fully loved; dear; beloved. 3. the wife of Vidura and mother of Anaśva (*M.Bh.*).

Sampūjā (S) (F) reverence; esteem.

Sampuṣṭi (S) (F) perfect prosperity.

Sararāj (S) (F) 1. ruling over all. 3. a daughter of Priyavrata (*V. Purāṇa*).

Sararāṭ (S) (F) 1. universal queen. 3. a daughter of Priyavrata (*V. Purāṇa*).

Samṛddhī (S) (F) prosperity; welfare; fortune; perfection; excellence; wealth.

Samṛddhin (S) (F) 1. accomplished; perfect; happy; blessed; full of riches. 3. another name for the Gaṅgā.

Samṛti (S) (F) coming together; meeting.

Samudramahiṣī (S) (F) 1. chief wife of the ocean. 3. another name for the Gaṅgā.

Samudranemī (S) (F) 1. surrounded by the ocean. 2. the earth.

Samudraśrī (S) (F) 1. beauty of the ocean. 2. mermaid.

Samudrasubhagā (S) (F) 1. favourite of the ocean. 3. another name for the Gaṅgā.

Sāmudrī (S) (F) 1. born of the ocean. 3. the daughter of Samudra and wife of Prāćīnabarhis.

Sānandā (S) (F) 1. full of pleasure. 2. pleasant; joyful. 3. a form of Lakṣmī.

Sanātanī (S) (F) 1. eternal; ancient; permanent. 3. another name for Durgā, Lakṣmī and Sarasvatī.

Sanćāranī (S) (F) 1. conveying; bringing near; delivering a message. 3. one of the 6 Buddhist goddesses of magic.

Saṅdhyā (S) (F) 1. holding together; union; juncture of day and night. 2. religious acts performed at the 3 divisions of the day; reflection; meditation. 3. twilight personified as a daughter of Brahmā and consort of Śiva, the sun, Kāla, Pulastya, and Pūṣan; the deity presiding over the divisions of the day; the mother of the rākṣasī Śālakataṅkā who married Vidyutkeśa (*U. Ramāyaṇa*); a river whose goddess sits in Varuṇa's assembly (*M. Bh.*); the goddess of dusk (*M. Bh.*); Arundhatī in her previous birth; a river (*M. Bh.*).

Sāṅdhyakusumā (S) (F) flower of the twilight (*Hibiscus rosa sinensis*).

Saṅdhyārāgā (S) (F) 1. the colour of twilight. 3. the red colour in the evening sky per-sonified as a daughter of Himavān.

Saṅdhyāvalī (S) (F) 1. period of twilight. 3. the wife of King Rukmāṅgada.

Śāṅḍilī (S) (F) 1. collector. 3. a Brāhmaṇī worshipped as the mother of Agni; a daughter of Dakṣa and wife of Dharma and mother of Vasu Anala (*M. Bh.*); a yoginī famous in the Purāṇas.

Śāṇḍilī (S) (F) 1. goddess of curd. 3. another name for Pārvatī.

Saṅganī (S) (F) companion.

Sanghamitrā (S) (F) 1. sun of the assembly; friend of society; period of the Buddhist order. 3. the daughter of Emperor Aśoka.

Saṅgir (S) (F) assent; promise.

Saṅgīti (S) (F) concert; symphony.

Sānikā (S) (F) a flute.

Śaniprasū (S) (F) 1. mother of Saturn. 3. another name for Ćhāyā.

Saniti (S) (F) acquisition; obtainment.

Sanitrā (S) (F) gift; oblation.

Sānjali (S) (F) with hands hollowed and joined in prayer.

Sañjanā (S) (F) one who joins; creator.

Sañjitī (S) (F) complete victory.

Saṅjñā (S) (F) 1. well known; perfect knowledge; noun. 2. agreement; harmony; consciousness; clear understanding; sign; token; gesture. 3. a daughter of Tvaṣṭṛ or Viśvakarman and the wife of the sun, she was the mother of Manu, Yama and Yamī, the aśvins and Revanta.

Sañjogitā (S) (F) 1. attached; related; conjoined. 3. a wife of King Prithvīrāja.

Saṅkalpā (S) (F) 1. will; vow; resolution; determination. 3. a daughter of Dakṣa and the wife of Dharma, she was the mother of Saṅkalpa (*Bhāgavata*); Manu's wife (*H. Purāṇa*).

Śankarā (S) (F) 1. causer of tranquillity; auspicious, causing prosperity. 3. Śankara's wife; a rāga.

Śankarī (S) (F) 1. the wife of Śiva. 2. *Mimosa suma*; *Prosopis spicigera.*

Saṅkaṭā (S) (F) 1. goddess who removes dangers. 3. a yoginī; a goddess worshipped in Benaras.

Śaṅkhā(S) (F) a kind of flute.

Śaṅkhadhavala (S) (F) as white as a conchshell; Jasmine flower (*Jasminum auriculatum*).

Śaṅkhakumbhaśravas (S) (F) 1. producing the sound of conchshell and a pitcher. 2. loud voiced. 3. a mother in Skanda's retinue (*M. Bh*).

Śaṅkhalikā (S) (F) 1. as perfect as a conchshell. 2. flawless. 3. a mother in Skanda's retinue (*M. Bh.*).

Śaṅkhamuktā (S) (F) conchshell and pearl conjoined; mother of pearl.

Śākhaliṇī (S) (F) 1. one that has branches; supreme among the branches; *Jasminum sambac.* 2. best; excellent.

Śaṅkhaśravas (S) (F) **1.** shell eared. **3.** an attendant of Skanda (*M. Bh.*).

Śaṅkhayūthikā (S) (F) a collection of conchshells; a garland of jasmine flowers (*Jasminum auriculatum*).

Śaṅkhinī (S) (F) **1.** mother of pearls. **3.** a Śakti worshipped by the Buddhists; a kind of semi divine being or fairy.

Sankhya (S) (F) welfare; comfort; health; happiness; felicity.

Saṅmati (S) (F) nobleminded.

Saṅnam (S) (F) favour; kindness.

Saṅnatī (S) (F) **1.** bending down; humility. **3.** humility personified as a daughter of Dakṣa and wife of Kratu and mother of Bālakhilyas (*A. Purāṇa*); wife of King Brahmadatta (*P. Purāṇa*).

Saṅnihatī (S) (F) **1.** destroying easily. **3.** a river.

Sanojā (S) (F) eternal.

Sanolī (S) (F) possessed with self penance; introspective.

Saṅraktā (S) (F) **1.** full of blood; red coloured. **2.** coloured; red; charming; beautiful.

Śansā (S) (F) praise; invocation; charm; blessing; recitation; wish.

Saṅśatī (S) (F) **1.** doubting. **3.** the wife of the agni Pavamāna and the mother of Sabhya and Avasathya (*M. Purāṇa*).

Sansiddhi (S) (F) perfection; success; complete accomplishment.

Sansitā (S) (F) **1.** wished; desired; longed for. **2.** praised; celebrated.

Śāntā (S) (F) **1.** peaceful; calm. **3.** a daughter of Daśaratha and wife of Ṛṣyaśṛṅga (*M. Bh.*); a jaina goddess who executes the orders of the 7th Arhat (*J. Literature*); a Śakti.

Saṅtani (S) (F) continuing; forming an uninterrupted line; harmony; music.

Saṅtānikā (S) (F) **1.** stretching. **2.** cobweb; cream; foam; the blade of a sword. **3.** an attendant of Skanda (*M. Bh.*).

Santānikī (S) (F) made from the flowers of the Kalpa tree.

Saṅtatī (S) (F) **1.** continuity; race; progeny; offspring. **3.** a daughter of Dakṣa and wife of Kratu.

Śānti (S) (F) **1.** tranquillity; peace. **3.** quiet personified as a daughter of Śraddhā and the wife of Atharvan or as a daughter of Dakṣa and Prasūti and wife of Dharma (*V. Purāṇa*).

Śāntidevī (S) (F) **1.** goddess of peace. **3.** a daughter of King Devaka and a wife of Vasudeva (*Vā. Purāṇa*).

Śāntivā (S) (F) **1.** bearer of peace. **2.** beneficient; friendly; kind. **3.** a deity.

Santoṣā (S) (F) **1.** content; satisfied. **3.** the mother of Gaṅgādāsa.

Saṅtoṣī (S) (F) satisfied; contented.

Santuṣṭi (S) (F) complete satisfaction; contentment.

Sānumatī (S) (F) **1.** mountain. **3.** an apsarā.

Saṅvegadhāriṇī (S) (F) **1.** bearer of passion; passionate. **3.** a kinnarī.

Sanvitti (S) (F) knowledge; intellect; understanding; harmony.

Saṅvṛttī (S) (F) **1.** fulfilment. **2.** being; existing; becoming; happening. **3.** fulfilment per-sonified as a devī in Brahmā's court (*M. Bh.*).

Saṅyuktā (S) (F) relating to; conjoined; united; a kind of metre.

Saparyā (S) (F) worship; homage; adoration.

Saptajit (S) (F) **1.** winning the 7 elements namely, earth, water, fire, air, ether, mind and ego. **3.** a daughter of Kaśyapa and Danu (*M. Purāṇa*).

Sārā (S) (F) hard; firm; solid; precious; valuable; best; excellent.

Śāradā (S) (F) **1.** a vīṇā or lute bearer. **3.** a Sarasvati; a daughter of evaratha; another name for Durgā.

Śaradaćandrikā (S) (F) autumnal moonshine.

Śāradāmaṇi (S) (F) **1.** jewel among the lutes. **2.** the best lute. **3.** the wife of Rāmākṛṣṇa Paramahaṇsa.

Śaradaśrī (S) (F) **1.** beauty of autumn. **3.** a wife of Kuṇala.

Śaradayāminī (S) (F) a night in autumn.

Śāradī (S) (F) autumn; modest; sky; the day of full moon in the month of Kārtika.

Śaradī (S) (F) as lovely as autumn.

Śāradikā (S) (F) autumnal.

Śāradvatī (S) (F) 1. with a lute; autumnal. 3. an apsarā (*H. Purāṇa*); another name for Kṛpī.

Saraghā (S) (F) 1. Indian beech tree (*Pongamia glabra*). 3. wife of Bindumat and mother of Madhu (*Bh. Purāṇa*).

Śarajjyotsnā (S) (F) autumnal moonshine.

Saralā (S) (F) 1. straight. 2. right; correct; honest; simple; *Pinus longifolia*; fire. 3. a river.

Saramā (S) (F) 1. the fleet footed one. 3. the bitch of the gods and the mother of Syāma and Śabala who are the messengers of Yama; the daughter of the gandharva Śailūṣa and life of Vibhīṣana (*V. Rāmāyaṇa*); a daughter of Dakṣa and Asiknī and the wife of Kaśyapa, she is considered the mother of ferocious animals (*Bhāgavata*).

Sāraṅgī (S) (F) 1. a spotted doe. 3. a rāgini.

Śaraṇī (S) (F) 1. protecting. 2. guarding; defending; housing. 3. another name for the earth; *Paederia foetida*.

Saraṇi (S) (F) a road; path.

Śaraṇyā (S) (F) 1. defender; protectress; giving shelter. 3. another name for Durgā.

Saraṅyū (S) (F) 1. quick; nimble; fleet footed. 3. a daughter of Tvaṣṭṛ represented in the Ṛg Veda as the wife of Vivasvat and mother of the 2 aśvins.

Sārasākṣī (S) (F) lotus eyed.

Sarasavāṇī (S) (F) 1. sweet voiced. 3. the wife of Maṇḍanmiśra.

Sarasijamukhī (S) (F) lotus faced.

Sarasvatī (S) (F) 1. region abounding in pools; full of essences. 3. a river celebrated in the *Ṛg Veda*; the river goddess who is the mother of streams, the best among the mothers of rivers and of goddesses, in the earlier hymns she formed a triad with the goddesses Iḍā and Bhāratī; in the Brāhmaṇas she is connected with speech and later becomes the goddess of learning and eloquence identified with Durgā, considered the wife and daughter of Brahmā born from his face and also his consort, she is the mother of Svāyambhuva; according to the Purāṇas she assumed the form of the river Sarasvatī (*Ṛg Veda*); the wife of Manu (*M. Bh.*); the wife of sage Dadhīca and the mother of Sarasvata (*Br. Purāṇa*); Intellect tree (*Celastrus paniculata*).

Śarāvatī (S) (F) 1. full of reeds. 3. a river (*M. Bh.*).

Sarayū (S) (F) 1. moving fast. 2. air; wind. 3. a Purāṇic river which is considered the source of Agni and in which Rāma drowned himself; the wife of Agni Vīra and the mother of Siddhi (*M. Bh.*).

Śārdūlī (S) (F) 1. tigress. 3. a daughter of Kaśyapa and Krodhavaśā who is the mother of tigers and leopards (*V. Rāmāyaṇa*).

Sargiṇī (S) (F) composed of parts.

Śarī (S) (F) 1. bird; arrow. 3. a daughter of Māthara and wife of Tiṣya and mother of the 1st disciple of Gautama Buddha (*B. Literature*).

Saridvarā (S) (F) 1. best of rivers. 3. the Gaṅgā.

Sarikā (S) (F) a string of pearls; jewel; pond; lake; the sky.

Sārikā (S) (F) 1. the Mynah bird (*Turdus salica*). 2. confidante; the bridge of a stringed instrument; a form of Durgā (*K. Sāgara*) 3. a rākṣasī.

Sarit (S) (F) 1. river; stream. 3. another name for Durgā.

Saritā (S) (F) 1. moving. 2. stream; river.

Sarju (S) (F) lightning.

Śarmilā (S) (F) shy.

Śarmiṣṭhā (S) (F) 1. most fortunate. 3. a daughter of Vṛṣaparvan and wife of Yayāti and mother of Druhyu, Anu and Purū.

Sarojinī (S) (F) abounding in lotuses.

Sarpāsyā (S) (F) 1. snake faced. 2. one who eats snakes. 3. a yoginī.

Sarpī (S) (F) **1.** crawling. **2.** snake. **3.** the wife of a rudra.

Sarūpā (S) (F) **1.** uniform; similar; embodied; beautiful; handsome. **3.** a wife of Bhūta and mother of many rudras (*Bh. Purāṇa*).

Śarvā (S) (F) **1.** consort of Śiva. **3.** another name for Umā.

Sarvā (S) (F) **1.** while; complete; perfect. **3.** a Purāṇic river (*M. Bh.*).

Sarvajñā (S) (F) **1.** knower of all. **2.** omnicient. **3.** a yoginī; another name for Durgā.

Sarvakāmadughā (S) (F) **1.** fulfiller of all desires. **3.** a daughter of Surabhi (*M. Bh.*).

Sarvamaṅgalā (S) (F) **1.** universally auspicious. **3.** another name for Durgā and Lakṣmi.

Sarvāṇī (S) (F) **1.** omnipresent. **2.** perfect. **3.** another name for Śiva's wife or Durgā.

Śarvāṇī (S) (F) Śiva's wife.

Sarvapā (S) (F) **1.** drinking everything. **3.** the wife of the daitya Bali.

Śarvapatni (S) (F) **1.** the wife of Śiva. **3.** another name for Pārvatī.

Śārvarī (S) (F) night.

Śarvarī (S) (F) **1.** the star spangled night; evening; twilight. **3.** the wife of Doṣa and mother of Śiśumāra.

Sarvasahā (S) (F) **1.** one who endures all. **2.** all enduring. **3.** another name for the earth; *Commiphora mukul.*

Sarvasaṅgā (S) (F) **1.** going with all. **3.** a river (*M. Bh.*).

Sarvāstrā (S) (F) **1.** with all weapons. **3.** one of the 16 Jaina vidyādevīs.

Sarvayaśā (S) (F) **1.** famous among all. **3.** a queen of Ayodhyā who was the mother of Anantanātha Jaina. Tīrthaṅkara (*J. Literature*).

Sarveśā (S) (F) goddess of all.

Sarveśī (S) (F) desired by all.

Sarvikā (S) (F) **1.** universal. **2.** all; whole; entire.

Śaśāṅkavatī (S) (F) like the moon.

Śaśī (S) (F) **1.** hare marked. **3.** an apsarā.

Śaśibhās (S) (F) moonbeam.

Śaśikalā (S) (F) **1.** digit of the moon. **3.** the daughter of King Subāhu of Kāśī and the wife of Emperor Sudarśana.

Śaśikāntā (S) (F) **1.** beloved of the moon. **2.** the white lotus flower (*Nelumbium speciosum*) **3.** a river.

Śaśilekhā (S) (F) **1.** a digit of the moon. **3.** an apsarā (*Brah. Purāṇa*); *Psoralia corylifolia.*

Śaśimukhī (S) (F) moon faced.

Śaśinī (S) (F) containing the moon; a digit of the moon.

Śaśiprabhā (S) (F) moonlight.

Śaśiraśmī (S) (F) moon beam.

Śaśokūlamukhī (S) (F) **1.** with a face like a sweetmeat. **3.** an attendant of Skanda.

Saśrīkā (S) (F) possessed with beauty, grace and fortune; lovely; splendid.

Ṣaṣṭhī (S) (F) **1.** a praise; a hymn. **3.** another name for Durgā.

Ṣaṣṭhidevī (S) (F) **1.** protectress of a 6 day-child. **3.** folk goddess form of Durgā.

Ṣaṣṭhīdevī (S) (F) **1.** one sixth. **3.** a goddess who is the patron of children and is considered the wife of Subrahmaṇya and the daughter of Brahmā (*D. Bhāgavata*).

Ṣaṣthikā (S) (F) the 6th day after a child's birth personified as a divine mother regarded as a form of Durgā supposed to protect children.

Śāstī (S) (F) praise; hymn.

Śasti (S) (F) praise; hymn.

Śastradevatā (S) (F) **1.** weapon. **3.** deity of weapons personified as the daughter of Kṛśāśva.

Śatabāhu (S) (F) **1.** 100 armed. **3.** a goddess.

Śatadalā (S) (F) **1.** with a 100 petals. **2.** the Indian White Rose (*Rosa alba*).

Śatadrutī (S) (F) **1.** flowing in branches. **3.** a daughter of Varuṇa and wife of Barhiṣada (*Bhā. Purāṇa*).

Śataghantā (S) (F) **1.** with a 100 spears. **3.** a mother attending on Skanda (*M. Bh.*).

Śatahradā (S) (F) **1.** containing a 100 sounds. **2.** thunderbolt. **3.** a daughter of Dakṣa and wife of Bahuputra; the mother of the rākṣasa Virādha (*V. Rāmāyaṇa*).

Śatakārā (S) (F) **1.** knower of a 100 skills. **3.** a gandharvī.

Śatākṣi (S) (F) **1.** 100 eyed. **2.** the night. **3.** another name for Durgā; Dill (*Peucedanum graveolens*).

Śatakumbhā (S) (F) **1.** with a 100 pitchers. **3.** a sacred river (*M. Bh.*).

Śatamukhī (S) (F) **1.** with a 100 faces. **3.** another name for Durgā.

Śatananā (S) (F) **1.** 100 faced. **3.** a goddess.

Śatānandā (S) (F) **1.** delighting 100s. **3.** an attendant of Skanda.

Śatapadmā (S) (F) **1.** a lotus with a 100 petals; consisting of hundred lotuses. **2.** very beautiful; tender; soft; loving. **3.** the wife of Śukra.

Śataparvā (S) (F) **1.** with a 100 portions. **3.** the wife of Śukraćārya (*M. Bh.*).

Sataprabhā (S) (F) radiant; brilliant lustre.

Śatapuṣkarā (S) (F) consisting of a 100 blue lotus flowers.

Śatapuṣpā (S) (F) **1.** consisting of 100 flowers. **2.** extremely beautiful; having a fragrant body.

Śatarūpā (S) (F) **1.** with a 100 forms. **3.** the daughter of Brahmā and sister and wife of Svāyambhuva Manu and the mother of Priyavrata, Uttānapāda, Prasūti and Ākūti (*V. Purāṇa*).

Śataśīrṣā (S) (F) **1.** 100 headed. **3.** the wife of Vāsuki (*M. Bh.*).

Satī (S) (F) **1.** truthful. **2.** a virtuous and faithful wife; a female ascetic. **3.** the wife of Viśvāmitra; the goddess Durgā described as truth personified or as a daughter of Dakṣa and wife of Bhava; a wife of Aṅgiras; a wife of Viśvāmitra (*Ṛg Veda*).

Sāti (S) (F) gaining; obtaining; gift; oblation.

Ṣaṭkūtā (S) (F) **1.** eater of 6. **3.** a form of Bhairavī.

Śātodara (S) (F) slender waisted.

Śatodarī (S) (F) **1.** with a 100 bellies. **3.** an attendant of Skanda (*M. Bh.*).

Satpṛītikā (S) (F) beloved of truth.

Śatruñjayā (S) (F) **1.** conquering enemies. **3.** a mother in Skanda's retinue (*M. Bh.*).

Sattvavatī (S) (F) **1.** pregnant. **3.** a tāntric deity.

Sāttvikī (S) (F) **1.** of true essence. **2.** spirited; vigorous; energetic; pure; true; honest. **3.** another name for Durgā.

Satvantī (S) (F) **1.** full of truth. **2.** faithful.

Śatvarī (S) (F) night.

Sātvatī (S) (F) **1.** pleasant. **2.** delighted. **3.** princess of the Satvata tribe; the mother of Śiśupāla (*M. Bh.*).

Satvatī (S) (F) truthful; faithful.

Satvī (S) (F) **1.** existent; real. **3.** a daughter of Vainateya and wife of Bṛhanmanas (*H. Purāṇa*).

Satyā (S) (F) **1.** truthful; sincere. **3.** the wife of Manthu and mother of Bhauvana (*Bh. Purāṇa*); a daughter of Nagnajit and the wife of Kṛṣṇa, the daughter of Dharma who was the wife of the agni Śanyu and mother of Bharadvāja (*M. Bh.*); another name for Durgā and Sītā.

Satyabelā (S) (F) time of truth.

Satyabhāmā (S) (F) **1.** having true lustre. **3.** a daughter of Śatrajit and one of the 8 wives of Kṛṣṇa (*M. Bh.*).

Satyadevī (S) (F) **1.** goddess of truth; shining with truth. **3.** a daughter of King Devaka and a wife of Vasudeva (*M. Purāṇa*).

Satyaratā (S) (F) **1.** devoted to truth. **3.** a Kekaya princess who married King Triśaṅku of Ayodhya (*Vā. Purāṇa*).

Satyarathā (S) (F) **1.** with a chariot of truth. **2.** truthful; honest; pious; virtuous. **3.** a wife of Triśanku (*H. Purāṇa*).

Satyasandhā (S) (F) **1.** true in promise. **3.** another name for Draupadi.

Satyāśīṣā (S) (F) a realized wish or prayer.

Satyavādinī (S) (F) **1.** always speaking the truth. **3.** a form of Dākṣāyāṇī; a goddess of the Bodhi tree (*L. Vistara*).

Satyavatī (S) (F) **1.** truthful. **3.** the daughter of the apsarā Ādrikā who became the mother of Vyāsa by sage Parāśara, she married King Śantanu of the lunar dynasty and became the mother of Vićitravīrya and Ćitrāṅgada (*M. Bh.*); a sister of Viśvāmitra; a Kekaya princess who married Triśaṅku and was the mother of Hariśćandra (*M. Bh.*); a wife of Nārada (*M. Bh*); a daughter of Gādhi and wife of Rćika who is fabled to have become the Kauśikī river (*M. Bh.*).

Saubālī (S) (F) **1.** daughter of the powerful. **3.** a wife of Dhṛtarāṣṭra (*D. Bhāgavata*).

Saubhāgyā (S) (F) **1.** welfare; success; good fortune. **2.** beauty; charm; happiness.

Saubhāgyagaurī (S) (F) **1.** goddess of fortune. **3.** a form of Pārvatī (*A. Purāṇa*).

Saubhāgyamañjarī (S) (F) beautiful blossom.

Saubhāgyasundarī (S) (F) **1.** beautiful maiden of fortune. **3.** the feminine form of Nārada.

Saudāmanī (S) (F) **1.** lightning. **3.** a daughter of Kaśyapa and Vinatā (*V. Purāṇa*); a daughter of the gandharva Hāhā (*K. Sāgara*); the consort of Indra's elephant Airāvata; an apsarā; a yakṣiṇī (*K. Sāgara*).

Saugandhikā (S) (F) **1.** fragrant. **3.** the flower garden of Kubera (*M. Bh.*); Blue Lotus (*Nymphaea stellata*); Geranium grass (*Cymbopogon schoenanlhus*).

Saujanyā (S) (F) good; kind; generosity; gentle; friend; compassionate; loving.

Saumyā (S) (F) **1.** related to the moon. **2.** calm; tranquil; beautiful; pleasing; gentle; a pearl. **3.** the 5 stars in Orions head; another name for Durgā; Arabian Jasmine (*Jasminum sambac*).

Saumyī (S) (F) moonshine.

Saunandā (S) (F) **1.** sweet natured. **3.** the wife of Vatsaprī (*Mā. Purāṇa*).

Saurabheyī (S) (F) **1.** of Surabhī. **3.** an apsarā (*M. Bh.*).

Saurabhī (S) (F) **1.** possessing fragrance. **3.** the cow daughter of Surabhi and one of the 4 cows that protect the 4 directions, hers being the east (*M. Bh.*).

Saurati (S) (F) **1.** always pleasing. **3.** a rāgiṇi.

Sauvarṇa (S) (F) made of gold.

Sauvasa (S) (F) a fragrant species of Tulasi (*Ocimum sanctum*).

Sauvīrī (S) (F) **1.** daughter of a hero; princess of the Sauvīras. **3.** the wife of King Manasyu of the Purū dynasty (*M. Bh.*).

Savadammā (S) (F) goddess of the weavers in Coimbatore who is regarded as an incarnation of Pārvatī.

Savarammā (Kannada) (F) **1.** mother of weavers; goddess who rides on horseback. **3.** another name for Maheśvarammā or Pārvatī.

Savarṇā (S) (F) **1.** similar in colour; of the same appearance. **3.** the woman substituted by Saraṇyū for herself as the wife of Sūrya and later called Ćhāyā; the daughter of Samudra and wife of sage Prāćīnabarhis, she was the mother of the Praćetas (*V. Purāṇa*).

Sāverī (S) (F) **1.** with saffron. **3.** a rāgiṇī.

Sāvinī (S) (F) **1.** one who prepares soma; nectar giving. **3.** a river.

Savitrī (S) (F) **1.** producer. **2.** mother.

Sāvitrī (S) (F) **1.** solar power. **2.** a hymn addressed to the sun; ray of light; solar ray; the ring finger. **3.** a prayer dedicated to Savitṛ or Sūrya (*Ṛg Veda*); the daughter of the sun married to Brahmā in some Purāṇas, Sāvitrī, Gāyatrī and Sarasvatī are the same; a hand-maid of Devī Umā (*M. Bh.*); the daughter of King Aśvapati and Mālatī of Madra and the wife of Satyavān of Śālva, she is considered a model of devotion (*M. Bh.*); a wife of Śiva; a form of Prākṛti; a daughter of Dakṣa and the wife of Dharma (*V. Purāṇa*); a wife of Kaśyapa; the wife of King Bhoja of Dhārā; the daughter of Aṣṭāvakra (*K. Sāgara*).

Sāvitrikā (S) (F) **1.** solar power. **3.** a Śakti.

Śāyamā (S) (F) **1.** sleeping goddess. **3.** a form of Durgā worshipped by the tāntrikas; a daughter of Meru considered an incarnation of Gaṅga; a goddess who executes the commands of the 6th Arhat; another name for Yamunā.

Semantī (S) (F) the Indian White Rose (*Rosa alba*).

Semantikā (S) (F) the Indian White Rose (*Rosa alba*).

Śemuśī (S) (F) intellect; understanding; wisdom.

Senā (S) (F) **1.** missile; dart. **2.** spear; army. **3.** Indra's wife personified as his thunderbolt (*T. Samhitā*); Kārttikeya's wife personified as armed force (*Ṛg Veda*); a queen of Śrāvasti and mother of Śambhavanātha Jaina Tīrthaṅkara (*J. Literature*).

Senajitā (S) (F) **1.** vanquishing armies. **3.** an apsarā.

Śephālī (S) (F) **1.** with drowsy bees. **2.** very fragrant; the Coral Jasmine tree (*Nyctanthes arbortristis*).

Śephālikā (S) (F) the fruit of *Nyctanlhes arbortristis*.

Sevā (S) (F) worship; homage; reverence; devotion.

Śevā (S) (F) prosperity; happiness; homage.

Śevalinī (S) (F) **1.** with a moss like surface. **3.** a river.

Sevatī (S) (F) the Indian White Rose (*Rosa alba*).

Śiċi (S) (F) flame; glow.

Siddhā (S) (F) **1.** one who has attained power in penance. 3. a form of the devī; a yoginī.

Siddhalakṣmī (S) (F) **1.** perfect fortune. 3. a form of Lakṣmī.

Siddhambā (S) (F) **1.** blessed mother. 3. another name for Durgā.

Siddhāṅganā (S) (F) an accomplished woman; a female siddha.

Siddharthā (S) (F) **1.** attainer of meaning; attainer of wealth. 3. the queen of Ayodhyā and mother of Abhinanda Jaina Tīrthaṅkara (*J. Literature*).

Siddhavatī (S) (F) **1.** achieving perfection. **3.** a goddess.

Siddhayoginī (S) (F) **1.** perfect yoginī. 3. another name for Manasā.

Siddheśvarī (S) (F) goddess of accomplishment.

Siddhi (S) (F) **1.** accomplishment; performance; fulfilment; prosperity; luck; the acquisition of magical powers; success personified. **3.** the wife of Bhaga and mother of Mahiman (*Bhā. Purāṇa*); a daughter of Dakṣa and wife of Dharma (*V. Purāṇa*); a wife of Gaṇeśa; a goddess worshipped for the attainment of any object, she is believed to have been reborn as Kuntī the mother of the Pāṇḍavas (*M. Bh.*); another name for Durgā.

Siddhidātrī (S) (F) **1.** giver of perfection. 3. a form of Durgā.

Siddhirūpinī (S) (F) goddess of achieving all.

Siddhyāyikā (S) (F) **1.** accomplisher; fulfiller; effector. 3. one of the 24 goddesses who execute the commands of the Arhats.

Śikhā (S) (F) crest; plume; topknot; flame; ray of light; pinnacle; peak.

Śikhaṇḍī (S) (F) **1.** crested. **2.** Rosary Pea (*Abruts precatorius*); Yellow Jasmine (*Jasminum humile*).

Śikhaṇḍinī (S) (F) **1.** peahen. **3.** an apsarā daughter of Kaśyapa; the wife of King Antardhāna and the mother of Havirdhāna (*V. Purāṇa*).

Śikharavāsinī (S) (F) **1.** dwelling on a peak. 3. another name for Durgā.

Śikharinī (S) (F) **1.** eminent; excellent. 2. Arabian Jasmine.

Śikra (S) (F) skilful; clever; artistic; able.

Śīlā (S) (F) **1.** calm; tranquil; good natured; good character. **3.** the wife of Kauṇḍinya.

Śilā (S) (F) **1.** rock. **3.** a daughter of Dharma and wife of Marīći (*Vā. Purāṇa*).

Śīlavatī (S) (F) **1.** virtuous; moral. 3. the wife of Ugraśravas renowned for her fidelity and chastity.

Śilpā (S) (F) variegated.

Śilpī (S) (F) artisan.

Śilpikā (S) (F) skilled in art.

Sīmā (S) (F) boundary; boundary of a field; bank; shore; horizon; summit; rule of morality.

Sīmantinī (S) (F) **1.** with hair parted. **3.** a wife of King Ćitratāngada (*M. Bh.*).

Simbala (S) (F) **1.** a small pod. **2.** the flower of the Śālmali tree (*Bombax malabaricum*); the preparer of sacrificial food.

Śimidā (S) (F) **1.** giving work. **3.** a demon.

Sindhū (S) (F) **1.** ocean; sea; river. **3.** a river famous in the Purāṇas whose goddess sits in the court of Varuṇa.

Sindhujā (S) (F) **1.** ocean born. **3.** another name for Lakṣmī.

Sindhukanyā (S) (F) **1.** daughter of the ocean. **3.** another name for Lakṣmī.

Sindhumātṛ (S) (F) **1.** mother of streams. **3.** another name for Sarasvatī.

Siṅhagāminī (S) (F) **1.** walking with a lion's gait. **3.** a gandharva maiden (*K. Vyūha*).

Sinhamati (S) (F) lion hearted; brave.

Sinhavāhinī (S) (F) **1.** drawn by lions. **3.** another name for Durgā.

Siṅhayānā (S) (F) **1.** with a car drawn by lions. **3.** another name for Durgā.

Siṅhī (S) (F) lioness.

Siṅhīkā (S) (F) **1.** lioness. **3.** a daughter of Dakṣa and wife of Kaśyapa and mother of Rāhu (*M. Bh.*); a form of Dakśāyaṇī; a rākṣasī who was the daughter of Kaśyapa and Diti and the wife of Vipraćitti and the mother of Rāhu and Ketu (*M. Bh.*).

Siṅhinī (S) (F) **1.** lioness. **3.** a Buddhist goddess.

Sinīvālī (S) (F) **1.** the day before the new moon. **2.** goddess of easy birth; goddess of fecundity. **3.** a daughter of Aṅgiras and Smṛtī, she is invoked in the *Ṛg Veda* with Sarasvatī and Rākā; in later Vedic texts she is the deity of the 1st day of the new moon and a wife of Viṣṇu; the wife of Dhātṛ and mother of Darśa (*Bhā. Purāṇa*); a river (*Mā. Purāṇa*); a daughter of Bṛhaspatī and Śubhā given in marriage to Kardama but abandoned him and lived with Soma the moon (*Vā. Purāṇa*).

Śiñjā (S) (F) **1.** tinkle; jingle. **2.** the tinkling of silver ornaments.

Śinśapā (S) (F) **1.** the Sheesham tree (*Dalbergia sissoo*); Aśoka tree (*Saraca indica*). **3.** a daughter of a king of Gāndhāra and a wife of Kṛṣṇa.

Śinśumar (S) (F) **1.** porpoise. **3.** a daughter of a Gāndhāra king and wife of Kṛṣṇa.

Śiphā (S) (F) **1.** the lash of a whip. **2.** a tuft of hair on the crown of the head. **3.** a river extolled in the *Ṛg Veda.*

Śīphālikā (S) (F) the Coral Jasmine tree (*Nyctantes arbor tristis*).

Śiprā (S) (F) **1.** cheeks. **2.** the visor of a helmet; the nose. **3.** a holy river.

Śiriṇā (S) (F) night.

Śisugandha (S) (F) **1.** with a youthful fragrance. **2.** Double Jasmine.

Śiśukumāramukhī (S) (F) **1.** with a face like a young prince. **3.** a mother in Skanda's retinue (*M. Bh.*).

Śiśumāramukhī (S) (F) **1.** dolphin faced. **3.** a mother in Skanda's retinue.

Sītā (S) (F) **1.** furrow; the track of a plough-share. **3.** a form of Dākṣāyaṇī; the eastern branch of the 4 mythical branches of the heavenly Gaṅgā; the wife of Rāma who is considered the incarnation of Māhālakṣmī, found in a field by King Janaka of Mithilā, she married Rāma of Ayodhyā and was the mother of Lava and Kuśa (*Rāmāyaṇa*).

Sitā (S) (F) **1.** white. **2.** white sugar; moonlight; handsome woman; Durvā Grass; Arabian Jasmine; the Gaṅgā river. **3.** one of the 8 Buddhist devīs.

Śītalā (S) (F) **1.** of cold disposition. **2.** sand. **3.** the goddess of smallpox.

Sītālakṣmī (S) (F) Sītā and Lakṣmī as one; purity of fortune.

Sītalammā (T) (F) **1.** mother of purity. **3.** village goddess of water.

Śitalatā (S) (F) cooling power.

Śītamañjarī (S) (F) **1.** blossom of the cold. **3.** the Coral Jasmine tree (*Nyctantes arbor tristis*).

Śītāṣī (S) (F) **1.** cold eater. **3.** a river famous in the *Purāṇas* (*M. Bh.*).

Sitasindhu (S) (F) **1.** pure river. **3.** another name for the Gaṅgā.

Sitayāminī (S) (F) moonlight.

Śītikā (S) (F) coldness.

Sītormilā (S) (F) Sīta and her sister Ūrmilā conjoined.

Śītoṣṇā (S) (F) **1.** cold and hot. **3.** a demon.

Śivā (S) (F) **1.** auspicious power; goddess of grace; final emancipation. **3.** the wife of Aṅgiras (*M. Bh.*); the wife of the vasu Anila and mother of Manojava and Avijñātagati (*M. Bh.*); the mother of the 22nd Arhat of the present Avasarpinī; a river (*M. Bh.*); a Purāṇic river (*M. Bh.*); the energy of Śiva personified as his wife, Pārvatī, Durgā, Kālī, Umā, and Gaurī.

Śivadevī (S) (F) **1.** goddess of grace; prosperity and welfare. **3.** a queen of Dvārakā and mother of Neminātha Jaina Tīrthaṅkara (*J. Literature*).

Śivadūtī (S) (F) **1.** Śiva's messenger. **3.** a form of Durgā (*Mā. Purāṇa*); a yoginī.

Śivadūtikā (S) (F) **1.** messenger of Śiva. **3.** a mother in Skanda's retinue.

Śivagaṅgā (S) (F) the Gaṅgā flowing through Śiva's hair.

Śivakāntā (S) (F) **1.** beloved of Śiva. **3.** another name for Durgā.

Śivakāriṇī (S) (F) **1.** doer of benevolent deeds. **2.** goddess of welfare. **3.** a form of Durgā.

Śivakarṇī (S) (F) **1.** procurer of prosperity. **3.** a mother in Skanda's retinue (*M. Bh.*).

Śivāli (S) (F) **1.** beloved of Śiva. **3.** another name for Pārvatī.

Śivānī (S) (F) Pārvatī the wife of Śiva.

Śivapriyā (S) (F) **1.** beloved of Śiva. **3.** another name for Durgā; Rudrakśa tree (*Eleocarpus ganitrus*).

Śivasundarī (S) (F) **1.** wife of Śiva. **3.** another name for Pārvatī.

Śivātmikā (S) (F) soul of Śiva; consisting of the essence of Śiva.

Śivavallabhā (S) (F) **1.** loved by Śiva; the Indian white rose (*Rosa alba*). **3.** another name for Pārvatī.

Śivikā (S) (F) palanquin.

Smaradhvajā (S) (F) a bright moonlit night.

Smaradūtī (S) (F) **1.** messenger of love. **3.** a maid of Vṛndā the wife of Jalandhara (*P. Purāṇa*).

Smaranī (S) (F) **1.** act of remembering. **2.** a rosary of beads.

Smarapriyā (S) (F) **1.** dear to Kāma. **3.** another name for Rati.

Śmaśānabhairavī (S) (F) **1.** terrible goddess of crematoriums. **3.** a form of Durgā.

Śmaśānakālikā (S) (F) **1.** black goddess of crematoriums. **3.** a form of Durgā.

Smerā (S) (F) smiling; friendly; blossomed; evident; apparent.

Smiti (S) (F) a smile; laughter.

Smṛti (S) (F) **1.** remembrance. **2.** a code of laws; desire; wish; understanding. **3.** memory personified as the daughter of Dakṣa and wife of Aṅgiras and the mother of Sinīvālī, Kūhū, Rākā and Anumatī (*V. Purāṇa*); in later texts she is the daughter of Dharma and Medhā.

Smṛtimālā (S) (F) garland of memories.

Snehala (S) (F) full of affection.

Snehalatā (S) (F) vine of love.

Snehamayī (S) (F) loving.

Snigdhā (S) (F) adhesive; tender; friendly; charming; agreeable; loving; attached; glossy; shining; intent; resplendant.

Śobhā (S) (F) splendour; brilliance; lustre; beauty; grace; loveliness.

Śobhanā (S) (F) **1.** beautiful. **2.** turmeric. **3.** an attendant of Skanda.

Śobhikā (S) (F) brilliant; beautiful.

Śobhinī (S) (F) graceful; splendid.

Śobhiṣṭhā (S) (F) most beautiful; splendid.

Sobodhinī (S) (F) waking the gods.

Śoćayantī (S) (F) **1.** inflaming. **3.** an apsarā (*T. Brāhmaṇa*).

Śoći (S) (F) flame.

Śoḍaṣī (S) (F) **1.** 16 year old; having the length of one sixteenth of a man. **3.** one of the 12 forms of Durgā; one of the 10 mahāvidyās.

Sohanā (H) (F) graceful; beautiful.

Sohanī (H) (F) **1.** beautiful. **3.** a rāga.

Sohelā (H) (F) beautiful.

Sohinī (S) (F) splendid; adorned; beautiful.

Śokarahitā (S) (F) **1.** griefless; without troubles. **3.** a form of Durgā.

Śolī (S) (F) the night.

Somā (S) (F) **1.** the Soma plant; moonlike. **2.** beautiful. **3.** an apsarā (*M. Bh.*).

Somābhā (S) (F) like the moon.

Somadā (S) (F) **1.** like a moon. **2.** giver of tranquility; procurer of nectar. **3.** a gandharvī (*Rāmāyaṇa*).

Somadevī (S) (F) **1.** goddess of nectar. **3.** the wife of Kāmapāla.

Somadhārā (S) (F) **1.** stream of Soma. **3.** the Milky Way.

Somāhuti (S) (F) a Soma sacrifice.

Somalatā (S) (F) **1.** the creeper from which Soma is extracted. **3.** another name for the river Godāvarī; Common Rue (*Ruta graverlens*).

Somālī (S) (F) beloved of the moon.

Somapatnī (S) (F) wife of Soma; wife of the moon.

Somaśṛī (S) (F) divine nectar.

Somasutā (S) (F) daughter of the moon; the river Narmadā.

Somavatī (S) (F) containing Soma.

Somilā (S) (F) **1.** moonlike. **2.** calm.

Śoṇā (S) (F) **1.** redness; blooded; fiery. **3.** a Purāṇic river supposed to be a source of Agni (*M. Bh:*)

Sonā (H) (F) gold.

Sonākṣi (H) (F) **1.** golden eyed. **3.** another name for Pārvatī.

Sonālī (H) (F) Indian laburnum; golden.

Sonālikā (H) (F) golden.

Sonam (H) (F) **1.** goldlike. **2.** beautiful; lucky.

Śoṇamaṇī (S) (F) **1.** red gem. **2.** ruby.

Soni (H) (F) golden; beautiful.

Sonikā (H) (F) with golden beauty.

Śoṇitā (S) (F) **1.** blooded; red. **2.** Saffron (*Crocus sativus*).

Śoṇitapriyā (S) (F) **1.** lover of blood. **3.** a goddess (*S. Dvatrinśikā*).

Sovā (S) (F) one's own.

Spandanā (S) (F) throbbing; heart throb; pulsating beauty.

Sparśānanda (S) (F) **1.** delighting the touch. **3.** an apsarā.

Śraddhā (S) (F) **1.** faith; confidence; reverence; trust; loyalty. **3.** reverence personified as a daughter of Dakṣa and Prasūtī and wife of Dharma and mother of Kāma (*V. Purāṇa*); daughter of Sūrya also known as Sāvitrī (*Ś. Brahmaṇa*); wife of Vaivasvata Manu; a daughter of Prajāpati Kardama and Devahūtī who married Aṅgiras and was the mother of Utathya and Bṛhaspati (*Bhāgavata*).

Sragviṇī (S) (F) **1.** wearing a wreath of flowers. **3.** a goddess.

Śrāvaṇī (S) (F) the day of the fullmoon in the month of Śrāvaṇa (July/August).

Sravantī (S) (F) **1.** flowing. **2.** a river.

Śraviṣṭhā (S) (F) **1.** most famous. **3.** a nakṣatra (*V's B. Samhitā*); the daughter of Ćitraka (*H. Purāṇa*).

Śreyā (S) (F) best; beautiful; excellent.

Śrī (S) (F) **1.** diffusing radiance. **2.** prosperity; beauty and grace conjoined; light; grace; splendour; glory; welfare; power; majesty. **3.** Lakṣmī as goddess of prosperity (*Ś. Brāhmaṇa*); a Buddhist goddess; another name for Sarasvatī; a daughter of King Suśarman (*K. Sāgara*); Indian Lotus (*Nelumbium nucifera*).

Śrībālā (S) (F) divine maiden.

Śrībhadrā (S) (F) **1.** best among people. **3.** a goddess; a wife of Bimbisāra (*B. Literature*).

Śrīdā (S) (F) **1.** given by Lakṣmī; bestowing fortune. **3.** another name for Rādhā.

Śrīdevā (S) (F) **1.** fortune giver. **3.** a daughter of King Devaka and wife of

Vasudeva and mother of Nandaka (*Bhāgavata*).

Śrīdevī (S) (F) 1. goddess of prosperity. 3. another name for Lakṣmī; a queen of Ayodhyā.

Śrīgarbhā (S) (F) 1. having welfare as the inner nature. 3. another name for Rādhā.

Śrīhara (S) (F) 1. excelling all in beauty. 3. another name for Rādhā.

Śrīhastinī (S) (F) 1. in the hands of fortune. 2. the sunflower (*Heliotropium indicum*) supposed to be held by Śrī.

Śrikā (S) (F) prosperity; fortune; wealth; beauty.

Śrīkalā (S) (F) a portion of Lakṣmī.

Śrīkāma (S) (F) 1. desirous of glory. 3. another name for Rādhā.

Śrīkaṇṭhikā (S) (F) 1. graceful voiced. 3. a rāga.

Śrīkriyārūpiṇi (S) (F) 1. incarnation of goddess of fortune. 3. another name for Rādhā.

Śrilā (S) (F) given by Lakṣmī; prosperous; happy; beautiful; eminent.

Śrīlakṣmi (S) (F) divine Lakṣmī.

Śrīlalitā (S) (F) graceful; prosperous.

Śrīlatā (S) (F) divine vine.

Śrīmahādevī (S) (F) 1. divine Pārvatī. 3. the mother of Śankara.

Śrīmaṅgalā (S) (F) goddess of prosperity.

Śrīmaṇī (S) (F) 1. best among the jewels. 2. beautiful jewel. 3. a rāga.

Śrīmātā (S) (F) 1. divine mother. 3. a form of the devī (*Sk. Purāṇu*).

Śrīmatī (S) (F) 1. bearer of prosperity; beauty and grace. 2. pleasant; royal; divine; beautiful. 3. a gandharva maid; a mother in Skanda's retinue (*M. Bh.*); Spanish Jasmine (*Jasminum grandiflorum*).

Śrīmukhī (S) (F) with a radiant face.

Śrīṇā (S) (F) night.

Śrīnandinī (S) (F) daughter of prosperity.

Śrīnitambā (S) (F) 1. with beautiful hips. 3. another name for Rādhā.

Śrīvāni (S) (F) divine speech.

Śrīvidyā (S) (F) 1. divine knowledge. 3. a form of Durgā.

Śrivṛddhī (S) (F) 1. increasing fortune. 3. a Buddhist goddess; the mother of the 17th Arhat; a deity of the Bodhi tree (*L. Vistara*).

Śriyā (S) (F) prosperity and happiness personified as the wife of Śrīdhara.

Śṛngārāvalli (S) (F) 1. garland of love. 3. the mother of the Tamil poet Kambar.

Śṛṅgārikā (S) (F) 1. horned. 2. love.

Śṛṅginī (S) (F) 1. horned; crested. 2. cow; *Jasminum sambac.*

Śṛṅgotpādinī (S) (F) 1. producer of horns. 3. a yakṣinī who changes men into animals.

Sṛñjayī (S) (F) 1. giving victory. 3. a wife of Bhajamāna (*H. Purāṇa*).

Sṛti (S) (F) road; path.

Śrutā (S) (F) 1. famous; glorious; celebrated. 2. heard; known. 3. a daughter of Dīrghadanṣtra (*K. Sāgara*); sacred knowledge personified as a daughter of Dharma and Medha (*Purāṇa*).

Śrutadevā (S) (F) 1. with divine knowledge. 3. a daughter of Sūra (*H. Purāṇa*).

Śrutadevī (S) (F) 1. goddess of knowledge. 3. name of a sister of Vasudeva and aunt of Kṛṣṇa (*Bhāgavata*); another name for Sarasvatī.

Śrutakīrtī (S) (F) 1. of well known glory. 2. famous. 3. a wife of Śatrughna and daughter of Kuśadhvaja (*K. Rāmāyaṇa*); a sister of Vasudeva and aunt of Kṛṣṇa (*Bhāgavata*).

Śrutasenā (S) (F) 1. with a famous army. 3. a wife of Kṛṣṇa (*H. Purāṇa*).

Śrutasomā (S) (F) 1. of the moon. 3. a wife of Kṛṣṇa (*H. Purāṇa*).

Śrutaśravas (S) (F) 1. listener of the scriptures. 3. a sister of Vasudeva and aunt of Kṛṣṇa (*Bhāgavata*); a wife of King Damaghoṣa of Ćedi and mother of Śiśupāla.

Śrutavatī (S) (F) 1. favourably known. 3. a daughter of sage Bharadvāja and Ghṛtāćī (*M. Bh.*)

Śrutavindā (S) (F) **1.** knower of the scriptures. **3.** a river (*Bhā. Purāṇa*).

Śrutī (S) (F) hearing; ear; knowledge of the Vedas.

Śrutibuddhī (S) (F) **1.** with knowledge of scriptures. **3.** a daughter of Atri and wife of Kardama (*V. Purāṇa*).

Stambhakī (S) (F) **1.** post; pillar. **3.** a goddess.

Stāvā (S) (F) **1.** praiser. **3.** an apsarā.

Sthāvarā (S) (F) **1.** stable; immovable; standing still; firm; constant. **3.** a Buddhist goddess (*L. Vistara*).

Sthirā (S) (F) **1.** strong minded. **3.** another name for the earth.

Strīratna (S) (F) **1.** jewel of a woman. **3.** another name for Lakṣmī.

Strītamā (S) (F) a complete woman.

Stuti (S) (F) **1.** praise; eulogy; adulation. **3.** the wife of Pratihartṛ; another name for Durgā.

Subāhū (S) (F) **1.** with beautiful arms. **3.** an apsarā daughter of Kaśyapa and Prādhā (*M.Bh.*).

Subalī (S) (F) very strong; very powerful.

Subāndhava (S) (F) **1.** good friend. **3.** another name for Śiva.

Subbālakṣmī (S) (F) divine fortune.

Śubhā (S) (F) **1.** splendour; beauty; ornament; decoration; light; lustre; desire. **2.** an assembly of the gods. **3.** a companion of the goddess Umā; another name for Dhruva's mother.

Subhā (S) (F) **1.** prosperous; auspicious. **3.** a wife of Aṅgiras and mother of Bṛhatkirti (*M. Bh.*).

Śubhadantī (S) (F) **1.** with good teeth. **3.** the elephant consort of Puṣpadanta.

Subhadrā (S) (F) **1.** glorious; splendid; auspicious. **3.** a form of Durgā (*H. Ć. Ćintāmaṇi*); a wife of Durgama (*Mā. Purāṇa*); a daughter of Balin and wife of Avīkṣit; a grand daughter of Rukmin and wife of Aniruddha (*V. Purāṇa*); a daughter of the asura Sumāya (*K. Sāgara*); the daughter of Vasudeva and Devakī and the sister of Kṛṣṇa and the wife of Arjuna and the mother of Abhimanyu (*M. Bh.*); a daughter of Surabhi and guardian of the western region (*M. Bh.*).

Subhāgā (S) (F) **1.** fortunate; rich. **3.** a daughter of Raudrāśva.

Subhagā (S) (F) **1.** good fortune. **2.** wild Jasmine; Sacred Basil (*Ocimum sanctum*); honoured mother; beloved by husband. **3.** a daughter of Kaśyapa and Prādhā (*M. Bh.*); a mother in Skanda's retinue.

Śubhagā (S) (F) **1.** going well. **2.** gracious; elegant. **3.** a Śakti (*H. Ć. Ćintāmaṇi*).

Śubhagābhīrī (S) (F) **1.** deep and virtuous. **3.** a rāgiṇī.

Śubhalakṣmī (S) (F) radiant Lakṣmī.

Śubhalocanā (S) (F) fair eyed.

Śubhamālā (S) (F) **1.** with a splendid garland. **3.** a gandharvī (*K. Vyuha*).

Śubhamayī (S) (F) **1.** full of splendour. **2.** splendid; beautiful.

Śubhānandā (S) (F) **1.** beauty and pleasure conjoined. **2.** delighting in virtues. **3.** a goddess said to be a form of Dākṣāyāṇī.

Śubhāṅgī (S) (F) **1.** handsome limbed. **3.** the daughter of Rukmin and wife of Pradyumna (*H. Purāṇa*); a wife of Kubera; a wife of Kuru of the lunar dynasty and the mother of Vidura (*M. Bh.*); another name for Rati.

Śubhaṅkarī (S) (F) **1.** doer of good deeds; virtuous. **3.** another name for Pārvatī.

Subhāryā (S) (F) **1.** prosperous lady. **2.** graceful lady. **3.** a daughter of Śvaphalka and sister of Akrūra (*Bhāgavata*).

Subhāsaṇī (S) (F) soft spoken.

Subhaṣitā (S) (F) spoken well of.

Śubhasūćanī (S) (F) **1.** indicating good. **3.** a deity worshipped by women in times of calamity.

Śubhavaktrā (S) (F) **1.** of auspicious face. **3.** a mother in Skanda's retinue (*M. Bh.*).

Śubhikā (S) (F) a garland of auspicious flowers.

Subhīmā (S) (F) **1.** very dreadful or terrible. **3.** a wife of Kṛṣṇa (*H. Purāṇa*).

Śubhrā (S) (F) **1.** radiant. **3.** another name for the Gaṅgā.

Śubhrāvatī (S) (F) **1.** fair complexioned. **3.** a river (*H. Purāṇa*).

Śubhrū (S) (F) **1.** lovely browed woman. **3.** an attendant of Skanda (*M. Bh.*).

Subuddhī (S) (F) **1.** of good intellect. **2.** understanding; wise; clever.

Sućārā (S) (F) **1.** very skilful. **2.** a good performer. **3.** a daughter of Śvaphalka.

Sućarā (S) (F) **1.** with a beautiful gait. **3.** an apsarā (*V. Purāṇa*).

Suććhāyā (S) (F) **1.** throwing a beautiful shadow. **2.** beautiful; shining brightly; splendid. **3.** the wife of Śliṣṭi (*V. Purāṇa*).

Śućī (S) (F) **1.** shining; bright; clean; holy; virtuous. **3.** a daughter of Tāmrā and wife of Kaśyapa regarded as the mother of waterfowl (*H. Purāṇa*).

Śućikā (S) (F) **1.** puritan; sacred. **3.** an apsarā (*M. Bh.*).

Śućimallikā (S) (F) **1.** the white vine. **2.** Arabian Jasmine.

Śućmukhī (S) (F) **1.** pure faced. **3.** the maid of princess Prabhāvatī the daughter of Vajranābha.

Sućintā (S) (F) deep thought.

Śućiṣmatī (S) (F) **1.** shining; radiant. **3.** the mother of Agni; an apsarā in Kubera's assembly (*M. Bh.*).

Śućismitā (S) (F) **1.** with a pious smile. **3.** an apsarā in Kubera's assembly (*M. Bh.*).

Sućitā (S) (F) sacred; propitious.

Sudāmā (S) (F) **1.** bountiful. **3.** a mother in Skanda's retinue; a river *(Rāmāyaṇa)*.

Sudāminī (S) (F) **1.** as bright as lightning. **2.** bright; light; wealthy. **3.** a wife of Śamīka (*Bhā. Purāṇa*).

Sudantā (S) (F) **1.** with good teeth. **3.** an apsarā.

Sudantī (S) (F) **1.** with good teeth. **3.** the female elephant of the northwest quarter.

Sudarulakṣmī (S) (F) goddess of beauty.

Sudarśanā (S) (F) **1.** lovely in appearance; pleasing to eyes. **3.** a gandharva maiden, the daughter of Ikṣvāku dynasty king, Duryodhana and Narmadā and wife of the god Agni, she is said to have been the most beautiful woman born (*M. Bh.*).

Sudarśinī (S) (F) **1.** lovely in appearance; pleasing to eyes. **2.** a lotus pond.

Sudattā (S) (F) **1.** well given. **3.** a wife of Kṛṣṇa (*M. Bh.*).

Śuddhā (S) (F) **1.** clean; pure; holy; sacred. **3.** a daughter of Sinhahanu (*B. Literature*).

Śuddhī (S) (F) **1.** purification; holiness; truth; clearness. **3.** a Śakti of Viṣṇu; Dākṣāyāṇī in Kapālamoćana; another name for Durgā.

Sudeṣṇā (S) (F) **1.** born in a good place. **3.** the daughter of the king of Kekaya and wife of King Virāṭa of Matsya and the mother of Uttarā (*M. Bh.*); the wife of King Bali and the mother of Aṅga, Vaṅga, Kaliṅga, Puṇḍra and Suhma by the hermit Dīrghatamas (*Bhāgavata*).

Sudevā (S) (F) **1.** a real goddess. **3.** the daughter of King Ariha of Aṅga and the father of King Ṛkṣa (*M. Bh.*); the wife of King Vikuṇṭha of the Purū dynasty and the mother of King Ajamīdha (*M. Bh.*); the daughter of King Devarāta of Kāśī and the wife of Ikṣvāku, she is supposed to have been an incarnation of Lakṣmi (*P. Purāṇa*).

Sudevī (S) (F) **1.** real goddess. **3.** the wife of Nābhi and mother of Ṛṣabha (*Bhā. Purāṇa*).

Sudhā (S) (F) **1.** good drink; welfare; ease, comfort. **2.** nectar; lightning; honey, Soma, water. **3.** the wife of a rudra; another name for the Gaṅga; *Desmodium gangeticum*; Prickly Pear (*Opuntia dillenii*); Black Myrobalan (*Terminalia chebula*).

Sudhāmukhī (S) (F) **1.** nectar mouthed. **3.** an apsarā.

Sudhānśuratna (S) (F) **1.** jewel of the moon. **2.** pearl.

Sudharmā (S) (F) **1.** of right path; follower of law. **3.** the assembly hall of the gods (*Bhāgavata*); the wife of Mātali and the mother of Guṇakeśī (*M. Bh.*).

Sudhī (S) (F) good sense; intelligence.

Sudīkṣā (S) (F) **1.** beautiful consecration. **3.** another name for Lakṣmī.

Suditi (S) (F) bright flame.

Śudrā (S) (F) **1.** a woman of the 4th caste. **3.** a daughter of Raudrāśva.

Sudṛśī (S) (F) **1.** pleasing to the eye. **2.** pretty; with beautiful eyes.

Sugaṇā (S) (F) **1.** good attendant. **3.** a mother in Skanda's retinue (*M. Bh.*).

Sugandhā (S) (F) **1.** fragrant; Sacred Basil (*Ocimum sanctum*) **3.** a form of Dākṣāyāṇī; an apsarā (*M. Bh.*); Fleabane (*Artemisia vulgaris*); Caraway (*Carum carvi*); *Hiptage madoblata*.

Sugandhī (S) (F) **1.** fragrant. **2.** the small banana; the blue lotus (*Nymphaea slellata*); sandal. **3.** a wife of Vasudeva and mother of Puṇḍra (*Vā. Purāṇa*); *Elellaria cardomomum*.

Sugandhikā (S) (F) fragrant.

Sugatī (S) (F) welfare; happiness; bliss.

Sugātrī (S) (F) fair limbed; graceful; beautiful.

Sugtṣṇā (S) (F) **1.** singing well. **3.** a kinnarī.

Sugrīvī (S) (F) **1.** beautiful necked. **3.** a daughter of Kaśyapa and Tāmrā and mother of horses, camels and donkeys (*H. Purāṇa*); an apsarā (*H. Purāṇa*).

Suhā (S) (F) **1.** rejoicing. **3.** a rāga.

Suhāsinī (S) (F) smiling beautifully.

Suhelā (S) (F) easily accessible.

Suhitā (S) (F) **1.** beneficial. **2.** suitable. **3.** one of the 7 tongues of fire.

Sujasā (S) (F) **1.** of good fame. **3.** mother of Anantanātha.

Sujātā (S) (F) **1.** well born. **2.** noble; beautiful. **3.** a daughter of Uddālaka and wife of Kahoda (*M. Bh.*).

Sukalā (S) (F) a good part; very skilled.

Sukaṇṭhi (S) (F) **1.** sweet voiced. **2.** the female Indian cuckoo. **3.** an apsarā (*B. Rāmāyaṇa*).

Sukanyā (S) (F) **1.** beautiful maiden. **3.** the daughter of Śaryāti and wife of ṛṣi Ćyavana (*H. Purāṇa*); the wife of sage Mātariśvan and the mother of Maṅkaṇa.

Śukavāṇi (S) (F) with a voice like the note of a parrot.

Sukeśī (S) (F) **1.** with beautiful hair. **3.** the daughter of the king of Gāndhāra and a wife of Kṛṣṇa (*M. Bh.*); an apsarā (*M. Bh.*); a daughter of King Ketuvīrya of Magadha and wife of Marutta (*Mā. Purāṇa*).

Sukhā (S) (F) **1.** piety; virtue; ease; comfort; pleasure. **3.** one of the 9 Śaktis of Śiva.

Sukhadā (S) (F) **1.** bestower of happiness. **3.** an apsarā; another name for the Gaṅgā; Mimosa suma; Prosopis spicigera.

Sukhajammā (**Kannada**) (F) **1.** the mother who grants happiness. **3.** the village goddess of smallpox.

Sukhavatī (S) (F) **1.** happy. **3.** the paradise of Amitābha (*B. Literature*); the wife of Sūryaprabhā (*K. Sāgara*).

Śukī (S) (F) **1.** parrot. **2.** bright; talkative; quickwitted. **3.** a daughter of Kaśyapa and Tāmrā and the mother of Natā (*V. Rāmāyaṇa*); the mythical mother of parrots and wife of Kaśyapa; the wife of Saptarṣi (*Bh. Purāṇa*).

Sukīrtī (S) (F) well praised; hymn of praise.

Śuklā (S) (F) **1.** white; bright; pure; white cow. **3.** another name for Sarasvatī.

Sukrīḍā (S) (F) **1.** sporting. **3.** an apsarā.

Sukṛtā (S) (F) **1.** a pious deed; doing good; pious. **3.** a river (*V. Purāṇa*).

Sukṛtī (S) (F) kindness; good conduct; virtue; kindness; auspiciousness.

Sukṣa (S) (F) with good eyes.

Sūkti (S) (F) beautiful verse; a wise saying.

Śukti (S) (F) **1.** shining; bright. **2.** an oyster shell.

Śuktimatī (S) (F) **1.** having oyster shells. **3.** a river (*M. Bh.*).

Sukukṣī (S) (F) **1.** born from a good womb. **2.** noble. **3.** a gandharva maiden (*K. Vyuha*).

Sukumārī (S) (F) **1.** very tender; very delicate; with soft and delicate skin. **2.** *Jasminum sambac.* **3.** a river (*M. Bh.*); a daughter of King Sṛñjaya and a wife of sage Nārada.

Sukusumā (S) (F) **1.** ornamented with beautiful flowers. **3.** a mother in Skanda's retinue (*M. Bh.*).

Sulabhā (S) (F) **1.** easily available. **2.** attainable; *Jasminum sambac; Ocimum sanctum.* **3.** an ascetic who held discourse with King Janaka (*M. Bh.*).

Sulabhalalitā (S) (F) easily obtainable pretty woman.

Śūladharā (S) (F) **1.** consort of Śiva. **3.** another name for Durgā.

Śūladhāriṇī (S) (F) **1.** holding a spear. **3.** another name for Durgā.

Sulakṣaṇā (S) (F) **1.** with auspicious marks. **2.** fortunate; with good qualities. **3.** a wife of Kṛṣṇa; a friend of Umā; a wife of Ćaṇḍaghoṣa.

Sulakṣmī (S) (F) **1.** divine Lakṣmī. **3.** one of the 4 divine women who rose out of the Ocean of Milk (*P. Purāṇa*).

Sulekhā (S) (F) **1.** having auspicious lines. **2.** fortunate.

Śūlinī (S) (F) **1.** armed with a spear. **3.** another name for Durgā.

Sulocanā (S) (F) **1.** with beautiful eyes. **3.** a wife of Indrajit; an apsarā (*H. Purāṇa*); a yakṣiṇī (*K. Sāgara*); the wife of King Mādhava (*P. Purāṇa*).

Sulohitā (S) (F) **1.** very red. **3.** one of the 7 tongues of fire.

Sulomā (S) (F) **1.** with beautiful hair. **2.** Indian Redwood (*Soymida febrifuga*).

Sumadātmajā (S) (F) **1.** daughter of passion. **3.** an apsarā.

Sumadhyā (S) (F) **1.** graceful woman; slender waisted. **3.** daughter of Madirākṣa (*M. Bh.*).

Sumālinī (S) (F) **1.** well garlanded. **3.** a gandharvī (*K. Vyuha*).

Sumāllikā (S) (F) a special kind of geese; a beautiful shuttle.

Sumanā (S) (F) **1.** charming; lovely; beautiful; wheat; Spanish Jasmine (*Jasminum grandiflorum*); *Rosa glandulifera.* **3.** a wife of Dama (*Mā. Purāṇa*); the wife of Madhu and mother of Vīravrata.

Sumaṅgalā (S) (F) **1.** auspicious. **3.** an apsarā; a mother in Skanda's retinue (*M. Bh.*); a river (*K. Purāṇa*); a queen of Ayodhyā and mother of Sumatīnātha Jaina Tīrthaṅkara (*J. Literature*).

Sumaṅgalī (S) (F) **1.** auspicious. **3.** another name for Pārvatī.

Sumatī (S) (F) **1.** good mind; benevolence; kindness; devotion. **3.** a daughter of Kratu (*V. Purāṇa*); a wife of Viṣṇuyaśas and mother of Kalkin (*K. Purāṇa*); a wife of Lava.

Sumāvalī (S) (F) a garland of flowers.

Sumāyā (S) (F) **1.** with excellent plans. **3.** a daughter of Maya.

Śumbhamathanī (S) (F) **1.** Śumbha destroying. **3.** another name for Durgā.

Sumirā (S) (F) much remembered; overtly praised.

Sumitā (S) (F) well measured; having a balanced form; one who has a beautiful body.

Sumitrā (S) (F) **1.** a nice friend; having many friends. **3.** a wife of Daśaratha and mother of Lakṣmaṇa and Śatrughna (*Rāmāyaṇa*); a wife of Kṛṣṇa (*M. Bh.*); a yakṣiṇī (*K. Sāgara*); the mother of Mārkaṇḍeya; the mother of Jayadeva.

Sumnāvarī (S) (F) **1.** bringing joy. **3.** another name for Uṣās (*Ṛg Veda*).

Sumonā (S) (F) calm; quiet.

Sumukhī (S) (F) **1.** bright faced; lovely; pleasing; learned; mirror. **3.** the mother of a serpent called Aśvasena on the arrow of Karṇa (*M. Bh.*); an apsarā (*M. Bh.*).

Sumuṇḍīka (S) (F) **1.** with a good head. **3.** an asura.

Sunakṣatrā (S) (F) **1.** born under an auspicious constellation. **3.** a mother in Skanda's retinue.

Sunāmī (S) (F) **1.** well named. **3.** a daughter of Devaka and wife of Vasudeva (*H. Purāṇa*).

Sunandā (S) (F) **1.** pleasing; delighting. **3.** a wife of Kṛṣṇa (*H. Purāṇa*); the mother of Bāhu and Vālin; a river (*Bhā. Purāṇa*); a club made by Tvaṣṭṛ (*Mā. Purāṇa*); a Kekaya princess who was married to King Sārvabhauma of the Kuru dynasty and the mother of Jayatsena (*M. Bh.*); a daughter of King Sarvasena of Kāśī and a wife of King Bharata and the mother of Bhaumanyu (*M. Bh.*); a princess of Śibi who married King Pratīpa and was the mother of Devāpi, Śāntanu and Bālhīka (*M. Bh.*); a daughter of Vīrabāhu and sister of King Subāhu of Ćedi (*M. Bh.*); another name for Umā.

Sunandī (S) (F) pleasing; delighting.

Sunayā (S) (F) **1.** very just; well conducted. **3.** the mother of Jaina Tīrthaṅkara Sitalanatha and queen of Bhadrikapuri (*J. Literature*).

Sunayanā (S) (F) with beautiful eyes.

Sundaravatī (S) (F) **1.** having beauty. **3.** a river.

Sundarī (S) (F) **1.** beautiful. **3.** a yoginī; an apsarā (*B. Rāmāyaṇa*); a daughter of Svaphalka (*H. Purāṇa*); a daughter of Vaiśvānara (*V. Purāṇa*); a rākṣasi who was the wife of Mālyavat (*Rāmāyaṇa*).

Sundarīvallī (S) (F) **1.** beautiful vine. **3.** a daughter of Mahāviṣṇu (*Sk. Purāṇa*).

Sunehrī (H) (F) golden.

Sunīlā (S) (F) of blue colour; very blue; dark.

Sunīlimā (S) (F) bright blue; dark.

Suniṣkā (S) (F) with beautiful ornaments.

Sunītā (S) (F) **1.** well conducted; well behaved. **2.** polite; civil.

Sunīthā (S) (F) **1.** well disposed; righteous; virtuous; moral. **3.** the firstborn mental daughter of Mṛtyu or death who became the wife of King Aṅga and was the mother of Veṇa (*H. Purāṇa*).

Sunīti (S) (F) **1.** good conduct. **2.** wisdom; discretion. **3.** the wife of Uttānapāda and mother of Dhruva (*Bhā. Piirāṇa*).

Suṅkalammā (Kannada) (F) **1.** mother of diseases. **3.** the village goddess of smallpox.

Sūnṛtā (S) (F) **1.** gladness; joy; exultation; song of joy; kindness. **3.** the daughter of Dharma and wife of Uttānapāda (*H. Purāṇa*); an apsarā; truth personified as a goddess (*Ṛg Veda*).

Suparṇā (S) (F) **1.** with beautiful leaves. **2.** a lotus plant. **3.** the mother of Garuḍa (*Bhā. Purāṇa*); another name for Pārvatī.

Suphulla (S) (F) with beautiful blossoms.

Suprabhā (S) (F) **1.** very bright. **2.** beautiful; splendid. **3.** a wife of Kṛṣṇa (*M. Bh.*); an asura who was the daughter of Kaśyapa and Svarbhānu (*A. Purāṇa*); the river Sarasvatī when it flows through Puṣkara; a daughter of sage Vadānya and wife of Aṣṭāvakra; a daughter of Dakṣa and mother of arrows; a daughter of King Suratha and wife of Nābhāga and the mother of Bhalandana (*Mā. Purāṇa*); one of the 7 tongues of fire; a mother in Skanda's retinue (*M. Bh.*); *Psoralia corylifolia.*

Suprabhāta (S) (F) illuminated by dawn; a morning prayer.

Suprajā (S) (F) **1.** with many children. **3.** a wife of the agni Bhānu (*M. Bh.*).

Suprasādā (S) (F) **1.** auspicious; propitious; gracious. **3.** a mother in Skanda's retinue (*M. Bh.*).

Supratīkinī (S) (F) **1.** with a beautiful form. **3.** the wife of the elephant Supratīka.

Supratiṣṭhā (S) (F) **1.** well established. **2.** famous; glorious; installation; consecration. **3.** a mother in Skanda's retinue (*M. Bh.*).

Supratiṣṭhitā (S) (F) **1.** standing firm; consecrated; celebrated; with beautiful legs. **3.** an apsarā (*V. Purāṇa*).

Suprayogā (S) (F) **1.** well practised. **2.** well managed; dextrous. **3.** a sacred river believed to be a source of Agni (*M. Bh.*).

Supremā (S) (F) very loving.

Suprīti (S) (F) great joy or delight.

Supriyā (S) (F) **1.** very dear. **2.** lovely. **3.** an apsarā daughter of Kaśyapa and Prādhā (*M. Bh.*); Indian Pennywort (*Hydrocotyle asiatica*).

Supuṇyā (S) (F) **1.** bearer of good deeds; of great religious merit. **3.** a river (*M. Bh.*).

Supuṣpā (S) (F) with beautiful flowers; Indian Coral tree (*Erythrina indica*).

Surā (S) (F) **1.** spirituous liquor. **3.** wine personified as a daughter of Varuṇa.

Surabhi (S) (F) **1.** sweet smelling; agreeable; shining; charming; pleasing; famous; good; beautiful; beloved; wise; virtuous. **2.** Campaka tree; nutmeg; Kadamba tree; spring; Sacred Basil (*Ocimum sanctum*); Jasmine. **3.** a fabulous cow who was the daughter of Dakṣa and wife of Kaśyapa and the mother of Kāmadhenu, cattle and of the rudras (*M. Bh.*); cow of the gods formed from a syllable of Brahmā whose daughters Surūpā, Hansikā, Subhadrā and Sarvakāmadughā are protectors of the 4 regions (*M. Bh.*); another name for the earth; Curryleaf tree (*Murraya koenigii Mimusops elengi*); *Prosopis spicigera.*

Surabhū (S) (F) **1.** born of the gods. **3.** a daughter of Ugrasena and sister of Kansa (*Bhāgavata*)

Surādevī (S) (F) **1.** goddess of wine. **3.** a daughter of Varuṇa and Devī and who is the presiding goddess of liquor (*M. Bh.*).

Surajā (S) (F) **1.** born of gods. **3.** an apsarā daughter of Kaśyapa and Prādhā (*M. Bh.*)

Surajanī (S) (F) beautiful night.

Surājīva (S) **1.** livelihood of the gods. **3.** another name for Viṣṇu.

Surakāminī (S) (F) **1.** desired by the gods. **3.** an apsarā.

Suralā (S) (F) **1.** one who brings the gods. **3.** another name for the Gaṅgā.

Suramohinī (S) (F) attracting the gods.

Suramyā (S) (F) **1.** very beautiful. **3.** a queen of Kāmpīlya and mother of Vimalanātha Jaina Tīrthaṅkara (*J. Literature*).

Suraṇā (S) (F) **1.** joyous; gay; making a pleasing sound. **3.** a river.

Suranandā (S) (F) **1.** joy of the gods. **3.** a river.

Surāṅganā (S) (F) celestial woman.

Surapriyā (S) (F) **1.** dear to the gods. **3.** an apsarā (*Bh. Purāṇa*).

Śūraputiā (S) (F) **1.** with a heroic son. **3.** another name for Aditi.

Surāraṇī (S) (F) **1.** mother of the gods. **3.** another name for Aditī.

Surasā (S) (F) **1.** of good essence. **2.** well flavoured; lovely; sweet; elegant; Sacred Basil (*Ocinum sanctum*). **3.** a rāgiṇī; a daughter of Raudrāśva (*H. Purāṇa*); a daughter of Kaśyapa and Krodhavaśā and the mother of serpents who was reborn as Rohiṇī the wife of Vasudeva (*Bhāgavata*); an apsarā (*M. Bh.*); another name for Durgā; Indian Snakeroot (*Ophiorrhiza mungos*).

Sūrasenī (S) (F) **1.** with an army of warriors. **3.** the wife of Pravīra and mother of Manasyu of the Purū dynasty (*M. Bh.*).

Surastrī (S) (F) celestial woman.

Surasū (S) (F) mother of gods.

Surasundarī (S) (F) **1.** celestial beauty. **3.** a yoginī; another name for Durgā.

Surathā (S) (F) **1.** with a good chariot. **3.** an apsarā daughter of Kaśyapa and Prādhā (*M. Bh.*); a river (*Mā. Purāṇa*); the mother of Emperor Śibi (*M. Bh.*).

Suratnā (S) (F) possessing rich jewels.

Suravāhinī (S) (F) **1.** river of the gods. **3.** another name for the heavenly Gaṅgā.

Suravallī (S) (F) **1.** vine of the gods. **2.** Sacred Basil (*Ocimum sanctum*).

Suravāni (S) (F) earth as the mother of the gods.

Suravara (S) (F) **1.** best among the gods. **3.** another name for Indra.

Suravilāsinī (S) (F) heavenly nymph; apsarā.

Surayuvatī (S) (F) celestial maiden; apsarā.

Surejyā (S) (F) worshipped by the gods; the Sacred Basil (*Ocimum sanctum*); bowthread of the gods.

Surekhā (S) (F) **1.** having beautiful lines; a beautiful line. **2.** fortunate; auspicious.

Sureṇū (S) (F) **1.** very small. **2.** dust particle; an atom. **3.** a daughter of Tvaṣṭṛ and wife of Vivaśvat; a river regarded as one of the 7 Sarasvatīs (*M. Bh.*).

Sureśi (S) (F) **1.** supreme goddess. **3.** another name for Durgā.

Sūrī (S) (F) **1.** consort of the sun. **3.** another name for Kuntī as being married to the Sun before her marriage of Pāṇḍu.

Suri (S) (F) goddess.

Surīlā (H) (F) melodious.

Surīśvarī (S) (F) **1.** goddess of the gods. **2.** pious; pure. **3.** another name for the celestial Gaṅgā.

Surocanā (S) (F) **1.** much liked. **2.** enlightening beautifully. **3.** a son of Yajñabāhu (*Bh. Purāṇa*); an attendant of Skanda (*M. Bh.*).

Surohiṇī (S) (F) beautifully red.

Surottamā (S) (F) **1.** best among the goddesses. **3.** an apsarā (*V. Purāṇa*).

Śūrpaṇakhā (S) (F) **1.** with fingernails like winnowing fans. **3.** the daughter of Viśravas and Kaikasī and sister of Rāvaṇa and wife of Vidyujjīhva and mother of Śambhukumāra (*K. Rāmāyaṇa*).

Suṛtā (S) (F) divine truth.

Suruca (S) (F) bright light; with fine tastes.

Surucī (S) (F) **1.** taking great delight in. **3.** a wife of Uttānapāda and mother of Uttama (*Purāṇas*).

Surukhī (S) (F) having a beautiful face.

Surūpā (S) (F) **1.** well formed. **2.** lovely; beautiful. **3.** a daughter of Viśvakarman and wife of Priyavrata; an apsarā (*H. Purāṇa*); Spanish Jasmine (*Jasminum grandiflorum*).

Surūpikā (S) (F) **1.** well formed. **2.** beautiful.

Sūryā (S) (F) wife of Sūrya.

Sūryabhā (S) (F) as bright as the sun.

Sūryajā (S) (F) 1. born of the sun. **3.** another name for the river Yamuna.

Sūryakalā (S) (F) a portion of the sun.

Sūryakāntī (S) (F) sunshine; sunlight.

Sūryalocanā (S) (F) **1.** eye of the sun. **2.** one whose eyes are as bright as the sun. **3.** a gandharvī.

Sūryamukhī (S) (F) **1.** sun faced. **2.** with a face as bright as the sun; *Helianihus annus.*

Sūryāṇī (S) (F) the wife of the sun.

Sūryaprabhā (S) (F) as bright as the sun.

Sūryaputrī (S) (F) **1.** daughter of the sun. **3.** patronymic of the Yamunā river; lightning.

Sūryaśobhā (S) (F) sunshine.

Suṣamā (S) (F) exquisite beauty; splendour.

Susangatā (S) (F) a good companion; easily attainable.

Suśāntā (S) (F) **1.** very calm; placid. **3.** a wife of Śaśidhvaja.

Suśānti (S) (F) perfect calm.

Susatyā (S) (F) **1.** always truthful; nice and truthful. **3.** wife of Janaka (*K. Purāṇa*).

Suśīlā (S) (F) **1.** well disposed; good tempered. **3.** a wife of Kṛṣṇa (*H. Purāṇa*); a female attendant of Rādhā; wife of Yama; a daughter of Harisvāmin; daughter of the gandharva named Suśīla; a cow sister of Surabhi.

Suśīlikā (S) (F) of a good character; a bird.

Susīmā (S) (F) **1.** with the hair well parted. **3.** mother of the 6th Arhat.

Susmitā (S) (F) with a pleasant smile.

Suśobhanā (S) (F) **1.** very charming; very graceful. **3.** a wife of King Parīkṣit and the mother of Śala, Dala and Bala.

Suśravā (S) (F) **1.** much heard of; abounding in fame. **3.** a wife of King Jayatsena of the Purū dynasty and the mother of Arvaćīna (*M. Bh.*).

Suśrī (S) (F) very splendid; very rich.

Suśroṇī (S) (F) **1.** with beautiful hips. **3.** a goddess.

Suśubhā (S) (F) very beautiful; very auspicious.

Susvarā (S) (F) **1.** sweet voiced. **3.** a gandhara.

Suśyāmā (S) (F) **1.** very beautiful; very dark. **3.** an apsara who married Ṛtadhvaja and became the mother of Vṛddha (*Br. Purāṇa*).

Sutā (S) (F) **1.** begotten. **2.** daughter.

Sutanu (S) (F) **1.** possessing a slender body. **2.** delicate; slender; lovely woman. **3.** a daughter of Āhuka (*M. Bh.*); a concubine of Vasudeva (*H. Purāṇa*); a daughter of Ugrasena (*H. Purāṇa*); a daughter of Yudhiṣṭhira and wife of King Aśvasuta of Vajra (*Vā. Purāṇa*); wife of Akrūra.

Sutārā (S) (F) **1.** very bright. **2.** shining star; cat's eye. **3.** a daughter of Śvaphalka (*V. Purāṇa*); an apsarā; a gandharvī.

Sutārakā (S) (F) **1.** with beautiful stars. **3.** one of the 24 goddesses who executes the commands of the 24 Arhats.

Sutasomā (S) (F) **1.** offerer of Soma. **3.** a wife of Kṛṣṇa.

Sutoyā (S) (F) **1.** with beautiful water. **2.** a river.

Sutrāmā (S) (F) **1.** protecting well. **3.** another name for the earth.

Suvaćā (S) (F) **1.** speaking well. **3.** a gandharva.

Suvaćanī (S) (F) **1.** always speaking well. **3.** a goddess.

Suvalī (S) (F) graceful.

Suvāmā (S) (F) **1.** beautiful woman. **3.** a famous river of the Purāṇas (*M. Bh.*).

Suvapus (S) **1.** with a handsome body. **3.** an apsarā (*V. Purāṇa*).

Suvarćalā (S) (F) **1.** abode of a glorious life. **3.** daughter of sage Devala and the wife of Śvetaketu (*M. Bh.*); a wife of Sūrya (*M. Bh.*); wife of Pratīha (*Bh. Purāṇa*); wife of Parameṣṭhin and mother of Pratīha (*Bh. Purāṇa*).

Suvarćas (S) (F) **1.** full of life; very glorious. **3.** wife of sage Dadhīći and the mother of Pippalāda.

Suvarṇā (S) (F) **1.** of beautiful colour. **2.** gold; turmeric. **3.** one of the 7 tongues of fire; daughter of Ikṣvāku and wife of King Suhotra and the mother of Hastī (*M. Bh.*); Prickly Poppy (*Argemone mexicana*); Ironwood tree (*Mesua ferrea*); *Curcuma longa*.

Suvarṇabhāsa (S) (F) **1.** golden glitter. **3.** a gandharva maiden.

Suvarṇamekhalī (S) (F) **1.** golden girdled. **3.** an apsarā.

Suvarṇarekhā (S) (F) **1.** golden line. **3.** a river.

Suvārtā (S) (F) **1.** good news. **2.** one who brings good news. **3.** a wife of Kṛṣṇa (*H. Purāṇa*).

Suvāsu (S) (F) **1.** fragrant. **3.** an apsarā.

Suvedā (S) (F) **1.** very intelligent; knower of scriptures; very knowledgeable. **3.** wife of Priyavrata's son Savana.

Suveṇā (S) (F) **1.** with a beautiful plait of hair. **3.** a Purāṇic river which sage Mārkaṇḍeya saw in the stomach of child Kṛṣṇa (*M. Bh.*).

Suviśālā (S) (F) **1.** very large. **3.** an attendant of Skanda (*M. Bh.*).

Suvitti (S) (F) **1.** good knowledge. **3.** a divine being.

Suvratā (S) (F) **1.** very religious; a virtuous wife. **3.** a queen of Ratnapuri and mother of Dharmanātha Jaina Tīrthaṅkara; a daughter of Dakṣa and Vīraṇī (*Br. Purāṇa*); an apsarā.

Suvṛttā (S) (F) **1.** well conducted. **2.** virtuous. **3.** an apsarā (*H. Purāṇa*).

Suvyūhā (S) (F) **1.** halo. **3.** an apsarā.

Suyajñā (S) (F) **1.** good sacrificer. **3.** a daughter of King Prasenajit of the Purū dynasty and wife of King

Mahābhauma and the mother of Ayutanāyī (*M. Bh.*).

Suyaśā (S) (F) **1.** very famous. **3.** a daughter of King Bahudā and wife of Parīkṣit who was the son of Anaśva (*M. Bh.*); an apsarā (*V. Purāṇa*).

Suyaśas (S) (F) **1.** very famous. **3.** a wife of King Divodāsa (*H. Purāṇa*).

Svadhā (S) (F) **1.** self power. **3.** the offerings to the gods and ancestors personified as the daughter of Dakṣa and wife of the Pitṛs or Manes and the mother of Menā and Dhāraṇī (*V. Purāṇa*).

Svadhi (S) (F) well minded; thoughtful.

Svāhā (S) (F) **1.** oblation personified as the daughter of Dakṣa and wife of Agni and supposed to be the goddess presiding over burnt offerings, also represented as the wife of the rudra Paśupati. **3.** a daughter of Bṛhaspati (*M. Bh.*).

Svāhādevī (S) (F) **1.** goddess of oblation. **3.** wife of Agni and the mother of Pāvaka, Pavamāna and Śuci.

Svākṛtī (S) (F) good looking.

Svaladā (S) (F) **1.** giving a little. **3.** a daughter of Raudrāśva.

Svāminī (S) (F) lady of the house.

Svapnā (S) (F) dream.

Svapnasundarī (S) (F) dream girl.

Svarā (S) (F) **1.** goddess of sound or a musical note. **3.** the chief wife of Brahmā.

Svaravedī (S) (F) **1.** knower of music. **3.** an apsarā. Śeṣa (*V. Purāṇa*).

Svarbhānavī (S) (F) **1.** daughter of the divine. **3.** daughter of the sun; daughter of Svarbhānu who married Āyus and was the mother of Nahuṣa (*M. Bh.*).

Svareṇū (S) (F) **1.** beautiful note. **3.** wife of the sun.

Svargaṅgā (S) (F) the celestial Gaṅgā; the Milky Way.

Svarṇā (S) (F) **1.** golden. **3.** an apsara and mother of Vṛndā (*P. Purāṇa*).

Svarṇadāmā (S) (F) **1.** gold girdled. **3.** a tutelary goddess.

Svarṇalatā (S) (F) **1.** golden vine. **2.** Climbing Staff Plant (*Celastrus paniculata*).

Svarṇamālā (S) (F) golden necklace.

Svarṇambha (S) (F) white light; golden light.

Svarṇapadmā (S) (F) **1.** bearing golden lotuses. **3.** another name for the celestial Gaṅgā.

Svarṇapuṣpikā (S) (F) **1.** golden flower. **2.** jasmine.

Svarṇarekhā (S) (F) **1.** golden streak. **3.** a river (*V. Purāṇa*); a vidyādharī (*Hitopadeśa*).

Svārṣā (S) (F) celestial; winning heaven; bestowing light.

Svarūptā (S) (F) beautiful.

Svarvadhū (S) (F) celestial woman; apsarā.

Svarvīthī (S) (F) **1.** heavenly path; abode of music. **3.** a wife of Vatsara (*Bhā. Purāṇa*).

Svaryoṣit (S) (F) celestial woman.

Śvāsā (S) (F) **1.** the breath; hissing; panting; breathing. **3.** the mother of Śvasana (*M. Bh.*); a daughter of Dakṣa and wife of Dharma and mother of Anila (*M. Bh.*).

Svasti (S) (F) well being; fortune; success sometimes personified as a goddess.

Svastidevī (S) (F) **1.** goddess of welfare. **3.** a goddess represented as the wife of Vāyu and said to have sprung from the essence of Prākṛtī; a mystical cross.

Svasū (S) (F) **1.** self created. **3.** the earth.

Svāti (S) (F) **1.** the star Arcturus. **3.** a wife of the Sun; one of the 27 constellations.

Svayamhārikā (S) (F) **1.** self seizing. **3.** a daughter of Nirmārṣṭi and Dusśaha (*Mā. Purāṇa*).

Svāyamprabhā (S) (F) **1.** self shining. **3.** an apsarā (*M. Bh.*); the daughter of Hemasāvarṇi (*Rāmāyaṇa*); a daughter of the asura Maya (*K. Sāgara*).

Śvenī (S) (F) white.

Śvetā (S) (F) **1.** white. **3.** one of the 7 tongues of fire; a mother in Skanda's retinue (*M. Bh.*); the mother of the elephant Śveta (*M. Bh.*); a daughter of Dakṣa and Krodhavaśā (*V. Rāmāyaṇa*); *Aconitum heterophyllun*; Blue Pea (*Clitoria ternatea*).

Śvetāmbarā (S) (F) clad in white.

Śvetāśvā (S) (F) **1.** with a white horse. **3.** a goddess.

Śvetī (S) (F) **1.** silver. **3.** a river.

Śvetyā (S) (F) **1.** white; brilliant as the dawn. **3.** a river.

Svīkṛtī (S) (F) acceptance.

Sviṣṭi (S) (F) a successful sacrifice.

Śviti (S) (F) whiteness.

Śvitrā (S) (F) white.

Śyāmā (S) (F) **1.** blue; black; dark; beautiful. **2.** consort of Śyāma. **3.** a goddess who executes the commands of the 6th Jaina Arhat; a daughter of Meru and wife of Agnīdhra (*Bhāgavata*); another name for Yamunā; *Aglaia odoratissima*; *Curcuma longa*; Common Indigo (*Indigofera hinctoria*); Couch grass (*Cynodon dactylon*); Rādhā as the beloved of the dark one.

Śyāmalā (S) (F) **1.** dark. **3.** a form of Durgā.

Śyenī (S) (F) **1.** female hawk. **3.** the daughter of Kaśyapa regarded as the mother of hawks (*M. Bh.*).

Śyeti (S) (F) white.

T

Tāḍakā (S) (F) **1.** beater; murderer. **3.** a fierce rākṣasī who was the daughter of the yakṣa Suketu and the wife of Sunda and mother of Marīci and Subāhu, she was killed by Rāma whereupon she was restored to being a gandharvī (*V. Rāmāyaṇa*).

Taḍitprabhā (S) (F) **1.** a flash of lightning. **3.** a mother attending on Skanda (*M. Bh.*).

Tālākākṣi (S) (F) with green eyes.

Tālākhyā (S) (F) perfume; with the scent of a palm tree.

Tālikā (S) (F) **1.** the palm of the hand. **2.** nightingale (*Curculigo orchioides*).

Talinodarī (S) (F) slender waisted.

Tallī (S) (F) **1.** youthful; boat. **3.** a wife of Varuṇa.

Talunī (S) (F) maiden.

Tamā (S) (F) night.

Tamahariṇī (S) (F) **1.** remover of darkness. **3.** a deity who destroys darkness.

Tamasā (S) (F) **1.** dark coloured. **3.** a river that merges with the Gaṅgā and on whose banks was the āśrama of Vālmiki (*V. Rāmāyaṇa*).

Tāmasī (S) (F) **1.** night; sleep. **3.** a river (*M. Bh.*); another name for Durgā.

Tamasvinī (S) (F) night.

Tamī (S) (F) night.

Tāmrā (S) (F) **1.** copper crested. **3.** a follower of Skanda.

Tāmrakarṇī (S) (F) **1.** copper eared. **3.** the consort of Añjana the elephant of a quarter.

Tāmrapakṣā (S) (F) **1.** copper coloured. **3.** a daughter of Kṛṣṇa (*H. Purāṇa*).

Tāmraparṇī (S) (F) **1.** with red leaves. **3.** a holy river of Kerala on whose banks the devas did penance (*M. Bh.*).

Tāmrarasā (S) (F) **1.** of red juice. **3.** a daughter of Raudrāśva (*Vā. Purāṇa*).

Tāmrāvatī (S) (F) 1. coppery. **3.** an ancient river which is supposed to have generated fire (*M. Bh.*).

Tāmrikā (S) (F) **1.** coppery. **2.** Rosary Pea (*Abrus precatorius*); Indian Madder (*Rubia cordifolia*).

Tanūbhavā (S) (F) daughter.

Tanūjā (S) (F) **1.** born of the body. **2.** daughter.

Tanulatā (S) (F) **1.** with a vine like body. **2.** slender; flexible; elastic.

Tanuśṛī (S) (F) with a divine body.

Tanuvī (S) (F) a slender woman.

Tanvangī (S) (F) slender limbed.

Tanvī (S) (F) **1.** slender; beautiful; delicate; fine. **2.** *Desmodium gangeticum*; *Uraria lagopoides*.

Tapā (S) (F) **1.** consuming by heat; one who performs penance. **2.** doer of penance. **3.** one of the 8 deities of the Bodhi tree (*L. Vistara*).

Tapanasutā (S) (F) **1.** daughter of the sun. **3.** another name for the Yamunā river.

Tapanatanayā (S) (F) **1.** daughter of the sun. **3.** the rivers Yamunā and Godāvarī conjoined.

Tapanātmajā (S) (F) **1.** daughter of the sun. **3.** another name for the Yamunā river.

Tāpanī (S) (F) **1.** heat. **3.** a river.

Tapantī (S) (F) **1.** warming. **3.** a river.

Tapasvinī (S) (F) **1.** ascetic. **2.** Spikenard (*Nardostachys jatamansi*).

Tapatī (S) (F) **1.** warming. **3.** the daughter of Sūrya and Saṁjñā and goddess of the river Tāpati, she is the wife of Saṁvaraṇa and the mother of Kuru, she was transformed into the river Narmadā (*Bh. Purāṇa*).

Tāpatī (S) (F) **1.** of Tapatī. **3.** a river.

Tāpī (S) (F) **1.** heat; glow. **3.** another name for the Tāpatī river.

Tapuṣi (S) (F) a burning weapon.

Tārā (S) (F) **1.** star. **2.** the pupil of the eye; meteor; perfume. **3.** Dākṣāyāṇī worshipped in Kiṣkindhā (*M. Purāṇa*); wife of Buddha Amoghasiddha; a female monkey who was the daughter of Suṣeṇa and the wife of Bāli, she was the mother of Aṅgada (*M. Bh.*); the wife of Bṛhaspati who eloped with Ćandra and became the mother of Budha or Mercury who became the ancestor of the lunar race of kings (*Bhāgavata*); a tāntric goddess who figures predominantly in the Jaina and Buddhist traditions as the great mother goddess and one of the 10 mahāvidyas; a yoginī (*H. Ć. Cintamaṇi*); a Śakti (*J. Literature*); a rāga.

Tārābhūṣā (S) (F) **1.** decorated with stars. **2.** the night.

Tārādatta (S) (F) **1.** given by the stars. **3.** the wife of King Kalingadatta of Takṣaśila and mother of an incarnation of the apsarā Surabhidattā.

Tārakā (S) (F) **1.** star; falling star; meteor; the eye. **3.** Bṛhaspati's wife (*V. Purāṇa*).

Tārakiṇī (S) (F) **1.** starry. **2.** night.

Taralā (S) (F) **1.** spirituous liquor. **2.** a bee. **3.** a yoginī (*H. Ć. Ćintāmaṇi*).

Taralalekhā (S) (F) a tremulous line.

Tārāmati (S) (F) **1.** with a glorious mind. **3.** the wife of Hariśćandra and the mother of Rohita.

Tārāmbā (S) (F) mother star (*Br. Purāṇa*).

Tarānā (S) (F) song.

Taraṅgiṇī (S) (F) **1.** full of waves; restless; moving. **3.** a river.

Taraṇī (S) (F) raft; boat.

Taraṇitanaya (S) (F) **1.** daughter of the sun. **3.** another name for the river Yamunā.

Tārāpuṣpa (S) (F) star blossom; jasmine.

Tārāvalī (S) (F) **1.** a multitude of stars. **3.** the daughter of the yakṣa prince Maṇibhadra.

Tārāvatī (S) (F) **1.** surrounded by stars. **3.** a daughter of Kakutstha and wife of King Ćandraśekhara; the wife of Dharmadhvaja; a form of Durgā.

Tārikā (S) (F) belonging to the stars.

Tāriṇī (S) (F) **1.** enabling to cross over; saving. **3.** another name for Durgā.

Tārinīrā (S) (F) **1.** having the quality of liberation; crossing over the water. **3.** a Buddhist goddess.

Taritā (S) (F) **1.** the forefinger; the leader. **3.** another name for Durgā.

Tarpiṇi (S) (F) **1.** satisfying; offering oblations. **2.** *Hibiscus mutabilis.*

Tarulatā (S) (F) vine.

Taruṇī (S) (F) **1.** young girl. **2.** *Rosa alba.*

Taruṣī (S) (F) victory.

Taṭinī (S) (F) **1.** with banks. **2.** a river.

Tātṛpi (S) (F) intensely satisfying.

Taviṣī (S) (F) **1.** power; strength; violence; courage; river; heavenly virgin. **3.** a daughter of Indra; another name for the earth.

Tejaśrī (S) (F) with divine power and grace.

Tejasvatī (S) (F) **1.** splendid; bright; glorious; energetic. **3.** the daughter of King Vikramasena of Ujjayinī and the wife of Somadatta (*K. Sāgara*); the wife of King Ādityasena of Ujjayinī; *Zanthoxylum budrunga.*

Tejini (S) (F) **1.** sharp; bright; energetic. **2.** touchstone; whetstone.

Tejomayī (S) (F) consisting of light and splendour.

Tejovatī (S) (F) **1.** sharp; bright; splendid. **3.** the city of Agni (*D. Bhāgavata*).

Tīkṣṇakantā (S) (F) **1.** fond of cruelty. **3.** a form of Ćaṇḍikā (*K. Purāṇa*).

Tilabhāvanī (S) (F) **1.** beautiful dot. **3.** jasmine.

Tilakā (S) (F) a type of necklace.

Tilakalatā (S) (F) **1.** ornamental vine. **2.** the *Chlerodendron phlomoides.*

Tilakāvatī (S) (F) **1.** decorated. **3.** a river.

Tilikā (S) (F) a small mark of sandalwood.

Tillā (S) (F) **1.** one who has gone before. **3.** a deity.

Tilottamā (S) (F) **1.** one of the guardians of the sun; the best sesamum seed. **3.** a form of Dākṣāyānī (*M. Purāṇa*); an apsarā who was the daughter of Kaśyapa and Prādhā and was created by Viśvakarmān from small particles of all the best things in the world, Śiva developed his 4 heads and Indra his 1000 eyes in order to see her beauty always (*M. Bh.*).

Timi (S) (F) **1.** fish. **3.** a daughter of Dakṣa and wife of Kaśyapa and the mother of the sea monsters.

Timilā (S) (F) a musical instrument.

Tīrtha (S) (F) passage; way; ford; stairs for descent into a river; a place of pilgrimage; sacred object; a worthy person.

Tīrthamayī (S) (F) containing pilgrimage centres.

Tīrthanemi (S) (F) **1.** encircling the sacred place; carrying sacred objects. **3.** an attendant of Skanda (*M. Bh.*).

Tīrthapūjā (S) (F) the washing of Kṛṣṇa's statue in water.

Tīrthaseni (S) (F) **1.** with an army of sanctified ones. **3.** a mother in Skanda's retinue (*M. Bh.*).

Tīrthavatī (S) (F) **1.** holy; pious; flowing through a sacred place. **3.** a river (*Bhā. Purāṇa*).

Tiṣyarakṣitā (S) (F) **1.** protected by luck. **3.** Aśoka's 2nd wife.

Titikṣā (S) (F) **1.** patience; endurance. **3.** patience personified as the daughter of Dakṣa and Prasūti and the wife of Dharma, she was the mother of Kshema (*Skandha Bhagāvata*).

Titli (S) (F) butterfly.

Toḍikā (S) (F) **1.** splitting; breaking. **3.** a rāgiṇī.

Toṣaṇī (S) (F) **1.** satisfying; gratifying; appeasing; pleasing. **3.** another name for Durgā.

Totalā (S) (F) **1.** repeating. **3.** another name for Gaurī and Durgā.

Toya (S) (F) **1.** water. **2.** *Pavonia odoralā.*

Toyanīvī (S) (F) **1.** ocean girdled. **2.** the earth.

Trailokyadevī (S) (F) **1.** goddess of the 3 worlds. **3.** the wife of King Yaśakara (*R. Taraṅginī*).

Trailokyaprabhā (S) (F) **1.** splendour; grace; light of the 3 worlds. **3.** the daughter of a dānava.

Trasareṇu (S) (F) **1.** the mote in the sunbeam. **3.** a wife of the sun.

Trayī (S) (F) **1.** intellect; understanding. **3.** the 3 Vedas.

Treyā (S) (F) walking in 3 paths.

Triambikā (S) (F) **1.** consort of the 3 eyed Śiva. **3.** another name for Pārvatī.

Tribhuvanaprabhā (S) (F) **1.** glory and grace; light of the 3 worlds. **3.** a daughter of a dānava (*K. Sāgara*).

Tridaśeśvarī (S) (F) **1.** chief of the gods. **3.** an attendant of Durgā; another name for Durgā.

Tridhārā (S) (F) **1.** 3 streamed. **3.** another name for the Gaṅgā river.

Tridivā (S) (F) **1.** heaven; cardamoms. **3.** a river of ancient Bhārata (*M. Bh.*).

Trigartā (S) (F) woman; a pearl.

Trihāyanī (S) (F) **1.** returning in 3 years. **3.** Svargalakṣmī who was reborn 3 times as Draupadī, Vedavatī and Sītā.

Trijagatī (S) (F) **1.** mother of the 3 worlds. **3.** another name for Pārvatī.

Trijaṭā (s) (F) **1.** with 3 locks of hair. **3.** a rākṣasī who was friendly to Sītā (*Rāmāyaṇa*).

Trikalā (S) (F) **1.** 3 pieces. **3.** a goddess produced by the union of 3 gods for the destruction of Andhaka.

Trilocanā (S) (F) **1.** consort of Śiva; the 3 eyed one. **3.** another name for Pārvatī.

Trimukhā (S) (F) **1.** 3 faced. **3.** Śākyamuni's mother.

Tripathagā (S) (F) **1.** flowing through 3 regions. **3.** another name for the Gaṅgā.

Tripathagaminī (S) (F) **1.** flowing through three regions. **3.** another name for Gaṅgā.

Tripurā (S) (F) **1.** triply fortified. **2.** kind of cardamom. **3.** another name for Durgā.

Tripurasundari (S) (F) **1.** damsel of gold, silver and iron. **3.** another name for Durgā.

Triputā (S) (F) **1.** 3 fold. **2.** Arabian Jasmine (*Jasminum sambac*). **3.** another name for Durgā.

Triśalā (S) (F) **1.** 3 pointed. **3.** the mother of Mahāvīra also known as Priyakarṇi.

Triśūlagaṅgā (S) (F) **1.** coming from Śiva's trident **3.** the trifurcated streams of the Gaṅgā; a river.

Triśulinī (S) (F) **1.** consort of Triśulin. **3.** another name for Durgā.

Trivakrā (S) (F) **1.** bent at 3 places. **3.** a hunch backed woman who gave her scents to Kṛṣṇa and was cured by him (*Bhāgavata*).

Triveṇī (S) (F) **1.** triple braided. **3.** the confluence point of the 3 rivers Gaṅgā, Yamunā and Sarasvatī.

Triyā (S) (F) young woman.

Trotaki (S) (F) **1.** angry speech. **3.** a rāgiṇī.

Tṛptā (S) (F) **1.** satiety; contentment. **3.** the wife of Kālu and the mother of Guru Nānak who founded the Sikh religion; another name for the Gaṅgā.

Tṛptī (S) (F) **1.** satisfaction; contentment; water. **3.** a gandharvī.

Tṛṣā (S) (F) **1.** thirst. **3.** desire personified as the daughter of Kāma.

Tṛṣlā (S) (F) making thirsty; desiring.

Tṛṣṇā (S) (F) **1.** thirst; desire. **3.** avidity personified as the mother of Dambha and the daughter of Mṛtyu.

Tṛtīya (S) (F) **1.** the 3rd. **3.** a river personified as a goddess who sits in the court of Varuṇa (*M. Bh.*).

Truṭi (S) (F) **1.** atom; a minute period of time. **3.** an attendant of Skanda (*M. Bh.*).

Tuḍi (S) (F) **1.** satisfying. **3.** a rāgiṇī.

Tuhi (S) (F) a cuckoo's cry.

Tuja (S) (F) thunderbolt.

Tulasāriṇī (S) (F) a quiver.

Tulasī (S) (F) **1.** matchless. **2.** Sacred Basil (*Ocimum sanctum*) produced from the ocean when churned (*P. Purāṇa*) or from the hair of the goddess Tulasī (*Brahma Purāṇa*); the Basil plant is held sacred by the Hindus as it is regarded as an incarnation of Mahālakṣmī who was born as the daughter of King Dharmadhvaja and Mādhavī, she prayed for many thousand years to obtain Māhāviṣṇu as her husband, she became the wife of the demon Śaṅkhaćuḍa who was an incarnation of Sudāmā and ascended to Vaikuṇṭha with Mahāviṣṇu.

Tūlinī (S) (F) the Cotton tree.

Tuṅgā (S) (F) **1.** strong; elevated; high. **3.** a river in Mysore.

Tuṅgabhadrā (S) (F) **1.** very noble; sacred. **3.** the river in Mysore which is formed by the junction of the Tuṅgā and Bhadra.

Tuṅgaveṇā (S) (F) **1.** loving heights. **3.** a river in the Deccan.

Tuṅgī (S) (F) night; turmeric.

Turī (S) (F) **1.** a painter's brush. **3.** a wife of Vasudeva (*H. Purāṇa*).

Turyā (S) (F) superior powers.

Tuṣitā (S) (F) **1.** satisfied; pleased. **3.** the wife of Vedaśiras and mother of the tuśitas.

Tuṣṭi (S) (F) **1.** satisfaction. **3.** contentment personified as a daughter of Dakṣa, wife of Dharma and mother of Santoṣa or Mudā (*V. Purāṇa*) or as daughter of Paurnamāsa (*Vā. Purāṇa*) or as a deity sprung from Prakṛtī (*Brahma Purāṇa*) or as a mātrika or a Śakti; a digit of the moon.

Tuvikṣatra (S) (F) **1.** ruling powerfully. **3.** another name for Aditi.

Tvaritā (S) (F) **1.** hasty; quick; swift; expeditious. **3.** another name for Durgā and a magical formula named after her.

Tveṣā (S) (F) brilliant; glittering; impetuous; vehement.

Tviṣā (S) (F) **1.** light; splendour. **3.** a daughter of Marīći and Sambhūti (*Vā. Purāṇa*).

Tviṣi (S) (F) vehemence; impetuousity; splendour; light; brilliance; energy.

U

Uććadevatā (S) (F) **1.** superior god. **2.** time personified.

Uććaihpaurṇamāsi (S) (F) **1.** the lofty full moon day. **2.** a particular full moon day when the moon appears before sunset.

Uććatā (S) (F) height; superiority; the apex of the orbit of a planet.

Uććhiṣṭaćāṇḍālinī (S) (F) **1.** the fierce goddess of the eater of remains. **3.** Durgā as worshipped by Uććhiṣṭas; a goddess.

Uććhṛta (S) (F) raised; lifted up; erect; arising; growing powerful.

Udadhisutā (S) (F) **1.** daughter of the ocean. **3.** another name for Lakṣmī and Kṛṣṇa's capital Dvārakā (*Bhā. Purāṇa*).

Udalākāśyapa (S) (F) **1.** giving water to the earth. **3.** a tutelary goddess of agriculture.

Udankanyā (S) (F) **1.** daughter of the ocean. **3.** another name for Lakṣmī and Dvārakā the capital of Kṛṣṇa.

Udantikā (S) (F) satiety; satisfaction.

Udāramatī (S) (F) noble minded; highly intelligent; wise; virtuous; chaste.

Udayantī (S) (F) risen; virtuous; excellent.

Udayatī (S) (F) **1.** of Udaya. **2.** daughter of the mountain. **3.** the daughter of Udayatuṅga.

Udbhūtī (S) (F) coming forth; existence; appearance; fortune giver.

Uddīptī (S) (F) excited; inflamed.

Udgīta (S) (F) **1.** sung; announced; celebrated; highly praised. **2.** hymn of glory; ultimate song.

Udgīti (S) (F) singing.

Uditi (S) (F) rising of the sun.

Udu (S) (F) water; star.

Udvahā (S) (F) **1.** continuing; carrying on. **2.** daughter.

Udvahni (S) (F) gleaming; sparkling.

Udyati (S) (F) raised; elevation.

Ugraćaṇḍā (S) (F) **1.** powerful and fierce. **3.** a violent form of Durgā (*K. Purāṇa*).

Ugraćāriṇī (S) (F) **1.** moving impetuously. **3.** another name for Durgā.

Ugradaṅṣṭrī (S) (F) **1.** with terrible teeth; with sharp teeth. **3.** a daughter of Mahāmeru and wife of a son of Agnīdhra (*J.S. Koṣa*).

Ugraduhitṛ (S) (F) daughter of a powerful man; daughter of Śiva.

Ugrajit (S) (F) **1.** victor of passion. **3.** an apsarā (*A. Veda*).

Ugrakālī (S) (F) **1.** fierce and black. **3.** goddess Durgā in her dreadful form (*D. Bh. Purāṇa*).

Ugrakarṇikā (S) (F) with large earrings.

Ugrapaśyā (S) (F) **1.** frightful; hideous; fierce looking; malignant. **3.** an apsarā (*A. Veda*).

Ugraśekharā (S) (F) **1.** crest of the ferocious. **3.** the Gaṅgā as the crest of Ugra or Śiva (*Ś. Purāṇa*).

Ugrasenī (S) (F) **1.** wife of a powerful leader. **3.** wife of Akrūra.

Ugratā (S) (F) violence; passion; anger; pungency; acrimony.

Ugratārā (S) (F) **1.** ferocious star. **2.** having terrible eyes. **3.** a tāntric goddess (*K. Purāṇa*).

Ugrī (S) (F) **1.** angry. **3.** a being belonging to a class of demons (*A. Veda*).

Ujjayatī (S) (F) **1.** one who has won. **2.** winner; conqueror; victorious.

Ujjeṣā (S) (F) victorious.

Ujjiti (S) (F) victory.

Ujjīvati (S) (F) brought to life; full of life; jubilant; optimist; to return to life.

Ujjīvayatī (S) (F) restored to life; animated.

Ujjṛmbhitā (S) (F) opened; stretched; expanded; blown.

Ujjūṭitā (S) (F) with upgoing hair; wearing the hair twisted together and coiled upwards.

Ujjvalā (S) (F) brightness; clearness; splendour.

Ujjvalata (S) (F) splendour; radiance; beauty; clarity.

Ujjvalitā (S) (F) lighted; shining; flaming.

Uktapratyukta (S) speech and reply; discourse; conversation; a kind of anthem or alternate song.

Ukthāmada (S) praise and rejoicing conjoined.

Ukthārkā (S) (F) recitation and hymn conjoined; praise of the sun; hymn of the sun.

Ukthasampadā (S) (F) **1.** wealth of hymns. **2.** a particular concluding verse of a Śāstra (*A. Araṇyaka*).

Ukthaśansin (S) (F) reciter of hymns; praising; uttering the Ukthas.

Ukthavīrya (S) power of the verse; a particular part of Śāstra, conversant in speech.

Ukthīn (S) (F) uttering verses; lauding; accompanied by praise or in ritual by Ukthas.

Ukthyasthālī (S) (F) place of Uktha; a place for the preparation of an Uktha libation.

Ukti (S) (F) sentence; proclamation; speech; expression; word; a worthy speech; idiom.

Ulkā (S) (F) meteor; fire; falling from heaven; firebrand; torch.

Ulkuśi (S) (F) a brilliant phenomenon in the sky; a meteor; firebrand.

Ulūkī (S) (F) **1.** she owl. **3.** a daughter of Kaśyapa and Tāmrā (*H. Purāṇa*).

Ululi (S) (F) **1.** loud. **2.** a cry indicative of prosperity.

Ulūpī (S) (F) **1.** with a charming face. **2.** a species of soft grass; one who lives in water. **3.** the daughter of the nāga Kauravya and the wife of Arjuna and mother of Irāvān (*M. Bh.*).

Ulūtī (S) (F) **1.** she falcon. **3.** a wife of Garuḍa (*M. Bh.*).

Umā (S) (F) **1.** O, do not! splendour; light; fame; reputation; quiet; tranquillity; night. **3.** Pārvatī born as the daughter of Himavat and Menā who became the wife of Śiva and is also known as Pārvatī and Durgā, the name is derived from the exclamation 'O Child, do not practice austerities' supposed to have been said to Pārvatī by her mother (*Ś. Purāṇa*); Turmeric (*Curcuma longa*); Flax (*Linum usitatissimum*).

Umāmaheśvarī (S) (F) **1.** Umā, the consort of Maheśvara. **3.** another name for Pārvatī.

Umloća (S) (F) **1.** with questioning eyes. **3.** an apsarā in the court of Śiva (*S. Purāṇa*).

Unmadā (S) (F) **1.** with intoxicating beauty; passionate. **3.** an apsarā who was reborn as Hariṇī the daughter of King Videha (*V. Rāmāyaṇa*).

Unmādinī (S) (F) betwitching; intoxicating.

Unmuktī (S) (F) deliverance.

Unnati (S) (F) **1.** prosperity; progress; dignity. **2.** rising; ascending. **3.** a daughter of Dakṣa and wife of Dharma (*Bhā. Purāṇa*); the wife of Garuḍa.

Upabhukti (S) (F) enjoyment; the daily course of a star (*P. Ratra*).

Upaḍā (S) (F) present; offering; benevolent.

Upadānavi (S) (F) **1.** near a dānava. **3.** a daughter of the dānava Vṛṣaparvaṇ (*H. Purāṇa*); a daughter of Vaiśvānara (*Bhā. Purāṇa*).

Upadevī (S) (F) **1.** a secondary deity. **3.** a wife of Vasudeva.

Upadhrtī (S) (F) ray of light.

Upakārikā (S) (F) protectress.

Upakośā (S) (F) **1.** like a treasure. **3.** a daughter of Upavarṣa and wife of Vararući (*K. Sāgara*).

Upamā (S) (F) resemblance; similarity; equality.

Upaṇāyika (S) (F) fit for an offering.

Upanīti (S) (F) initiation.

Upāsāna (S) (F) devotion; worship; homage.

Upaśruti (S) (F) **1.** listening attentively. **3.** a goddess of the sun's progress towards the north in the first half of the year (*M. Bh.*); the secondary Vedas.

Upāsti (S) (F) adoration; worship.

Upaveṇā (S) (F) **1.** with small tributaries. **3.** a river who is considered the mother of Agni (*M. Bh.*).

Upendrā (S) (F) **1.** younger sister of Indra. **3.** a river (*M. Bh.*).

Urdhvakeśā (S) (F) **1.** with erect hair. **3.** a goddess.

Ūrdhvaveṇīdharā (S) (F) **1.** with hair tied at the top of the head. **3.** an attendant of Skanda (*M.Bh.*).

Ūrja (S) (F) **1.** energy; strength; vigour. **2.** food; water; power; breath; heartborn; loving daughter. **3.** a daughter of Dakṣa and wife of sage Vasiṣṭha and the mother of the 7 ṛṣis of the 2nd Manvantara (*V. Purāṇa*); the month of Kārttika; another name for Pārvatī.

Ūrjāni (S) (F) **1.** belonging to energy; energy personified. **3.** a daughter of the sun (*Ṛg Veda*); goddess of strength.

Ūrjasvatī (S) (F) juicy; vigorous; powerful; strong.

Ūrjjasvatī (S) (F) **1.** full of energy; energetic; strong. **3.** a daughter of Priyavrata and Surūpā she became the wife of Śukra and the mother of Devayānī (*Bhāgavata*).

Ūrmī (S) (F) wave; ripple; light.

Ūrmikā (S) (F) wave; finger ring; humming of bees.

Ūrmilā (S) (F) **1.** of the waves of passion; beautiful; enchanting. **3.** the daughter of King Janaka and the sister of Sītā, she married Lakṣmaṇa and was the mother of Takṣaka and Ćitraketu (*U. Rāmāyana*).

Ūrmyā (S) (F) **1.** wavy. **2.** night. **3.** a Vedic goddess of light (*V. Rāmāyaṇa*).

Ūrṇā (S) (F) **1.** woollen. **2.** warm; ever excited. **3.** a wife of Ćitraratha; a wife of Marīći (*D. Bhāgavata*).

Ūrnāvatī (S) (F) **1.** rich in sheep. **3.** a tributary river of the Indus (*Ṛg. Veda*).

Ūrubilvā (S) (F) **1.** broad leaved. **3.** the place to which the Buddha retired for meditation and obtained supreme knowledge, it was later known as Bodhagayā (*B. Literature*).

Urukīrti (S) (F) of far reaching fame.

Urunjirā (S) (F) **1.** pleaser of heart; heart winning. **3.** another name of the river Vipās.

Uruṣā (S) (F) granting much; producing abundantly.

Urutā (S) (F) greatness; vastness.

Uruvī (S) (F) **1.** great; large; spacious; excellent; broad. **3.** another name for the earth.

Urvarā (S) (F) **1.** fertile soil. **2.** the earth. **3.** an apsarā in the palace of Kubera (*M. Bh.*).

Urvaśī (S) (F) **1.** widely extending. **3.** an apsarā considered the most beautiful in the 3 worlds who was born from the thigh of Narāyaṇa and married Purūravas and had 6 sons; another name for Gaṅgā as she sat on the thigh of Bhagīratha (*M. Bh.*).

Urvī (S) (F) **1.** the wide one. **2.** the earth; river; heaven and earth conjoined.

Uṣā/Uṣas (S) (F) **1.** daybreak. **2.** dawn. **3.** morning light personified as the daughter of heaven and sister of the ādityas and night; the evening light; night; the period between the setting of the stars and the rising of the sun; a wife of Rudra or Bhava; a daughter of Bāṇa and wife of Aniruddha (*A. Purāṇa*).

Uṣalākṣī (S) (F) dawn eyed; large eyed; with piercing eyes.

Uśanā (S) (F) **1.** with desire. **3.** a wife of Rudra (*H. Purāṇa*); Ceylon Leadwort (*Plumbago zeylanica*).

Uśanā (S) (F) **1.** wish; desire. **2.** the plant from which the Soma juice is produced.

Uṣasī (S) (F) twilight.

Uśī (S) (F) wish.

Uśijā (S) (F) **1.** desire born. **2.** wishing; desiring; zealous; lovely; charming; amiable; desirable. **3.** the mother of Kakṣīvat (*V. Purāṇa*).

Uṣikā (S) (F) **1.** dawn worshipper. **3.** a wife of Dīrghatamas and the mother of Kakṣīvān.

Usṛ (S) (F) morning light; daybreak; day.

Usrā (S) (F) morning light; daybreak; brightness personified as a red cow; earth as the source of all good things.

Ūti (S) (F) help; protection; kindness; enjoyment.

Utī (S) (F) wish; enjoyment; desire.

Utkalā (S) (F) 1. coming from Utkala. 3. a wife of Samrāj (*Bh. Purāṇa*).

Utkalikā (S) (F) longing for glory; a bud; ungrown flower; a wave.

Utkalitā (S) (F) unbound; loosened; opened; blossoming; brilliant.

Utkaṇikā (S) (F) desire; longing.

Utkānti (S) (F) excessive splendour.

Utkarikā (S) (F) made of precious material; made of milk treacle and ghee.

Utkārthinī (S) (F) 1. fulfilling one's ambitions. 3. an attendant of Skanda (*M. Bh.*).

Utkāśaṇā (S) (F) giving orders; commanding.

Utkaṭa (S) (F) exceeding the usual measure; immense; gigantic; richly endowed with; abounding in; superior; high; uneven; difficult.

Utkhalā (S) (F) perfume.

Utkṣīptikā (S) (F) lifted; a crescent shaped ornament worn on the upper ear.

Utkūjā (S) (F) a cooing note as of the Kokila.

Utpalā (S) (F) 1. filled with lotuses. 3. a river (*H. Purāṇa*).

Utpalākṣī (S) (F) 1. lotus eyed. 3. a goddess (*M. Purāṇa*); another name for Lakṣmī.

Utpalamālā (S) (F) a garland of lotus flowers.

Utpalāvatī (S) (F) 1. made of lotuses. 3. an apsarā; a river (*M. Bh.*).

Utpalinī (S) (F) 1. an assemblage of lotuses; 3. a river flowing near the Naimiṣāraṇya forest (*M. Bh.*).

Uttamā (S) (F) best; excellent; affectionate.

Uttamikā (S) (F) best worker.

Uttarā (S) (F) 1. upper; higher; northern. 2. future; result. 3. daughter of King Virāṭa of Matsya and wife of Abhimanyu, she was the mother of Parīkṣit (*M. Bh.*).

Uttarikā (S) (F) 1. crossing over. 2. coming out; delivering; conveying; a boat. 3. a river (*Rāmāyaṇa*).

Uttejinī (S) (F) 1. exciting; animating. 3. a follower of Skanda (*M. Bh.*).

V

Vāća (S) (F) **1.** speech. **2.** word; voice; oath; sacred text. **3.** language personified in the Vedas as having been created by Prajāpati and married to him, she is also represented as the mother of the Vedas and wife of Indra and as the daughter of Dakṣa and wife of Kaśyapa, she is most frequently identified with Sarasvatī (*A. Brāhmaṇa*).

Vāćaknavī (S) (F) **1.** with the power of speech. **2.** an orator; a speaker; eloquent. **3.** a preceptress of the family of Gārgi (*Ṛg Veda*).

Vāćyā (S) (F) **1.** blamed. **3.** another name for Sītā.

Vaḍabā (S) (F) **1.** mare. **3.** the apsarā Aśvinā in her form as marewife of Vivasvān; a wife of Vasudeva (*V. Purāṇa*).

Vadhrimatī (S) (F) **1.** with an impotent husband. **3.** a Ṛg Vedic princess and devotee of the aśvins and mother of Hiraṇyahasta (*Ṛg Veda*).

Vadhūsarā (S) (F) **1.** roaming woman. **3.** a river made of the tears of Pulomā that flowed through the hermitage of Ćyavana (*M. Bh.*).

Vādṛmatī (S) (F) with Viṣṇu.

Vāgadevī (S) (F) **1.** goddess of speech. **3.** another name for Sarasvatī.

Vagalā (S) (F) **1.** slow; limping. **3.** a tāntric goddess.

Vāgavādinī (S) (F) **1.** disputing speech. **2.** one who takes part in discussion. **3.** a goddess (*Panćatantra*).

Vāgīśvarī (S) (F) **1.** goddess of speech. **3.** another name for Sarasvatī.

Vāhinī (S) (F) **1.** army; body of force. **3.** the wife of King Kuru (*M. Bh.*).

Vahnijāyā (S) (F) **1.** conqueror of fire. **3.** the wife of the agni Vahni (*Ṛg Veda*).

Vahnikanyā (S) (F) **1.** daughter of fire. **2.** air; wind.

Vahnipriyā (S) (F) **1.** beloved of fire. **3.** the wife of Vahni (*M. Bh.*).

Vahnīśvarī (S) (F) **1.** goddess of fire. **3.** another name for Lakṣmī.

Vahnivadhū (S) (F) **1.** wife of fire. **3.** the wife of Agni (*Ṛg Veda*).

Vahnīvallabha (S) (F) **1.** beloved of fire. **3.** another name for Svāhā.

Vāhyakā (S) (F) **1.** chariot. **2.** venomous insect. **3.** the 2 daughters of King Sṛnjaya who were married to the Yādava king Bhajamāna and became the mothers of Nimi, Vṛṣṇi and Kṛmila (*M. Purāṇa*).

Vaidagdhī (S) (F) grace; beauty.

Vaidarbhī (S) (F) **1.** of Vidarbha. **3.** a wife of King Sagara and the mother of 60,000 sons; the wife of King Kuśa and the mother of Kuśāmba, Kuśanābha, Asūrtarajas and Vasu (*V. Rāmāyaṇa*); the wife of Agastya; another name for Damayantī; another name for Rukmiṇī.

Vaidehī (S) (F) **1.** princess of the Videhas. **3.** another name for Sītā.

Vaidhṛtī (S) (F) **1.** with a similar disposition. **2.** properly adjusted. **3.** the wife of Āryaka and mother of Dharmasetu (*Bhā. Purāṇa*).

Vaijayantī (S) (F) **1.** gift of victory. **2.** flag; banner; garland of victory. **3.** the necklace of Viṣṇu; the bells of Airāvata presented by Indra to Subrahmaṇya (*M. Bh.*).

Vaijayantikā (S) (F) **1.** bestowing victory. **2.** flag; banner; pearl necklace.

Vaijayantimālā (S) (F) **1.** garland of victory. **3.** the 5 gemmed garland worn by Viṣṇu (*Bhā. Purāṇa*).

Vaikuṇṭhā (S) (F) **1.** without hindrance; abode of the absolute. **3.** consort of Viṣṇu (*Bhā. Purāṇa*).

Vaikuṇṭha (S) (F) **1.** abode of the absolute. **2.** without hindrance. **3.** another name for Mahāviṣṇu and the name of his dwelling place on the eastern peak of Mount Meru.

Vaimitrā (S) (F) **1.** friend of the universe. **3.** one of the Saptamātṛs or 7 mothers of Skanda (*M.Bh.*).

Vaiṁṛdhī (S) (F) consecrated to Indra.

Vaiṇavī (S) (F) **1.** of Veṇu. **2.** gold from the Veṇu river.

Vairāgī (S) (F) **1.** free from passions. **3.** a rāgiṇī.

Vairaṇī (S) (F) **1.** of Viraṇa. **3.** a wife of Dakṣa (*H. Purāṇa*).

Vaiśakā (S) (F) lioness.

Vaiṣākhī (S) (F) **1.** the day of full moon in the month of Vaiṣākha. **3.** a wife of Vasudeva (*H. Purāṇa*).

Vaiśālī (S) (F) **1.** the great. **2.** princess of Viśālā. **3.** a wife of Vasudeva (*V. Purāṇa*); an east Indian kingdom where the Buddha lived.

Vaiśālinī (S) (F) **1.** daughter of the great. **3.** the daughter of King Viśāla and the wife of Avikṣit and the mother of Marutta (*Mā. Purāṇa*).

Vaiṣṇavī (S) (F) **1.** worshipper of Viṣṇu. **3.** the Śakti of Viṣṇu; the Nakṣatra Śravana; *asparagus racemosus*; another name for Manasā.

Vaitaraṇī (S) (F) **1.** crossing over the world. **2.** one who helps in crossing over the world; one who takes the devotees up to the other world. 3. the river Gaṅgā when it flows through the world of the manes (*M. Bh.*); a river which gives the lustre of the moon to bathers (*M. Bh.*); a river in Orissa (*M. Bh.*).

Vaivasvatī (S) (F) **1.** belonging to the sun. **3.** another name for the Yamunā river (*M. Bh.*).

Vajrā (S) (F) **1.** mighty; strong; hard. **3.** another name for Durgā; a daughter of Vaiśvānara (*Ṛg Veda*).

Vajrabhṛkuṭi (S) (F) **1.** with a thunderous frown. **3.** one of the 6 Buddhist goddesses of magic.

Vajradehā (S) (F) **1.** hard bodied. **2.** diamond bodied. **3.** a goddess.

Vajradhātṛ (S) (F) **1.** bearer of the thunderbolt. **3.** a Buddhist Śakti.

Vajrahastā (S) (F) **1.** thunderbolt handed; mighty. **2.** diamond handed. **3.** a Buddhist goddess.

Vajrajvālā (S) (F) **1.** illuminated by a thunderbolt. **2.** shining like lightning. **3.** a granddaughter of Vairoćana (*Rāmāyaṇa*).

Vajrakālī (S) (F) **1.** black goddess of lightning. **3.** a Jina Śakti (*V. Purāṇa*).

Vajrakālikā (S) (F) **1.** black goddess of lightning. **3.** the mother of Gautama Buddha (*B. Literature*).

Vajrakāmā (S) (F) **1.** wishing for thunderbolts. **3.** a daughter of Maya (*V. Purāṇa*).

Vajramālā (S) (F) **1.** with a diamond necklace. **3.** a gandharvī (*K. Vyuha*).

Vajrāmbujā (S) (F) **1.** thunderbolt of Indra. **3.** a goddess (*D. Purāṇa*).

Vajraṅkuśī (S) (F) **1.** diamond hooked. **2.** stern controller. **3.** a goddess.

Vajraprastāriṇī (S) (F) **1.** extender of the thunderbolt. **3.** a tāntric goddess (*Ṛg Veda*).

Vajraśrī (S) (F) **1.** divine diamond. **3.** a gandharvī (*K. Vyuha*).

Vajraśrnkhalā (S) (F) **1.** diamond chain. **3.** one of the 16 Jaina vidyādevīs.

Vajravālā (S) (F) **1.** stern maiden; a maiden with diamonds. **3.** a daughter of Mahābalī and wife of Kumbhakarṇa (*U. Rāmāyaṇa*).

Vajravallī (S) (F) valuable vine; Sunflower (*Heliotropium indicum*).

Vajravārāhī (S) (F) **1.** as strong as a boar. **3.** a tantric goddess.

Vajravidrāviṇī (S) (F) **1.** defeating with a thunderbolt. **3.** a Buddhist goddess.

Vajrayoginī (S) (F) **1.** stern meditator. **3.** a goddess.

Vajreśvarī (S) (F) **1.** goddess of the thunderbolt. **3.** a Buddhist goddess.

Vajrodarī (S) (F) **1.** hard bellied. **3.** a rākṣasī (*Bhā. Purāṇa*).

Vākā (S) (F) **1.** word; speech. **2.** text; recitation. **3.** the daughter of Malyavān and the wife of Viśravas she was the mother of Triśiras, Dūṣana, Vidyujjihvā and Anupālikā.

Vākaprada (S) (F) **1.** giver of speech. **3.** another name for the river Sarasvatī (*V. Rāmāyaṇa*).

Vākinī (S) (F) **1.** one who recites. **3.** a tāntric deity.

Vakṣanā (S) (F) the nourisher; the bed of a river; refreshment; oblation; flame.

Vakṣani (S) (F) strengthening.

Vakṣī (S) (F) strength; nourishment; flame.

Vakti (S) (F) speech.

Valaśiphā (S) (F) **1.** curled hair. **3.** a yoginī (*D. Purāṇa*).

Valayā (S) (F) **1.** coiled. **2.** bracelet; armlet; ring.

Valgukī (S) (F) very beautiful.

Vālinī (S) (F) **1.** tailed. **3.** the constellation Aśvinī (*M. Bh.*).

Vallabhā (S) (F) beloved.

Vallakā (S) (F) a lute.

Vallarī (S) (F) **1.** cluster of blossoms. **2.** creeper. **3.** another name for Sītā.

Vallārī (S) (F) **1.** vine. **3.** a rāgiṇī.

Vallarīkā (S) (F) vine.

Vallī (S) (F) **1.** creeper; vine. **2.** lightning. **3.** a daughter of Ira and mother of vines; another name for the earth.

Vallikā (S) (F) **1.** covered with vines; covered with plants, greenery. **3.** diminutive for the earth; Velvet Leaf (*Cissampelos pareira*).

Vāmā (S) (F) **1.** beautiful. **3.** a form of Durgā; a mother in Skanda's retinue; a queen of Kāśī and mother of Jaina Tīrthaṅkara Pārśvanātha; a village goddess who represents a fierce class of yoginīs (*Purāṇas*); another name for Lakṣmī and Sarasvatī.

Vāmākṣī (S) (F) fair eyed.

Vāmaloćanā (S) (F) **1.** fair eyed. **3.** a daughter of Vīraketu (*V. D. Ćaritam*).

Vāmanā (S) (F) **1.** short. **3.** an apsarā (*M. Bh.*).

Vāmanī (S) (F) **1.** bringing wealth; short; dwarf. **3.** a yoginī (*H. Ć. Ćintāmaṇi*).

Vāmanikā (S) (F) **1.** dwarfish; small. **3.** an attendant of Skanda (*M. Bh.*).

Vāmikā (S) (F) **1.** situated on the left side; consort of Vāma. **3.** another name for Durgā (*D. Purāṇa*).

Vanaćandrikā (S) (F) **1.** moon rays of the jungle. **2.** *Jasminum Sambac.*

Vanadurgā (S) (F) **1.** goddess of the forest; dweller of the forest. **3.** a form of Durgā (*D. Purāṇa*).

Vanajā (S) (F) **1.** forest born; sylvan; wild; water born. **3.** Blue Lotus flower (*Nymphaea stellata*).

Vanajākṣi (S) (F) blue lotus eyed.

Vanajāyata (S) (F) resembling a lotus.

Vanajyotsnī (S) (F) **1.** light of the jungle. **2.** Jasmine.

Vanalakṣmī (S) (F) **1.** ornament of the forest; fortune of the forest; treasure of the forest. **2.** Banana (*Musa sapientum*).

Vanalatā (S) (F) creeper of the forest; vine.

Vanalikā (S) (F) **1.** of forest. **3.** Sunflower (*Heliotrope indicum*).

Vanamālā (S) (F) garland of the forest; a garland of wild flowers; flower braid.

Vanamālikā (S) (F) **1.** garland of the forest. **2.** garland of wild flowers. **3.** a friend of Rādhā; a river (*H. Purāṇa*); *Michelia champaka.*

Vanamālīśā (S) (F) **1.** desired by the gardener of forest. **2.** lady of the forest gardener; with Kṛṣṇa as consort. **3.** another name for Rādhā.

Vanamallī (S) (F) wild Jasmine.

Vanamallikā (S) (F) *Jasminum sambac.*

Vanāmbikā (S) (F) **1.** mother of forest. **3.** the tutelary deity of the family of Dakṣa (*K. Sāgara*).

Vanapuṣpā (S) (F) flower of the forest; wild flower.

Vanaraśmi (S) (F) light of forest; a ray of light.

Vanasarojinī (S) (F) lotus of the forest; the wild cotton plant; collection of wild lotuses.

Vanaśobhana (S) (F) **1.** water; beautifying. **2.** lotus (*Nelumbo speciosum*).

Vanaspatī (S) (F) **1.** protector of the forest. **2.** plants; trees; vegetables. **3.** a gandharvī (*K. Vyūha*).

Vanathi (S) (F) of the forest.

Vānća (S) (F) wish; desire.

Vandanā (S) (F) **1.** praise; worship; adoration. **3.** a river famous in the Purāṇas (*M. Bh.*).

Vandinīkā (S) (F) 1. honoured; praised. 3. another name for Dākṣāyānī.

Vanditā (S) (F) praised; worshipped.

Vandyā (S) (F) 1. praiseworthy; adorable. 3. a yakṣi.

Vāṅgālī (S) (F) 1. belonging to Bengal. 3. a rāgiṇī.

Vāṇī (S) (F) 1. speech; praise; sweet in voice. 2. sound; voice; music. 3. another name for Sarasvatī (*Ṛg Veda*).

Vānī (S) (F) wish; desire.

Vāṇići (S) (F) speech.

Vāṇimayī (S) (F) 1. goddess of speech. 3. another name for Sarasvatī.

Vāṇinī (S) (F) soft voiced; a clever and intriguing woman.

Vāṇīśrī (S) (F) 1. divine speech. 3. another name for Sarasvatī.

Vanitā (S) (F) wished for; desired; loved; woman.

Vanjulā (S) (F) 1. a cow that has an abundance of milk. 3. a river (*Ma. Purāṇa*).

Vaṅksu (S) (F) 1. arm. 2. a tributary of the Gaṅgā.

Vanmayi (S) (F) 1. goddess of speech. 3. another name for Sarasvatī.

Vanśā (S) (F) 1. offspring; daughter; bamboo; lineage. 3. an apsarā daughter of Kaśyapa and Prādhā (*M. Bh.*); Indian Dammer tree (*Shorea robusta*); Solid Bamboo (*Dendrocalamus strictus*).

Vanśadhārā (S) (F) 1. perpetuating the race. 3. a river rising from the Mahendra mountain.

Vanśalakṣmī (S) (F) the family fortune.

Vanśī (S) (F) flute; pipe; artery.

Vanśikā (S) (F) flute.

Vanu (S) (F) 1. zealous; eager. 2. friend. 3. a river of heaven (*Ṛg Veda*).

Vānyā (S) (F) 1. sylvan. 3. Rosary Pea (*Arbus precatorius*).

Vaprā (S) (F) 1. garden bed. 3. the mother of the Arhat Nimi (*J. S. Koṣa*).

Vapu (S) (F) 1. body. 3. an apsarā (*M. Bh.*).

Vapuṣā (S) (F) 1. embodied. 2. wonderfully beautiful; handsome; beauty; nature. 3. a daughter of Dakṣa and wife of Dharma (*V. Purāṇa*); an apsara who was reborn as the daughter of Kundhara and Menakā (*Mā. Purāṇa*).

Vapuṣī (S) (F) 1. embodied. 2. wonderfully beautiful. 3. beauty personified as a daughter of Dakṣa (*V. Purāṇa*); an apsarā (*V. Purāṇa*).

Vapuṣmatī (S) (F) 1. having a form. 2. beautifully formed. 3. a mother attending on Skanda; the daughter of the king of Sindhu and wife of Mārutta (*Mā. Purāṇa*).

Vapuṣṭamā (S) (F) 1. best among the embodied. 2. wonderfully beautiful. 3. the daughter of King Suvarṇavarmā of Kāṣī and wife of Janamejaya and the mother of Śatānika and Śankukarṇa (*M. Bh.*); *Hibiscus mutabilis*.

Varā (S) (F) 1. boon; choice; gift; reward; benefit; blessing. 3. a river; another name for Pārvatī and Ćhāyā.

Varadā (S) (F) 1. giver of boons. 2. girl; maiden. 3. a deity; a river (*M. Bh.*); a yoginī (*H. Ć. Ćintāmaṇi*).

Vārāhī (S) (F) 1. consort of boar. 2. sow. 3. the female energy of the boar form of Viṣṇu; a mother attending on Skanda (*M. Bh.*); Bulb bearing Yam (*Dioscorea bulbifera*); Nut Grass (*Cyperus rotundis*).

Varajākṣī (S) (F) with lotus eyes.

Varālikā (S) (F) 1. goddess of power. 2. controller of the army. 3. another name for Durgā.

Varaṇā (S) (F) 1. surrounding; enclosing. 2. rampart. 3. a holy river flowing past north Benaras now called Barnā (*M. Bh.*).

Varānanā (S) (F) 1. beautiful faced. 3. an apsarā (*M. Bh.*).

Varanārī (S) (F) best woman.

Varāṇasī (S) (F) 1. granting boons. 3. holy place of pilgrimage between the rivers Varaṇā and Asi, it was also known as Prayāga and Kāśi.

Varaṅganā (S) (F) beautiful.

Vārāṅgī (S) (F) **1.** having a beautiful body. **3.** the wife of Vajrāṅga and mother of Tārakāsura; the wife of King Saṁyati of the lunar dynasty and the mother of Ahaṁyati (*M. Bh.*).

Varāṅgi (S) (F) **1.** with an elegant form. **2.** turmeric. **3.** the daughter of Dhṛṣadvata; the wife of the asura Vajrānga.

Varapakṣiṇī (S) (F) **1.** well feathered. **3.** a tāntric goddess.

Varapradā (S) (F) **1.** granting wishes. **3.** a yoginī (*H. C. Ćintāmaṇi*); another name for Lopāmudrā.

Varārohā (S) (F) **1.** handsome; elegant; fine rider; fine hipped. **3.** Dākṣāyānī in Someśvara.

Varastrī (S) (F) **1.** noble woman. **3.** a sister of Bṛhaspati and wife of the vasu Prabhāsa (*M. Bh.*).

Varasyā (S) (F) request; wish; desire.

Varavarṇinī (S) (F) **1.** with a beautiful complexion. **3.** another name for Durgā, Lakṣmī and Sarasvatī.

Varayoṣita (S) (F) a beautiful woman.

Vareṇyā (S) (F) **1.** desirable. **3.** Śiva's wife (*Ś. Purāṇa*); Saffron (*Crocus sativus*).

Vargā (S) (F) **1.** belonging to a division; belonging to a set or group. **3.** an apsarā changed into a crocodile who was released from her curse by Arjuna.

Vārī (S) (F) **1.** rich in gifts; goddess of speech; water. **3.** another name for Sarasvatī (*Ṛg Veda*).

Varī (S) (F) stream; river.

Vārijākṣā (S) (F) lotus eyed.

Variṣā (S) (F) the rainy season.

Varivasyā (S) (F) service; devotion; obedience; honour.

Varjā (S) (F) **1.** water born. **2.** lotus (*Nelumbo speciosum*).

Varṇamātṛkā (S) (F) **1.** mother of speech. **3.** another name for Sarasvatī.

Varṇapuṣpī (S) (F) **1.** the coloured flower. **2.** Amaranth Lily (*Echinops echinatus*).

Varṇika (S) (F) of fine colour; fine gold; the purity of gold.

Varṣā (S) (F) rain; the rainy season.

Vārṣikī (S) (F) **1.** belonging to the rainy season; yearly. **2.** *Jasminum sambac.*

Vārttā (S) (F) news; intelligence; tidings.

Varuṇānī (S) (F) **1.** goddess of water. **3.** wife of Varuṇa (*Ṛg Veda*).

Varuṇavegā (S) (F) **1.** with the speed of Varuṇa. **3.** another name for a kinnarī.

Varuṇāvī (S) (F) **1.** water born. **3.** another name for Lakṣmī.

Vāruṇī (S) (F) **1.** of water; resembling water; liquor; wine. **3.** the daughter of Varuṇa who married the devas (*P. Purāṇa*); a river (*V. Rāmāyaṇa*) the Śakti or female energy of Varuṇa said to have been produced from the churning of the Ocean of Milk and is regarded as the mother of spirituous liquor (*Ṛg Veda*).

Varūthinī (S) (F) **1.** multitude; troop; army. **3.** an apsara (*M. Bh.*).

Varūtrī (S) (F) **1.** protectress. **3.** a tutelary goddess (*Ṛg Veda*).

Varyā (S) (F) treasure; wealth; chosen; valuable.

Vaśa (S) (F) obedient; willing.

Vāsanā (S) (F) **1.** knowledge derived from past perception; fancy; imagination; notion; idea; desire; inclination. **3.** the wife of the vasu Arka (*Bhāgavata*); another name for Durgā.

Vasantajā (S) (F) **1.** born in spring. **2.** Jasmine; the Mādhavi creeper.

Vasantakusuma (S) (F) spring flower.

Vasantalatā (S) (F) the vine of spring.

Vasantalekhā (S) (F) written by spring; spring born.

Vasantasenā (S) (F) **1.** with spring as the commander. **2.** as charming as the spring.

Vasantaśrī (S) (F) the beauty of spring.

Vāsantī (S) (F) **1.** of the spring season; vernal; light yellow; saffron. **3.** a rāgiṇī; a sylvan deity; the Navamallikā Jasmine (*Jasminum officianale*); a daughter of King Bhūmiśukla; another name for the mother of Vyāsa (*M. Bh.*); *Hiptage Madoblata.*

Vasantikā (S) (F) **1.** goddess of the spring. **3.** a forest deity; *Gaertnera racemosa.*

Vasātī (S) (F) **1.** dawn. **3.** a son of Ikṣvāku (*H. Purāṇa*); a lunar dynasty king and son of Janamejaya (*M. Bh.*); a king on the side of the Kauravas (*M. Bh.*).

Vāsavadattā (S) (F) **1.** enticing; fragrance born; given by Indra. **3.** the wife of King Udayana (*K. Granthāvali*)

Vāsavī (S) (F) **1.** daughter of the all pervading. **3.** the mother of Vyāsa who was the daughter of King Vasu and the apsarā Adrikā (*M. Bh.*).

Vasāvi (S) (F) treasury.

Vasordhārā (S) (F) **1.** stream of wealth. **3.** the celestial Gaṅgā (*M. Bh.*); the wife of the vasu named Agni (*Bhā. Purāṇa*).

Vastṛ (S) (F) shining; illumining.

Vastu (S) (F) dawn; morning.

Vasu (S) (F) **1.** light; radiance. **3.** a daughter of Dakṣa and mother of the vasus (*H. Purāṇa*).

Vasudā (S) (F) **1.** granting wealth. **3.** another name for the earth; a mother in Skanda's retinue (*M. Bh.*); a gandharvī (*M. Bh.*).

Vasudāmā (S) (F) **1.** controlling the divine beings. **3.** an attendant of Skanda (*M. Bh.*).

Vasudattā (S) (F) **1.** given by the gods. **3.** the mother of Vararuci (*K. Sāgara*).

Vasudevā (S) (F) **1.** goddess of wealth. **3.** a daughter of Śvaphalka (*V. Purāṇa*).

Vasudevatā (S) (F) **1.** goddess of wealth. **3.** a goddess granting wealth (*Bhā. Purāṇa*); the lunar mansion Dhaniṣṭha.

Vasudhā (S) (F) **1.** producing wealth. **3.** the daughter of gandharvī Narmadā (*M. Bh.*); another name for the earth and Lakṣmī.

Vasudharā (S) (F) **1.** bearing wealth. **3.** a Buddhist goddess (*B. Literature*); a Jaina Śakti; a river (*J.S. Koṣa*).

Vasudhāriṇī (S) (F) **1.** bearer of treasures. **3.** another name for the earth.

Vasudhitī (S) (F) possessing wealth.

Vāsukeśvarī (S) (F) **1.** sister of Vāsukī. **3.** another name for Manasā.

Vasulaksmi (S) (F) **1.** divine goddess of wealth. **3.** a sister-in-law of Agnimitra (*K. Granthāvali*).

Vasumatī (S) (F) **1.** possessing treasure. **3.** another name for the earth.

Vasundharā (S) (F) **1.** abode of wealth. **2.** containing wealth. **3.** a portion of the goddess Prakṛti; a daughter of Śvaphalka (*Ṛg Veda*); another name for the earth.

Vasundhareśā (S) (F) **1.** consort of the lord of the earth. **3.** another name for Rādhā.

Vasundhareyī (S) (F) **1.** daughter of the earth. **3.** another name for Sītā.

Vasuprabhā (S) (F) **1.** divine light. **3.** one of the 7 tongues of fire (*M. Bh.*).

Vāsurā (S) (F) **1.** valuable. **2.** night; the earth; woman.

Vasuśrī (S) (F) **1.** divine grace. **3.** a mother in Skanda's retinue (*M. Bh.*).

Vasvī (S) (F) the divine night.

Vasvoksārā (S) (F) **1.** essence of the divine waters. **3.** one of the 7 branches of the Gaṅgā (*M.Bh.*)

Vātansā (S) (F) garland; crest; ring.

Vātarūpā (S) (F) **1.** with the form of the wind. **2.** subtle; transparent. **3.** a rākṣasi who was the daughter of Līkā (*Mā. Purāṇa*).

Vatśā (S) (F) calf; daughter; breast.

Vatsalā (S) (F) **1.** child loving. **2.** affectionate; tender; devoted. **3.** an attendant of Skanda (*M. Bh.*).

Vatsamitra (S) (F) **1.** friend of children; friend of calves. **3.** an apsarā (*H. Purāṇa*).

Vatū (S) (F) **1.** who speaks the truth. **3.** a river of heaven.

Vatyā (F) gale; storm; hurricane.

Vayā (S) (F) **1.** a branch; twig. **2.** child; vigour; strength; power.

Vāyavyā (S) (F) the northwest presided over by Vāyu.

Vayodhā (S) (F) strengthening; invigorating.

Vayunā (S) (F) **1.** moving; active; alive; mark; aim; goal; knowledge; wisdom. **3.** a daughter of Svadhā (*Y. Veda*).

Vāyuvegā (S) (F) **1.** swift as the wind. **3.** a yoginī; a kinnarī; a sister of Vāyupatha (*K. Sāgara*).

Vedā (S) (F) **1.** well known; meritorious; pious; famous. **3.** a river (*Ṛg Veda*).

Vedabhā (S) (F) obtained from knowledge; a magic charm which brings jewels from the sky.

Vedagarbhā (S) (F) **1.** womb of the Vedas. **3.** another name for Durgā (*A. Purāṇa*) and Sarasvatī (*Bhā. Purāṇa*).

Vedajananī (S) (F) **1.** mother of the Vedas. **2.** the Gayatri mantra.

Vedamātṛ (S) (F) **1.** mother of the Vedas. **3.** another name for Sarasvatī, Sāvitrī and Gāyatrī.

Vedanā (S) (F) **1.** knowledge; perception; pain. **3.** the goddess of pain who is the daughter of Nirṛti and the mother of Duhkha (*A. Purāṇa*).

Vedāsinī (S) (F) **1.** carrying wealth. **3.** a river.

Vedasmṛtā (S) (F) **1.** remembrance of the scriptures. **3.** a river (*M. Bh.*).

Vedaśrutī (S) (F) **1.** heard about in the Vedas; famous in Vedas. **3.** a famous river of the Purāṇas (*Purāṇas*).

Vedavatī (S) (F) **1.** familiar with the Vedas. **3.** a daughter of Kuśadhvaja who was reborn as Sītā; an apsarā (*V. Rāmāyaṇa*).

Vedeśvā (S) (F) **1.** born of the sacred texts. **3.** a river.

Vedeśvara (S) (F) lord of the Vedas.

Vedhasyā (S) (F) worship; piety.

Vedī (S) (F) **1.** knowledge; science; altar. **3.** the wife of Brahmā (*M. Bh.*).

Vedikā (S) (F) **1.** a seal ring; making known; restoring to consciousness. **3.** an apsarā.

Vedinī (S) (F) **1.** knowing; feeling; proclaiming. **3.** a river (*Rāmāyaṇa*).

Vedyā (S) (F) knowledge.

Vegavāhinī (S) (F) **1.** flowing fast. **3.** a river whose deity lives in the court of Varuṇa (*M.Bh.*).

Vegavatī (S) (F) **1.** rapid. **3.** a river (*V. Rāmāyaṇa*); an apsarā.

Veginī (S) (F) **1.** going swiftly. **3.** a river (*M. Bh.*).

Vekā (S) (F) **1.** offspring of a bird. **3.** a rākṣasī who was the sister of Puṣpotkaṭa and Kaikaśī

Velā (S) (F) **1.** limit; coast; shore. **3.** boundary of sea and land personified as the daughter of Meru and Dhāriṇī and the wife of Samudra (*M. Bh.*); the wife of the Buddha (*L. Vistara*); a princess (*K. Sāgara*).

Veṇā (S) (F) **1.** yearning; longing; to go; to move; discern; to play on an instrument. **3.** a famous Purāṇic river which is among those where fire originated and worthy of being mentioned morning and evening (*M. Bh.*).

Veṇī (S) (F) **1.** a braid of hair; stream; the confluence of rivers. **3.** Luffa echinata.

Veṇika (S) (F) **1.** flowing. **2.** a continuous stream. **3.** a holy river of the Purāṇas (*H. Purāṇa*).

Veṇuvīṇādharā (S) (F) **1.** bearer of flute and lute. **3.** an attendant of Skanda (*M. Bh.*).

Veṇya (S) (F) to be loved; desirable.

Vetālajananī (S) (F) **1.** mother of the phantom. **3.** an attendant of Skanda (*M. Bh.*).

Vetravatī (S) (F) **1.** full of reeds. **3.** a form of Durgā (*H. Purāṇa*); a river now called Betwā (*Bhā. Purāṇa*); the mother of Vetrāsura (*M. Bh.*).

Vibalī (S) (F) **1.** young. **3.** a river.

Vibhā (S) (F) light; lustre; splendour; glory.

Vibhāsvatī (S) (F) brilliant; resplendant.

Vibhāvā (S) (F) **1.** cause of emotion. **3.** a wife of Svaroćis.

Vibhāvari (S) (F) **1.** brilliant; bright. **2.** dawn; most illuminated. **3.** a mindborn daughter of Brahmā considered a personification of a star filled night (*M. Bh.*).

Vibhīṣaṇa (S) (F) **1.** terrifying. **3.** an attendant of Skanda (*M. Bh.*); the son of Viśravas and Mālinī and the brother of Rāvaṇa and the husband of Saralā, he joined the side of Rāma and was made king of Laṅkā after the battle (*U. Rāmāyaṇa*).

Vibhrāṣṭī (S) (F) radiance; flame; blaze.

Vibhūṣā (S) (F) **1.** ornament; decoration. **2.** light; splendour; beauty.

Vibhūsanā (S) (F) decorated; ornamented; splendour; beauty.

Vibhūṣita (S) (F) decorated; adorned.

Vibhūtī (S) (F) **1.** expansion; abundance; splendour; fortune; welfare; plenty. **3.** another name for Lakṣmī.

Vićitrā (S) (F) **1.** strange; variegated; wonderful. **2.** a white deer. **3.** a river (*V. Purāṇa*).

Vidarbhā (S) (F) **1.** without darbhā grass. **3.** a daughter of Ugra and wife of Manu Ćakṣusa (*Mā. Purāṇa*).

Vidarśanā (S) (F) right knowledge; right perception; true philosophy.

Vidhivadhū (S) (F) **1.** wife of Brahmā **3.** another name for Sarasvatī.

Vidhumukhi (S) (F) moon faced.

Vidhupriyā (S) (F) **1.** dear to the moon. **2.** a lunar mansion.

Vidīpitā (S) (F) **1.** illuminated. **2.** bright.

Vidiśā (S) (F) **1.** an intermediate region. **3.** a river whose deity lives in the palace of Varuṇa (*M. Bh.*).

Viditā (S) (F) **1.** known; understood; perceived. **3.** a Jaina goddess (*J.S. Koṣa*).

Vidujjvalā (S) (F) flash of lightning.

Vidulā (S) (F) **1.** wise; intelligent. **3.** a heroic Kṣatriya woman who sent her fleeing son back into the battlefield (*M. Bh.*); the mother of Sanjaya the narrator of the battle to Dhṛtarāṣṭra (*M. Bh.*); Calamus rotang; Acacia rigata.

Viduṣī (S) (F) wise.

Vidveśi (S) (F) **1.** having resentment. **3.** a rākṣasī daughter of Duhsaha (*Mā. Purāṇa*).

Vidyā (S) (F) **1.** knowledge; learning; science; philosophy. **3.** a maid of Devī Umā (*M. Bh.*); a deity of the 3 Vedas (*Ṛg Veda*); another name for Durgā.

Vidyādevī (S) (F) **1.** goddess of learning. **3.** a Jaina divinity (*J.S. Koṣa*).

Vidyādharī (S) (F) **1.** bearing knowledge. **3.** a daughter of Śūrasena (*Bhā. Purāṇa*); attendants of Śiva.

Vidyādhidevatā (S) (F) **1.** presiding god of knowledge. **3.** Sarasvatī as the tutelary deity of science.

Vidyāgaurī (S) (F) goddess of knowledge.

Vidyāvadhū (S) (F) a goddess presiding over learning.

Vidyāvati (S) (F) **1.** learned. **3.** an apsara (*V. Purāṇa*).

Vidyotā (S) (F) **1.** consisting of lightning; shining; glittering. **3.** an apsarā (*M. Bh.*).

Vidyudambhas (S) (F) **1.** shining water. **3.** a river (*V. Purāṇa*).

Vidyudvallī (S) (F) a flash of lightning.

Vidyudvarṇā (S) (F) **1.** lightning coloured. **3.** an apsarā (*V. Purāṇa*).

Vidyudyotā (S) (F) with the brightness of lightning.

Vidyujjihvā (S) (F) **1.** lightning tongued. **3.** a mother attending on Skanda (*M. Bh.*).

Vidyullatā (S) (F) creeper of lightning.

Vidyullekhā (S) (F) a streak of lightning.

Vidyunmālā (S) (F) **1.** a wreath of lightning. **3.** a yakṣi; a daughter of Suroha (*K. Sāgara*).

Vidyutā (S) (F) **1.** lightning; a flashing thunderbolt; the dawn. **3.** the 4 daughters of Prajāpati Bahuputra; an apsarā (*M. Bh.*).

Vidyutapuñjā (S) (F) **1.** heap of lightning. **3.** the daughter of the dānava Vidyutprabha (*M. Bh.*).

Vidyutparṇā (S) (F) **1.** bearing lightning as wings. **3.** an apsarā daughter of Kaśyapa and Prādhā (*H. Purāṇa*).

Vidyutprabhā (S) (F) **1.** flashing like lightning. **3.** a daughter of the king of the rākṣasas; a daughter of the king of the yakṣas (*K. Sāgara*); a nāga maiden; an apsarā (*M. Bh.*); the granddaughter of Māhābali (*K. Sāgara*).

Vihā (S) (F) heaven.

Vihasatikā (S) (F) gentle laughter; smiling.

Vijarā (S) (F) **1.** never growing old. **3.** a river in Brahmā's world.

Vijayā (S) (F) **1.** victorious; triumphant. **3.** a friend of Durgā (*M. Bh.*); Kṛṣṇa's birthday (*H. Purāṇa*); the wife of Yama (*M. Bh.*); a yoginī (*H. Koṣa*); a daughter of Dakṣa (*Rāmāyaṇa*); Kṛṣṇa's garland (*M. Bh.*); the daughter of King Dāśārha and wife of Emperor Bhumanyu (*M. Bh.*); the daughter of Dyutimān and the wife of the Pāṇḍava Sahadeva and the mother of Suhotra (*M. Bh.*); the queen of Ćampāpuri and mother of Jaina Tīrathaṅkara Vasupūjya (*J.S. Koṣa*); another name for Durgā.

Vijayalakṣmī (S) (F) **1.** goddess of victory. **3.** one of the 8 Lakṣmīs who keeps the treasury of Brahmā and was reborn as Laṅkalakṣmī guarding Rāvaṇa until hit by Hanumān when she resumed her original form (*V. Rāmāyaṇa*); the mother of Venkaṭa (*R. Taraṅginī*).

Vijayantikā (S) (F) **1.** victorious in the end. **3.** a yoginī (*A. Koṣa*).

Vijayaśrī (S) (F) **1.** glory of victory. **3.** the goddess of victory; a kinnarī (*K. Vyuha*).

Vijayavatī (S) (F) **1.** victorious. **3.** the daughter of the nāga Gandhamālin (*K. Sāgara*).

Vijitī (S) (F) **1.** victory; triumph. **3.** a goddess (*M. Bh.*).

Vijittāri (S) (F) **1.** vanquisher. **3.** a rākṣasa (*V. Rāmāyaṇa*).

Vijitvarā (S) (F) **1.** best among the conquerors. **3.** a goddess (*Ć. Upaniṣad*).

Vijñatī (S) (F) knowledge; understanding.

Vikaćalambā (S) (F) **1.** radiant mother. **3.** another name for Durgā (*D. Purāṇa*).

Vikaćaśrī (S) (F) with radiant beauty.

Vikarālā (S) (F) **1.** formidable; terrible. **3.** another name for Durgā.

Vikāśini (S) (F) **1.** shining. **2.** radiant; illuminating. **3.** a mother in Skanda's train (*H. Purāṇa*).

Vikaṭā (S) (F) **1.** huge; large; great; terrible; ugly; dreadful. **3.** the mother of Gautama Buddha (*B. Literature*); a Buddhist divinity (*B. Literature*); a rākṣasi in the harem of Rāvaṇa (*V. Rāmāyaṇa*)

Vikāthinī (S) (F) **1.** boasting. **3.** an attendant of Skanda (*M. Bh.*).

Vikeśī (S) (F) **1.** hairless; with dishevelled hair. **3.** the wife of Śiva manifested in the form of Mahī or the earth (*Purāṇas*).

Vikhyāti (S) (F) fame; celebrity.

Vikrānti (S) (F) **1.** all pervading power. **2.** heroism; prowess; strength; might.

Vikṛtā (S) (F) **1.** deformed; changed; strange. **3.** a yoginī (*H. Koṣa*).

Vīkṣā (S) (F) knowledge; intelligence.

Vikuṇṭhā (S) (F) **1.** inward glance; mental concentration; penetration. **3.** the mother of the devatas or minor gods of the Raivata Manvantara (*Br. Purāṇa*).

Vilāsamayī (S) (F) playful; full of grace; charming.

Vilāsantī (S) (F) flashing; shining; glittering.

Vilāsinī (S) (F) **1.** radiant; shining; playful; charming; lively. **3.** another name for Lakṣmī.

Vilohitā (S) (F) **1.** deep red. **3.** one of the 7 tongues of fire (*M. Upaniṣad*).

Vimala (S) (F) **1.** stainless. **2.** clean; pure; bright; spotless; sacred. **3.** a calf who was the daughter of Rohiṇī and the granddaughter of Surabhi (*M. Bh.*), Dākṣāyānī in Puruṣottama; a yoginī; a daughter of Gandharvī (*M. Bh.*).

Vimalamati (S) (F) pure in heart.

Vimoćanī (S) (F) **1.** liberation; emancipation; freedom. **3.** a river.

Vīṇā (S) (F) **1.** lightning; lute. **3.** the Indian lute supposed to have been invented by Nārada (*Bhā. Purāṇa*); a yoginī (*A. Koṣa*); a river (*M. Bh.*).

Vinadī (S) (F) **1.** noisy. **3.** a river (*M. Bh.*).

Vinamratā (S) (F) politeness; gentleness; modesty.

Vinatā (S) (F) **1.** humble; one who bows. **2.** hunchback. **3.** a daughter of Dakṣa and wife of Kaśyapa and mother of Aruṇa, Garuḍa, Sumati (*M. Bh.*); a rākṣasī (*Ś. Purāṇa*).

Vinati (S) (F) prayer; entreaty; humility; modesty.

Viṇāyavatī (S) (F) **1.** polite; gentle; modest. **3.** a queen of Kāmarūpa and wife of Bhūtivarman.

Vināyikā (S) (F) the consort of Gaṇeśa.

Vindhyānilayā (S) (F) **1.** wind of the Vindhyas; resident of the Vindhyas. **3.** a form of Durgā (*A. Koṣa*).

Vindhyāvalī (S) (F) **1.** row of Vindhya mountains. **3.** the wife of Mahabali and the mother of Bāṇa and Kumbhīnāśī (*M. Purāṇa*).

Vindhyavāsinī (S) (F) **1.** dwelling in the Vindhyas. **3.** a form of Durgā (*D. Purāṇa*).

Vīndu (S) (F) dot; point; intelligent; wise.

Vinīti (S) (F) modesty; good behaviour; training.

Vinoditā (S) (F) diverted; amused; delighted.

Vipā (S) (F) speech.

Vipañcī (S) (F) **1.** remover of troubles. **2.** the Indian lute.

Vipāśā (S) (F) **1.** fetterless; unbound. **3.** a river, famous in the Purāṇas for having saved sage Vasiṣṭha, now known as Beas (*H. Purāṇa*).

Vipodhā (S) (F) giving inspiration.

Vipracitti (S) (F) **1.** sagacious. **3.** an apsarā (*V. Purāṇa*).

Vipsā (S) (F) succession; repetition.

Vipulā (S) (F) **1.** large; great; abundant. **3.** another name for the earth.

Vipulekṣaṇā (S) (F) large eyed.

Vīrā (S) (F) **1.** brave; wise; heroic; strong; powerful; excellent. **3.** the wife of the Agni named Bharadvāja and the mother of the agni Vīra (*M. Bh.*); a famous river of the Purāṇas (*M. Bh.*); the wife of King Karandhama and mother of Aviksit (*Mā. Purāṇa*).

Vīrabālā (S) (F) brave maiden.

Virajā (S) (F) **1.** free from dust; clean. **2.** pure. **3.** the wife of Nahuṣa (*H. Purāṇa*); Durvā grass (*Panicum dactylon*); a rākṣasi (*H. Purāṇa*); a gopi or cowherdess who melted due to Radha's anger and became a river (*D. Bhāgavata*).

Virajeśvarī (S) (F) **1.** goddess of the pure. **3.** another name for Rādhā.

Virājinī (S) (F) brilliant; splendid; queen.

Vīraṇī (S) (F) **1.** brave woman. **3.** a daughter of Brahmā born of his left thumb who married Dakṣa and was the mother of Nārada (*D. Bhāgavata*); a disciple of Yājñavalkya (*Vā. Purāṇa*); the daughter of Vīraṇa and mother of Manu Ćākṣuṣa (*Bhā. Purāṇa*).

Viraviṇī (S) (F) **1.** crying; weeping. **3.** a river.

Vīrendrī (S) (F) **1.** goddess of the brave. **3.** a yoginī (*A. Koṣa*).

Vīrikā (S) (F) **1.** possessed with bravery. **3.** a wife of Harṣa.

Vīriṇī (S) (F) **1.** of whom the brave are born. **2.** a mother of sons. **3.** a wife of Dakṣa also called Aśikni and mother of a 1000 sons (*M. Bh.*).

Viroćanā (S) (F) **1.** shining upon; illuminating. **3.** an attendant of Skanda (*M. Bh.*); a daughter of Prahlāda the asura king and the wife of Tvaṣṭā and the mother of Viraja (*Bhāgavata*) and Tṛśiras (*Vā. Purāṇa*).

Vīrūdhā (S) (F) **1.** sprouting; grown; formed. **3.** a daughter of Ira or of Surasā the mother of the serpents and who became the mother of vines.

Virūpā (S) (F) **1.** manifold; variegated; changed. **3.** the wife of Yama; a tāntric deity.

Vīryā (S) (F) **1.** vigour; energy; strength. **3.** a nāga maiden.

Vīryavatī (S) (F) **1.** powerful. **3.** a mother in Skanda's retinue (*M. Bh.*).

Viṣaharā (S) (F) **1.** removing venom. **3.** another name for Manasā.

Viśala (S) (F) **1.** large; spacious; extensive; wide. **3.** the wife of the lunar dynasty king Ajamīḍha (*M. Bh.*); the wife of Bhīma the son of Mahāvirya and the mother of Trayyāruṇi, Puṣkarī and Kapi (*Vā. Purāṇa*); the city Ujjayinī (*K. Granthāvali*); an apsarā (*V. Purāṇa*); a daughter of Dakṣa and wife of Ariṣṭhanemi (*Mā. Purāṇa*).

Viśalākṣi (S) (F) **1.** large eyed. **3.** a mother in Skanda's retinue (*M. Bh.*); a yoginī (*A. Koṣa*); a daughter of Śandilya; a subordinate female deity of Trichinopoly; another name for Durgā.

Viśalyā (S) (F) **1.** freed from pain. **3.** a wife of Lakśmana (*V. Rāmāyaṇa*); a holy river whose deity lives in the palace of Varuṇa (*M. Bh.*); *Tinospora cordifolia.*

Viśirā (S) (F) **1.** with no prominent veins. **3.** an attendant of Skanda (*M. Bh.*).

Viṣṇu (S) (F) **1.** omnipresent. **3.** the queen of Simhapuri and mother of Jaina Tiranthakara Śreyansanātha (*J.S. Koṣa*).

Viṣṇugaṅgā (S) (F) **1.** the river of the omnipresent. **3.** a river (*Bhā. Purāṇa*).

Viṣṇumatī (S) (F) **1.** with omnipresent intelligence. **3.** the wife of King Śatānīka and the mother of Sahaśrānīka (*K. Sāgara*).

Viṣṇumāyā (S) (F) **1.** the illusion of Viṣṇu. **3.** a form of Durgā (*K. Purāṇa*).

Viṣṇupadī (S) (F) **1.** emerging from the foot of Viṣṇu. **3.** the Gaṅgā river which flows from Viṣṇu's foot (*V. Purāṇa*).

Viṣṇupatnī (S) (F) **1.** wife of Viṣṇu. **3.** another name for Aditi and Lakṣmī.

Viṣṇupriyā (S) (F) **1.** beloved of Viṣṇu. **2.** Sacred Basil (*Ocimum sanctum*); Wax Flower (*Ervatomia coronaria*). **3.** another name for Lakṣmī.

Viṣṇuśakti (S) (F) **1.** power of Viṣṇu. **3.** another name for Lakṣmī.

Viṣṇuvallabhā (S) (F) **1.** beloved of Viṣṇu. **3.** another name for Lakṣmī and Tulasī.

Viśobhaginā (S) (F) **1.** prosperous. **3.** another name for Sarasvatī.

Viśokā (S) (F) **1.** exempted from grief. **3.** a wife of Kṛṣṇa (*M. Bh.*); a mother in Skanda's train (*M. Bh.*).

Viśrutī (S) (F) celebrity; fame.

Viṣṭāriṇī (S) (F) **1.** extensive; spreading; mighty; large. **3.** a goddess (*Mā. Purāṇa*).

Viśuddhī (S) (F) purity; holiness; virtue; perfect knowledge.

Viśvā (S) (F) **1.** the earth. **3.** a tongue of Agni (*Mā. Purāṇa*); a daughter of Dakṣa and the wife of Dharmā and mother of the viśvadevas (*M. Bh.*).

Viśvācī (S) (F) **1.** universal. **3.** an apsarā in the palace of Kubera (*M. Bh.*).

Viśvadāsā (S) (F) **1.** servant of the world. **3.** one of the 7 tongues of fire (*T. Samhita*).

Viśvadhāriṇī (S) (F) **1.** abode of the universe. **2.** all maintaining. **3.** another name for the earth.

Viśvadhenā (S) (F) **1.** cow of the universe. **2.** all feeding. **3.** another name for the earth.

Viśvagandhā (S) (F) **1.** fragrance of the universe. **2.** giving out fragrance everywhere. **3.** another name for the earth (*A. Kośa*).

Viśvakāyā (S) (F) **1.** the universal form. **2.** one whose body is the universe. **3.** a form of Dākṣayāṇī (*D. Purāṇa*).

Viśvamadā (S) (F) **1.** enchanting the universe; all delighting; all consuming. **3.** one of the 7 tongues of fire (*A. Koṣa*).

Viśvambharī (S) (F) **1.** feeding the universe. **2.** all bearing. **3.** another name for the earth.

Viśvamukhī (S) (F) **1.** of the universe. **3.** Dākṣāyāṇī in Jalandhara (*D. Purāṇa*).

Viśvapāvani (S) (F) **1.** pious in the world. **2.** Sacred Basil (*Ocimum sanctum*).

Viśvapūjitā (S) (F) **1.** worshipped by all. **2.** Sacred Basil (*Ocimum sanctum*).

Viśvarucī (S) (F) **1.** illuminator of the universe. **2.** all glittering. **3.** one of the 7 tongues of fire (*M. Upaniṣad*).

Viśvarūpā (S) (F) **1.** with the form of the universe. **2.** many coloured. **3.** a wife of sage Dharma and the mother of Dharmavratā (*Vā. Purāṇa*).

Viśvarūpī (S) (F) **1.** of the form of universe. **2.** multicoloured. **3.** one of the 7 tongues of fire.

Viśvarūpikā (S) (F) 1. with the form of the universe. 3. a yoginī (*H. Koṣa*).

Viśvarūpiṇī (S) (F) 1. with the form of the universe; creator of universe. 3. a goddess (*A. Koṣa*).

Viśvasahā (S) (F) 1. enduring all. 3. one of the 7 tongues of fire (*M. Upaniṣad*); another name for the earth.

Viśvāvatī (S) (F) 1. possessing the universe. 2. universal. 3. another name for th Gaṅgā.

Viśveśā (S) (F) 1. lady of the universe; desired by all. 3. a daughter of Dakṣa and wife of Dharma (*Mā. Purāṇa*).

Vītā (S) (F) wish; desire.

Vitana (S) (F) 1. extension; heap; performance; oblation; plenty; abundance. 3. the wife of Sattrāyana (*Bhā. Purāṇa*).

Vitastā (S) (F) 1. a measure of length which is from the wrist to the tip of the fingers. 3. a river now known as the Jhelum whose deity was once an advisor to Pārvatī and stays in the palace of Varuṇa (*M. Bh.*).

Vīti (S) (F) enjoyment; light; lustre; fire.

Vitolā (S) (F) 1. very calm. 3. a river (*R. Taraṅgiṇī*).

Vittadā (S) (F) 1. wealth giver. 3. a mother attending on Skanda. (*M. Bh.*).

Vitti (S) (F) consciousness; understanding; intelligence.

Vitti (S) (F) finding; acquisition; gain.

Vivandiṣā (S) (F) the wish to worship.

Vivasvatī (S) (F) 1. shining forth; diffusing light. 3. a city of the sun.

Vivitsā (S) (F) desire for knowledge.

Viyadgangā (S) (F) the celestial Gaṅgā; the galaxy.

Vṛćayā (S) (F) 1. searching. 3. a woman given by Indra to Kakṣīvat.

Vṛddhā (S) (F) great; large; wise; learned; experienced; eldest.

Vṛddhakanyā (S) (F) 1. daughter of a preceptor. 3. the daughter of the hermit Kuṇigarga.

Vṛddhasenā (S) (F) 1. with mighty hosts. 3. a wife of Sumalin (*Bh. Purāṇa*).

Vṛndā (S) (F) 1. heap; swarm; flocks; cluster of flowers; many; much; all; a chorus of singers; Sacred Basil (*Ocimum sanctum*). 3. the wife of the asura Jalandhara (*Bhā. Purāṇa*); another name for Rādhā.

Vṛndāvaneśvarī (S) (F) 1. goddess of Vṛndāvan. 3. consort of Kṛṣṇa; another name for Rādhā.

Vṛṣadevā (S) (F) 1. goddess of the bulls. 3. a wife of Vasudeva (*Bhā. Purāṇa*).

Vṛṣadhvajā (S) (F) 1. bull bannered. 3. another name for Durgā.

Vṛṣakā (S) (F) 1. cow. 3. a yakṣi who is the tutelary divinity of fertility.

Vṛttamallikā (S) (F) 1. the encircling creeper. 2. *Jasminum sambac.*

Vṛttī (S) (F) 1. being; existence; state; moral conduct. 3. a wife of Rudra (*Bhā. Purāṇa*).

Vūrnā (S) (F) chosen; selected.

Vyādhi (S) (F) 1. disease; trouble; epidemic. 3. the daughter of Mṛtyu (*V. Purāṇa*).

Vyāgheśvarī (S) (F) goddess of a tiger; goddess who rides a tiger.

Vyāghrāsyā (S) (F) 1. tiger faced. 3. a Buddhist goddess.

Vyāghravadhū (S) (F) tigress.

Vyāghrī (S) (F) 1. tigress. 3. a Buddhist being attending on the mātṛs.

Vyāhṛrī (S) (F) 1. utterance; speech. 2. declaration. 3. mystical utterances personified as the daughters of Sāvitṛ and Pṛṣṇi.

Vyāpti (S) (F) accomplishment; attainment; omnipresence.

Vyaṣṭi (S) (F) attainment; success; singleness; individuality.

Vyatibhā (S) (F) shining forth.

Vyenī (S) (F) 1. variously tinted. 2. the dawn.

Vyomagaṅgā (S) (F) the celestial Gaṅgā.

Vyominī (S) (F) celestial; apsarā.

Vyuṣṭi (S) (F) the 1st gleam of dawn; grace; beauty; fruit; reward; prosperity; felicity.

Y

Yādavī (S) (F) 1. woman of the Yādava tribe. 3. wife of Subāhu and mother of Sagara; another name for Durgā.

Yadunandinī (S) (F) daughter of the Yadus.

Yadvā (S) (F) perception; mind; intelligence.

Yahvā (S) (F) heaven and earth; the flowing water.

Yahvat (S) (F) the everflowing waters.

Yahvī (S) (F) heaven and earth conjoined.

Yajā (S) (F) 1. worshipper. 2. sacrificer. 3. a tutelary goddess.

Yājñasenī (S) (F) 1. sister of Dhṛṣṭadyumna. 3. another name for Draupadī.

Yajñavatī (S) (F) 1. worshipping. 3. a queen of Kāmarupa.

Yajñeśvarī (S) (F) 1. lord of the sacrifice. 3. a goddess.

Yājñikā (S) (F) 1. used in an oblation. 2. Flame of the Forest (*Butea frondosa*); Bastard Teak (*Butea monosperma*); Black Catechu tree (*Acacia catechu*).

Yakṣāngī (S) (F) 1. alive; speedy. 3. a river.

Yakṣī (S) (F) 1. a female yakṣa. 3. Kubera's wife.

Yakṣiṇī (S) (F) 1. a female yakṣa. 3. attendants of Durgā; another name for Kubera's wife.

Yamabhaginī (S) (F) 1. sister of Yama. 3. another name for the river Yamunā.

Yamahārdikā (S) (F) 1. heart piercing. 3. one of Durgā's attendants.

Yamajihvā (S) (F) 1. Yama's tongue. 3. a yoginī.

Yamakālindī (S) (F) 1. blossoming. 3. another name for Saṁjñā the mother of Yama.

Yamalā (S) (F) 1. a twin; a hiccough. 3. a tāntric deity; a river.

Yamāṅgikā (S) (F) 1. destroyer of Yama. 3. a yoginī.

Yamasvasṛ (S) (F) 1. Yama's sister. 3. another name for the river Yamunā and Durgā.

Yamī (S) (F) 1. the elder twin sister; brace; pair; couple. 3. a daughter of Sūrya and Saṁjñā and the twin sister of Yama who is identified in post Vedic mythology with the river Yamunī (*V. Purana*).

Yāmī (S) (F) 1. motion; course; progress; road; path; carriage. 3. a daughter of Dakṣa and wife of Dharma (*V. Purāna*); an apsara (*H. Purāṇa*).

Yaminī (S) (F) 1. consisting of watches. 2. night. 3. daughter of Prahlāda (*K. Sāgara*); wife of Tarakṣa and the mother of Śalabha (*Bh. Purāṇa*); a daughter of Daksa and wife of Kaśyapa (*Bhāgavata*).

Yamunā (S) (F) 1. a river commonly called Jamunā which is identified with Yamī, it rises in the Himalayas among the Jamnotri peaks and flows down to join the Gaṅgā in Allahabad. 3. the daughter of sage Mataṅga (*K. Sāgara*); another name for the Kālindī river which is personified as a black goddess on a tortoise with a water-pot in her hand (*M. Bh.*).

Yamyā (S) (F) night.

Yaśasvatī (S) (F) illustrious; famous.

Yaśasvinī (S) (F) 1. beautiful; splendid; illustrious; famous. 3. a mother of Skanda's retinue; a sister of Draupadī (*Bhāgavata*).

Yaśodā (S) (F) 1. conferring fame. 3. the wife of the cowherd Nanda and the foster mother of Kṛṣṇa she is considered the incarnation of Dharā; the wife of Mahāvīra and the daughter of Samaravīra; another name for Durgā.

Yaśodevī (S) (F) 1. goddess of fame and beauty. 3. a wife of Bṛhanmanas (*H. Purāna*).

Yaśodhā (S) (F) conferring splendour and fame.

Yaśodharā (S) (F) 1. maintaining fame or glory. 3. the wife of Tvaṣṭṛ and the mother of Tṛśiras and Viśvarupa; the 4th night of the month; a daughter of King Trigarta and married to King

Hasti of the Purū dynasty, she was the mother of Vikaṇṭha (*M. Bh.*); wife of Gautama Buddha and mother of Rāhula.

Yaśolekhā (S) (F) a narrative of glorious deeds.

Yaśomatī (S) (F) **1.** having fame. **3.** the foster-mother of Kṛṣṇa; the 3rd lunar night.

Yaśovatī (S) (F) **1.** possessing glory and fame. **3.** a mythical city on Mount Meru of Iśāna's the ruler of the north eastern part (*D. Bh. Purāṇa*).

Yaṣṭikā (S) (F) a string of pearls.

Yatanā (S) (F) **1.** torment; agony. **3.** the pains of hell personified as the daughter of Bhaya and Mṛtyu.

Yati (S) (F) restraint; control; guidance.

Yatudhani (S) (F) **1.** magician; conjurer. **3.** a rākṣasī born from a sacrificial fire who was killed by Indra (*M. Bh.*).

Yavakṣā (S) (F) **1.** with barley in abundance. **3.** a river (*M. Bh.*).

Yavyavatī (S) (F) **1.** to have barley and fruit in abundance. **3.** a river (*Ṛg Veda*)

Yelemelā (T) (F) **1.** wealthy. **3.** Rukmini as an incarnation of Lakṣmī.

Yogā (S) (F) **1.** total; conjunction; meditation. **3.** a Śakti; another name for Pīvari daughter of the Pitṛs called Barhiṣads (*H. Purāṇa*).

Yogadīpikā (S) (F) light of meditation.

Yogakanyā (S) (F) **1.** born of meditation. **3.** the infant daughter of Yaśoda who was substituted for Kṛṣṇa and killed by Kaṅsa.

Yogamāyā (S) (F) **1.** the magical power of abstract meditation. **3.** another name for Durgā.

Yogamāyādevī (S) (F) the form of Devī in the state of yoga, she transferred the 7th child of Devaki, Balarāma, from her womb to that of Rohiṇī (*D. Bh. Purāna*).

Yoganidrā (S) (F) **1.** meditation sleep. **3.** Viṣṅu's sleep personified as a goddess said to be a form of Durgā.

Yogapatnī (S) (F) **1.** wife of Yoga. **3.** another name for Pīvarī.

Yogaratna (S) (F) a magical jewel.

Yogasiddhā (S) (F) **1.** perfected through yoga. **3.** a sister of Brhaspati.

Yogatārā (S) (F) the chief star of any constellation.

Yogavatī (S) (F) **1.** united; joined. **2.** one who is versed in yoga. **3.** the 3rd daughter of Meṇā who was the wife of the sage Jaigīṣavya (*P. Purāṇa*).

Yogeśvari (S) (F) **1.** adept in yoga. **3.** a form of Durgā (*H. Ć. Ćintāmani*); a vidyādharī (*K. Sāgara*); *Mimordica balsamina.*

Yogin (S) (F) meditator; devotee; ascetic.

Yoginī (S) (F) **1.** a being endowed with magical power. **2.** fairy; witch; sorceress. **3.** attendants created by Durga (*H. Purāṇa*)

Yogitā (S) (F) bewitched; enchanted; wild.

Yojanagandhā (S) (F) **1.** diffusing fragrance to the distance of a Yojana (about 9 miles). **3.** another name for Satyāvatī and Sītā.

Yoṣā (S) (F) young woman; maid.

Yoṣaṇā (S) (F) girl; young woman.

Yoṣidratnā (S) (F) a jewel among women.

Yoṣitā (S) (F) woman; wife.

Yugala (S) (F) **1.** pair. **2.** a double prayer to Lakṣmī and Nārāyaṇa.

Yugandharā (S) (F) **1.** bearing an era. **3.** another name for the earth.

Yūthikā (S) (F) **1.** multitude. **2.** Common White Jasmine (*Jasminum officianale*)

Yuvatī (S) (F) young girl applied as an adjective in the *Ṛg Veda* to Uṣās; night; morning; heaven and earth; the zodiac sign of Virgo; *Curcuma longa.*

Yuvatīṣṭa (S) (F) Yellow Jasmine (*Jasminum humile*)

Yuvikā (S) (F) young girl.

List of the Sources

Āśvālayana Gṛhyasūtra	–	*Ā. Gṛhyasūtra*
Āpasthambha Srantasūtra	–	*Ā. Śrantasūtra*
Ātma Prabodha	–	*A. Prabodha*
Āryabhaṭīya	–	*Āryabhṭīya*
Bāla Bhārata	–	*B. Bhārata*
Buddhist Jātakas	–	*B. Jātakas*
Bhartṛhari Śatakam	–	*B. Śatakam*
Devi Bhāgavata	–	*D. Bhāgavata*
Devi Bhāgvata Purāna	–	*D. Bh. Purāna*
Mahādevi Bhāgavata	–	*M. Bhāgavata*
Aitareya Brāhmaṇa	–	*A. Brāhmaṇa*
Kauśītaki Brāhmaṇa	–	*K. Brāhmaṇa*
Pañćavimśa Brāhmaṇa	–	*P. Brāhmaṇa*
Śatapatha Brāhmaṇa	–	*Ś. Brāhmaṇa*
Tāṇḍya Brāhmaṇa	–	*Tā. Brāhmaṇa*
Vanśa Brāhmaṇa	–	*V. Brāhmaṇa*
Bhāva Prakāśa	–	*B. Prakāśa*
Ćaitya Vandana	–	*Ć. Vandana*
Ćandrāloka	–	*Ćandraloka*
Naisadha Ćarita	–	*N. Ćarita*
Mahāvīra Ćarita	–	*M. Ćarita*
Buddha Ćarita	–	*B. Ćarita*
Bhadrabāhu Ćarita	–	*Bha. Ćarita*
Vīra Ćarita	–	*V. Ćarita*
Chandraswamy Ćarita	–	*Ć. Ćarita*
Divyāvadāna	–	*Divyāvadāna*
Datta Ćandrikā	–	*D. Ćandrikā*
Durgāsaptaśati	–	*D. Saptaśati*
Gaṇaratna Mahodadhi	–	*G. Mahodadhi*
Gautama's Dharmaśāstra	–	*G's. Dharmaśāstra*
Gobhila's Śraddhā Kalpa	–	*G's Ś. Kalpa*
Gṛhya Samigraha	–	*G. Samigraha*
Gṛhya Sūtra	–	*G. Sūtra*
Hitopadeśa	–	*Hitopadeśa*
Hemendrīya Ćaturvarga Ćintāmaṇi	–	*H.Ć. Ćintāmaṇi*

Īśa Tantra	–	*Ī. Tantra*
Jaimini Aśvamedha	–	*J. Aśvamedha*
Jaimuni Bhārata	–	*J. Bhārata*
Jātākam	–	*Jātakam*
Jaina Sāhitya	–	*J. Literature*
Kāvya Prakāśa	–	*K. Prakāśa*
Kalpa Sūtra	–	*K. Sūtra*
Kālidasa Granthāvali	–	*K. Granthāvali*
Kaṇvādi	–	*Kaṇvādi*
Kādambari	–	*Kādambari*
Kathārṇava	–	*Kathārṇava*
Kharatara Gaccha	–	*K. Gaccha*
Kathāsaritasāgara	–	*K. Sāgara*
Karaṇḍvyūha	–	*K. Vyūha*
Amar Koṣa	–	*A. Koṣa*
Hatayudha Koṣa	–	*H. Koṣa*
Hemaćandra Koṣa	–	*He. Koṣa*
Jainendra Siddhānta Koṣa	–	*J. S. Koṣa*
Lalita Vistara	–	*L. Vistara*
Buddha Sāhitya	–	*B. Literature*
Maskāra Stava	–	*M. Stava*
Mṛcchakaṭikam	–	*M. Katikam*
Manu Smṛti	–	*M. Smṛti*
Mahābhārata	–	*M. Bh*
Naćiketupākhyana	–	*N. Pākhyāna*
Nirukta	–	*Nirukta*
Nalopākhyāna	–	*Nalopākhyāna*
Nīti Śataka	–	*N. Śataka*
Pañćdaṇḍa Ćatraprabandha	–	*P. Ćatraprabandha*
Agni Purāṇa	–	*A. Purāṇa*
Bhāgvata Purāṇa	–	*Bhā. Purāṇa*
Bhaviṣya Purāṇa	–	*Bh. Purāṇa*
Bhīṣma Purāṇa	–	*Bhī. Purāṇa*
Brahmāṇḍa Purāṇa	–	*Br. Purāṇa*
Brahmavaivarta Purāṇa	–	*Brah. Purāṇa*

Brahma Purāṇa	–	*Brahma Purāṇa*
Devī Purāṇa	–	*D. Purāṇa*
Gaṇeśa Purāṇa	–	*G. Purāṇa*
Garuḍa Purāṇa	–	*Gar. Purāṇa*
Harivaṁśa Purāṇa	–	*H. Purāṇa*
Harivaṅśa Purāṇa	–	*H. Purāṇa*
Kalkī Purāṇa	–	*K. Purāṇa*
Liṅga Purāṇa	–	*L. Purāṇa*
Matsya Purāṇa	–	*M. Purāṇa*
Mārkaṇḍeya Purāṇa	–	*Mā. Purāṇa*
Nārada Purāṇa	–	*N. Purāṇa*
Nahni Purāṇa	–	*Nah. Purāṇa*
Padma Purāṇa	–	*P. Purāṇa*
Śiva Purāṇa	–	*Ś. Purāṇa*
Skanda Purāṇa	–	*Sk. Purāṇa*
Subāhu Purāṇa	–	*Su. Purāṇa*
Vasiṣṭha Purāṇa	–	*V. Purāṇa*
Viṣṇu Purāṇa	–	*V. Purāṇa*
Vāyu Purāṇa	–	*Vā. Purāṇa*
Vāmana Purāṇa	–	*Vam. Purāṇa*
Varāha Purāṇa	–	*Var. Purāṇa*
Varuṇa Purāṇa	–	*Varuṇa Purāṇa*
Purāṇas	–	*Purāṇas*
Prabhodha Ćandrodaya	–	*P. Ćandrodaya*
Pāṇinī	–	*Pāṇinī.*
Pañćatantra	–	*Pañćatantra*
Pārśavanatha Ćaritra	–	*P. Ćaritra*
Ānanda Rāmāyaṇa	–	*A. Rāmāyaṇa*
Bāla Rāmāyaṇa	–	*B. Rāmāyaṇa*
Kamba Rāmāyaṇa	–	*K. Rāmāyaṇa*
Uttar Rāmāyaṇa	–	*U. Rāmāyaṇa*
Vālmīki Rāmāyaṇa	–	*V. Rāmāyaṇa*
Rāja Taraṅgiṇī	–	*R. Taraṅgiṇī*
Rasa Gaṅgādhara	–	*R. Gaṅgādhara*
Raghuvanśa	–	*Raghuvanśa*
Ṛg Veda Anukramaṇikā	–	*R. Anukramaṇikā*
Āpastamba Samhitā	–	*Ā. Samhitā*
Pārāśara Samhitā	–	*P. Samhitā*
Suśruta Samhita	–	*S. Samhitā*

Taittirīya Samhita	–	*T. Samhitā*
Vājasaneyī Samhita	–	*V. Samhitā*
Varāhamihira's Bṛhat Samhitā	–	*V's B. Samhitā*
Yajurveda Samhitā	–	*Y. Samhitā*
Śiva Rāja Vijaya	–	*Ś R. Vijaya*
Suvarṇa Prābhāsa	–	*S. Prābhāsa*
Saddharma Puṇḍarīkā	–	*S. Puṇḍarīkā*
Sinhāsanadvātrinśikā	–	*S. Dvātrinśikā*
Śatruñjaya Mahātmya	–	*Ś. Mahātmya*
Śaṅkaravijaya	–	*Ś. Vijaya*
Svapna Vāsavadattam	–	*S. Vāsavadattam*
Sarvadarśana Saṁgraha	–	*S. Saṁgraha*
Sānkhyayan Śrauta Sūtra	–	*S. Ś. Sūtra*
Tantra Śāstra	–	*T. Śāstra*
Dharma Śāstra	–	*D. Śāstra*
Jyotiṣa Śāstra	–	*J. Śāstra*
Tīrthyāditya	–	*Tīrthyāditya*
Taittirīya Prātiśākhya	–	*T. Prātiśākhya*
Taittirīya Āraṇyaka	–	*T. Āraṇyaka*
Bṛhadāraṇyaka Upaniṣad	–	*Br. Upaniṣad*
Ćhandogya Upaniṣad	–	*Ć. Upaniṣad*
Kaṭhopaniṣad	–	*K. Upaniṣad*
Kauśitaki Upaniṣad	–	*Kau. Upaniṣad*
Maitreya Upaniṣad	–	*M. Upaniṣad*
Muṇḍaka Upaniṣad	–	*Mu. Upaniṣad*
Rāmatapanīya Upaniṣad	–	*Rā. Upaniṣad*
Vetāla Pañćavinśatikā	–	*V. Pañćavinśatikā*
Vikramorvaśiyam	–	*Vikramorvaśīyam*
Vićārāmṛta Saṁgraha	–	*V. Saṁgraha*
Vikramāṅka Deva Ćaritam	–	*V.D. Ćaritam*
Atharva Veda	–	*A. Veda*
Ṛg Veda	–	*Ṛg. Veda*
Sāma Veda	–	*S. Veda*
Yajur Veda	–	*Y. Veda*
Yogavāsiṣṭha	–	*Yogavāsiṣṭha*